CIVILIZATION OR BARBARISM

CIVILIZATION OR BARBARISM
AN AUTHENTIC ANTHROPOLOGY

Cheikh Anta Diop

Translated from the French by Yaa-Lengi Meema Ngemi
Edited by Harold J. Salemson and Marjolijn de Jager

LAWRENCE HILL BOOKS

First published by Présence Africaine, Paris, copyright © 1981
Translated by Yaa-Lengi Meema Ngemi

Published by Lawrence Hill Books
An imprint of Chicago Review Press Incorporated
814 North Franklin Street
Chicago, Illinois 60610
ISBN 978-1-55652-048-8

This edition has been made possible through the financial help of the French Ministry of Culture.

Library of Congress Cataloging-in-Publication Data
Diop, Cheikh Anta.
[Civilisation ou barbarie. English]
Civilization or barbarism : an authentic anthropology / Cheikh Anta Diop : translated from the French by Yaa-Lengi Meema Ngemi : edited by Harold J. Salemson and Marjolijn de Jager. — 1st ed.
p. cm.
Translation of: Civilisation ou barbarie.
Includes bibliographical references.
ISBN 978-1-55652-048-8
1. Africa—Civilization. 2. Egypt—Civilization—To 332 B.C.
I. Salemson, Harold J. II. De Jager, Marjolijn. III. Title.
DT14.D5613 1991
960–dc20 90-4141 CIP

Printed in the United States of America
20 19 18 17 16 15 14

I dedicate this book to the memory of
Alioune Diop

who died on the battlefield of African culture.

Alioune, you knew what you came to do on this earth: A life entirely dedicated to others, nothing for yourself, everything for others, a heart filled with goodness and generosity, a soul steeped in nobility, a spirit always serene, simplicity personified!

Did the demiurge want to provide us with an example, an ideal of perfection, by calling you into existence?

Alas, the terrestrial community, to which you knew how to convey, better than anyone else, the message of human truthfulness that sprang from the inmost depths of your being, was deprived of you too soon. But the remembrance of you will never be erased from the memory of the African peoples, to whom you dedicated your life.

That is why I am dedicating this book to your memory, in witness to a brotherly friendship that is stronger than time.

Cheikh Anta Diop
Dakar, Senegal

CONTENTS

Acknowledgments
(French edition)

Thanks to Amar Samb, director of the IFAN, and to Mahady Diallo, general secretary of the University of Dakar, for their crucial contribution to the development of the structures of African research.

I warmly thank Willy Girardin, who had the kindness to fully dedicate himself to the completion of this work. His meticulous technical preparation and his creation of the index greatly facilitate the reading of this book.

List of Figures

FOREWORD

Cheikh Anta Diop is considered to be one of the greatest scholars to emerge in the African world in the twentieth century. He was born in Diourbel, Senegal, a town on the west coast of Africa, in 1923. His birthplace has a long tradition of producing Muslim scholars and oral historians. This is where his inspiration and interest in history, the humanities, and the social sciences from an African point of view began.

The years of his life (1923–86) and the creation of his work were years of transition and change for the whole of the African world. In the United States, the Pan-African Congresses, under the leadership of W. E. B. Du Bois, were well under way. African Americans were still debating Booker T. Washington's theory of education, favorably, while dismissing his theory of participation. The first of the trials of Marcus Garvey, in relationship to the Black Star Line, had already started, and the largest Africa-oriented movement ever to be built was well under way in spite of the trials and tribulations of Garvey.

In the Caribbean, the intellectuals on the larger islands, especially Jamaica, Trinidad, and Barbados, were fighting for a constitutional government. From the French-speaking islands, Guadeloupe and Martinique, and from what was then called French Guyana, representatives were being sent to the French Parliament who spoke clearer and more precise French than most Frenchmen.

In Africa, most of the warrior-nationalists of the nineteenth century had either been driven into exile, imprisoned, or removed from power. Missionary-trained Africans were capturing the attention of the colonial administrations. While the physical fight against colonialism had abated, the intellectual fight continued. From this period until the eve of the African independence explosion in the late 1950s, African political literature appeared mainly in South Africa and in West Africa—in Ghana, Nigeria, and Sierra Leone.

In 1945, Caribbean Islanders and Africans in England convened the Fifth Pan-African Congress in Manchester. In attendance at this congress were Kwame Nkrumah, who was one of the conveners, Jomo Kenyatta, Nambi Azikiwe of Nigeria, Peter Abrams of South Africa, and Amy Ashwood Garvey, the first wife of Marcus Garvey. Not one of these participants had forgotten the restimulation in African thought brought on by the Italian-Ethiopian War of 1935–36 and the death of Marcus Garvey in 1940. They were meeting, in part, to pay tribute to Marcus Garvey and as a reminder that Africans had to reclaim Africa for Africans.

Cheikh Anta Diop lived through the African independence explosion that began with the independence of Ghana in March 1958. The aftermath of this event was bright and hopeful, but unfortunately short-lived. Diop lived to see Africa turned against itself, motivated in part by its former colonial masters, who were still behind the scenes controlling the destiny of the continent. He lived to plan a solution that came to the attention of a few serious scholars. On the eve of his unfortunate passing, he was just beginning to reach the audience that would give him the recognition he deserved. All African people, everywhere, are closer to a better understanding of their history and destiny because of the personality and work of Cheikh Anta Diop.

Using the disciplines on linguistics, cultural and physical anthropology, history, chemistry, and physics that his research required, he forged new theoretical pathways and revealed new evidence in the quest to uncover the ancient origins and unifying principles of classical African civilization. He was not only an innovative theoretician, but he was also a pragmatist. He published works that offered programmatic suggestions for the political and economic unification of Africa. For example, in his book, *Black Africa: The Economic and Cultural Basis for a Federated State*, he presented a blueprint for saving the mineral wealth of Africa for generations still unborn. This book is neither widely read nor understood, and this is unfortunate because it is one of his more useful books. In some ways he went beyond Pan-Africanism: he was a scholar-activist, dedicated to science in the interest of his people. He saw Africa and its people as the hope of humanity.

Civilization or Barbarism is Cheikh Anta Diop's magnum opus and the last of his great contributions to the clarification of African world history. In many ways this book is a summation and an extension of his previous research; it is a refinement of his analyses and a final statement reflecting the completion of his mission. Through this book he has left us an historical legacy that will inspire future historians and researchers who seek the truth about the role of Africa in world history. Before his untimely death he had stated that this would be his last scholarly work. His intent was to devote the remainder of his life to the development of a political master plan that would save Africa for the Africans.

I first became aware of the writings of Cheikh Anta Diop in 1958, while reading the proceedings of the First and Second Conferences of Negro Writers and Artists. His work was a revelation to me, because I had not encountered, in print, an African scholar so forthright in challenging prevailing misconceptions about African history and in putting forth a new creative view, with documentation. When I read his contribution to this first conference, "The Cultural Contribution and Prospects of Africa," I began to inquire about his other writings. I discovered later that the content of this article was part of a chapter of a future book. In reading the proceedings of the second conference, held in Rome in 1959, my curiosity grew concerning this new voice in the wilderness of African historiography. I then discovered that Présence Africaine had published a comprehensive work by him on African history: *The African Origin of Civilization: Myth or Reality*.

When I attended the second meeting of the International Congress of Africanness in Dakar, Senegal, which met at the University of Dakar in 1967, I sought out Dr. Diop. I was surprised to learn that his office and laboratory were located on the campus of the university, less than three hundred yards from the assembly hall where the Congress was being held, yet he was not one of the participants at the conference. The sponsoring organization, the African Studies Association, was then dominated by white scholars, and to this day it has not recognized the scholarship of Cheikh Anta Diop and his contributions to a new concept of African history. Neither his name nor his work was mentioned at the conference.

I visited him in his laboratory and discussed the long effort that African Americans and Caribbean Americans had engaged in to write about and preserve African history. Some of the names that I mentioned he had never heard of. This first meeting went quite well—better than I had expected because we had to speak to each other through an interpreter.

I returned to the United States and spent the next seven years trying to convince American publishers that the books of Cheikh Anta Diop should be translated into English and published in the United States. I first mentioned my efforts to my friend and colleague, the late Alioune Diop, who encouraged me to continue in spite of repeated disappointments. It was not until 1974 that an American publisher, Lawrence Hill and Company, saw fit to publish Diop's book *The African Origin of Civilization*.

The African Origin of Civilization is a one-volume translation of the major sections of two other books by Diop, *Nations nègres et Culture*, and *Antériorité des civilisations nègres*. These two works have challenged and changed the direction of attitudes about the place of African people in history in scholarly circles around the world. It was largely due to these works that Cheikh Anta Diop, with W. E. B. Du Bois, was honored as "the writer who had exerted the greatest influence on African people in the twentieth century," at the World Black Festival of Arts and Culture held in Dakar, Senegal, in 1966.

The main thrust of *The African Origin of Civilization* is a redefinition of the place of Egypt in African history. Here Diop calls attention to the historical, archaeological, and anthropological evidence that supports his thesis. Diop states:

> The history of Africa will remain suspended in air and cannot be written correctly until African historians connect it with the history of Egypt.

I wrote a review of this book, which reads, in part:

> Cheikh Anta Diop, one of the most able of present-day scholars writing about Africa, is also one of the greatest living African historians. His first major work, *Nations nègres et Culture* (1954), is still disturbing the white historians who have made quick reputations as authorities on African history and culture. In this book Dr. Diop shows the interrelationships between African nations, North and South, and proves, because in this case proof is needed, again and again, that ancient Egypt was a distinct African nation and was not historically or culturally a part of Asia or Europe.

This book and others of recent years, all by African writers, have called for a total reconsideration of the role that African people have played in history and their impact on the development of early societies and institutions. In a review of Martin Bernal's book, *Black Athena*, the English writer Basil Davidson makes the following statement about how Egypt, as a part of Africa, was left out of world history:

> But isn't Egypt, other issues apart, quite simply a part of Africa? That, it seems, is a merely geographical irrelevance. The civilisation of Pharaonic Egypt, arising sometime around 3500 B.C. and continuing at least until the Roman dispositions, has been explained to us as evolving either in more or less total isolation from Africa or as a product of West Asian stimulus. On this deeply held view, the land of ancient Egypt appears to have detached itself from the delta of the Nile, some five and a half thousand years ago, and sailed off into the Mediterranean on a course veering broadly towards the coasts of Syria. And there it apparently remained, floating somewhere in the seas of the Levant, until Arab conquerors hauled it back to where it had once belonged.

> Now what is one to make of this unlikely view of the case, coming as it has from venerable seats of learning? Does its strength derive from a long tradition of research and explanation? Is it what Europeans have always thought to be true? Have the records of ancient times been found to support it? As Martin Bernal has now most ably shown in his *Black Athena*, the remarkable book about which I am chiefly writing here, the answer to such questions is plainly and unequivocally in the negative. That the ancient Egyptians were Black (again, in any variant you may prefer)—or, as I myself think it is more useful to say, were African—is a belief which has been denied in Europe since about 1830, not before. It is a denial, in short, that belongs to the rise of modern European imperialism, and has to be explained in terms of the "new racism," especially and even frantically an anti-Black racism, which went together with and was consistently nourished by that imperialism. I say, "new racism" because it followed and further expanded the older racism which spread around Europe after the Atlantic slave trade had reached its high point of "take-off" in about 1630.

If we understand Davidson's statement, we must also understand the consequences of the second rise of Europe and its recovery from the Middle Ages. In the fifteenth and sixteenth centuries, Europe not only began to colonize most of the world, but also instituted a systematic colonization of information about the world. Consequently, the work of Cheikh Anta Diop and other African historians, both in Africa and in the United States, is a restoration project, an attempt to restore what slavery and colonialism had taken away. While the main focus of Diop's book *Civilization or Barbarism* is Egypt and its relationship to early world history, he gives us a panoramic view of how Africa, its nations, peoples, and culture relate to the whole world. In a previous work, *L'Antiquité* (Evolution of the Black World From Prehistory to the End of Antiquity), Diop had documented a little-known aspect of the African-European connection. He dealt with the Grimaldi Man and his presence in Europe over six thousand years ago. In both works, *L'Antiquité* and *Civilization or Barbarism*, he raises some questions that are both topical and historical, mainly the African origin of the people who are now referred to as Europeans.

In the introduction to *Civilization or Barbarism*, Diop explains the methodology he used in putting the book together, the conclusions he reached, and how he documented these conclusions, both with fact and logic. In setting forth his arguments, he had to deal with the contradictions that relate to Egyptian history and to African history in general. He repeatedly refers to the Southern African origins of the Egyptians. He infers that the Nile River was the world's first cultural highway, stretching four thousand miles into the body of Africa, bringing culture and people out of the heart of Africa who gave stimulus to Egypt and constantly renewed its energy.

In chapter 1, "Prehistory—Race and History: Origin of Humanity and Racial Differentiation," Diop explains the early development of Africa and how its cultures and religions eventually influenced the Western world, in particular, and the whole world, in general. Diop states:

> The general problem confronting African history is this: how to reorganize effectively, through meaningful research, all of the fragments of the past into a single ancient epoch, an origin which will reestablish African continuity; if the ancients were not victims of a mirage, it should be easy enough to draw upon another series of arguments and proofs for the union of history of Ethiopian and Egyptian societies with the rest of Africa. Thus combined, these histories would lead to a properly patterned past in which it would be seen that (ancient) Ghana rose in the interior (West Africa) of the continent at the moment of Egyptian decline, just as the western European empires were born with the decline of Rome.

While using Africa as the vantage point and the basis for his thesis, Diop does not neglect the broader dimensions of history. He shows that history cannot be restricted by the limits of ethnic group, nation, or culture. Roman history is Greek, as well as Roman, and both Greek and Roman history are Egyptian because the entire Mediterranean was civilized by Egypt; Egypt in turn borrowed from other parts of Africa, especially Ethiopia.

As Diop explains, Africa came into the Mediterranean world mainly through Greece, which had been under African influence. The first Greek invasion of Africa was peaceful. This invasion brought in Herodotus. Egypt had lost its independence over a century before his visit. This was the beginning of the period of foreign domination over Egypt that would last, in different forms, for two thousand years.

Diop approaches the history of Africa frontally, head-on, with explanations but no apologies. In locating Egypt on the map of human geography he asks and answers the question: Who were the Egyptians of the ancient world?

The Ethiopians said that Egypt was one of their colonies, which was brought to them by the deity Osiris. The Greek writer Herodotus repeatedly referred to the Egyptians as being dark-skinned people with woolly hair. He said they have the same tint of skin as the Ethiopians. The opinion of the ancient writers on the Egyptians is more or less summed up by Gaston Maspero (1846–1916) in *The Dawn of Civilization*, where he says:

> By the almost unanimous testimony of ancient historians, they (the Egyptians) belong to an African race which first settled in Ethiopia on the middle Nile, following the course of the river they gradually reached the sea.

"The Greek writer, Herodotus, may be mistaken," Cheikh Anta Diop tells us, "when he reports the customs of a people, but one must grant that he was at least capable of recognizing the skin color of the inhabitants of countries he visited." His descriptions of the Egyptians were the descriptions of a Black people. At this point the reader needs to be reminded of the fact that at the time of Herodotus' visit to Egypt and other parts of Africa (between 484 and 425 B.C.) Egypt's Golden Age was over. Egypt had suffered several invasions, mainly the Kushite invasions, coming from within Africa in 751 B.C., and the Assyrian invasions from Western Asia (called the Middle East), starting in 671 B.C. If Egypt, after years of invasions by other peoples and nations was a distinct Black African nation at the time of Herodotus, should we not at least assume that it was more so before these invasions occurred?

If Egypt is a dilemma in Western historiography, it is a created dilemma. The Western historians, in most cases, have rested the foundation of what is called "Western Civilization" on the false assumption, or claim, that the ancient Egyptians were white people. To do this they had to ignore great masterpieces of Egyptian history written by other white historians who did not support this point of view, such as Gerald Massey's great classic, *Ancient Egypt, The Light of the World* (1907), and his subsequent works, *The Book of the Beginnings* and *The Natural Genesis*. Other neglected works by white writers are *Politics, Intercourse, and Trade of the Carthaginians and Ethiopians* by A. H. L. Heeren (1833) and *The Ruins of Empires* by Count C. F. Volney (1787).

In his book, *Egypt*, Sir E. A. Wallis Budge states:

> The prehistoric native of Egypt, both in the old and new Stone Ages, was African, and there is every reason for saying that the earliest settlers came from the South.

He further states:

> There are many things in the manners and customs and religions of the historic Egyptians that suggest that the original home of their ancestors was in a country in the neighborhood of Uganda and Punt.

European interest in Ethiopia and the origin of civilization dates from the early part of the nineteenth century and is best reflected in a little-known, though important, paper in Karl Richard Lepsius's *Incomparable*

Survey of the Monumental Ruins in the Ethiopian Nile Valley in 1843–1844.

The records found by Lepsius tend to show how Ethiopia was once able to sustain an ancient population that was numerous and powerful enough not only to challenge, but on a number of occasions to conquer completely the populous land of Egypt. Further, these records show that the antiquity of Ethiopian civilization had a direct link with civilizations of ancient Egypt.

Many of the leading antiquarians of the time, based largely on the strength of what the classical authors, particularly Diodorus Siculus and Stephanus of Byzantium, had to say on the matter, were exponents of the view that the ancient Ethiopians, or at any rate the Black people of remote antiquity, were the earliest of all civilized peoples, and that the first civilized inhabitants of ancient Egypt were members of what is referred to as the Black race, who entered the country as emigrants from Ethiopia. A number of Europe's leading African historians are Bruce, Count Volney, Fabre, d'Olivet, and Heeren. In spite of the fact that these writers defended this thesis with all the learning at their command and documented their defense, most present-day African historians continue to ignore their findings.

In 1825, German backwardness in this respect came definitely to an end. In that year, Arnold Hermann Heeren (1760–1842), professor of history and politics at the University of Göttingen and one of the ablest of the early exponents of the economic interpretation of history, published in the fourth and revised edition of his great work, *Ideen Uber die Politik, den Verkehr und den Handel der Vornehmsten Volker der Alten Weld*, a lengthy essay on the history, culture, and commerce of the ancient Ethiopians. This essay profoundly influenced contemporary writers in its conclusion that it was among the ancient Black people of Africa and Asia that international trade first developed, and that, as a by-product of these international contacts, there was an exchange of ideas and cultural practices that laid the foundations of the earliest civilizations of the ancient world.

The French writer Count C. F. Volney in his important work *The Ruins of Empires* extended this point of view by saying that the Egyptians were the first people to "attain the physical and moral sciences necessary to civilized life." In referring to the basis of this achievement he states further that,

> It was, then, on the borders of the Upper Nile, among a Black race of men, that was organized the complicated system of worship of the stars, considered in relation to the productions of the earth and the labors of agriculture; and this first worship, characterized by their adoration under their own forms and national attributes, was a simple proceeding of the human mind.

Over a generation ago African-American historians, such as Carter G. Woodson, W. E. B. Du Bois, Willis N. Huggins, J. A. Rogers, and Charles C. Seifort read the works of these radical writer-historians and began to expand on their findings. This tradition has continued and is reflected in the works of present-day Black historians, such as John G. Jackson's *Introduction to African Civilizations* (1970), Yosef ben-Jochannan's *Black Man of the Nile* (1972), and Chancellor Williams's *The Destruction of Black Civilization: Great Issues of a Race from 4500 B.C.–2000 A.D.* (1971).

Until the publication of James Spadys's article, "Negritude, Pan-Benegritude and the Diopian Philosophy of African History," in *A Current Bibliography on African Affairs*, vol. 5, no. 1, January 1972, and the interview by Harun Kofi Wangara, published in *Black World*, in February 1974, Cheikh Anta Diop was known to only a small group of African-American writers, historians, and teachers in the United States. With the publication of his last work he has left us a mission and a legacy. Carrying out this mission and honoring this legacy is the greatest monument that we can erect to him. He will rest in peace only when his people are free of foreign domination and are secure in their understanding of their role in world history.

John Henrik Clarke
Professor Emeritus
Department of Africana and Puerto Rican Studies
Hunter College, New York City
August 1990

INTRODUCTION

This introduction is intended to facilitate the reading of this book and to underscore what is new about it as compared to our previous publications.

It is a further contribution to the work that allowed us to elevate the idea of a Black Egypt to the level of an operational scientific concept. For all the writers who preceded the ludicrous and vicious falsifications of modern Egyptology, and the contemporaries of the ancient Egyptians (Herodotus, Aristotle, Diodorus, Strabo, and others), the Black identity of the Egyptian was an evident fact that stood before their eyes, so obvious that it would have been superfluous to try to demonstrate it.

Around the 1820s, just before the birth of Egyptology, the French scholar Count Constantin de Volney, a universal and objective spirit, if ever there were one, tried to refresh the memory of humanity, who, because of the recent enslavement of Blacks, had forgotten the past of this people.

Since then, the line of ill-intentioned Egyptologists, equipped with ferocious erudition, have committed their well-known crime against science, by becoming guilty of a deliberate falsification of the history of humanity. Supported by the governing powers of all the Western countries, this ideology, based on a moral and intellectual swindle, easily won out over the true scientific current developed by a parallel group of Egyptologists of good will, whose intellectual uprightness and even courage cannot be stressed strongly enough. The new Egyptological ideology, born at the opportune moment, reinforced the theoretical bases of imperialist ideology. That is why it easily drowned out the voice of science, by throwing the veil of falsification over historical truth. This ideology was spread with the help of considerable publicity and taught the world over, because it alone had the material and financial means for its own propagation.

Thus imperialism, like the prehistoric hunter, first killed the being spiritually and culturally, before trying to eliminate it physically. The negation of the history and intellectual accomplishments of Black Africans was cultural, mental murder, which preceded and paved the way for their genocide here and there in the world. So that between the years 1946 and 1954—when our project for the restitution of the authentic history of Africa and the reconciliation of African civilizations with history was elaborated—the distorted perspective caused by the blinders of colonialism had so profoundly warped intellectuals' views of the African past that we had the greatest difficulty, even among Africans, in gaining acceptance for ideas that today are becoming commonplace. One can hardly imagine the degree of alienation of the Africans of that period.

Therefore, for us the new, important fact is less to have stated that the Egyptians were Blacks, as one of our principal sources, the ancient writers, already did, than to have contributed to making this idea a conscious historical fact for Africans and the world, and especially to making it an operational scientific concept: this is where our predecessors did not succeed.

There will always be some rearguard actions, and it can be seen, now that the battle is practically won, that even some Africans are strutting around on this conquered ground while giving us some pinpricks and some lessons in "scientific objectivity."

Race does not exist! But we know that Europe is populated by Whites, Asia by Yellows and Whites, who are all responsible for the civilizations of their respective countries and homelands. The race of the ancient Egyptians alone must remain a mystery. Western ideology believed it could decide that it was to be so. Today, the data of molecular biology are used indiscriminately to try to complicate the problem. But it just so happens that the methods of this new discipline can cast a singular light on the ethnic identity of the ancient Egyptians, if one ever cares to apply them judiciously. It is recognized that a biased anthropologist can whiten a Black or blacken a White by a tendentious interpretation of measurements and carefully selected partial analyses.

Notwithstanding the genetic polymorphism of populations revealed by molecular biology, which has led generous and humanistic scholars like Jacques Ruffie, A. Jacquard, and others to deny the existence of race, hematology, which is the finest flower of this science, informs us of the existence of "racial markers." The system of blood groups *A*, *B*, and *O* is common to all races and predates the racial differentiation of humanity. *Rh* factors also exist in all races, though with variable frequency; thus the *r* chromosome is present in all Whites and "culminates" in the Basques; *Ro* can be found in everybody, but its frequency is particularly high among the Blacks south of the Sahara.

A third category is even more specific. These are in fact the "racial markers": the Diego factor is characteristic of the Yellow race and is found only in American Indians, Yellows of the Far East, and certain Nepalese people (of probable mixed blood). "The Sutter and Henshaw factors are detectable almost exclusively among Blacks."[1] The Kell factor is mainly observed among Whites.[2]

Therefore, those desiring to learn more of the ethnicity of the ancient Egyptians should look for the above-mentioned factors in the truly autochthonous ancient population, and not in foreign mummies, Ptolemaic, Greek, or others. . . . The team in charge of this work, to be credible, should include African scientists. A pure race does not exist anywhere, but one eagerly refers to the Whites of Europe and the Yellows of Asia: in the same way, we refer to the Blacks of Egypt.

If the town of Dakar were to become a new Pompei due to some cataclysm, in two thousand years, in analyzing the petrified debris of William Ponty Avenue[3] one might seriously defend the idea that the Senegal of the late twentieth century was a multiracial community whose civilization was created by a White element strongly represented in the population, and Blacks were only an enslaved element. Today, Africans have become invulnerable to these kinds of falsifications, so common at the birth of Egyptology. We have intentionally reproduced the table of races that was known to the Egyptians and represented by them. In referring to it (fig. 17), one will see that only those who have shameless reasons to doubt this will do so, be they Africans or others.

At this point we must underscore the abyss that separates us from those Africans who believe that it can be enough to flirt with Egyptian culture. For us, the return to Egypt in all domains is the necessary condition for reconciling African civilizations with history, in order to be able to construct a body of modern human sciences, in order to renovate African culture. Far from being a reveling in the past, a look toward the Egypt of antiquity is the best way to conceive and build our cultural future. In reconceived and renewed African culture, Egypt will play the same role that Greco-Latin antiquity plays in Western culture.

Insofar as Egypt is the distant mother of Western cultures and sciences, as it will emerge from the reading of this book, most of the ideas that we call foreign are oftentimes nothing but mixed up, reversed, modified, elaborated images of the creations of our African ancestors, such as Judaism, Christianity, Islam, dialectics, the theory of being, the exact sciences, arithmetic, geometry, mechanical engineering, astronomy, medicine, literature (novel, poetry, drama), architecture, the arts, etc.[4]

One can see then how fundamentally improper is the notion, so often repeated, of the importation of foreign ideologies in Africa. It stems from a perfect ignorance of the African past. Just as modern technologies and sciences came from Europe, so did, in antiquity, universal knowledge stream from the Nile Valley to the rest of the world, particularly to Greece, which would serve as a link.

Consequently, no thought, no ideology is, in essence, foreign to Africa, which was their birthplace. It is therefore with total liberty that Africans can draw from the common intellectual heritage of humanity, letting themselves be guided only by the notions of utility and efficiency.

This is also the place to say that no thought, and particularly no philosophy, can develop outside of its historical terrain. Our young philosophers must understand this, and rapidly equip themselves with the necessary intellectual means in order to reconnect with the home of philosophy in Africa, instead of getting bogged down in the wrong battles of ethnophilosophy.[5] By renewing ties with Egypt we soon discover an historical perspective of five thousand years that makes possible the diachronic study, on our own land, of all the scientific disciplines that we are trying to integrate into modern African thought.

The history of African thought becomes a scientific discipline where "ethnophilosophical" cosmogonies occupy their chronological place like the mummy in its sarcophagus. The Gods are appeased. Hegel and Marx did not have a "German quarrel" with St. Thomas or with the obscure Heraclitus; for without the stammerings of the latter, they would not have been able to construct their philosophical systems. It is essential, therefore, to break away from the atemporal structural study of African cosmogonies, because by isolating oneself from the historical framework, one becomes exhausted in a false battle without knowing it, slicing the air with sharp sword's lashes.

Without the historical dimension, we would never have had the possibility of studying the evolution of the societies,[6] and the means to go back and forth from the ethnological level to the sociological one. Of course it is not the kind of ethnology the descriptions of which would turn a monkey red. In our report to the Symposium on "Lenin and Science," organized by UNESCO in 1971 in Helsinki to commemorate the centennial of Lenin's birth, we emphasized the unique difficulties encountered by the African sociologist: often he is obliged to take into account the two levels mentioned above and deal with them, as Engels did a little bit, either by using Morgan's works on the Indians who had remained at the Ethnographic Age, or by studying the social structures of the German tribes. The works are quickly hit with caducity if the ethnological materials are badly analyzed. In general, the ethnological phase is absent in the works of Western Marxists who study the contradictions of European societies that have entered the industrial phase.

WHAT DOES THIS BOOK CONTAIN?

An ideological tactic currently in use consists of modifying, of recasting one's conceptual apparatus in order to make only concessions of form, and not of substance, when faced with the new scientific facts. Such a tendency becomes clear where the thesis that places the cradle of humanity in Africa is concerned. It is now being said and written, in a manner more general than one can imagine, that Africa is the cradle of humanity only at the *Homo erectus* stage and that "sapientization" took place from the adaptation of this primitive African stock under geographical conditions of the different continents.

It appeared indispensable for us to demonstrate how this new point of view is scientifically untenable. The reader who so desires can follow the details of our reasoning in chapter 2.

By basing our work on the data of absolute chronology, of physical anthropology, and of prehistoric archaeology, we believe we have shown that Africa is the birthplace of humanity, both at the stage of *Homo erectus* and *Homo sapiens sapiens.*

Chapter 1 gives a readable general summary of this idea, and chapter 2 discusses it in depth. Thus, it is possible to go from the first to the third chapter, or to read the second chapter in order to further edify oneself.

The so-called "on wheels" cradle of humanity is not as mobile as it is pretended to be. In thirty years it has passed in its entirety from Asia to Africa, and it has never been placed in Europe, or in America.

Chapter 3 shows in what manner archaeology, based on the radiocarbon dating method, has introduced the myth of Atlantis into the domains of science and history.

In this chapter, we also show that the XVIIIth Egyptian Dynasty, contemporaneous with the explosion of the island of Santorini in the Cyclades, which gave birth to the myth of Atlantis, did in fact colonize Crete and the whole Eastern Mediterranean in the same period. This enables us to understand the appearance of *Linears A* and *B* and many other facts that have remained puzzling until now, because nobody wanted to connect them to their historical background.

Chapter 4 deals with the archeological masterpiece proving that Egyptian civilization originated from the heart of Africa, going from south to north, and that the Nubian kingdom predated and gave birth to that of Upper Egypt.

Chapters 5 through 13 are devoted to the description of the laws that govern the evolution of societies in their different phases: clans, tribes, nations; the identification of the different types of states and of the historical motor in the AMP states; and the study of the different revolutions in history, especially the revolutions that apparently failed and that were never taken into account by classical theory.

In chapter 12, we have furnished the theoretical elements that permit a surpassing, based on knowledge, of the caste system in the regions of the Sahel.

The study of these revolutions is important at this moment when African society is entering the phase of the true struggle of classes in the modern sense of the term. In fact, the process of accumulation, the confiscation of wealth, is very much advanced. This wealth, in an unequal distribution, is passed from the hands of the old colonialists to those of the new African bourgeoisie which, for now, is investing in the parasitic sectors such as real estate. But the first strike of African workers against an African industrialist employer would mark the beginning of the new era in the class struggle.

Chapters 14 and 15 give respectively a definition of cultural identity and an approach to intercultural relations.

Chapter 16 surveys the scientific contribution of the Black Egyptian world to Greece in particular, and shows that Egyptian science, despite the tenacious legend to the contrary, was highly theoretical. This chapter, like the ensuing one, allows us to appreciate the numerous unacknowledged achievements that Greek scholars borrowed from Egyptian science and philosophy.

It will be shown that an exact and rigorous type of mathematics is necessarily theoretical: this is the case with Egyptian mathematics, and particularly with Egyptian geometry. Inversely, a grossly false mathematics is necessarily empirical. This is particularly the case with Mesopotamian geometry.

Chapter 17 defines Egyptian philosophical currents and their obvious connections to those of Greece. It underscores the historical kinship of Islam, Christianity, and Judaism with Egyptian religious thought. It also tries to reveal the premises of a new philosophy largely founded on the sciences and the scientific experience and which could, perhaps one day, reconcile humanity with itself.

Finally, chapter 18 is a kind of appendix that defines a proper method for identifying the Greek vocabulary of Black African–Egyptian origin, even if some of the terms cited sometimes lack pertinence.

Thanks to the direct knowledge that it confers, the existence of an African Egyptology alone will allow us to move for good beyond the frustrating and destructive theories of obscurantist or agnostic historians who, lacking solid information acquired right from the source, seek to save face by proceeding with a hypothetical dosage of influences as if they were dividing an apple.

Only the implanting of such a scientific discipline in Black Africa would, one day, lead to the grasping of the richness and the novelty of the cultural conscience that we want to awaken, its quality, its depth, its creative power.

The African who has understood us is the one who, after the reading of our works, would have felt a birth in himself, of another person, impelled by an historical conscience, a true creator, a Promethean carrier of a new civilization and perfectly aware of what the whole Earth owes to his ancestral genius in all the domains of science, culture, and religion.

Today each group of people, armed with its rediscovered or reinforced cultural identity, has arrived at the threshold of the postindustrial era. An atavistic, but vigilant, African optimism inclines us to wish that all nations would join hands in order to build a planetary civilization instead of sinking down to barbarism.

PART 1

PALEONTOLOGICAL APPROACH

1

PREHISTORY

RACE AND HISTORY: ORIGIN OF HUMANITY AND RACIAL DIFFERENTIATION

The research conducted in humanistic paleontology, particularly by the late Dr. Louis Leakey, has helped to place the birthplace of humanity in East Africa's Great Lakes region, around the Omo Valley.

Two ramifications that have not been sufficiently emphasized until now have come to light as a result of this research:

1. Humankind born around the Great Lakes region, almost on the Equator, is necessarily pigmented and Black; the Gloger Law calls for warm-blooded animals to be pigmented in a hot and humid climate.
2. All the other races derive from the Black race by a more or less direct filiation, and the other continents were populated from Africa at the *Homo erectus* and *Homo sapiens* stages, 150,000 years ago. The old theories that used to state that Blacks came from somewhere else are now invalid.

The first Black who went out to populate the rest of the world exited Africa through the Strait of Gibraltar, the Isthmus of Suez, and maybe through Sicily and Southern Italy.[1] The existence of a cave and parietal African art of the Upper Paleolithic period has confirmed this point of view (figs. 1, 2, 3).

The Djebel Ouenat carvings in Libya were dated as those of the Upper Paleolithic Age, according to Abbé Henri Breuil. In Egypt, the most ancient

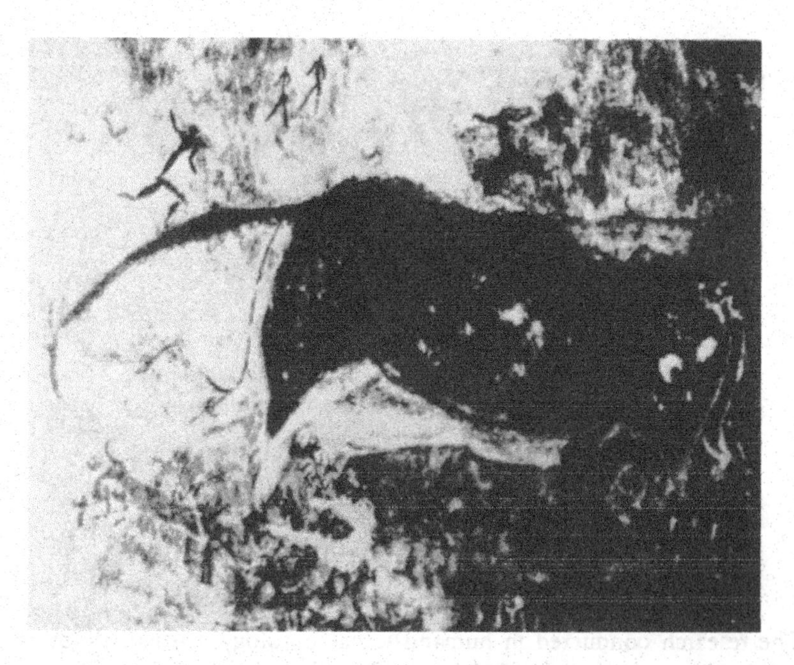

Figure 1: Typical art of the African Upper Paleolithic period. Graven cave image, Botswana, Southern Africa. (Leo Frobenius, *Histoire de la civilisation africaine*, fig. 44)

carvings are of the Upper Paleolithic period. In Ethiopia, near the Dire Dawa site, the paintings discovered in the Porcupine Cavern are of the type found in Egypt and in Libya. According to Leakey, the most ancient art form, in East Africa, is from the Upper Paleolithic period. The presence of the Stillbayen in districts rich in paints (west shores of Lake Victoria, Eyassi, and Central Tanganyika) attest to their antiquity. The archaeological layers containing colored pallets and other coloring materials descend to about five meters. In Swaziland, the men of the Upper Paleolithic Age mined iron 30,000 years ago in order to extract the red ore.[2] It is the most ancient mine in the world.

It is the advent of absolute chronology, meaning the radioactive dating methods, particularly that of Potassium-Argon, that allowed science to make great progress and thereby disparage the dogmatism that prevailed not long ago in this domain. In fact, the stratigraphical methods did not

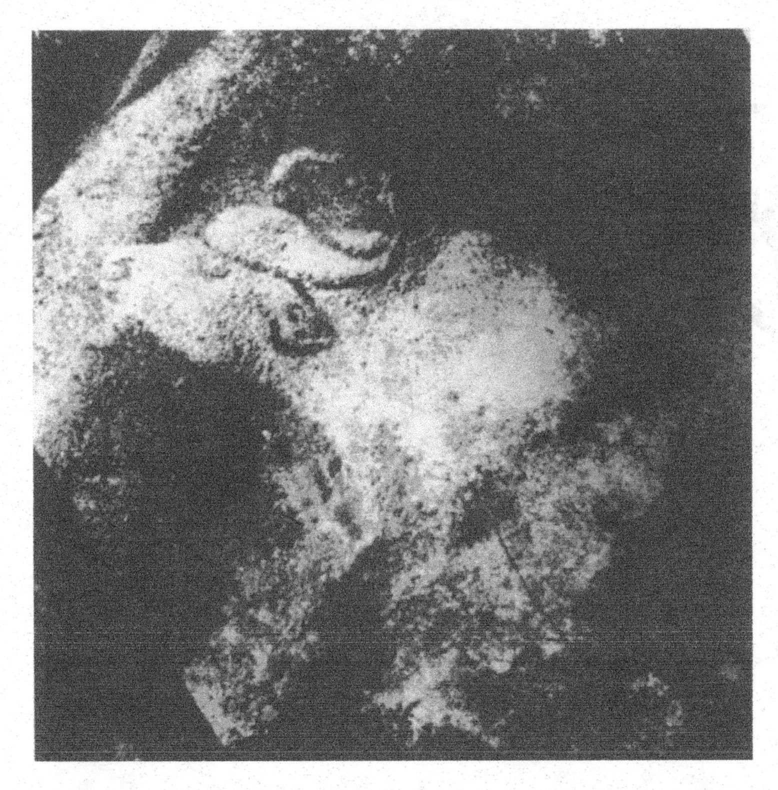

Figure 2: Prehistoric African painting. Cave painting, Khotsa Cave, Lesotho, Southern Africa, (Leo Frobenius, *Histoire de la civilization africaine*, fig. 45)

offer a clear-cut choice between the scholars' differing views. Thus, as pertaining to the main issue, it has been shown that the first inhabitant of Europe was a migrating Black: the *Grimaldi* Man. But a prominent authority, the late French scholar Raymond Vaufrey, had decreed that Africa was backward. From then on, to the eyes of the scholar, the prehistorical facts of Africa were made to appear more recent in order for them to explain a prior antiquity of Europe. Obviously, neither the Grimaldi Man nor the Combe-Capelle Man, both being Black, could have been indigenous to Europe. However, a chronological difficulty related to the limits of the stratigraphical methods would not allow that these men originate from Africa.

Racial differentiation took place in Europe, probably in southern France and in Spain, at the end of the last Würm glaciation, between 40,000 and 20,000 years ago (fig. 4). We understand now, because of the above-cited facts, why the first inhabitant of Europe was the Grimaldi Black man,[3] who was responsible for the first lithical industry of the European Upper

Figure 3: *Left:* Dancing sorcerer of Afvallingskop, Southern Africa (according to L. S. B. Leakey).
Right: Dancing sorcerer in the Cave of the Three Brothers, France (according to Count Begouen and Abbé Breuil).
The resemblance between these two figures separated by more than 10,000 km is striking. Even today, these "masterly" disguises of men as animals in the secret societies of initiation contribute to maintaining, even among university-trained Africans, naturalists moreover, the superstitious belief according to which human beings can change into animals and vice versa, like the *Neurres* who, according to a legend recorded by Herodotus, changed themselves into wolves: relics from prehistory. (Raymond Furon, *Manuel de préhistoire générale*, fourth edition [Paris: Payot, 1959], fig. 57, p. 213 and fig. 105, p. 316)

Paleolithic period called Aurignacian industry. Some believed they saw in the Lower Perigordian a strictly European industry anterior to the previous one, whose creator would have been truly indigenous to Europe, as opposed to the Grimaldi Black invader. This refers to the Combe-Capelle Man. It has been forgotten that the latter is as typical a Black as the Grimaldi Man himself and that both individuals belong to the same an-

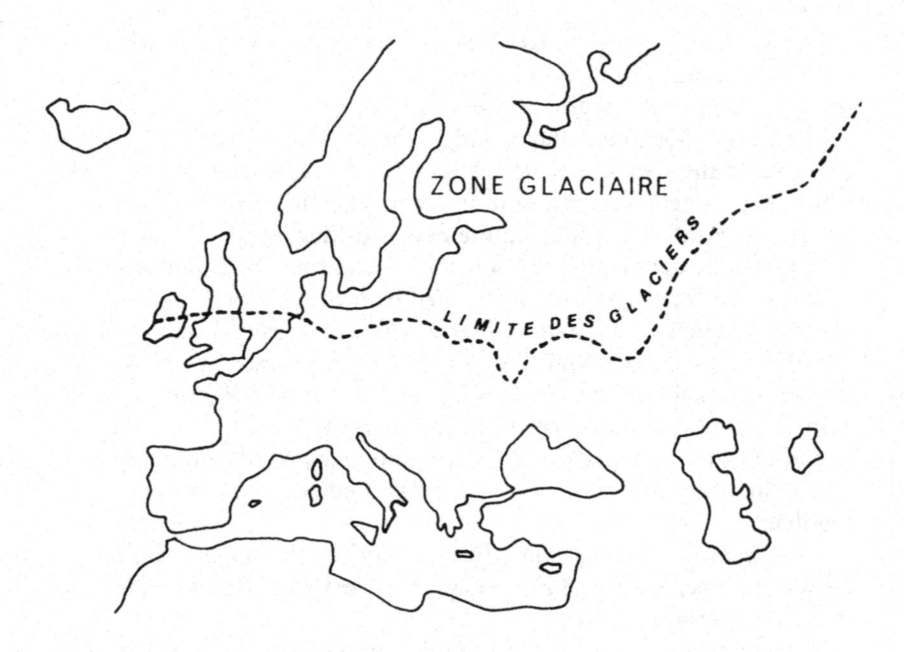

Figure 4: The boundaries of habitable Europe during the Würm glacial period. (Zone Glaciaire = Glacial Zone; Limite Des Glaciers = Boundary of the Glaciers.)

thropological type. This is the reason why the Lower Perigordian and the Aurignacian were first viewed as forming a sole and same industry. It is not possible to give here all the reasons that led to the making of these later distinctions. We refer you to our article cited above[4] and to the following discussion.

The Grimaldi Negroids have left their numerous traces all over Europe and Asia, from the Iberian Peninsula to Lake Baykal in Siberia, passing through France, Austria, the Crimea, and the Basin of Don, etc. In these last two regions, the late Soviet Professor Mikhail Gerasimov, a scholar of rare objectivity, identified the Negroid type from skulls found in the Middle Mousterian period. Marcellin Boule and Henri-Victor Vallois insist on the fact that the localizing layers of the Grimaldians are always in direct contact with those of the Mousterian period in which the last Neanderthal lived; in other words, there is no other variety of *Homo sapiens* that precedes the Grimaldi Negroid in Europe or in Asia.

If one bases one's judgment on morphology, the first White appeared only around 20,000 years ago: the Cro-Magnon Man. He is probably the result of a mutation from the Grimaldi Negroid due to an existence of

20,000 years in the excessively cold climate of Europe at the end of the last glaciation.

The Basques, who live today in the Franco-Cantabrian region where the Cro-Magnon was born, would be his descendants; in any case there are many of them in the southern region of France.

The Chancelade Man, who would be the prototype of the Yellow race, appeared in the Reindeer period, about 15,000 years ago in the Magdalenian Age. Is he a mongrel, born in a cold climate, from both stocks of the last Grimaldi in Europe and the new Cro-Magnon?

In any case, considering his dolichocephalic trait, he could only have been a Paleosiberian and not a true Yellow man (like the Chinese or the Japanese), because the latter is a brachycephalus in general, and we know that this morphological trait did not exist in the Upper Paleolithic Age; the mesocephalic trait appeared during the Mesolithic Age (around 10,000 years ago) and the brachycephalic trait much later.

The brachycephalic races—Yellow, Semites—appeared only around the Mesolithic Age, probably following great migratory currents and interbreeding.

Thus, humanity was born in Africa and differentiated itself into several races in Europe, where the climate was sufficiently cold at the end of the Würmian glaciation.

If the human being had been born in Europe, it would have been first white and then it would have negrified (darkened) under the Equator, with the appearance of the formation of melanin at the level of the epidermis, protecting the organism against the ultraviolet rays.

Therefore, this is not a value judgment: there is no particular glory about the cradle of humanity being in Africa, because it is just an accident. If the physical conditions of the planet had been otherwise, the origin of humanity would have been different.

Hence the interest of this exposé resides solely in the necessity to show, with the most possible scientific rigor, the unfolding of the facts relative to the human past, in order to restore to them all their meaning and also to extricate from them the foundation of both science and civilization.

One can thus measure the greatness of the damage perpetrated by ideologies that knowingly falsify their data.

In light of the above-mentioned facts, it seems normal that Africa, which did not see the birth of the Cro-Magnon and Chancelade men, did not know their respective industries: the Solutrean and the Magdalenian. Instead, Africa had an Aurignacian industry (Egypt, Kenya, etc.) whose age would have to be reexamined in light of the new dating techniques.

But as one would expect, physical anthropology, using the latest findings of genetics, molecular biology, and linear analysis, denies race and admits only the reality of differing populations. It is sophisticated science strongly coated with ideology! But when dealing with the transmission of a hereditary defect as in the case of sickle-cell anemia, the notion of race reappears: sickle-cell anemia, genetically speaking, strikes only Black people, says the same science that denies race. In the case of thalassemia, another hereditary defect that afflicts the Alpine race, or the White Mediterraneans, physical anthropology asserts that this disease attacks only the inhabitants of the Mediterranean periphery.

Race does not exist! Is it to say that nothing allows me to distinguish myself from a Swede, and that, a Zulu can prove to Botha (Prime Minister of the White minority government of South Africa) that they both are of the same genetic stock, and that consequently, at the genotypical level, they are almost twins, even if accidentally their phenotypes, meaning their physical appearances, are different?

Certainly, the dilution of the human species' genes during prehistoric times is very important; but from there to deny race, in the sense that it impacts on history and on social relations, meaning at the phenotypical level, which is of interest solely to the historian and to the sociologist, is a step that the daily facts of life prohibit anyone from taking.

Why does a certain physical anthropology use this scholarly manner to duck the questions? Is it loathe to rigorously derive all the implications of the monogenetic origin of humanity and, in the same vein, to take into consideration the real development of the appearance of the races? But an avant-garde West has already begun to courageously spread these ideas; and it was a White American who wrote: "I proceeded to explain that the first human beings were Black, and that light-skinned people developed later, by natural selection, to survive in temperate climates; it made us all feel much closer."[5]

The Paleolithic industry has been attested to in the Nile Valley. It therefore appears that this valley was necessarily populated solely by Blacks from the origin of humanity up to the appearance of the other races (20,000 to 15,000 years ago). Prior to some infiltrations at the end of the fourth millenium, Whites were absent from Egypt, and it practically remained that way until 1300 B.C., the period of the great invasions from the peoples of the sea under the XIXth Dynasty, not taking into account the Hyksos's invasions.[6]

The genetic table of the races represented in the tomb of Ramses III (twelfth century B.C.) shows that the Egyptians perceived themselves as Blacks (fig. 17). In fact, the Egyptian artist does not hesitate to represent the genetic type of the Egyptian as a typical Black, a Nubian; Karl Lepsius, a White scholar from Germany who made this discovery, was surprised and wrote: "Where we expected to see an Egyptian, we are presented with an authentic Negro."[7] This ruins all of the tendentious studies of ideologists and demonstrates that the Egyptians did not establish any ethnic difference between themselves and other Africans; they belonged to the same ethnic universe.

What then happened, from an anthropological standpoint, after the appearance of the Cro-Magnon in Europe? This question will be debated for a long time to come. But there is sufficient reason to suppose that the Alpine race is indigenous to Europe and therefore the descendant of the Cro-Magnon, whose survivors are the Basques. Thus, the Basques's language could very well be the oldest in Europe.

With the abatement of the cold toward the end of the Ice Age (about 10,000 years ago), a group of these Cro-Magnons moved to the North. This stock would give rise to the Scandinavian and the Germanic branches.

A first group detached itself from the northern branch at a yet undetermined time, but surely at a time posterior to 10,000 years ago. This group occupied the eastern part of Europe, and then descended all the way to Scythia, at the outskirts of the Meridional cradle: the Slavs.

Other branches probably descended the Rhine and the Danube Rivers to Caucasia and the Black Sea; from thence would originate the secondary migrations of the Celts, the Iberians, and the other Indo-European tribes who did not under any circumstance come from the heart of Asia. One therefore sees how this illusion was created.

Around 2200 B.C., the Greeks separated themselves from the northern branch, and in a north-south migration, arrived in Hellas.

The Latins, much later perhaps, occupied Italy where they found the descendants of the Alpine race (Ombrians) mixed probably with the Sicilians, the Scytheans, and the Pelasgians who must have been of a type close to that of the pre-Latins.

In 1421 B.C., the explosion of the Santorini Island of the Cyclades had migratory consequences that have been neglected and not studied until now. This event may explain the great migration of the Nordics toward India, whence the name Indo-European or Indo-Aryan? (See p. 102, as well as my work: *l'Unité culturelle de l'Afrique Noire*, Présence Africaine, 1959).

A fraction of the group that migrated toward India, and who had to pass between the Caspian and Black Seas, must have necessarily lived near the Greeks, as witnessed by the study of their mores and customs (see p. 122, and *l'Unité culturelle*, *op. cit.*).

Even in modern times, Goethe will sing of this irresistible pull toward the south of France on northern Europeans.

Do you know the land where the lemon tree blooms,
  Where the golden oranges in the somber foliage shines,
A soft wind in the blue sky blows,
The myrtle is always erect and still and the laurel standing.
Do you know it?
Over there! Over there
I must take you there, oh! my love.[8]

The last migrations of the Nordics are those of the Vikings in the Middle Ages. Thule, Iceland, and the Polar Circle are the mythical lands of the ancestors of the gods Ossian, Wotan, etc.

The Saxons separated themselves from the trunk of continental Germany in order to populate England. Thus the Nordics and the Germans were born in the North following the on-site adaptation of the Cro-Magnon. They never came from Asia or from Caucasia; what happened was just the opposite, and the secondary gyratorial migrations that started from these regions complicated the facts and gave the impression, at times, of an initial movement from western Asia.

The England of the Megalithic period felt the impact of a strong Negroid Egyptian-Phoenician influence. In fact, the first Phoenician and Sidonian navigations of the Bronze Age are contemporaneous with the XVIIIth Egyptian Dynasty (see p. 95); the Phoenicians, subjects and brokers of the Egyptians, fetched tin from the Sorlinguan Islands, meaning from England. Today, long and deep mining tunnels have been found. They are so deep that they extend all the way down under the sea. It was in this period that a pre-Christian African vocabulary came into what was to become the English language: ancient Saxon. The population of the island was then very minimal, and this facilitated the penetration of Meridional culture: they numbered less than three million up to the One Hundred Years War.

It is interesting to note that according to Marija Gimbutas[9] there existed an ancient civilization referred to as "of ancient Europe," which came directly from the Upper Paleolithic and the Mesolithic periods, and which was characterized by a sedentary life, agriculture, a cult of the mother goddess, the fecundator of life, and other feminine divinities—a matriarchal, egalitarian, urbane, and peaceful society. It is said to have lasted for three millenia, from 6500 to 3500 B.C., and it never knew war: therefore a society which, in every aspect, brings to mind the sedentary, agrarian, and matrilineal African societies.

This civilization developed in central and southeastern Europe, in the Balkans along the Danube River and its tributaries with their fertile valleys so suited to agriculture. It gave birth, at different periods, to the cultural cycles known under the names of: Karanovo (Bulgaria), Stracevo (Hungary), Sesklo (Greece), Cucuteni (Romania), Vinca (north of Macedonia).

This civilization is said to have been destroyed by the nomadic proto-Indo-Europeans (called the "Kurgams" by Gimbutas), who came from the Eurasiatic Russian steppes between the Caspian and the Black Seas. These very crude people had a culture that was characterized by nomadism, patriarchy, the veneration of the warrior deities, the domestication of the horse, an armament until then unknown in ancient Europe. The newcomers literally erased the ancient European civilization originated by the Cro-Magnoids who were left in the South (the Alpines and others) and by the last Negroids who were still[10] present as far as Switzerland. There would have been three Kurgan invasions spaced between 3400 and 2900 B.C., the last twelve waves reaching the borders of the Baltic across the basin of the Danube. The excavation of the burial mounds, left by the invaders, and the carbon 14 dating furnished the precious information about this stratification of the civilizations of Europe.

These facts give evidence of a break in continuity. There was not, as Swiss philosopher Johann Bachofen supposed, internal passage from matriarchy to patriarchy during an evolution of the same society due to the simple play of endogenous factors. Rather it was a patriarchal, nomadic group that surprised a sedentary society and introduced patriarchy and all its corollary practices by force. This shows also that neither matriarchy nor patriarchy hinges on race but stems from the material conditions of life, as we have always maintained. This does not minimize the fact that patriarchy became solidly established in the Indo-European societies at the end of the Iron Age, with the arrival of the Dorians in Greece. This occurred in Rome, Persia, Arian India, Greece, etc.; and it is inconceivable to project a matriarchal past onto the very people who were the vehicles of patriarchy, particularly the Dorians. All evidence suggests that these were people who went from hunting to nomadic life without ever experiencing the sedentary phase. It was only afterward, with the conquest of the agricultural regions, that they became sedentary.

However, let us formulate some reservations about Gimbutas's thesis. As she acknowledges it herself, the culture that made ridged pottery, which developed from the one that made spherical amphora at the beginning of the third millenium B.C., is considered to be the first Indo-European culture typical of the North: "Germans, Celts, Illyrians, Baltics, and perhaps the Slavs."[11] It is not absolutely certain that the hypothetical Kurgan invaders, to whom she attributes this transformation in northern Europe, from making funnel-shaped goblets to making spherical amphora, were truly Indo-Europeans or proto-Indo-Europeans. It should be pointed out here that the invaded area, principally that of the Balkans, contains the most distant European branch and is quite different from the Nordic type, often revealing Negroid features, reminiscent of the Grimaldi type, or of the Asiatic traits resulting from the Asiatic invasions of which the Huns and the Hungarians were the last. In fact, Gimbutas writes:

> The analysis of the skeletons in the cemeteries of Budakalasz (famous for the four-wheel chariot in clay miniature)[12] and in Alsonemedia, near Budapest, has revealed the presence of populations connected to the steppes type[13] as well as to the Mediterranean type.[14]

Gimbutas believes that there existed already the beginning of writing consisting of a corpus of more than two hundred linear and hieroglyphic signs in the Vinca and the Karanovo cultures. "This writing precedes by three thousand years the Minoan linear and seems to have a certain kinship with it."[15]

In reality, however, they are merely symbolic drawings that in no way present the coherence of genuine writing; otherwise it would have been the first writing in the world, and one cannot understand then why Crete and the Aegean, located in the area spared from the destructive invasion of the "Kurgans," would not have known writing three thousand years earlier. Thus there is no credibility to this thesis. Crete, in spite of its so-called cultural heritage, did not come out of protohistory and would become acquainted with writing only under colonization by the XVIIIth Egyptian Dynasty (see chapter 3). Crete owes this writing to Egypt as evidenced by the following facts:

It is particularly noteworthy that on the linear tablets of Pilos, in continental Greece, during the Mycenaean epoch, there are two metrological signs that reveal the typical Egyptian influence: the *talent*, a measure of weight equivalent to 29 kg, is represented by the ideogram of the Egyptian balance . Also the measure of capacity equivalent to a quarter of a liter, the *kotyla*, is represented by another Egyptian ideogram = *nb* = basket = a semicircle, etc.[16] Likewise, the genitive form of the name of Dionysus, replica of Osiris, has been found on these tablets. Finally, the Aegean civilization, instead of migrating from north to south as one would have expected, moved rather from the extreme south toward the north of Greece, which had remained semibarbaric even during the time of Thucydides (see p. 162 and figs. 18, 19, 20).

Raymond Furon reminds us that Chartes Autran has particularly insisted on the Dravidians's role in the dissemination of the pre-Aryan myths in the West.[17]

The former predominance of the Black civilization around the Mediterranean region is attested to by the unexpected existence of the pre-Hellenic Black virgins and goddesses, such as "the black Demeter of Phigalia in Arcadia, the black Aphrodite of Arcadia and Corinth, the black virgin of Saint Victor of Marseilles, and the black virgin of Chartres, who once was honored as Our-Lady-under-the-Earth."[18]

Lastly, Marcellin Boule and Henri-Victor Vallois, citing Schreiner,[19] insist on the fact that *Homo nordicus* is of recent stock, who resulted from interbreeding that occurred south of Denmark at the beginning of the Neolithic Age, between a local element consisting of the descendants of Upper Paleolithic Man and a group of invaders who came from the South; a diverse dolichocephaly with, up to a certain point, slight Neolithic brachycephalic traits.[20]

Moreover, these authors think that the mesocephaly of Ofnet evolved into the world's first brachycephaly during the Neolithic period, at a time when the last of them were neither present in Russia, the Near East, nor in North Africa. There were fewer still during the Upper Paleolithic Age which was marked by the presence of dolichocephaly and mesocephaly.[21]

The third "Kurgan" ("Jamna" in Soviet terminology) invasion occurred around 2900 B.C. and "is attested to by the hundreds of tombs in Rumania, Bulgaria, Yugoslavia, and Central Hungary. These tombs, down to the tiniest details, resemble the Kurgan tombs of the lower Dnepr and those of the lower Don called 'Jamna' (tombs in a shaft, in the Russian language)."[22]

These invasions could very well have contributed in a significant way to the formation of the Slav branch or to its division into two groups: the Slavs of the North (Russians, Polish) and the Slavs of the South (the Balkan peoples).

It is important to emphasize the fact that these "Kurgan" people of the lower Dnepr and lower Don migrated recently to this region, probably at the beginning of the Neolithic Age. There is no evidence of their presence in the Upper Paleolithic Age. It is only after the abatement of the cold weather, at the end of the last Würm Glaciation, that the Cro-Magnoids were able to advance farther to the East and occupy these regions, and to set out again toward the West, after an adaptation to the conditions of nomadic life, thus giving the signal to the so-called Kurgan invasions.

On the other hand, in spite of Gimbutas's suppositions, ancient Europe did not know writing and did not transmit to posterity any evidence that it did—not a single readable sign. Also, the existence of matriarchy in this ancient society, though probable, remains purely a hypothesis that cannot be demonstrated today owing to a lack of documents.

This ancient culture founded on agriculture was completely destroyed and replaced by a patriarchal nomadic culture that came from the outside, the same one that Europe finally transmitted to history beginning with the Dorians, twelve hundred years before Christ.

The cult of the Black virgins, which the Church finally sanctified in modern times, derived directly from the cult of Isis, which preceded Christianity in the northern Mediterranean.[23] We lack scientific proof to connect them to the Aurignacian Venuses. But their existence confirms the southern origin of civilization.

Finally, Gimbutas could have assigned rough values to the carbon 14 dates next to the calibrated, or corrected, values according to highly technical procedures, but which are still contested. Calibration, according to the rough age found, can make any age younger or older at will, so much so that, for now, many laboratories limit themselves to supplying non-calibrated dates.

CHRONOLOGICAL TABLE
OF THE EVOLUTION OF HUMANITY IN GENERAL,
AND OF THE BLACK WORLD IN PARTICULAR
(Table to be read from bottom to top
in order to maintain chronological order)

Dates	Events	Comments
+639 years −31 −332 −525	Arrival of the Arabs into Egypt Conquest of Egypt by the Romans Conquest of Egypt by Alexander the Great Conquest of Egypt by Cambysis II	Period of decline and degradation of the Black world: Social disintegration and migrations
−663	The sacking of Thebes in Egypt by the Assyrians	Beginning of the decline of the Black world
−750 −1,300 −1,400 −2,400 −4,326	Was Homer a contemporary of the XXVth Egyptian Dynasty?[24] Invasion of the Sea Peoples; arrival of the white Libyans Testimony in the language of the Hittites: the oldest Indo-European language[25] Appearance of the first Semites; Sargon I of Akkad 1,460-year-old Egyptian astronomical calendar already in use	Supremacy of Blacks
−5,000	Semites do not yet exist.	
−10,000 −15,000 −20,000	Appearance of mesocephaly and brachycephaly Appearance of Chancelade Man (southern France): prototype of the yellow race? Appearance of the Cro-Magnon (Southern France), prototype of the leucoderm (White races).	Racial differentiation of humanity in Europe
−35,000 to −32,000 −40,000 −150,000 to −130,000	Grimaldian and Aurignacian cultures (C-14 dated) Arrival of the Grimaldian Negroid in Europe First Negroid *Homo sapiens sapiens* in Africa	Humanity is represented only by Negroid *Homo sapiens*
−5.5 million	Beginning of humanity	Diverse varieties of the Australopithecus
−14 million −3.5 billion	Population of monkeys Appearance of life in embryonic form	

2

CRITICAL REVIEW OF THE MOST RECENT THESES ON THE ORIGIN OF HUMANITY

The monogenetic and African origin of humanity is becoming, every day, a more tangible fact. What then remains to be done with ideology? Faced with scientific progress, the ideologists, instead of abandoning lost ground and indefensible positions, contrive to recast their conceptual apparatuses. This is the current practice. In so doing they think that they will be able to integrate all of the known facts without having to renounce the sacred ideas that are so dear to them. For some ideologists, this would amount to committing moral suicide.

Thus, timidly, the tendency now emerging is the one holding that the monogenetic, African origin of humanity stops at the *Homo erectus* stage. And that the "sapientization" of this African *Homo erectus* was brought about at the level of each continent, but in a paleolithic environment and under conditions of "cultural" adaptation that safeguard the necessary specificity, and thus the desirable hierarchy, of the races, which hyperfine sociobiological studies ought to demonstrate.

What we are briefly evoking here are the infinitely varied nuances of this position in order to show that the ideologists have not reached the end of their martyrdom, because logical coherence remains with science.

Let us recall, for history's sake, that this malaise was already present in the previous generation of eminent anthropologists, at a time when the methods of absolute chronology had not yet cast a singular light on the prehistorical archaeology of each continent. What was then known was still quite disturbing.

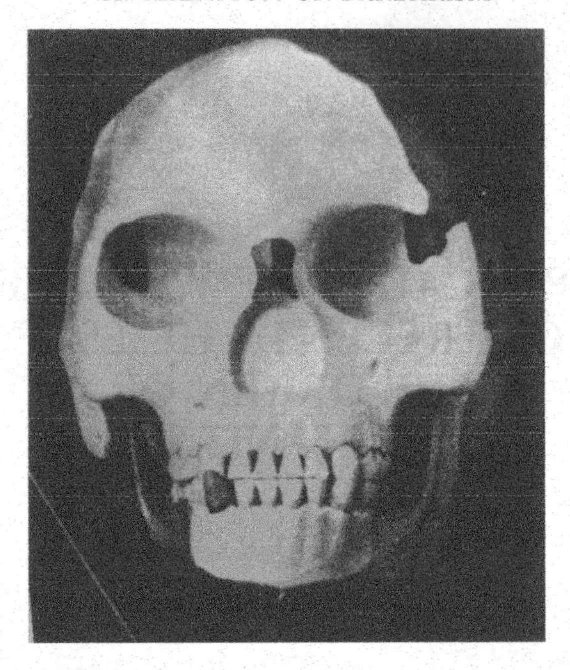

Figure 5: "Piltdown Man," the entirely fabricated falsehood, which ideology needed in order to support the thesis of the pre-*Sapiens*. It is made up of a juxtaposition of the skull of a modern man with a high forehead and the jawbone of a monkey whose canines can be seen. (Marcellin Boule and Henri-Victor Vallois, *Les Hommes fossiles*, fig. 119)

The first *Homo sapiens* who inhabited Europe was unquestionably a migrant Negroid who came from outside, about 40,000 years ago,[1] as René Verneaux[2] has demonstrated. The first "White," the Cro-Magnon Man, appeared in the same region 20,000 years later. Who was the ancestor of Cro-Magnon, if he did not derive from the Negroid through mutation? For neither the Cro-Magnon nor the Negroid descended from Neanderthal Man who preceded them and who lived 80,000 years ago, during the Würmian period.

Thus there was born, out of necessity, the theory of the existence of pre-*Sapiens*, corroborated by the discovery of three fossils, the principal one of which was a scientific hoax deliberately fabricated to supply ideology with the pertinent facts that it had lacked. This was the all too famous Piltdown Man (fig. 5) that was discovered—in reality fabricated—in 1912 by British geologist Charles Dawson.[3] Upon reflection, it was wrong that until now this talented forger, a true scholar, was allowed to pass as a "practical joker" who had no intention other than to mislead the specialists, whether for fun or for revenge. His aim was quite different, and for fifty years, scholars of good faith such as Henri-Victor Vallois, while formulating some reservations, adhered to the pre-*Sapiens* theory, because it was so greatly needed by cultural and political Europe. Thus Vallois wrote:

> The documentation on Piltdown Man is unfortunately incomplete. Its extremely difficult interpretation is still doubtful on some essential points. However, one cannot ignore the fact that this discovery is extremely important and most enlightening, especially now that we know that the jawbone belongs to the same skull. This discovery tells of the existence of a man whose skull more closely resembles that of *Homo sapiens* and thereby comes more directly from this *Homo sapiens* than from Neanderthal Man. His existence, though dated at a period less ancient than previously thought, is nevertheless from the Lower Pleistocene period. The origins of our direct ancestors should therefore go back to the very remote past. Up to now, a certain number of discoveries without geological support, and consequently with no demonstrative value, have been marshaled in support of this hypothesis. The Piltdown skull, for the first time, provides us with a well-observed fact whose significance is clear and precise, in spite of the uncertainties that still linger about its age.[4]

Thus, even a scholar of the caliber of Vallois believed that the simian jawbone of Piltdown and the skull belonged to the same individual. Moreover, he emphasized the geological guarantees surrounding the discovery of this fossil, which had been buried by the learned forger 1.5 meters under the gravel of the Ouse River in Sussex. It was not until 1954 that another British scientist of good faith, Kenneth P. Oakley, working at the British Museum, had the idea of measuring the quantity of fluorine contained in the two pieces in order to deduce the difference in the amount. The results showed with certainty that the specimen was a fake, that the jaw and skull did not belong to the same individual, because they did not contain the same amount of fluorine.[5] Oakley thus put an end to the bitter debate that had lasted for nearly fifty years over the authenticity of Piltdown Man. By the same token, he dealt—it is important to underscore this—the final blow to the theory of pre-*Sapiens*. Furthermore, this theory had relied on pieces of two faceless skulls—Swanscombe Man (1935–36) and Fontéchevade Man (1947)—specimens so unsatisfactory, as one can tell from the statement by Vallois quoted above, that these scholars had pinned all their hopes on Piltdown Man, the only piece in the series that apparently was convincing for the following reasons: It had a complete face; the high forehead typical of *Homo sapiens*, without the slightest trait of the supraorbital torus so characteristic of Neanderthal Man; it was more evolved than the latter, and it was indigenous to Europe, a true ancestor of *Homo europus*. It was also of a totally different extraction from the Negroid *Homo sapiens*, wherever it came from. Alas, this one (the Piltdown Man) turned out to be a fake.[6]

The x-ray spectrometer has confirmed the hoax of Piltdown by showing evidence of traces of chromium salt that is used when applying patina to bones.[7] The facts are even more ludicrous when one knows that several identical morphological traits were established among the fossils of Piltdown Man, Fontéchevade Man, and Swanscombe Man:

> Resemblances with the skull of Piltdown, demonstrated by A. Keith appear, on the contrary, to have to been retained. The English author had concluded from them that Swanscombe Man was a descendant of Piltdown Man, more evolved toward Homo sapiens. This hypothesis is incorrect, because we now know that Swanscombe man is older. Kinship between the two is nonetheless evident.[8]

Concerning the fossil of Fontéchevade Man, the same authors—Boule and Vallois—write:

> The foreheads of Fontéchevade men were like those of modern man and were totally different from that of Neanderthal Man. Here again there is a marked resemblance with Piltdown Man, because the piece of forehead corresponding to the second find at this site is also lacking a protruberance, and its profile is almost exactly congruent with that of the Fontéchevade piece.[9]

In reality the "modern" characteristics of this fossil were merely imagined by these scholars, rather than being genuine morphological traits, as pointed out by Bernard Vandermeersch:

> The piece discovered in the cave of Fontéchevade in Charente is represented by one part of the cranial arch the morphology of which, according to Vallois, is more modern than that of contemporaneous fossils, particularly in the area of the forehead. Unfortunately it is very incomplete and does not have a characteristic structure. The "modern" characteristics set forth are not the result then of direct observations, but are inferred from the proposed reconstruction and have often been contested.[10]

If *Homo sapiens* were indigenous to Europe, it should be possible to follow his evolution from his alleged ancestors of the interglacial Mindel-Riss period, who are supposed to have lived 350,000 years ago, to his descendant, the Cro-Magnon of the Solutrean period, who lived 20,000 years ago. However, the paleontological gap between the two has in no way been filled to this day.

So the "pre-*Sapiens*" disappeared for 350,000 years without leaving any descendants, and one has to wait until the beginning of the Würm glacial period, around 80,000 years ago, to see the emergence of Neanderthal, who then suddenly disappears around 40,000 years ago as well, without leaving any descendants either, at the same time that *Homo sapiens*, namely the Grimaldi Negroid, enters Europe, 20,000 years before the appearance (probably by mutation of the Negroid) of the first traces of Cro-Magnon, the ancestor of the present-day European.

The fossil found by Henri de Lumeley and named Tautavel Man brought no new element to the pre-*Sapiens* thesis. This fossil was dated using the amino acid method (Jeffrey Bada) and the uranium method (K. Furekian).[11] The deposits of the Tayacian and the Acheulean industries containing these fossils were said to be between 320,000 (G layer) and 220,000 (F layer) years old.[12]

This Tautavel Man, as his inventor seemed to think, was an intermediary between *Homo erectus* (Pithecanthropus) and Neanderthal Man. He had a prominent supraorbital protruberance, so characteristic of Neanderthal, with a cranial capacity inferior to that of the latter.

There is another fact that deserves to be pointed out: the industries associated with "pre-*Sapiens*" are characteristic of *Homo erectus*. And, by supreme contradiction, these industries are more primitive than those of the Neanderthal Man, the Mousterian. Indeed we are beginning to see that Tautavel Man is associated with both Tayacian industry and that of the Middle Acheulean; similarly, Fontéchevade industry is Tayacian, and that of Swanscombe, Acheulean.

So many facts often left in the dark have led paleontologists like Vandermeersch to reject the thesis of pre-*Sapiens*.

The evolutionary period just considered goes from the Mindel-Riss to the Riss-Würm. Vandermeersch thinks that it is untenable to state that during a span of 250,000 years both Neanderthal and the first pre-*Sapiens* could have evolved separately within the same European region, each developing his own specific features without any assimilation taking place; which, on the contrary, should have taken place and thus mitigated the differences, since the "specific barrier" no longer existed: interbreeding must certainly have taken place because Neanderthal Man is only a subspecies of *Homo sapiens*.

Likewise, no cultural barrier could play any role since both subspecies, the so-called pre-*Sapiens* and the Neanderthal, were associated with the same Acheulean and Tayacian industries.

Let us recall that the classical Mousterian industry of Neanderthal Man was definitely and paradoxically more highly developed than the abovementioned industries, attributed to pre-*Sapiens*. So much so that, at the

1969 UNESCO colloquium on the appearance of modern man, care was taken, to the best of my recollection, to dissociate cultural evolution (industry) from morphological evolution. This was done in order to eliminate the insurmountable obstacle just raised above, namely: how can a morphologically and physically more primitive being, such as Neanderthal Man, be responsible for an industry coming out of a materially more advanced and perfected culture than the more highly evolved pre-*Sapiens*?

The study of the Biache-Saint-Vaast skull, a new pre-Neanderthal recently discovered in the north of France, led Vandermeersch to conclude that Swanscombe, Fontéchevade, and all the other fossils found in Europe prior to the appearance of *Homo sapiens* about 37,000 years ago in this region belong to the Neanderthal lineage.

Let us add that, according to Vallois, the Ehringsdorf Man, the number 1 skull of Saccopastora, the Steinheim skull, and Heidelberg Man, all belong to that same lineage.[13] According to Vandermeersch,

> . . . because of the Biache skull, the gap that separated pre-Neanderthals from pre-Sapiens is considerably reduced. Of all the pre-Neanderthals, the Biache skull is the one that is closest to Swanscombe Man. All the more so because the cranial region of the Biache, which presents the most pronounced Neanderthalian features, is the mastoid region that is no longer present in the Swanscombe skull. The latter appears to be more "modern," or one might say more Archanthropic, for it is older and closer to the birth of the lineage, therefore less specialized in the Neanderthalian sense. This a general law of evolution.

Thus Archanthropic men, coming most probably from Africa, may have begun (during the Mindel-Riss interglacial period) to assume individual features on the order of the Neanderthal type, because of climatic conditions in the paleo-environment. At the beginning of the Riss-Würm period 80,000 years ago, the evolutionary process that was to end in the cul-de-sac of Neanderthal Man was completed and the Neanderthal population of Europe remained homogeneous during Würm I and II, practically speaking, from 80,000 to 40,000 years ago.

These facts led Vandermeersch to conclude that Neanderthal Man alone is specifically European, and that the origin of *Homo sapiens* must be found elsewhere, namely in the East and, to be precise, in Palestine, even though he does not pinpoint the exact location.[14]

As stated earlier, it is not impossible that Neanderthal Man resulted from a progressive adaptation of the African *Homo erectus* in Europe during the Riss-Würm interglacial period, and that afterward he migrated to the other continents, where he became extinct without leaving any descendants, contrary to what Vandermeersch thinks. If this were actually the case, prehistoric archaeology would have to prove that the Neanderthalian fossils of Europe are older than those found on other continents, to which this species migrated later. Now, no one can possibly make preemptorily such an affirmation.

Broken Hill Man (Rhodesian or Zimbabwean Man) is a Neanderthalian fossil, in some ways more primitive than the European skull of La Chapelle-aux-Saints, which it so unmistakably resembles (fig. 6).

I was not far from adopting the viewpoint above, but the fact that the African Neanderthal of Broken Hill, dated by the amino acid method to be 110,000 years old, is older than those of Europe, or in any case of comparable age, has again raised more questions. Now, it is no longer absurd to suppose that even Neanderthal Man could have come from Africa.

The oldest Neanderthalian fossils of Europe do not seem to date much beyond Würm I/II (80,000 years ago).

Through radiocarbon dating, we now know that Negroid *Homo sapiens sapiens*, with very voluminous skulls measuring up to 1,500cm^3 on average, if not more, lived in southern Africa between 50,000 and 100,000 years ago, and that they were probably the ones who were called the world's first miners: the iron mines of Swaziland, cited in chapter 1. The fossils of these *Homo sapiens* are represented by the large Boskop skull, the incomplete Florisbad head (one part of the skull and the face), and the bony Cape Flats head.[15] Thus the largest skulls discovered to this day are those of these Negroids of Southern Africa, contrary to the calculations of the authors of *Race et Intelligence*, a work that I will deal with later (see pp. 55–65).

The Florisbad fossil was dated as being more than 41,000 years old. It is therefore older than all of the European *Homo sapiens sapiens* and those from the other continents, when dated by a method of absolute chronology, without tendentious or biased interpretation.

Finally, the Oriental origin of *Homo sapiens*, as Vandermeersch asserts it, is today scientifically indefensible.

In fact, Vandermeersch took up the idea of Vallois, who, following Sir Arthur Keith and T. D. McCown, studied Palestine's Neanderthals and concluded that these fossils probably were not direct ancestors of Upper Paleolithic men, but rather that their existence "indicates that, while the transformation from Neanderthal man to modern man did not take place in Europe, it was able to take place somewhere else. This is a conclusion of extreme importance."[16] Vandermeersch himself recognized that there was a serious difficulty of a chronological nature, which, unfortunately, still persists. Indeed, in order for the hypothesis above to be acceptable, these fossils would have to belong at least to the Riss or the Riss-Würm period. However, we now know that this is not the case. The radiocarbon and amino acid datings conducted in this region agree and give an age that

Figure 6: Skulls of Broken Hill (top) and of La Chapelle-aux-Saints (bottom); three-quarters shown, almost from the same angle, in order to facilitate comparison. (Boule and Vallois, *Les Hommes fossiles*, fig. 282)

varies between 37,000 and 53,000 B.C.[17] Therefore, these would-be ancestors of *Homo sapiens* are much more recent than the African *Homo sapiens sapiens* who appeared at least 150,000 years ago (skulls of Omo I, Omo II; Kanjera Man).[18]

Before drawing conclusions from the anteriority of the African *Homo sapiens sapiens* in relation to the *Homo sapiens sapiens* on other continents, let us insist on the fact that the "evolved Neanderthals" of Qafzeh (37,000 years ago) are strictly contemporaries of the European *Homo sapiens* and therefore cannot be his ancestors. In a report presented to the Paris Colloquium of 1969, Vandermeersch writes that layer 17, which contains the three skeletons he discovered, also contains traces of coal and ashes in such abundance that their color has become a "uniform deep gray." In such conditions, it is absolutely possible to carry out radiometric dating of these ashes. But was this ever attempted?[19] M. Ottieno of Kenya and I represented the African continent at the Paris Colloquium, and the ideas that I presented against the polycentric thesis and the differentiation from *Homo erectus* onward are the same ones.

The Neanderthals of Palestine and Iraq are thus nothing but dead ends. They are too recent to be the origin of any species of *Homo sapiens sapiens*. Endocranial molds made from these fossils would enable one to understand better the still enormous gap that separates them from *Homo sapiens sapiens*. But until now, the making and studying of these molds have been neglected, even though I raised this question at the Paris Colloquium of 1969. If modern man was not born in Europe, he was going to be born in Palestine, according to the Biblical word, which is what these anthropologists seem to be saying to themselves subconsciously!

Compounding this irony, Palestine appears to constitute a paleontological vacuum during the period corresponding to the appearance of *Homo sapiens sapiens*. One will have to wait until the Mesolithic Age, around 8,000 or 10,000 years ago, to see the appearance there of *Homo sapiens sapiens* in the form of a Negroid: Dorothy Garrod's Natufian is, all ideology aside, the first example of *Homo sapiens sapiens* in this region. The gap that exists between him and the evolved Neanderthals of Qafzeh has not been filled to this day by prehistoric archaeology. However, during almost the same period, a Negroid culture known as Capsian, characterized by small blades in the shape of crescents, extended from Kenya to Tunisia and into Palestine. This was the period of the Negroids of the Capsian culture.

In Africa, this Capsian culture was immediately preceded by that of the Ibero-Maurusian, which disappeared ten thousand years ago without leaving any descendants. No demonstrable provable link exists between Ibero-Maurusian Man and the Guanches of the protohistorical Canary Islands. A gap of eight thousand years, which no one has tried to fill, separates them: the Guanches, who practiced mummification and were more or less imbued with Punic culture, must be considered a mere branch of today's Berbers who, in turn, are undoubtedly descendants of the White peoples of Europe, called the "Sea Peoples" in the Egyptian texts, who invaded Egypt under the XIXth Dynasty (1300 B.C.), precisely that of the Ramessides. Conquered by the Egyptians, they were driven back west of the Nile Delta, from whence they scattered progressively to the Atlantic Ocean, across Cyrenaica, from the Nasamons to the Gaetulians of southern Morocco.

As paradoxical as it may be, the thesis of the polycentric origin of humanity, which at first seems to make sense, cannot withstand an analysis of the facts, above all chronological facts. That is why, when adopting this view, even scholars of the caliber of Andor Thoma end up explaining humanity's evolution backward. Thoma, who adopts the views of Vandermeersch on Palestine Man, writes: "The Qafzeh VI skull recently described by Henri Vallois and Bernard Vandermeersch is the earliest representative of western Neanthropians."[21] Thus, the hypotheses of Keith and McCown, taken up by Vallois and Vandermeersch, become certitude, to be commented upon by Thoma and other polycentrists.

Thoma does not hesitate to connect the skull of the one-and-a-half-year-old infant of Starocelia, found in the Crimea and of the Aurignacian type according to Gerasimov,[22] to the Neanderthals of Palestine. In passing, one may note that the supraorbital protuberance so prominent in Qafzeh Man and the exaggerated width of his nasal orifice,[23] in short, the primitive and almost bestial aspect of the men of Palestine, which should eliminate all possibility of direct comparison with *Homo sapiens sapiens*, is minimized in the reproduction of the article. To see this, one can refer to figure 250 of H.V. Vallois (*op. cit.*, p. 395). For Thoma, Qafzeh and Starocelia are the proto-Cro-Magnons descending from the Paleoanthropians such as Steinheim and Swanscombe, dated as being more than 200,000 years old. Their descendants are the Cro-Magnons of Europe and North Africa. The latter, "on colonizing Africa, were rapidly 'Negroidized,' under the effect of the high selective pressure exerted by the new environment; for the distinctive alveolar prognathism, the considerable width of the nose, and the relatively low and very long neuroskull are already typically Negroid."[24]

That is how Thoma describes the morphological features of a series of skeletons dating from the last Paleolithic period (10,000 to 12,000 B.C.) which were discovered in Nubia and then studied by J. E. Anderson.

For Gerasimov, the Starocelia child is a typically Negroid *Sapiens sapiens*. Moreover, the dimensions and form of his forehead prohibit classifying him among the Neanderthals, even the evolved ones.

Still according to Thoma, the evolutionary passage from the Paleoanthropic to the Neanthropic phase was accomplished in at least three geographical centers: in Indonesia and in Australia, 600,000 years ago, during the Archanthropic phase, resulting in the individualization of the Australoid branch of humanity; in southern Siberia, 80,000 years ago resulting in the Mongoloid phylum; whereas the separation of the Europoids and the Negroids did not occur until the Neanthropic phase, about 12,000 years ago, in his view.

For Thoma, the study that he conducted on the resemblances between the digiti-palmar skin grooves of the "five" great races especially confirms the recent separation of the Negroid and the Europoid, or, as we might say, the Grimaldian and Cro-Magnon. If this latter fact is paleontologically true, it took place in the opposite direction from the process supposed by Thoma, in the south of France, and in any case in southern Europe, and not in Africa, between 40,000 and 20,000 years ago, namely during the interval that separates the arrival in Europe of the Grimaldi Man—a Negroid migrant who probably came by way of Gibraltar—from that of Cro-Magnon Man of the Solutrean Period. These *Homo sapiens* who entered Europe did not owe their existence to the men of Qafzeh, for they were either their predecessors or at least their contemporaries as proven by the radiometric datings conducted at the excavation sites.

Let us also add that immunological data have confirmed the hypothesis of a recent separation of Blacks and Whites, Negroids and Caucasoids,[25] although the latter term is improper, since the Caucasus is in no way the cradle of the White race (fig. 7).

According to Jacques Ruffie, quoting Nei Masatoshi and A. R. Roycoudhury, the separation of these racial groups occurred much earlier. These authors begin with several dozen blood markers in order to study both the inter- and intragroup genetic differences among Negroid, Caucasoid, and Mongoloid populations:

> They define, more or less approximately, the coefficients of correlations that allow dating of the time at which these groups separated from each other. The Negroid group became autonomous some 120,000 years ago, whereas the Mongoloids and Caucasoids branched off only about 55,000 years ago.[26]

Even though 55,000 years may appear to be too old an age for the formation of the Caucasoid and the Mongoloid branches, in view of the prehistoric data, 120,000 years fits in well with the appearance of the first African Negroid *Homo sapiens sapiens* in the Omo Valley and Kanjera.

According to Thoma, "the present-day Australoids can be related to the Pithecanthropes of Java by way of the Ngandong men of Java (at the beginning of the Upper Pleistocene period, about 150,000 years ago.)"[27] The Australian site of Kow Swanif (8000 B.C.) yielded twenty skeletons that corresponded morphologically to the population of Ngandong and provided proof of the existence of an Australian phylum.

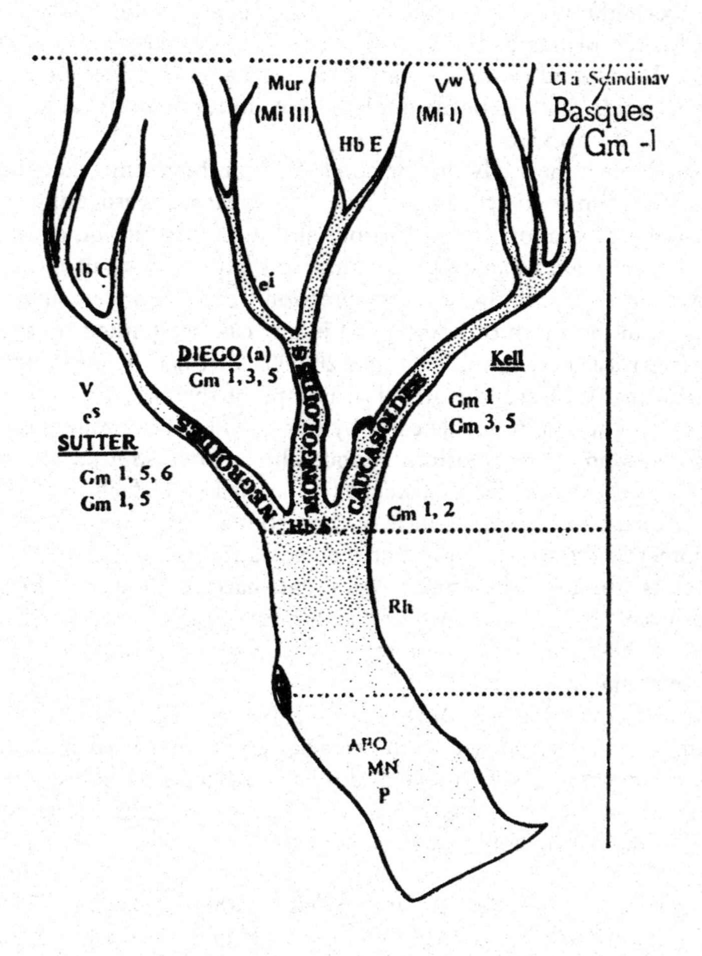

Figure 7: Racial differentiation according to hemotypological data. Altogether, racial markers exist that are significant enough to allow identification of the ancient Egyptians, if they have not already been identified. The three factors: Sutter (Negroid), Diego (Mongoloid), and Kell (Caucasoid) have been underlined on this diagram. (Jacques Ruffie, *De la biologie à la culture*, p. 395)

At the 1969 Paris Colloquium, the same tendency was displayed, which consisted of trying to isolate the Australoid phylum in order to make it a subhuman species, perhaps doomed to disappear. Addressing the colloquium in a plenary meeting for the adoption of conclusions, Dr. L. S. B. Leakey said that what they were in the process of doing had no relation to science, and he asked that the paragraph about the Australoid phylum be deleted from the final text, which was done.

Another great scholar told me: "Psychically, I do not know, but morphologically I know that the Australians are different from modern human beings."

However, the Australians are *Homo sapiens sapiens* in the strict sense of the term and do not constitute a branch apart. Their intellectual capacities have been tested, and we know that their performance is indeed identical to that of modern man.

They are not of an insular origin. They arrived at their present habitat in Australia by navigating from the Asian continent, about 30,000 years ago.[28]

According to Thoma, the Mongoloid fossils known to exist only in the recent Würm period (about 20,000 years ago) in southern Siberia (Atontova, Gora, Malta, Bouriet), where they are accompanied by human representations of the Mongoloid type, may have resulted from a "neanthropization" of the Near Eastern Neanderthal, when Siberia was habitable as far as 61 degrees latitude north. The author bases his reasoning on the fact that Paleosiberian and Mongoloid fossils, like the Neanderthals, generally do not have canine fossae, but have high, large, and rounded sockets. Yet the same author, in the same article, describes the Near Eastern Neanderthals as having precisely canine fossae, and therefore are able to be classified as proto-Cro-Magnons.

Still according to Thoma, it was not until the Neolithic period, 6,000 years ago, that the Mongoloids gained a definite selective advantage in their original environment. Consequently, one might expect to find Mongoloid features in many of the Asiatic populations not descended from the Mongoloid phylum.

Espousing the viewpoint of William W. Howells, according to which evolution always involves a certain amount of anagenesis (meaning perfecting without the possibility of diversification) and a certain amount of cladogenesis (meaning the birth of several branches of which only one advances to perfection), Thoma maintains that the most probable hypothesis for humanity's evolution is polycentrism, which is not to be confused with polyphyletism.

According to this perspective, a species can originate from several other species belonging to different families or ancestral types. Thus it was assumed at the beginning of this century that Whites descended from chimpanzees, Blacks from gorillas, and Yellows from orangutans. The three races would then have come respectively from three separate ancestral types: "Pan, Goullael, Pongo." This would allow one to say: "I, the Caucasoid, descend from the chimpanzee. I have nothing in common with the Black who descends from the gorilla, or the Yellow who descends from the orangutan, although all three of us are human!" The purpose of this was to find, at whatever cost, a difference in origin that might justify racial superiority. It was Vallois who demonstrated in 1929 the impossibility of polyphyletism.[29] Thoma showed that polycentrism began with Theodor Mollison of Munich in 1931 and was developed later by F. Weidenreich in 1943. He adds:

> Weidenreich's concept of human evolution was further developed by Sir A. Keith, then modernized by Prof. Carleton Coon in 1962.[30] But these authors never took into consideration the possibility of prehistoric migrations. This omission seemed unacceptable to many prehistorians and to myself. Since 1962,[31] I have developed another polycentric diagram of human evolution.[32]

Thus for Thoma and the defenders of the polycentric thesis, modern man originated several times from different Paleoanthropians, in widely separated areas of the ancient world, during the Upper Pleistocene period. Then, through secondary traits, he adapted to the ever varying local environment, from one center to another, and thus necessarily underwent a "cladogenetic" evolution. This hypothesis is also one of common sense; at first sight it imposes itself on good sense with an almost overbearing imperative.

However, this hypothesis is probably false and an objective analysis of the facts requires its rejection. If it were true, the American continent, which is as old as the other continents—particularly Africa and Europe—and which extends from the North Pole to the South Pole and consequently encompasses all the climatic transitions, should also be a multiple center for the genesis of humanity at the Australopithecus and *Homo erectus* stages as well as at that of *Homo sapiens.*

But we know that this is not so. There are no fossilized humans indigenous to America. This continent was populated from Asia, by way of the Bering Strait. All scholars agree on this fact.

The polycentric hypothesis leads to the insurmountable contradiction inherent in supposing that the children were born before the parents who begot them. It is this fundamental contradiction that is seen throughout all of Thoma's reasoning, albeit he has made a remarkable display of erudition in attempting to rejuvenate and adapt the polycentric thesis. He particularly called attention to the fact that authors like Keith and Coon neglected the migratory currents, and that their conceptions were thus rendered at least partially unacceptable.

For Thoma, as quoted above, Africa was populated later from Europe at the Neanthropic stage: ". . . Migratory Cro-Magnons, as they colonized Africa around 10,000 years ago, quickly became Negroidized due to a strong pressure of genetic selection."

There can be no better example of taking liberties with facts, especially chronological ones.

If the polycentric hypothesis were valid, we should be able find somewhere in the rest of the world at least one single center of the birth of *Homo erectus* or *Homo sapiens sapiens*, respectively more ancient than the centers in Africa. However, in the case of the polycentric hypothesis, chronological data oblige us to admit that the so-called ancestors of the Africans—Thoma's Cro-Magnons in this case—were born well after their "African sons," and even better yet, that in all probability they were descended from their so-called sons by mutation of the Grimaldi Negroid. The latter was completely ignored by Thoma throughout his entire development, as he tacitly perhaps assimilated him to Cro-Magnon, as is the current practice, particularly with the French ideologues.

African *Homo sapiens sapiens*, as we have seen above, is confirmed particularly by the Omo I skull, which is at least 150,000 years old. Richard Leakey explained to me, in May 1977 in Nairobi, Kenya, how these fossils were dated. They had been buried under layers of the African Middle Pleistocene Age in a region where the stratigraphy had not been disturbed by any tectonic movements. A piece of charcoal found at a distance one-third of the depth of these fossils was dated as being more than 50,000 years old. By extrapolation, multiplying this age by three gives the average age of the fossils. Dating by the uranium-thorium method has confirmed this result by conferring an age of 130,000 years.[33]

This Omo I specimen is to be associated, as Dr. Leakey has done, with Kanjera Man, a *Homo sapiens sapiens*[34] of the Middle Pleistocene Age that was discovered by Leakey in 1933.

A conference that was held in Cambridge at that time concluded that, in spite of their antiquity, the Kanjera fossils barely differ from modern man.[35] At the time, as a result of criticism voiced by the British geologist P. Boswell, some doubt was cast on the age of these fossils. These doubts have now been removed because we know that this is a specimen of *Homo sapiens sapiens* with modern man's forehead and without a supraorbital torus of any kind.

Even if these fossils were only 60,000 years old, they would still be the oldest of their species in the world.

On the other hand, we know that about 30,000 years ago the world's most ancient iron mine was being operated in South Africa, in Swaziland, for the extraction of hematite, red ocher, by a man who could be only a *Homo sapiens sapiens*.[35] The mine contained 23,000 stone tools, the analysis of which was to allow determining which type of man was responsible for the mining, for we know or suppose that Neanderthal Man also rubbed red ocher on his body. A block of hematite extracted from this mine was found on a piece of charcoal that Yale University dated as being 29,000 years old.[36]

These are the facts as they relate to Black Africa. Now let us look more closely at the chronology of *Homo sapiens sapiens*' appearance on the other continents.

The first *Homo sapiens sapiens* in Europe was, as we have already seen, the migratory Negroid who was responsible for Aurignacian industry. Now, the chronological facts relative to the antiquity of *Homo sapiens sapiens* on the African continent allow us to suppose that the Grimaldi Negroid came from Africa and that he entered Europe through the Iberian Peninsula rather than from the East. All along his path he left still visible traces in the form of parietal rock drawings, none of which are to be found on the other supposed itineraries.

His arrival in Europe was dated by the carbon 14 method by Prof. Hallam L. Movius, Jr.[37]

The excavations undertaken from 1958 to 1964 at the Pataud shelter (Les Eyzies, Dordogne), under the auspices of the Musée de l'Homme (Paris) on the one hand and the Peabody Museum of Harvard University on the other, resulted in the discovery of fourteen archaeological layers. These layers, most of which were dated using the radiocarbon method, are listed in the footnote.[38] The dates obtained range between 34,000 B.P., that is about 32,000 B.C. for the layer constituting the base of the ancient Aurignacian period, and 21,940 B.P., or 19,990 B.C., for the Proto-Magdalenian period.

Layer 1 of the Solutrean period in the same cave did not provide any datable sample; but at West Langerie-Haute, a neighboring site, layer 31, which would be equivalent to Solutrean I of the Pataud shelter, gave a date (20,890 B.P. + 300, or 18,940 B.C.), which coincides effectively with the preceding dates and confirms the anteriority of the Grimaldi as compared to the Cro-Magnon; for, as we must repeat, the latter is indeed Solutrean Man.

At Quina (Gardes, Charente), the Recent Mousterian period gave the date of 32,250 B.P. + 350 or 33,300 B.C.,[39] which agrees well with the ancient Aurignacian and illustrates the remark by Boule and Vallois, according to which, stratigraphically speaking, there is no difference between the Negroid Aurignacian race of Grimaldi Man and that of the Mousterian:

> It is nonetheless significant, in any case, that the Negroid skeletons [of Grimaldi Man] go back to the beginning of the Reindeer Age, to a period that borders on the Mousterian, if not coinciding with it. This fact must not be forgotten.[40]

For François Bordes, Aurignacian Man did not originate in Europe. He was an invader who arrived with his own ready-made industry:

> One thing appears likely: that the Aurignacian (industry) arrived in France fully developed. And while some of its tools are found in the Quina type of the Mousterian, or even earlier, there does not seem to be any possibility of the Aurignacian developing on the spot. One

clearly has the impression that, for once, there was an invasion that came from the East.[41]

In actuality, Aurignacian expansion went from West to East and not the other way, as confirmed by all the above-mentioned facts.

Bordes thinks that the truly indigenous industry of Europe in the Upper Paleolithic Age is the ancient Perigordian, characterized by the so-called Châtelperron point. It derived from the evolved Mousterian period and Acheulean type B tradition immediately anterior to Würm II. Thus it probably dated from the end of the Würm II/III interglacial period. This industry is mainly known from the excavations conducted by André Leroi Gourhan and Bordes himself.[42]

Bordes notes that this industry is interstratified with that of the Aurignacian period at at least two sites (Piage and Roc de Combe).

What can this mean, other than that it is difficult to distinguish between these two industries which were originally considered to be but two facets of the Aurignacian, as previously mentioned?

It is as delicate a task to separate Perigordian industry into a category of its own as it is to establish its anteriority in relation to the Aurignacian. Has not Bordes just told us that the tools of the Aurignacian period are found in the Quina type of the Mousterian period, which were dated, as we have seen, at 35,000 B.P., if not earlier? No absolute chronological dating method has as yet permitted us to establish in a precise manner this Perigordian anteriority, if it really is distinct from the Aurignacian, which has several facets, one of which might be Perigordian I, as stated earlier, and which extends incomparably beyond the Perigordian, as we shall see.

Movius is of this opinion when he writes with great politeness: "The following C-14 dates relative to the layers of Perigordian I in France suggest that this industry probably was, in part at least, contemporaneous with the Aurignacian period of the Pataud shelter and other places."[43]

The anthropological identity of this hypothetical indigenous European, situated somewhere between the final Mousterian and the Aurignacian periods and probably responsible for Perigordian I, is even more mysterious and constitutes a quasi-insolvable problem of prehistoric archaeology. Indeed, D. de Sonneville-Bordes notes that ". . . since the all too old discovery of the Rock of Combe-Capelle Man (1909), the Dordogne region of Southwest France has unfortunately not yielded any human remains that could be attributed to the Lower Perigodian period,"[44] and at the present time one is reduced to conjecture about who was responsible for that industry. As we have already said, the Grimaldi Negroid was responsible for Aurignacian industry, having obviously been an invader, as Bordes himself acknowledges. One is tempted to associate Perigordian I industry with the man of the Rock of Combe-Capelle, who would then be truly indigenous to Europe, representing the autochthonous race of Europe; a race that might have been born and developed on the spot from the "pre-*Sapiens*" independently of any foreign source, especially the Grimaldi African Negroid, between the Middle and Upper Paleolithic periods. Hence, as the foregoing shows, this is only pure gratuitous ideological speculation, unsupported by the least prehistoric archaeological fact.

To say that Combe-Capelle Man is a Europoid is to overlook his deep morphological affinities with the Grimaldi Negroid, particularly his subnasal prognathism (fig. 8). Those who seek to classify him in the Cro-Magnon series are obliged to postulate an extreme variability of this type, in other words, to modify the criteria to the point where they no longer characterize anything at all.

The description by Boule and Vallois is rather edifying and shows that we are indeed in the presence of a characteristically Negroid type:

> The Combe-Capelle skull, first described by Klaatch, who saw as it as a new species, *Homo aurignacensis*, has since been an object of study for numerous anthropologists. Moschi found Australoid characteristics in this species because of its pronounced superciliary arches. According to Giuffrida-Ruggeri, this skull is more dolichocephalic, more elevated, more prognathous, more platyrhinian, and thus displays Ethiopic affinities.[45] He was inclined to call it *Homo pre-aethiopicus*. Mendes Correa was of the same opinion.[46]

We are therefore in the presence of a Negroid specimen, which, moreover, was found at the bottom of an Aurignacian site, but under conditions that leave too much to be desired. The fact is that this fossil was discovered at a time when scientific prehistoric archaeology was in limbo (1909). It was discovered not by a professional, but rather by an antiques dealer who was a purveyor to the Berlin Museum to which he sold it. This specimen, whose inventors baptized it *Homo aurignacensis*, could not be older than the industry that it belonged to. The estimates that held it to be 50,000 years old were not based on any scientific data. They wanted to have it old enough to make it an autochthonous *Homo europeus*, a predecessor of the invading Grimaldi Negroid. Now, we are forced to recognize that it is not distinct from the latter, and that the dating of the Aurignacian industry by carbon 14 definitely accords it an age of about 32,000 years. Furthermore, dating by Jeffrey Bada's amino acid method is practically not destructive, is applicable to this fossil, and could bring to light precious additional information, as could also dating with carbon 14 by accelerator.

One might indeed expect that the industry of the so-called Lower Perigordian, attributable to a hypothetical indigenous European, would cover the whole continent. This is not the case: this role falls to the Aurignacian industry of the invading Grimaldi Negroid. At the Ninth UISPP Congress

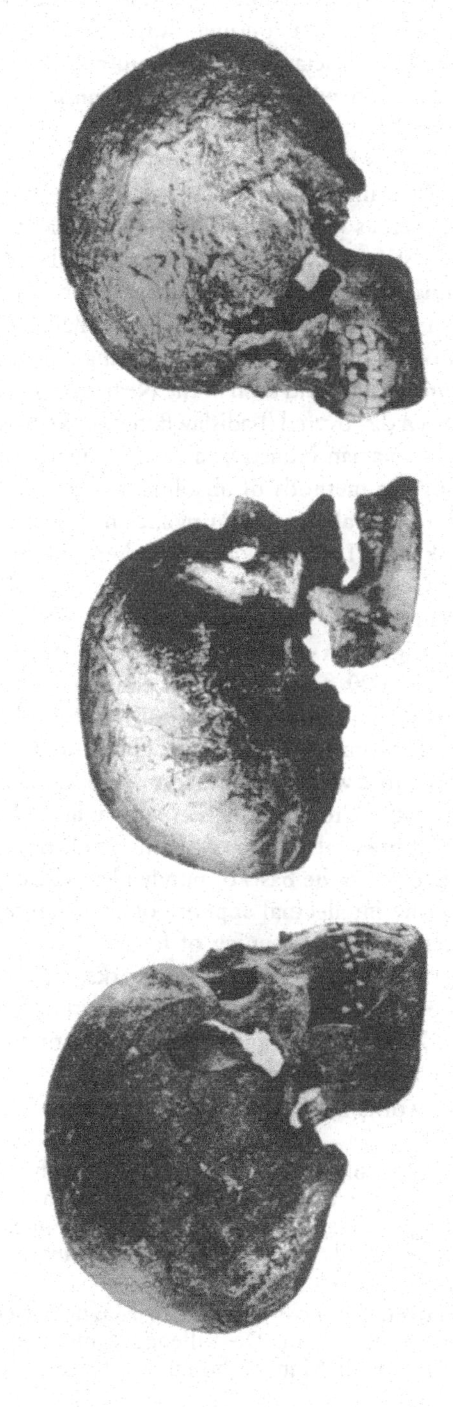

Figure 8: These are the three skulls of Combe Capelle (left), Cro-Magnon (center), and Grimaldi (right) seen from the same angle. Compare the prognathism of the two Negroids (Combe Capelle and Grimaldi) to the orthognathism of Cro-Magnon in the middle (mounting by the author). Some specialists think that Combe Capelle Man might be a fake sold to the German Museum by the supplier, Hauser! (See François Lévèque and Bernard Vandermeersch, in *La Recherche*, no. 119, *op. cit.*, p. 244.)

in Nice, the Sixteenth Colloquium, dealing with the Aurignacian industry in Europe, showed that that continent was literally covered with the various features of the Aurignacian, whereas Solutrean industry, attributable to the real Cro-Magnon who did not appear until 20,000 years later, was absolutely nonexistent.[47]

According to this study, Aurignacian industry is present in France; in the entire Upper Danube basin of Austria (Joachim Hahn), with nineteen indexed sites, such as the famous villages of Willendorf, Vogelherd, Klei-neofnet, Gopfelstein, etc.; in Slovakia (Ladislav Banesz); in northern Rumania (M. Bitiri) and in Banat (F. Mogosamu); in Poland (Elzbieta Sachse-Kozlowska); in Moravia (Karel Valoch), in the Balkans (Janusz Kozlowski); in eastern Europe (G. P. Grigoriev, text missing); in Belgium (Marcel Otte); in Bosnia (Djuro Basler); and even in the Near East where a pre-Aurignacian industry has been discovered (Ladislav Banesz). We have already mentioned the African Aurignacian industry, the age of which will have to be determined anew by the methods of absolute chronology.

Let us add to the above the Aurignacian industry of the Crimea and that of Irkutsk near Lake Baykal in southern Siberia, discovered by the late Professor Gerasimov, a scholar of exceptional objectivity; and finally the Aurignacian industry of Grimaldi and that of Java.

Although Aurignacian culture preceded that of the Solutrean Cro-Magnon by nearly 20,000 years, and even though no confusion is possible between the two physical types respectively responsible for these industries, Western ideologues, particularly the French, do not hesitate now to identify the Grimaldi Negroid with a Cro-Magnon, or else to ignore him completely while presenting the Cro-Magnon as the very first *Homo sapiens sapiens* of Europe. It is gross falsifications of this kind, trying to explain human evolution in reverse on the basis of purely ideological preoccupations, that end up killing the intellectual appetite of younger generations, disgusted by the destruction of the meaning of facts.

The list stretches daily longer of the works, all French, which attempt to remodel the skull of the Grimaldi Negroid in order to try to make him orthognathic like the Cro-Magnon, or to reconstruct its teeth for the same reasons, as evidenced by the note below.[48]

All of these works are fallacious for a number of reasons:

1. A pressure of the burial materials, which might have deformed the face of true Cro-Magnons, giving them a Negroid appearance by causing an accidental prognathism to appear, would surely not have left the skulls of the subjects unharmed. However, these skulls are absolutely unharmed.
2. Moreover, the most typical Cro-Magnon lived in that same Cave of the Children where De Villeneuve discovered him at the same time as Grimaldi Man, although at different strata. How did this

specimen and all the other Cro-Magnons like him miraculously escape the deforming effects of the materials?

3. The most serious problem is that these studies conceal all the other specific morphological differences between the Negroid and the Cro-Magnon. The osteology of Grimaldi is typically Negritic. Furthermore, Boule and Vallois note that "the nose, flattened at its base, is very broad (platyrrhinian). The base of the nasal fossae is joined to the interior side of the jawbone by a cradle-splint on each side of the nasal spine, as is the case with Blacks, instead of being delimited by a narrow edge, as with the White race. The canine fossae are deep."[49]

Concerning dentition, the same authors write:

> All of the upper back molars have four well-developed denticles, even the last one; there are only three in civilized races. All of the lower molars have five very distinct denticles, even the second and third; the White race ordinarily has only four.
>
> The mandible is robust, its body very thick, its ascending branches wide and low. The chin is a little accentuated; a strong alveolar prognathism, related to the upper prognathism, gives it a pronounced receding appearance.
>
> Most of these characteristics of both the skull and the face are, if not Negritic, at the least Negroid.[50]

In comparing the dimensions of the bones of their limbs, one sees that they had very long legs in relation to their thighs, and very long forearms in relation to their arms. Their lower limbs were extremely developed in length in relation to their upper limbs. And these types of proportions reproduce, in exaggerated form, the characteristics present in today's Blacks.[51]

Moreover, Aurignacian art faithfully reproduced the physical type of the race, not only that of the typical African woman, but also that of the typical African man. There exists in this regard at the Saint-Germain-en-Laye Museum a very typical Negroid head, which is almost never talked about (figs. 9, 10, 11, 12).

Lastly, the remains of two individuals conserved at the Monaco Museum—a woman and a child—are, respectively, 1.60 meters and 1.56 meters tall, which does not permit us to have any exact idea of the real height of the Grimaldian race (fig. 13). For this to be accomplished, it would be necessary to have an adult male subject.

Likewise, for Gerasimov,[52] Grimaldi Man and Combe-Capelle Man are obviously Negroid *Homo sapiens*. Predmost Man, whom he considers to be a crossbreed of Neanderthal and *Homo sapiens sapiens*, might merely be an Australoid *Homo sapiens sapiens*, for at that late period of the

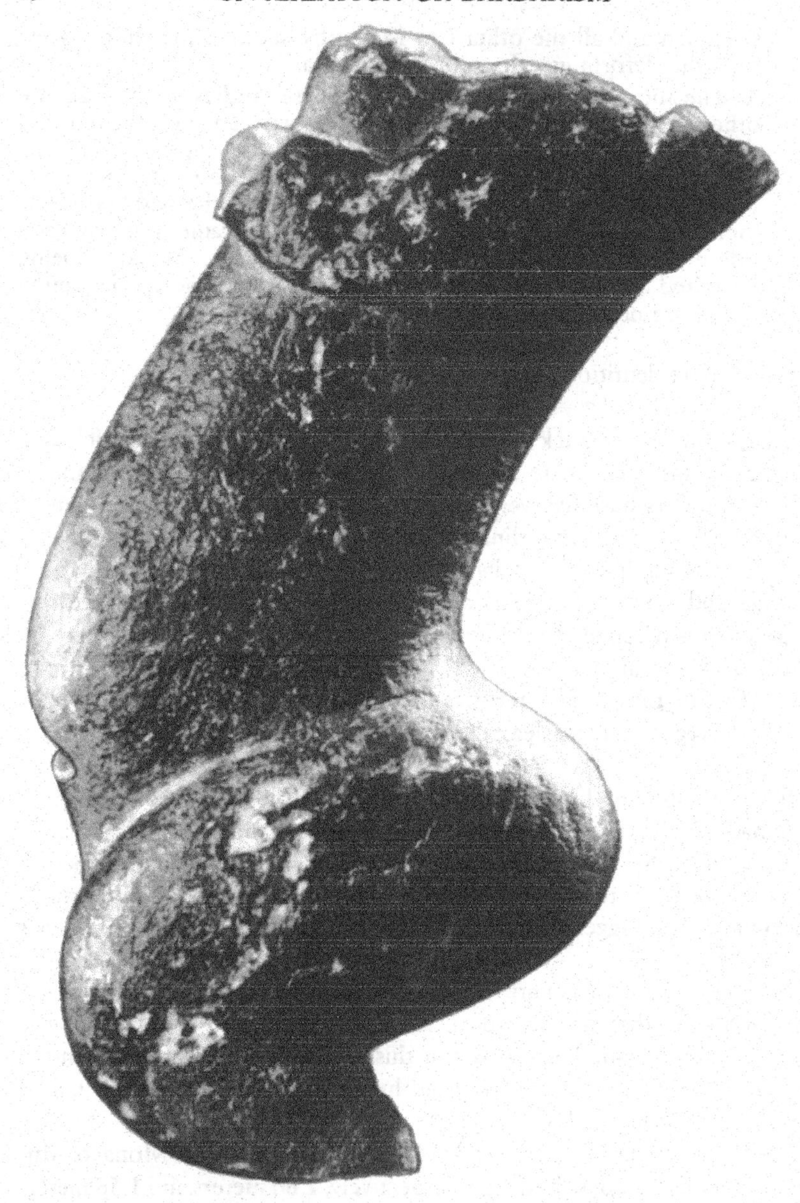

Figure 9: Negroid Aurignacian art of the European Upper Paleolithic period: Headless Venus of Sireuil, Dordogne. Notice the typically Negroid pelvis. (Musée des antiquités nationales, Saint-Germain-en-Laye)

Figure 10: Paleolithic art (Aurignacian-Perigordian): Venus of Willendorf. Notice the typically African hair style. (Museum of Natural History, Vienna)

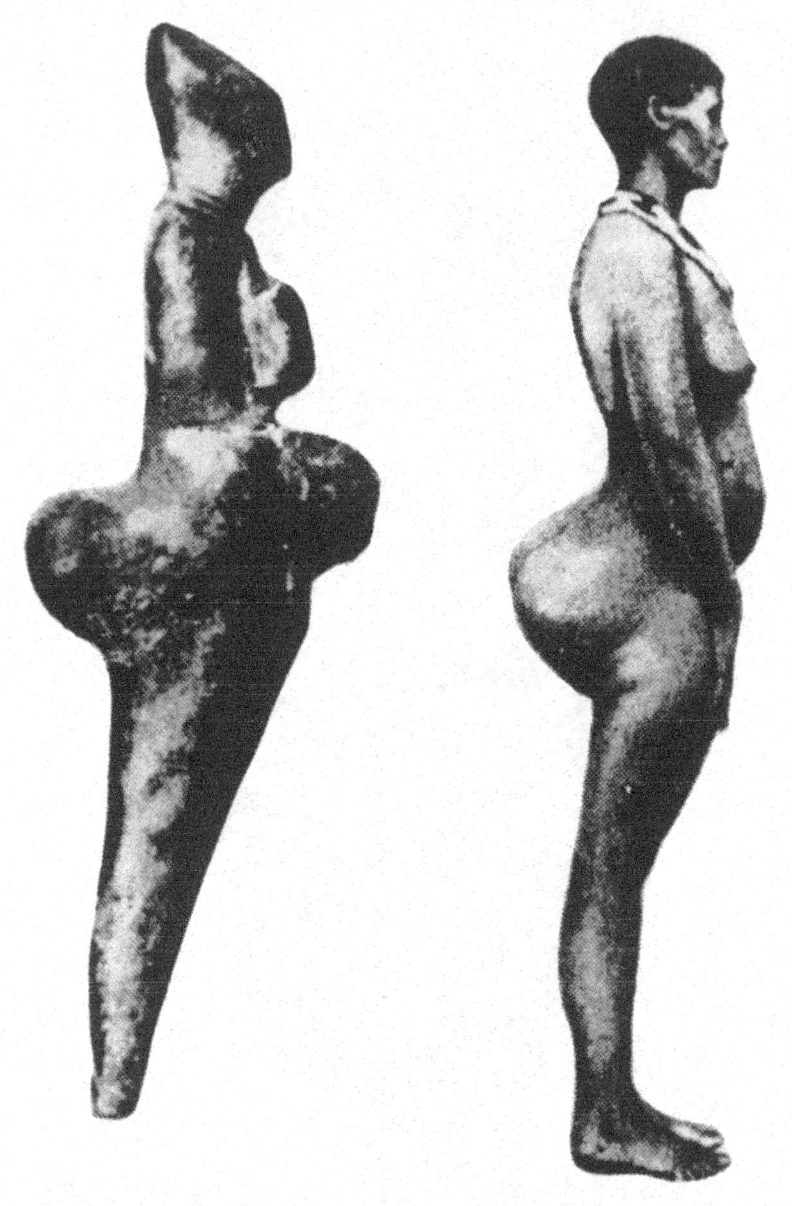

Figure 11: The shape of a statuette or an Aurignacian Venus compared to that of the celebrated Hottentot Venus (casting on the right), who lived in France between the two world wars. (Boule and Vallois, *Les Hommes fossiles*, p. 325)

Figure 12: Negroid Aurignacian art: Negroid head from the Saint-Germain-en-Laye Museum. (Musée des Antiquités nationales, Saint-Germain-en-Laye)

Upper Paleolithic all traces of Neanderthal would seem already to have disappeared. This man (Predmost) has all the appearances of a true Negroid, even though Vallois tries to classify him among the Cro-Magnons. The same can be said of Brno Man: Predmost and Brno seem to descend directly from the Aurignacians of the same region of the Danube and Central Europe.

Gerasimov also thinks that Grimaldi Man is a Negroid invader and not a native of Europe. He writes:

> It is particularly clear that Upper Paleolithic Man entered the territory of Western Europe already possessing diverse variants of the culture and the specific traits of Lower *Homo sapiens*, while displaying more or less equatorial traits. This pseudo-Negroid complex manifested itself in concert with specific features, not only of a physiognomical order, but also of a constitutional kind.

The mutation from Negroid to Cro-Magnon did not happen overnight. There was a long transition period of more than 15,000 years, corresponding to the appearance of numerous intermediate types between the Negroid and the Europoid, without any occurrence of interbreeding. In particular,

Figure 13: Negroid fossils of the Museum of Prehistoric Anthropology in Monaco. These are Aurignacian Negroids of Grimaldi (child and old woman) described by René Verneaux, Marcellin Boule, and Henri-Victor Vallois. Why would the pressure of the materials that supposedly made them prognathous miraculously have spared the skulls, which are intact, although they are not stronger than the bones of the jaws and the face? (Musée d'Anthropologie préhistorique de la Principauté de Monaco: Subjects of Grimaldi, Cave of the Children, Italian Liguria, *Homo sapiens* fossil of the Upper Paleolithic period)

the osteology of the very first Cro-Magnons is Negroid, which seems normal.

In fact, the Negroid osteology developed in the paleo-environment of the African savannah, where the giraffe appeared. This osteology took time to adapt to squatting in the caves of Europe during the glacial era, in other words, to pass from a life in the open air to a virtually subterranean one. The Negroid proportions of the original Grimaldi type become progressively inverted. Also Gerasimov notes:

> The classical Cro-Magnons can be named Europoids only under certain conditions: their bodily proportions are closer to those of the Negroids. Moreover, physiognomically, many of them have an abrupt forehead and lightly marked eyebrows, a strongly expressed prognathism, and as a consequence a protrusion of the lips. These characteristics of the equatorial type are more distinctly evident in the women.

Finally, the author, although a Soviet, in turn shows that the area covered by Negroid expansion extended from western Europe to Lake Baykal in Siberia, by way of the Crimea and the Don Basin. It was this same author who discovered the Aurignacian industry of Siberia, near Lake Baykal, the very industry of which Thoma speaks in his article.[53] Gerasimov continues:

> This "Negroidity" complex, although expressed in another form, is above all very clear in the Grimaldi skeletons. This specific equatorial complex is expressed in a particularly precise manner in the skeleton of "Maquina Gora" on the Don. The skull of this man practically cannot be distinguished from the skulls of today's Papuas, neither in terms of descriptive indicators, nor by mensurational data. The skeleton of Combe-Capelle Man is equally expressive even though it possesses different traits, those of the Australoid type.

It is interesting to note that the Combe-Capelle fossil, whom some see as the ancestor of the Europoids, is described here as an Australoid, especially if one remembers that Thoma would like to make the Australoids descend from the Archanthropians. It is easy to see how indefensible his viewpoint is. Today, the very recent character of the formation of the Australian branch is virtually demonstrated.[54]

But Gerasimov continues:

> The most "sapiential" skull related to Mousterian industry was discovered in the USSR, in the Crimea, near the town of Bakhchisaray, in the shelter of Starocelia.

> The skeleton of a buried child was discovered at this site. The stratigraphical data are impeccable, and the connection of the burial site to the Mousterian Period is incontestable. The skeleton is that of a one-and-a-half- to two-year-old child. For all practical purposes the skull is entirely intact (it has been able to be restored). Archaeologically speaking, it belongs to the final Mousterian period. Its *Homo sapiens* characteristics are of the equatorial type.

Moreover, bones belonging to an adult woman of the Mousterian period were discovered. Gerasimov analyzes these fossils in the following terms:

> The degree of development of the protuberant chin testifies to the presence of a fully formed *Homo sapiens*. The morphology of the child's skull and the fragment of the adult woman's maxilla allow us to suggest that these findings fix the nearly final stage of the formation of ancient *Homo sapiens* in his specific equatorial variant close to the man of "Maquina Gora" on the Don. The findings of Starocelia allow us to place back in the Middle Mousterian Period the formation of the *Homo sapiens* of antiquity.

It appears from the above that the most ancient *Homo sapiens* of Europe, as far as the borders of Asia, were Negroids, if one adheres to an objective analysis of the facts. When we move to Asia, the old Asia of the Orientalists, what strikes us, contrary to all expectations, is the extremely recent appearance of *Homo sapiens sapiens*. The carbon 14 analysis done by the Chinese themselves helped establish that Ziyang Man—estimated by scholars to be 100,000 years old—dates from 7500 + 130 B.P., or 5500 B.C. Likewise, the man of the Upper Cave of Choukoutien, whom specialists thought equally to be 100,000 years old, dates from 18,865 + 420 B.P., or 16,915 B.C.[55]

Weidenreich succinctly studied the fossils of this upper cave at the shelter where Sinanthropus was discovered. He found that one of the skulls, very dolichocephalic, presents both Cro-Magnon and Mongoloid affinities, which, in the author's view, would make it the primitive type of Mongol. Of the other two female skulls studied, one resembles the Melanesian type from New Guinea and the other, the modern Eskimo type. Weidenreich thinks that the above-mentioned dolichocephalic skull might be a very distant precursor of the present-day Chinese. But, notes Vallois:

> [The present-day Chinese] appeared only much later and in a sudden way, with all of their anthropological characteristics already well established. That is why the Neolithics of the Yang-Shaw period, with their polychrome pottery, dating from about 5,000 years ago, and whose skulls were found by Andersson in the provinces of Kansu

> and Honan and studied by Black, already belong to a type essentially similar to that of the North Chinese.[56]

All of the prehistoric Japanese sites, except perhaps one in the South, are of the Holocene Age. Matsumoto has exhumed Neolithic skeletons that rather resemble the Ainus, and the men of the recent paleolithic and the European neolithic periods.[57]

So all of the usual Eastern chronology falls apart with the advent of radiometric methods of dating. Here are, in review, the dates of the appearance of *Homo sapiens sapiens* in the various known centers in the world:

> Black Africa, Omo I and Kanjera, 150,000 years ago.
>
> Invasion of Europe by the Grimaldi Negroid from Africa, 33,000 years ago.
>
> First Cro-Magnon in Europe, 20,000 years ago (using only thoroughly verified dates).
>
> Arrival of Australians in Australia, 30,000 to 20,000 years ago.
>
> Appearance of first Paleosiberian (according to Thoma), 20,000 years ago.
>
> First *Homo sapiens* in China, 17,000 B.C.
>
> Appearance of the present Chinese type, around 6000 B.C.
>
> Appearance of the Nipponese type: Neolithic, perhaps around 5000 or 4000 B.C.

One can therefore grasp the impossibility of the polycentric thesis. The appearance of *Homo sapiens sapiens* in the various hypothetical centers ought to be approximately contemporaneous; some of these centers ought to be even older than those of Africa if they are to explain the independence of this polycentric genesis in relation to Africa. On the contrary, all of the so-called centers of the appearance of modern man are more recent than those of Africa and can therefore be explained with Africa as the starting point, by more or less direct filiation through migration and geographical differentiation, as a consequence of paleo-environmental adaptation. Thus, what is striking is not the independence of these centers, but rather their necessary connections to Africa in order for them to be scientifically explicable. One can now measure all that is unacceptable in the polycentric thesis as revised and improved by Thoma, following Keith and Coon.

The races that might be condemned to disappear because of the peopling by Whites would become living fossils descended from the Archanthropians: this was the case of the Bushmen and Australian aborigines, who are all *Homo sapiens sapiens*, having absolutely the same intellectual capacities as other races, except where they have degenerated individually because of chronic undernourishment.

Australia did not see the birth of *Homo sapiens*. He came there by sea, 30,000 years ago. Therefore, the idea of the local formation of an independent Australian type different from that of the invaders, who must have been a branch of the Aurignacians of Asia, is indefensible.

Negroids survived everywhere in Europe until the Neolithic period: Spain, Portugal, Belgium, the Balkans, etc. We have seen that during the Upper and Recent Paleolithic periods they were already in Siberia, in China (Upper Cave of Choukoutien, see above), even before the birth of the Chinese and the Japanese type. They would thus have coexisted in the Far East with a more or less Mongoloid Cro-Magnon type, in the same Cave of Choukoutien. There is no better way to delimit the conditions of crossbreeding (between Negroid and Mongoloid Cro-Magnon) in a defined paleo-environment, a crossbreeding which ultimately may have led to the formation of the recent branches of humanity: Yellows (Japanese, Chinese); Semites (Arabs and Jews in a different geographical context). The formation of the Semitic branch occurred between the fifth and fourth millennia. This was genuine interbreeding between White (non-Mongoloid Cro-Magnon) and Black at the beginning of the historical era.[58]

In the Riyadh Museum, in Saudi Arabia, one can see the reproduction of cave paintings showing the Negroid type that inhabited the Arabian Peninsula in Neolithic times. This type, who progressively crossbred with White elements, came from the northeast to give rise finally to the Arabian type. Not until the Sabean era, 1000 B.C., was this crossbreeding completed in the south (figs. 14, 15, 16).

No brachycephalic race could have been formed before the Mesolithic period, in other words, before 10,000 years ago. Therefore, we are able to distinguish the dolichocephalic races of the Upper Paleolithic period:

African Negroid (Omo I, Kanjera) 150,000 years ago
Grimaldi Negroid (Europe) 33,000 years ago
Cro-Magnon 20,000 years ago
Paleosiberian 20,000 years ago

The recent brachycephalic races that appeared during the Neolithic Period are yellow-skinned:

Chinese, Japanese 6,000 years ago
Semites (Akkadians, Arabs, Jews) 5,000 years ago

The mutation of the Grimaldi Negroid into the Cro-Magnon has become a quasi-patent fact for all scientists who are not shackled by ideological preoccupations, and molecular biology is now trying to isolate the process in the laboratory.

Thus, at the Bichat conference of 1976, a round-table discussion directed by Prof. B. Prunieras was devoted to this phenomenon, i.e., to the study of the depigmentation of Blacks, leading to the formation of the White type.

A great White American biochemist has just proposed a new explanation of this phenomenon based on the biosynthesis of vitamin D due to the action of ultraviolet rays.

The correlation between skin color and the latitude of origin of populations is a fact, but its interpretation by a mechanism of selection/adaptation remains a hypothesis that is plausible but not yet demonstrated.

Europe was not the birthplace of *Homo sapiens sapiens*, who came there as a migrant Negroid. His mutation into a Cro-Magnoid became more and more necessary, but the special mechanism of this mutation has not been fully understood, far from it. Molecular biology has just turned its attention to the problem.

In the first edition of the *Nations nègres et culture* (1954), I posited the hypothesis that the Yellow race must be the result of an interbreeding of Black and White in a cold climate, perhaps around the end of the Upper Paleolithic period. This idea is widely shared today by Japanese scholars and researchers. One Japanese scientist, Nobuo Takano, M. D., chief of dermatology at the Hammatsu Red Cross Hospital, has just developed this idea in a work in Japanese that appeared in 1977, of which he was kind enough to give me a copy in 1979, when, passing through Dakar, he visited my laboratory with a group of Japanese scientists.

Takano maintains, in substance, that the first human being was Black; then Blacks gave birth to Whites, and the interbreeding of these two gave rise to the Yellow race: these three stages are in fact the title of his book in Japanese, as he explained it to me.

Let us say a few words about a book published in 1977, entitled *Race et Intelligence*, which was edited by Jean-Pierre Hébert (Editions Copernic Factuelles, Paris). I will limit myself to pointing out only the inaccuracy of the fundamental facts on which it is based.

The contributors to this volume quote Coon's thesis according to which "the *erectus-sapiens* transformation must have taken place in Europe, about 200,000 years ago, well before the appearance of the African *sapiens*," and they remind us that Thoma called Coon's work "masterly" (p. 44).

To uphold their idea, these conservative anthropologists stopped at nothing; they did not hesitate to fabricate a counterfeit (Piltdown Man, whom the contributors completely and carefully fail to mention) in order to mislead the scientific world for half a century.

The motives that are today attributed to these scholarly counterfeitors strike us as being totally unacceptable. Therefore, the theory of European

Figure 14: Engraving from the Arabian desert. There are, in the Riyadh Museum, more typical reproductions of the Black populations of the prehistory of the Arabian Peninsula, populations whose fusion with a leucoderm element explains in large measure the birth of the Semite branch. (Leo Frobenius, *Ekade Ektab, Die afrikanischen Felsbilder* (Graz, Austria: Akademische Druck u. Verlagsanstalt, 1963), p. 49, fig. 63)

Figure 15: This Byzantine icon of the eleventh century A.D. shows that up to this relatively recent period, the remembrance of Black Egypt had not been erased from the memory of the people: it concerns the famous scene where Abraham, distinguished by his halo of sanctity, presents himself, with his wife Sarah, before the Black Pharaoh. The contrast of the colors is more striking in the original than in this black-and-white reproduction. There is no possible confusion; the Pharaoh and the dignitaries of his court are Blacks, Abraham and Sarah are leucoderms. (Reproduction of the *Octateuch*, folio 35, in Jean Devisse, *L'Image du Noir dans l'art occidental*, vol. II, Office du Livre, Fribourg, Switzerland, fig. 72, p. 102)

Figure 16: The Hebrews in Egypt: the first two individuals on the right are Blacks; they are the Egyptians; those who follow are Hebrews bringing offerings. The difference between the two communities at this time is clearly visible. In the reproductions in textbooks, the two Blacks, the Egyptians, are generally omitted. K. R. Lepsius, *Denkmäler aus Aegypten und Aethiopien*, vols. III and IV (Geneva: Éditions de Belles-Lettres, 1972), part II, p. 133.

pre-*Sapiens* was based on a hoax, and since its keystone has been shown to be false, willfully fabricated, the thesis has lost any coherence.

A scholar such as Carleton S. Coon does not hesitate to write a paragraph like the following one, in which all the figures, without exception, are false, radically false, as the chronological analysis of the facts has just proven to us. He writes:

> The oldest known skulls of *Homo sapiens*, probably both female, are those of Swanscombe and Steinheim, of the Mindel-Riss Interglacial period, dated today between 470,000 and 300,000 years old. In North Africa, the oldest *Homo sapiens* are between 100,000 and 47,000 years old, in East Africa between 60,000 and 30,000 years old, and in Java, Sarawak and China, not more than 40,000 years old.[59]

What can one call the *Homo sapiens* of 100,000 years ago in North Africa? In Java, the presence of an Aurignacian industry would seem to link the *Homo sapiens sapiens* to the same Negroid stock.

There is a very strong tendency among ideologues to arrange facts to suit themselves. Thus, another world-renowned British scholar, Sir Cyril Burt, did not hesitate to falsify the results of so-called IQ experiments on monozygotic and dizygotic twins. According to him, the correlation between the IQs of twins brought up separately was .771, when carried to the third decimal; whereas for twins raised together, it was as much as .944. A priori, such consistency in this relationship up to three decimal points seems surprising. A countercheck done by J. Kamin, professor of psychology at Princeton University, and A. Clarke of Hull University proved that this IQ study was merely a hoax, comparable in all aspects to that of Piltdown Man, having been put forth to prove the innate intelligence of some races and the inferiority of others.[60]

The contributors to *Race et Intelligence* are not naive: they have read Thoma's entire article, so they knew perfectly well that, when placed in context, Thoma's reference to Coon's work as "masterly" was not a compliment; it is a customary precaution taken by an author before demolishing an adversary's thesis. Thoma, while being an adherent of the polycentric thesis, avoids falling into the same trap as Coon, who, in order to safeguard the individuality of the European race, rejected any notion of migration. But Thoma nevertheless got bogged down in insurmountable difficulties, as we have shown, because polycentrism, a commonsense thesis, is scientifically indefensible today.

There is no need for us to return to the precise chronological data and the other facets already presented here that oblige us to reject polycentrism at the *Homo erectus* stage, unless we want to indulge in pure ideology.

SIMPLIFIED DIAGRAM OF THE PROBABLE PROCESS OF THE DIFFERENTIATION OF THE RACES UNDER THE INFLUENCE OF PHYSICAL FACTORS

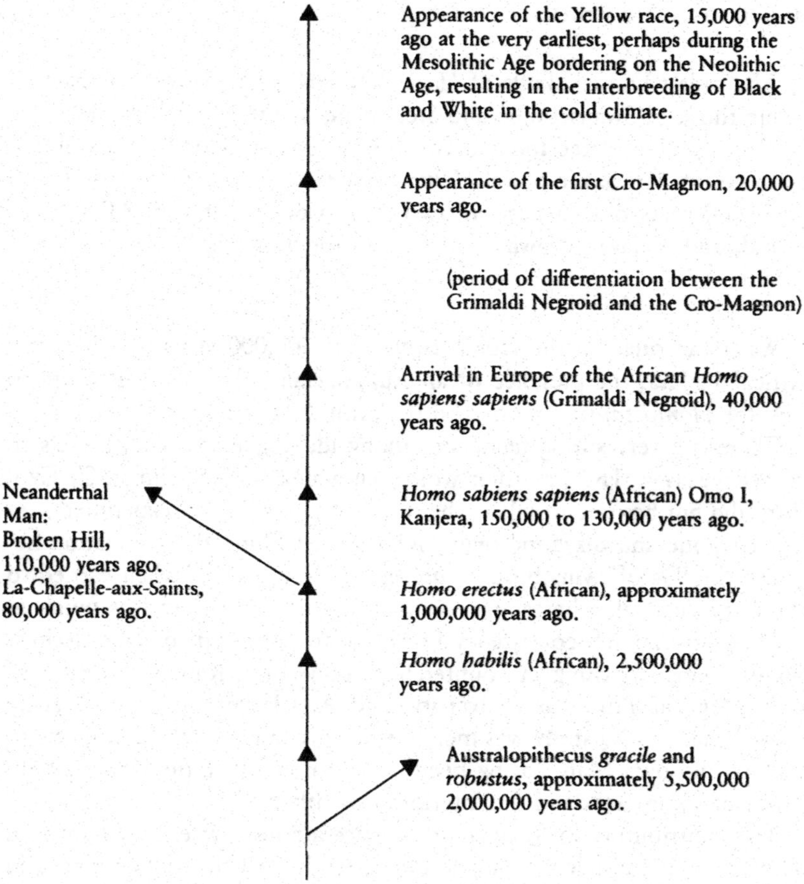

Appearance of the Yellow race, 15,000 years ago at the very earliest, perhaps during the Mesolithic Age bordering on the Neolithic Age, resulting in the interbreeding of Black and White in the cold climate.

Appearance of the first Cro-Magnon, 20,000 years ago.

(period of differentiation between the Grimaldi Negroid and the Cro-Magnon)

Arrival in Europe of the African *Homo sapiens sapiens* (Grimaldi Negroid), 40,000 years ago.

Homo sabiens sapiens (African) Omo I, Kanjera, 150,000 to 130,000 years ago.

Neanderthal Man:
Broken Hill,
110,000 years ago.
La-Chapelle-aux-Saints,
80,000 years ago.

Homo erectus (African), approximately 1,000,000 years ago.

Homo habilis (African), 2,500,000 years ago.

Australopithecus *gracile* and *robustus*, approximately 5,500,000 2,000,000 years ago.

Thoma, in order to defend polycentrism, used Penrose's method of calculating the formal differences between the various races, and found the Yellow race closer to Neanderthal Man than to Cro-Magnon. Ideology must certainly have flown to the author's rescue in order for him to find a greater gap between two *Homo sapiens* than between one of them (the Yellow) and *Homo faber* (Neanderthal), when one knows the profound morphological difference that exists between Neanderthal and *Sapiens.* "The difference of form between these two human variants (Paleosiberian and Neanderthal) is indeed less than that which separates Paleosiberians from Cro-Magnons; Neanderthals and Cro-Magnons are even further apart."[61]

Coon, Thoma, and all the polycentrists evade the major difficulty of explaining where European *Homo sapiens* had gone for 250,000 years, the time span that separates their hypothetical appearance in Europe and Grimaldi Man, the first true *Homo sapiens sapiens* to appear on the European continent. Indeed, these so-called European *Homo sapiens* vanished without leaving any descendants during this whole period. Why do the polycentrists never honestly discuss this question if they intend to do scientific work? No, there is a consensus: they know the difficulty is insurmountable, so they pretend not to see it and nobody raises the question. One need only refer to the presentation we have made above on this question.

The contributors to *Race et Intelligence* are masters of the art of deceiving the reader, as we have seen in the case of the expression "masterly work," deliberately interpreted in a tendentious and erroneous way. Indeed, they write: "A skull discovered at Vértesszöllös, studied by Professor Thoma, is some 500,000 years old. This individual knew how to make fire, and his cranial capacity reached 1,400 cc." Professor Thoma concludes that it belonged to a *Homo sapiens.* "Intelligent man, Homo sapiens, would therefore have appeared in Europe a very long time ago."[62] Here, one is within a hair's breadth of fraud, for the reader has no way of knowing that all these figures (500,000 years, 1,400 cc) are purely imaginary.

Indeed, the skull in question is merely an occipital bone found in Hungary in 1966–67 and associated with the fauna of the Middle Pleistocene period, whose morphological type is very debatable: the volume of the skull cannot be measured because it does not exist: it is a purely conjectural deduction. This is the reason why this fossil went almost unnnoticed at the UNESCO Colloquium of 1969. In order to give it any specific meaning, firm determination was necessary. The very fact that Thoma classified it in the same series as Heidelberg Man (Mauer's Jawbone), who is a *Homo erectus*, amply proves this.

Thoma writes: "Fragmentary fossils have provided a glimpse of the existence of a Western phylum, more uncertain than the previous two:

(Mauer?) —Vértesszöllös—Swanscombe—Fontéchevade—(Quinzano?)—Proto-Cro-Magnon of the Starocelia type—Qafzeh. . . .[63]

From all of the above we can see that this passage from Thoma is completely incoherent, and in any case inconsistent.

The fossil in question is without a face, without a forehead, without any feature that would allow it to be classified, except frivolously, among the *Sapiens*. And always the same question: What became of its descendants for 500,000 years? And Thoma, conscious of this abyss, even if he does not say so, uses terms so tentative that one clearly sees he does not fully believe what he writes in the paragraph quoted above: "Fragmentary fossils have provided a glimpse of the existence of a Western phylum, more uncertain than the previous two. . . ."

We have just seen it: in order to construct the pre-*Sapiens* theory, the contributors to *Race et Intelligence* boldly transform Thoma's hesitations into quasi-certainties.

If one wants to know the truth about the age of the Vértesszöllös occipital, all one needs to do is date it by the amino acid method, which is not very destructive.

Lastly, in order for the pre-*Sapiens* theory to be credible, it should be able to rely on the antiquity of *Homo sapiens* on the other continents, particularly Asia. That is why the contributors to *Race et Intelligence*, using imaginary stratigraphical estimates that allow them to make the fossils whatever age they wish, write: "In Asia . . . the first known *Sapiens* appeared 150,000 years ago at Tzuyang in the Szechuan province."[64] This statement is false. The fossil in question, dated by the Chinese themselves using the carbon 14 method, is only 7,500 years + 130 old. It therefore corresponds to the man of the African Neolithic period.

But the authors continue: "The cranial capacity of this man is 1,210 cc. He is therefore less precocious and has a smaller brain than Vértesszöllös Man (1,400 cc, 500,000 years)."[65]

Here the hoax is obvious. Vértesszöllös Man, a pure poetical fiction as far as his cranial volume and age are concerned, now becomes a palpable objective reality to be compared to an Asian type of equally fraudulent age.

The authors continue their masquerade: "He (Liu-Kiang Man) . . . lived 100,000 years ago."[66] This is also false, for this fossil was dated by the Chinese themselves as having an age of 16,915 years + 420. Thus, as demonstrated above, the whole theory of pre-*Sapiens* collapses. The differentiation of the races is a geographical phenomenon which, under the influence of physical factors, took place after the appearance of *Homo sapiens sapiens*, who was an African Negroid, and not at the *Homo erectus* stage as the Western ideologues wish to allege.

Let us now turn to the analysis of racial differences. They do not make sense and have no demonstrative value: anyone can see that the phenotype of a Black is not that of a Swede, thus, by making a list of all the real and imagined racial differences that may or may not be found in various areas, one gets merely a tedious compilation that appears to be scientific: such and such a blood group, for instance, is more frequent among Blacks than among Nordics. So what? Is it a revealing indicator of intellectual aptitude?

The Germans also believed in the "blue blood" that was supposed to distinguish them from the "degenerate French," the "Welch."

A sixteen-year-old young German, wounded during the Second World War at Strasbourg, preferred to die rather than "accept a transfusion of the impure blood of a Welsh" donor. The young German kindly thanked the French, then turned over and died. An admiring sonnet was dedicated to him in the *Mercure de France* of that time.

Jean-Pierre Hébert studies "the HLA system and its polymorphism among the different races" (p. 95), and "the pressure of the right hand and the pressure of the left hand among Whites, Blacks, American Indians, and the fellahs of Kargh (Egypt)" (p. 98).

That is the kind of absurd space-filler intended to condition the lay person, who gets from it the impression of having read a scientific work.

Enumerating anatomical differences among the races, which are by definition different in appearance, has no scientific meaning. For one would have to be able to demonstrate that these anatomical differences correspond to hierarchical differences in degree of humanization. If these authors could do this, they would no longer be masked authors, taking refuge in anonymity; they would rise to the dignity of "masked sorcerers," great miracle workers.

This is particularly true concerning the so-called anatomical differences found among the brains of different races, although here it is more important to distinguish reality from subtle fraud.

It has long been proven that all races of *Homo sapiens* have absolutely the same cerebral morphology. The big difference between *Homo erectus* and *Homo sapiens sapiens*, or between Neanderthal and *Homo sapiens sapiens*, is less the weight of the brain than the absence in Neanderthal Man of the brain's anterior lobe.

Molecular biology has just taught us that, at the individual level, there are no two identical human brains; and it is this polymorphism which constitutes "the luck of the draw" in the human species, i.e., its power of adaptation. But these individual differences, like the lines of one's hand, do not in any way translate into a racial hierarchism.

As we have already seen, it would then be necessary to find a hierarchical difference among the races, particularly between Black and White, at the level of the brain in general and the anterior part of the brain in particular. But this is not going to happen in the foreseeable future. And here again, the facts given are not simply false, they are cited only in order to mislead the uninitiated.

"From the arrangement and degree of complexity of the interneuronal connections of the frontal lobe, one can isolate, for instance, the primitive characteristics of the Australian aborigines and the pedomorphism of the Sanides" (Korsan, p. 113). This bit of pure fiction is simply a joke in very bad taste, since it is asserted at the expense of peoples whose lands were confiscated, and who are presumably condemned to disappear, like fossilized beings.

Any difference at the level of the brain can have only an individual, but never a racial, significance. To write then, on the basis of specious measurements of "hand-picked types," that there is such and such specific difference in weight or morphology (convolutions) among races, particularly between Black and White, smacks of scientific fraud (p. 105). These measurements would make sense only if they were developed by a mixed group of scholars (White, Black, Yellow) of equal competence, duly collecting their specimens from equally educated racial groups enjoying comparable social status.

Otherwise, take a homogeneous team of Blacks and Yellows working on White subjects, and all the results published in *Race et Intelligence* would be either reversed or at least called into question. Is it not rash to study the anatomy of a degenerate alcoholic Black Kenyan and conclude from it that Blacks are inferior, as was done by Dr. Vint of the Medical Research Laboratory of Nairobi? "Indeed, most of the brains that he (Dr. Vint) examined came from autopsies performed on diseased corpses, particularly victims of cirrhosis" (p. 115).

Only through manipulations of this type was it possible to assemble the fictive differences cited in *Race et Intelligence*, for what Western researcher has access to healthy brains of persons of other races?

Consistent with the racial character of the team making the investigation, the superior race comes out Nordic, Germanic, Anglo-Saxon, or Celtic. . . .

Thus, Brigham's 1923 investigation of two million Americans placed at the top of the intelligence test scores those of English origin, read: WASPs,[67] with an average of 14.87; then those from Scotland, the Netherlands, Germany, Denmark, etc. Mediterraneans and Slavs were at the bottom of the list, while the French were not even mentioned (p. 160). And we know that the still unrepealed American Immigration Act sharply limits immigration of southern Europeans to the United States. So the anonymous authors of *Race et Intelligence* would find it very difficult to immigrate to the United States, for they know that they have no place in the German Valhalla, where they are considered to be descendants of the prehistoric Negroids who settled in the Midi (southern region) of France. Thus the term "Nordic" used by the authors is a mere euphemism, which does not fully convey the sense of Germanic superiority before which "Celtism" appears only as a paltry reaction born of an inferiority complex.

A team of Blacks imbued with the same biased spirit would start by measuring Descartes's minuscule brain (the size of an apple), despite its numerous convolutions, and so on.

Now that Yellows, particularly the Japanese, are proving themselves in the scientific field, in spite of the so-called inferiority of their cranial measurements, racism toward them is tending to disappear. And racism is assuming a more and more bipolar—Black-White—character. At its cabinet meeting in July 1979, the French government assigned itself the task of catching up with Japan.

The Black race, historically, subjugated the White race for three thousand years. Visit the tomb of Ramses III, if you dare interpret correctly its murals. Today Blacks are on the eve of a new start, after having had their turn at being sold by the pound in the West.[68] Good luck to the racists, if they think they are the most intelligent; then what are they worrying about? (figs. 15, 17).

Race et Intelligence raises the question of miscegenation: Is it a positive or negative factor in the course of historic evolution? History has already answered the question. All Semites (Arabs and Jews), as well as the quasi-totality of Latin Americans, are mixed breeds of Blacks and Whites. All prejudice aside, this interbreeding can still be detected in the eyes, lips, nails, and hair of most Jews.[69]

The Yellows, the Japanese in particular, are also crossbreeds, and their own specialists today are acknowledging this important fact.[70]

Alongside the racist ideologues, there are impartial scholars who are advancing humanity's knowledge in this very delicate field of physical anthropology. The list would be too long to present here: A. Jacquard, F. Jacob, Franz Boas, Ashley Montagu, Jacques Ruffie, etc.

Jacquard notes that "determining intelligence with IQ is as ridiculous as confusing rectal temperature with health,"[71] and he adds: "The real problem is to understand why some pose this question. Their true aim is to justify social inequalities by means of alleged natural inequalities."[72]

ETHNICITY OF RAMSES II

We have just stated that the Egyptians were Blacks of the same species as all natives of tropical Africa (see fig. 17). This is particularly true of Ramses II, his father, Seti I, and Thutmose III.

The mummies of these three Pharaohs are well preserved at the Cairo Museum. I had occasion during the preparation of the Cairo Colloquium on the Ethnicity of the Ancient Egyptians, sponsored by UNESCO, to request one square millimeter of the skin of each of them in order to measure the percentage of melanin and thus determine their pigmentation. This is absolutely feasible.[73] Alas, the authorization to collect these samples was never given, so that my analyses in this area are based on the Egyptian mummies at the Paris Musée de l'Homme in Paris.

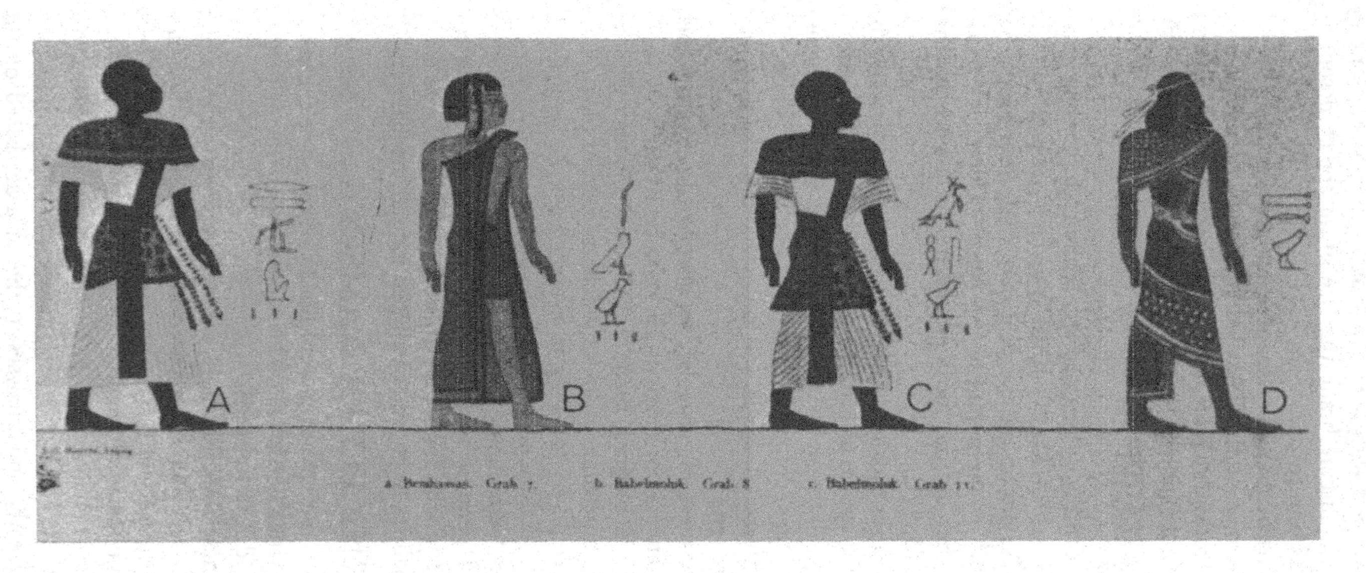

Figure 17: A) The Egyptian seen by himself, Black type
B) The "Indo-European"
C) The other Blacks of Africa
D) The Semite.
(K. R. Lepsius, *Denkmäler aus Aegypten und Aethiopien*, Erganzungsband, fig. 48.)

This painting from the tomb of Ramses III (1200 B.C.) shows that the Egyptians perceived themselves as Blacks, and represented themselves as such without possible confusion with the Indo-Europeans or the Semites. This is a representation of the races in minute detail, which guarantees the realism of the colors. Throughout their entire history, the Egyptians never dreamed of representing themselves by types B or D.

Even though the notion of race is very relative, molecular biology has isolated racial markers, which are factors almost exclusively localized in each racial group: the Diego factor among Yellows, the Kell factor among Whites, the Sutter and Gm6 factors among Blacks.[74]

Therefore science, by isolating the Sutter and Gm6 factors and analyzing the percentage of melanin, can determine precisely the race of Ramses II through the most objective of methods.

Dust sucked out of the mummy's stomach for analysis, during its stay in Paris, contained more organic debris and blood clots than required for such a study. But it seems to have been decided on principle not to carry out the only analyses that could have given us valid information about the race of the mummy, presumably out of concern for safeguarding its bodily integrity.

So, let nobody tell us that Ramses II was White and reddish-blond, for he was in fact the ruler of a people who systematically massacred reddish-blonds as soon as they met them, even on the street; the latter were considered strange beings, unwholesome, omens of bad luck, and unfit to live.[75] Anyway, how could one tell the original hair color of a ninety-year-old man? The fifty respected Parisian laboratories that studied this mummy have informed us that it had nicotine in its bowels, but that out of respect, they had used only the structure of one hair to determine its ethnicity. This structure should have been compared to the hair of a present-day jet black Nubian of Upper Egypt before reaching a conclusion.

The above shows that the determination of the ethnicity of Ramses II made in Paris is of no scientific value. It is certainly not conclusive. Even today, after radiation has turned the mummy yellow (before the experiment it was black, as I was able to verify), one can still determine the percentage of melanin in the skin, by using the products of melanin degradation, which remain on fossilized animals even after millions of years. Did they even question whether this was really the same mummy that was discovered by Gaston Maspero?

Ramses II was a Black. May he rest in peace in his black skin for eternity.[76]

The mother of Ramses II was a princess of the royal family, and his father, Seti I, was obliged to designate him as heir to the throne while he was still a child, for in the eyes of traditionalistic Egyptians, the child represented legitimacy.[77]

Finally, on another level, the nicotine found in the stomach of Ramses II is a major discovery. For, if tobacco is indeed a plant of American origin, as postulated by Raymond Mauny and A. Lucien Guyot,[78] it would mean that maritime relations existed between the Egypt of the Pharaohs and pre-Columbian America as early as the XIXth Dynasty. One cannot underestimate the importance of this fact, which we have already reported in *L'Afrique Noire précoloniale* (pp. 156–67) and in *L'Antiquité africaine par l'image.*

Furthermore, it is remarkable that one of the fads of today's young Senegalese women, with their use of xeesal (or kheesal = "lightening the complexion" through various cosmetics), has helped solve a four-thousand-year-old enigma: the fact that in the representations on ancient monuments Egyptian bourgeois women sometimes had lighter complexions than those of the men, was only the result of an affectation absent in their male counterparts. The urban bourgeoisie in Dakar and in Saint-Louis, with their neo-antique hair styles, are reproducing before our very eyes the exact profile of the Pharaonic Egyptian woman.

3

THE MYTH OF ATLANTIS RESTORED TO HISTORICAL SCIENCE THROUGH RADIOCARBON ANALYSIS

EXPLOSION OF THE ISLAND OF SANTORINI IN THE CYCLADES IN 1420 B.C.[1]

The volcanic eruption of the island of Santorini has been dated at 3050 + 150 B.P. or 3370 + 100 B.P. These two dates have been calculated from a piece of wood found under the thirty-meter-thick layer of ashes that had covered the whole group of the Cyclades Islands after the explosion. This wood is therefore contemporaneous with the volcanic explosion that was to give birth to the myth of Atlantis. The second date, 3370 + 100 B.P., was obtained after the extraction of the humic acid that had accumulated in the ligneous material with time, and which constitutes an organic impurity likely to engender false analytical results. Thus 3370 + 100 can be considered the most probable date of the eruption of Santorini.

Studies have shown, according to the authors already quoted on this subject, that the eruption of Santorini is comparable in intensity and typology to that of Krakatoa, an island in Indonesia, in 1883. The tidal wave of the latter reached a height of thirty-five meters on the neighboring coasts of Java and Sumatra, destroying 295 towns and drowning 36,000 people. After a very short time, the tidal wave was registered on the shores of almost all the oceans of the world. The explosion was heard over one-thirtieth of the earth's surface, and its vibrations broke windows 150 kilometers away and as far as 800 kilometers in the case of old houses. The clouds of dust darkened the sky the world over for years. It was the most powerful explosion known in historical times.

Yet, the 83 km^2 crater and the thirty-meter-thick layer of dust covering the group of islands surrounding Santorini allow us to conclude that the eruption of Santorini, in the Minoan period, was far more important and more catastrophic than that of Krakatoa in 1883. The ashes covered approximately 200,000 km^2, and the cloud of dust that formed must have covered Crete, a part of the Peloponnesus, and Asia Minor.

The northern coasts of Crete must have been submerged by the tidal wave (at more than 350 km/hr) half an hour after the explosion; the Tunisian coast and the Nile Delta must have been affected as well.

If the eruption were comparable only in power to that of Krakatoa in 1883, the noise of the explosion would have been heard in Gibraltar, in Scandinavia, in the Red Sea, and in Central Africa. The whole area south of the Aegean Sea and the Eastern Mediterranean must have been in complete darkness.

The established archaeological facts are the following:

Pre-Hellenic civilization in the Aegean Sea began at the end of the Neolithic period, around 3,000 years ago; this is the Minoan civilization, divided into three periods:

Ancient Minoan	3000–2200 B.C.	(Copper Age)
Middle Minoan	2200–1550 B.C.	(1st Bronze Age)
Recent Minoan	1550–1180 B.C.	(2nd Bronze Age)

The fall of Troy in 1180 B.C. marks the beginning of the Iron Age.

From 3000 to 1400 B.C., Crete was the political and cultural center of Aegean civilization. After the simultaneous destruction of all the Minoan cities around 1400 B.C., Cretan civilization declined and continental Greece began to emerge. Mycenaean civilization began around 1400 B.C. and marked the beginning of writing in Greece.

This sudden change in the history of Aegean civilization and the sudden appearance of writing in continental Greece are not explicable by archaeological facts.

The Recent Minoan is divided into three periods:

Recent Minoan I	1550–1450 B.C.
Recent Minoan II	1450–1400 B.C.
Recent Minoan III	1400–1180 B.C.

The destruction of all the cities and palaces of Crete occurred at the end of the Recent Minoan I period, around 1450 B.C.

According to Evans, Cnossus was not destroyed before the end of the Recent Minoan II period (1400 B.C.). But Dussaud, Pendlebury, and Hutchinson have proved that the Minoan I and Minoan II periods of Crete are contemporaneous with the Minoan I period of the other royal palaces, and that Cnossus must also have been destroyed at the same time as the other cities of Crete. The date of the destruction of Minoan Crete by the tidal wave on the the island of Santorini is 1400 B.C. After this destruction, some of the palaces were partially reoccupied, while others were abandoned for centuries. Evans thought that Cretan civilization was destroyed by an earthquake while Pendlebury thought it was the result of a revolution.

According to Pègues (1842), after the arrival of Cadmus on the island of Thera near Santorini around 1400 B.C., no major eruption occurred in the archipelago.

The prehistoric civilization destroyed by the eruption and buried under the thirty-meter-thick layer that covered the islands of Thera, Therapa, and Astronisi, existed between Middle Minoan III (1700 B.C.) and Recent Minoan I (1550 B.C.), according to the studies of Fouqué (1869–79) and Renaudin (pottery, 1922). The murals reveal a style already evolved in the Middle Minoan I (Marinatos, 1939).

It was a civilization of plowmen and fishermen. They cultivated cereals, made flour, extracted olive oil, raised sheep and goats, made decorated vases, and were familiar with gold and probably copper. Thus, archaeological and historical facts show that the eruption took place at the end of the Minoan prehistoric period.

The aforementioned authors think that royal power survived the cataclysm for a short period of time, at Cnossus, and that the king of that city may have been Evans's Minos, supposedly an Achaean who had no idea of his predecessors, like the Greeks of the later epoch.

But the Achaean origin of Minos is untenable for all the reasons we already know. The Minoan palace royalty was but a replica of Egyptian royalty, and the very name of Minos seems to be only a slight alteration of the name of the first semilegendary Egyptian king: Menes. No matter. Let us continue to summarize this important point, from which our remark removes none of its inestimable value.

The decline of Minoan civilization must be related to the desertion of the fertile valleys of Crete after the eruption of Santorini. Study of the marine sediments inclines us to think that this was due to volcanic fallout.

The quantity of ashes produced by the explosion was very great. All the islands in the Aegean Sea around Santorini, including the east and center of Crete, were covered with a layer of volcanic dust ten-centimeters thick.

The Minoan eruption must have been catastrophic for the Cretans. The initial cloud composed of volcanic ash, dust, gas, and fumes covered the entire south of the Aegean Sea, probably resulting in total darkness for several consecutive days, during which time the tidal wave (tsunami) destroyed the coastline, and extinguished lamps, setting fire to towns (Amnisos, Cnossus, Mallia, Gournia, Hagia Triada, etc.), while the gas and fumes poisoned the population, causing illnesses such as conjunctivitis, angina, bronchitis, and digestive disorders.

The majority of the surviving population probably left Crete the same year, immediately after the eruption, for continental Greece, because of its proximity, and perhaps for Asia Minor.

The first settlements in continental Greece probably date back to around 3000 B.C., and this civilization, called Helladic, is divided according to the model of the Minoan civilization into Ancient Helladic, Middle Helladic, and Recent Helladic.

In the period from 3000 to 1400 B.C., comprising Ancient, Middle, and the beginning of Recent Helladic, continental Greece was clearly backward in relation to Crete. Major progress in Helladic civilization began only around 1400 B.C., with the arrival of Cretan refugees bringing civilization in their wake. Not long before, these Cretans were using *Linear A*, and they would be the first scribes of Mycenaean civilization, with the invention of *Linear B*, which is only an adaptation of their writing to the Greek language, which was foreign to them (fig. 28).

Linear A was used in Crete from 1600 B.C. to 1400 B.C., whereas *Linear B* appeared in Greece only around 1400 B.C. (Ventris and Chadwick, 1959).

The tomb of Agamemnon, the treasure of the descendants of Atreus (or tomb of the genii), the tomb of Clytemnestra—these supreme models of Mycenaean architecture were built between 1400 B.C. and 1300 B.C. (Wace, 1949).

Frescoes found in Crete before 1400 B.C. appeared in Greece around this time (Pendlebury, 1939; Hutchinson, 1963) (figs. 18, 19, 20, 21).

Thus, contrary to the opinion of historians, according to whom the destruction and decline of Minoan civilization resulted from an Achaean invasion, it can be maintained, on the basis of archaeological and geological facts, that the important leap forward of the civilization of Recent Helladic III, commonly called Mycenaean civilization, after the eruption of the island of Santorini in 1420 B.C., was influenced by the presence of the Cretan refugees, who introduced the alphabet and the traditions of Minoan art.

The multiple effects of the eruption of Santorini were felt in Egypt, and they left traces in contemporaneous Egyptian literature. But until now this evidence has passed unnoticed or has been misinterpreted.

The explosion of Santorini took place under the XVIIIth Egyptian Dynasty (1580–1350 B.C.). This period can be divided into three different political periods:

1. 1580–1406 B.C., meaning from the beginning of the dynasty to the first five years of the reign of Amenophis III;

Figures 18 through 21 show the profound influence of Black Egypt on the Aegean Mediterranean, which it had effectively conquered under the XVIIIth Dynasty and particularly under Thutmose III. In fact, these frescoes were all painted according to the Egyptian canon and stylistic conventions, namely: the head in profile, the eye in front view, the bust in front view; refer to the preceding figure painted by the Egyptian artist or to the sketches of figures 61 to 65, if need be.

Figure 18: "Fisherman of Atlantis." Fresco from Thera. Notice the "totemic" hair style (Egyptian influence?). (*Excavations of Thera*, VI, from Spyridon Marinatos, University of Athens. See also *Santorini Island, Plato's Atlantis.*)

Figure 19: "Prince with Lily." Cretan fresco. (Palace of Cnossus)

Figure 20: "Ladies in Blue." Cretan fresco. (Palace of Cnossos, east site, from Costis Davaras, in *Musée d'Hérakleion*, Ekdotike Athenon, Athens)

Figure 21: Sarcophagus of Hagia Triada. It shows the religious influence of Egypt. (From J. A. Sakellarakis, University of Athens, in *Musée d'Hérakleion*)

2. The remainder of the reign of Amenophis III and the reign of Amenophis IV (1375–58 B.C.);
3. The end of the dynasty (1358–50 B.C.).

After the expulsion from Egypt of the Hyksos in 1580 B.C., the power of the new XVIIIth Dynasty increased progressively and reached its peak under the reign of Thutmose III (1501–1447 B.C.). This Pharaoh has been considered the greatest conqueror of ancient times. His empire extended from Babylon, on the Upper Euphrates, to the Upper Nile. The same expansionist policy was maintained by his successors, who succeeded in preserving the power of the empire until the Nubian campaign of Amenophis III, from 1407 to 1406 B.C. Around 1406 B.C., the political strategy of Amenophis III changed, and there suddenly began an era in international relations hitherto unknown in history, according to James Breasted (1951).

Relations between the Pharaoh and both the vassal princes and the neighboring kings became fraternal, instead of being based on force as was the case in preceding periods. They started calling each other "brothers" (tablets of Tel al-Amarna, Mercer, 1939). The Pharaoh appeared in public for the first time in history and the affairs of the divine royal house were dealt with in public. A period of literature began to flourish with its own art, architecture, and music. Amenophis III favored the cult of the sun god Aton, in the polytheistic Egypt of the time. The invasion of the Hittites (it might perhaps be more correct to say: the revolt) in the North marked the beginning of the collapse of the empire. Amenophis III did nothing in its defense. His successor, Amenophis IV, or Akhenaton (1375–58 B.C.), continued the peaceful politics of his father (tablets of Tel al-Amarna) while the Hittites invaded the northern part of the empire. Akhenaton was interested only in religious reform. He ordered the destruction of all polytheistic symbols, closed the ancient temples, and introduced the worship of a universal God, Aton. He is considered the first monotheist in history.

The last period of the XVIIIth Dynasty—Sakere, Tutankhamen, etc. (1358–50 B.C.)—was characterized by the rejection of monotheism, which was held responsible for the downfall of the empire.

James H. Breasted (1912, 1926, 1951) interpreted the history of the XVIIIth Dynasty as follows: After the conquest by Thutmose III, an idea of internationalism developed throughout the empire, and with it was born the concept of one God, imperial, universal, and common to all. These ideas reached their paroxysm under the reigns of Amenophis III and Amenophis IV (Akhenaton). But Breasted is not able to explain, many prominent authors think, why these ideas appeared all of a sudden in the middle of the reign of Amenophis III.

Important economic relations existed between Egypt and the Aegean Sea, during the XVIIIth Dynasty (Kantor, 1947; Vercoutter, 1954). Minoan ceramics were imported into Egypt until the end of the reign of Thutmose III. In fact, in the tomb of Rekhmira, vizier of Thutmose III, one sees Cretans bringing these vases as a tribute to Egypt, which had conquered their island (Fouqué, 1879); we know that the vases found under the ruins of Thera, after the eruption, resemble the vases of the Egyptian frescoes that we have just alluded to. These frescoes were commonplace during the reigns of Queen Hatshepsut and Thutmose III. They showed Cretans, called *Keftiu* in Egyptian texts, in Minoan costumes, bringing tribute to Egypt, in the form of vases and various "gifts" (figs. 22, 23). The frescoes appear for the last time, together with the ceramics of the Recent Minoan I period, in the tomb of Rekhmira, grand vizier of Upper Egypt, which was closed about 1450 B.C.

It is remarkable that the XVIIIth Dynasty was the only period in which the name *Keftiu* appeared in original Egyptian documents. Similar frescoes have been found in the palace of Cnossus (cup carrier of Recent Minoan I). The period of Akhenaton (Tel al-Amarna, 1375–58 B.C.) was already influenced by the Mycenaean art of continental Greece. Therefore, the destruction of Minoan Crete happened between the reign of Thutmose III and that of Amenophis IV (1450–1375 B.C.) in the Egyptian chronology (Dussaud, 1914; Evans, 1921, 1936). A circular seal of Queen Ti, wife of Amenophis III, has been found in a burial chamber at Hagia Triada, in Crete, with pottery of Recent Minoan I. This is the last datable object found in Crete, from the period preceding the destruction of the palaces of both Recent Minoan I and Recent Minoan II.

In addition, a vase and some fragments of a plaque bearing the name of Amenophis III, as well as a scarab bearing the name of Queen Ti, are the first and most ancient datable objects of Mycenaean Greece. This shows that the destruction of Minoan Crete by the volcanic eruption of Santorini island took place during the reign of Amenophis III, around 1400 B.C. (Myres, 1930; Pendlebury, 1939; Vercoutter, 1945; Hutchinson, 1963). Thus the date of the Minoan eruption of Santorini may be placed, within Egyptian chronology, between the Nubian War of Amenophis III and the beginning of the internationalization of monotheism and the decline of the empire of the XVIIIth Dynasty, the last great power of the Bronze Age.

No contemporary document attests to the influence of the eruption of Santorini on this sudden change of orientation in Egyptian history. A good part of Egyptian literature prior to the reign of Akhenaton was destroyed after his religious reform. The narrative songs and legends were all recorded after the XVIIIth Dynasty (Breasted, 1951), and some of them describe a period prior to Egyptian history. They were often written in a prophetic form. The composers of these texts claimed to have lived in an earlier period (Bennett, 1963). They predict the coming of an era of disasters, with prolonged darkness, thunder, storms, floods, a solar eclipse,

Figures 22, 23: The *Keftiu* (Cretans) paying their annual tribute to Thutmose III, Pharaoh of the XVIIIth Dynasty. The Cretans are particularly distinguishable by their costumes, but all the other Minoan peoples are also represented in the series, as the hieroglyphic text indicates. (Norman de Garis Davies; *Tomb of Rekh-Mi-Rê at Thebes*, vols. II, plates XIX and XVIII.)

pestilence, political changes, and the arrival of a savior and a good Pharaoh who will save his people.

> Trouble has beset the eyes. . . . For nine days nobody has left the palace. They have been nine days of violence and tempest. Nobody, neither God nor man, is able to see his neighbor's face. We do not know what has happened throughout the Earth. . . . It is a confusion that you brought upon the entire Earth with the sound of an uproar. . . . Oh, let the Earth stop rumbling. . . . Towns are destroyed. . . . Upper Egypt is devastated. . . . Blood is everywhere. . . . Pestilence, looting are everywhere on the Earth. (Griffith, 1890)

The same papyrus mentions the break in relations between Egypt and the Mediterranean coasts and Crete, using the term *Keftiu* for Crete, which is specific to the literature of the XVIIIth Dynasty to designate the Cretans.

> The men will not sail toward Byblos today. What will we do to obtain cedar wood for our mummies and the burial of priests, and oil from faraway Crete to embalm the dignitaries? They [these products] no longer come. What an important thing it is that the oasis people bring their spices during the feasts. (Gardiner, 1909)
>
> The sun is veiled and does not shine visibily in the eyes of men. No one can live when the sun is covered by clouds. God himself has abandoned men. If the sun shines, it is just for one hour. No one knows when it is noon; one cannot discern one's own shadow. . . . He [Ra] is in the sky looking like the moon. (Gardiner, 1914)

Greater certainty about the destructive effect of the Minoan tidal wave on the eastern coasts of the Mediterranean was provided by the archaeological discoveries in Syria. The port and half of the town of Ugarit were destroyed around 1400 B.C. Schaeffer (1936) suggested that this destruction could have been due to a tidal wave. A Phoenician poem found in the library of Ugarit speaks of a destruction provoked by tempest and tidal wave. Dussaud (1935) and Schaeffer suggest that this poem refers to the same event that destroyed the port of Ugarit.

Different dates have been proposed for the Biblical exodus: the end of the reign of Thutmose III (1450 B.C.), or during the reign of Ramses II (1292–25 B.C.).

Breasted, who translated Akhenaton's *Hymn to the Sun*, noted that this hymn and Psalm 104 in the Bible show a great similarity of form and content. The similitude between the events described in the Egyptian texts (Griffith, 1890; Gardiner, 1909, 1914) and the epidemics described in the Old Testament has already been pointed out by several historians. Breasted

(1951) concluded that specimens of this remarkable category of Egyptian literature can be found up to the first centuries of the Christian era, and we cannot resist the conclusion that they, in both form and substance, inspired the Hebrew prophets in the creation of their Messianic prophecies. Bennett (1963) was the first to suggest that the Egyptian calamities might have been a consequence of the Minoan eruption of Santorini. Galanopoulos thinks that the eruption took place during the summer, when the northeastern, high-altitude winds predominate, transporting dust from the island toward Egypt.

The Biblical name of Crete is Caphtor, which visibly derives from the Egyptian *Keftiu*, and the Cretans were called Philistines. Three Biblical chapters evoke the destruction of Minoan Crete, and one of them (Amos) shows that the Exodus is contemporaneous with destruction, therefore with the eruption. In fact, it came later.

> Did I not bring up Israel from the land of Egypt, and the Philistines from Caphtor and the Syrians from Kir? (Amos 9.7, written in the ninth century B.C.)

> A day of wrath is that day, a day of distress and anguish, a day of ruin and devastation, a day of darkness and gloom, a day of clouds and thick darkness. . . . And I will bring distress on men, so that they shall walk like the blind. . . . Land of the Philistines, I will destroy you till no inhabitant is left. (Zephaniah 1.15, 17 and 2.5, written in the seventh century B.C.)

> Behold the waters are rising out of the North . . . they shall overflow the land and all that fills it . . . because of the day that is coming to destroy all the Philistines. . . . For the Lord is destroying the Philistines, the remnants of the coastline of Caphtor. (Jeremiah 47.2, 4, written in the sixth century B.C.)

The eruption of Santorini had an impact on Greek mythology and legends. The long-term meteorological changes that accompanied it, affecting the aspect of the sun and the moon, must have given it a supernatural character in the eyes of witnesses, who would never have understood the exact nature of the event, which thus remained enshrouded in mythology.

Deucalion and Pyrrha, the mythological king and queen of Thessaly, ancestors of the Hellenic race, are the only survivors of the great flood provoked by Zeus. They sailed in a boat for nine days until they landed on Mount Parnassus. Myres (1930) attributed an age of 1,436 years to the flood of Deucalion, and Galanopoulos (1960, 1963) established a correlation between this flood and the eruption of Santorini.

Cadmus, son of Agenor, king of Phoenicia and brother of Europe, went in search of his sister who had been kidnaped by Zeus. After searching in vain, the Oracle of Delphi ordered him to make a stop in continental Greece. He founded the town of Thebes in Boeotia and is considered to be the most powerful [successful] man at the start of Mycenaean times, when the written history of Greece begins. Myres (1930) thinks that Cadmus belongs to the generation in 1400 B.C., and that he entered Greece immediately after the destruction of Minoan Crete. According to Herodotus, Cadmus stopped at the island of Thera, where he dropped off some Phoenicians and his own relative Menibliarus. The Phoenicians called the island *Kallisti* (the best). This Phoenician colony subsisted until 1089 B.C., when the Lacedaemonians, under the leadership of Theras, founded the second colony. They called the island by the name of their chief, Theras. This second colony survived until 623 B.C., when the inhabitants of the island set out to join the founders of Cyrene, in Libya.

Up to this date, neither the Santorini eruption nor any fact related to a pre-Mycenaean Aegean civilization has been mentioned in Greek history. The Greek legislator Solon visited Egypt in 590 B.C., and from there, introduced into Greece the legend of Atlantis. He learned from the Egyptian priests of the town of Sais that an island was swallowed up . . . somewhere in the ocean.

Two hundred years after Solon, around 395 B.C., the story was told by Plato in *Timaeus* and *Critias.* Following Solon, Plato discussed Greek history with Egyptian priests. The most ancient epoch that Plato could cite was that of Deucalion and Pyrrha, that of the great flood, but without being able to date this event. Then the priest told him that there had been several floods and that the largest one had completely destroyed an advanced Greek civilization.

> Don't you know that in your country had lived the most beautiful and the most noble race of men that ever lived? Race of which you and your town are the descendants, or a seed that survived. . . . But there were violent earthquakes and floodings, and in one day and one night of rain, all of your bellicose people, as one man, were buried under the ground, and the island of Atlantis, in the same manner, disappeared under the sea. . . . The result is that, in comparison to what was, there remain some small islets, nothing but the skeleton of a devastated body, all of the richest and the softest parts of the soil having been swallowed up, leaving only the skeleton of the country. . . . And this was unknown to you, because the survivors of this destruction have been dead for several generations without leaving any traces. (*Timaeus* and *Critias*)

Plato places Atlantis near Gibraltar. The event supposedly took place nine thousand years before Solon and was reported in the Egyptian texts one thousand years later. If we reduce everything by a factor of 10, we come back to its true age: the explosion of Santorini.

CONTEMPORANEITY OF THE EVENT WITH THE XVIIIth EGYPTIAN DYNASTY

It is important to first show that in the sixteenth century B.C., the XVIIIth Egyptian Dynasty, under Thutmose III (1504–1450 B.C.) in particular, had effectively conquered the whole eastern Mediterranean (Crete, Cyprus, the Cyclades, etc.) and all of western Asia (Hatti, or the Hittite country, Mittanni, Amourrou, Kadesh, Syria, the country of Akkad, and Babylonia).

In total, according to Thutmose III's *Hymn of Triumph*, written in verse and engraved on the "poetic stela" at Karnak, facing Thebes in Upper Egypt, 110 foreign states were conquered and integrated to different degrees into the Egyptian empire. In one year, under Thutmose III, the Egyptian treasury collected 3,500 kilos of gold (electrum), of which nine-tenths came from the tributes paid by vassals.[2] Western Asia was divided into administrative districts placed under the authority of Egyptian governors, charged with collecting the tributes, or annual taxes, that all these defeated and vassal states had to pay to the Egyptian treasury.

In some towns, as in Jaffa, the conquered princes were purely and simply replaced by Egyptian generals, and the administration was direct. Whereas Thutmose III discharged the conquered chief of the town of Aleppo, in Syria, he replaced him with another vassal "on whom he conferred sovereignty in a ceremony of investiture, by anointing him with oil," according to the Egyptian custom which Christianity would take over on a different level. These conquered states kept small territorial guards trained by the Egyptian officers. But the defense of this huge empire rested on the Egyptian army itself, so much so that, even under Amenophis III, the Phoenician towns would protest when they felt the Egyptian troops in charge of their protection were insufficient. Egyptian garrisons were stationed at strategic points, important towns and ports; the vassal chief of the country of the Amorites was authorized to organize a small defensive army. Fourteen hundred years before Rome, Egypt created the first centralized empire in the world. It might be believed that a vague bond, very loose and easily breakable, united the Egyptian emperor and his vassals; this was not the case. One can hardly imagine, today, the degree of centralization in the Egyptian empire and the efficacy of its administration.

"Royal messengers," a kind of *missi dominici*, went through the different regions of the empire delivering messages from the Pharaoh. The generals were in charge of regularly making inspection tours in the conquered territory. "A royal postal service circulates over roads created by the Egyptian administration, staked out with military stations and water tanks for resupply." The king maintained personal relations with his vassals and each year made inspection trips throughout the whole empire: the children of vassal princes were taken as "hostages" and educated in Egyptian style, at the court of the Egyptian emperor, in order to teach them Egyptian manners and tastes and to assimilate them to Pharaonic culture and civilization.

> A true ministry of foreign affairs, in charge of relations with foreign countries, was created at Thebes, and also included a special chancellery that was to centralize correspondence with the agents of the Egyptian administration in the provinces, with the vassal cities and princes, a correspondence carefully preserved in the archives of the department and part of which was discovered at Tel al-Amarna.[3]

The power of the Pharaoh over the vassals was absolute. The vassal had to be obedient and faithful and had to execute orders, whatever they might be. He had to respect the Pharaoh as a god, because, "according to the diplomatic formulary imposed on the vassal, the Pharaoh is his king, his god, his sun, at whose feet he bows seven and seven times."[4]

The tributes collected in one year under Thutmose III, by his vizier, or chancellor, Rekhmira, represented the colossal value for that period of 36,692 *deben* of gold, or more than three metric tons, of which 2,700 kilos came from the Asiatic provinces and the islands of the Aegean Sea alone. (figs. 22, 23, 24, 25)

In addition to the compulsory annual tribute representing the collective tax of the whole conquered nation, evaluated according to its wealth, the vassal owed other types of "help": gifts to the royal messengers, sending slaves (generally women) to the Egyptian king each time the vassal addressed the Pharaoh to ask a favor of him. The Pharaoh could at any moment require money, chariots, horses, compulsory war service; the vassal was constantly under the orders of the Egyptian generals. The Pharaoh judged and arbitrated conflicts between vassals; he could order one of them to arrest a disloyal peer. The vassals enjoyed only internal autonomy; in fact they had lost their international sovereignty: they could not directly deal with foreign lands. If his territory were invaded, the vassal had to report without delay to his lord, his sun, his god, the Pharaoh. He was declared a felon and beheaded if he separately made peace with an enemy of the Pharaoh. The felonious or supposedly guilty vassal was called to appear before Pharaoh's court to justify himself, failing which Pharaoh sent a faithful vassal to bring back the guilty one with his entire family in chains.

The Pharaoh, being the incarnation of the divine *Ka*, legitimately exercised the power that he received from the God Amon-Ra, creator of the universe, in order to maintain justice, peace, and law among mortals. The theory of individual will as a source of authority never existed in Egypt.

All the peoples had to obey Pharaoh Thutmose III, according to the divine will of Amon-Ra, who was not only the national Egyptian God, but God of the whole universe, his creation: that is what is affirmed by the Karnak stela, cited on p. 85 and, on which the 110 conquered states are enumerated:

> I have given you power and victory over all the nations
> you have conquered the rebel hordes as I commanded,
> the Earth in its length and its breadth, the peoples of the West and of the East are your subjects
> no one was subjected to your majesty without myself having been your guide, so that you would succeed.
> All the peoples come, bringing tribute to you on their backs, bowing before you as I have ordained.[5]

This was the philosophy of power that Thutmose III invented in order to create the first true empire in history:

"The king in the righteousness of his heart, reigns, accomplishing the divine will."

According to a theory similar to that of the kings of the XIIth Dynasty who succeeded in unifying the monarchy at the national level, the Egyptian solar cosmogony was imposed on all the conquered peoples of the empire, particularly in Asia where Amon became identified with the Babylonian Shamash.

Thus, the cult of Amon-Ra, the sun-king, became universal and heralded the religious revolution of Amenophis IV (Akhenaton).

The worshipers of Shamash, assimilated by Amon-Ra, the father of the Pharaoh, found it normal to obey him. The same was true for the local divinities of the vassal cities (Sidon, Tyre, Byblos, Berytus, Gaza, Askalon); the Pharaoh became recognized as the representative of the gods.

In this way, Pharaonic domination over all of western Asia was legitimized even in the view of the local religions.

On the other hand, we know that the individualistic Greek city-state was historically condemned and then declined because it was never able to overcome the superstructural obstacle of the hostility of foreign gods to individualism; it thus never grew to become a large national territory including several cities.

These new forms of dependency are revealed by the official manner in which the vassals of Asia addressed the Pharaoh. For instance, Radimur, the head of Byblos wrote: "To my lord, my king, my sun, Gebal [Byblos] your servant, Radimur your servant. . . . At the feet of my lord, the sun, seven and seven times I bow . . . may Baalat [the goddess] of Byblos give power to the king, my lord."

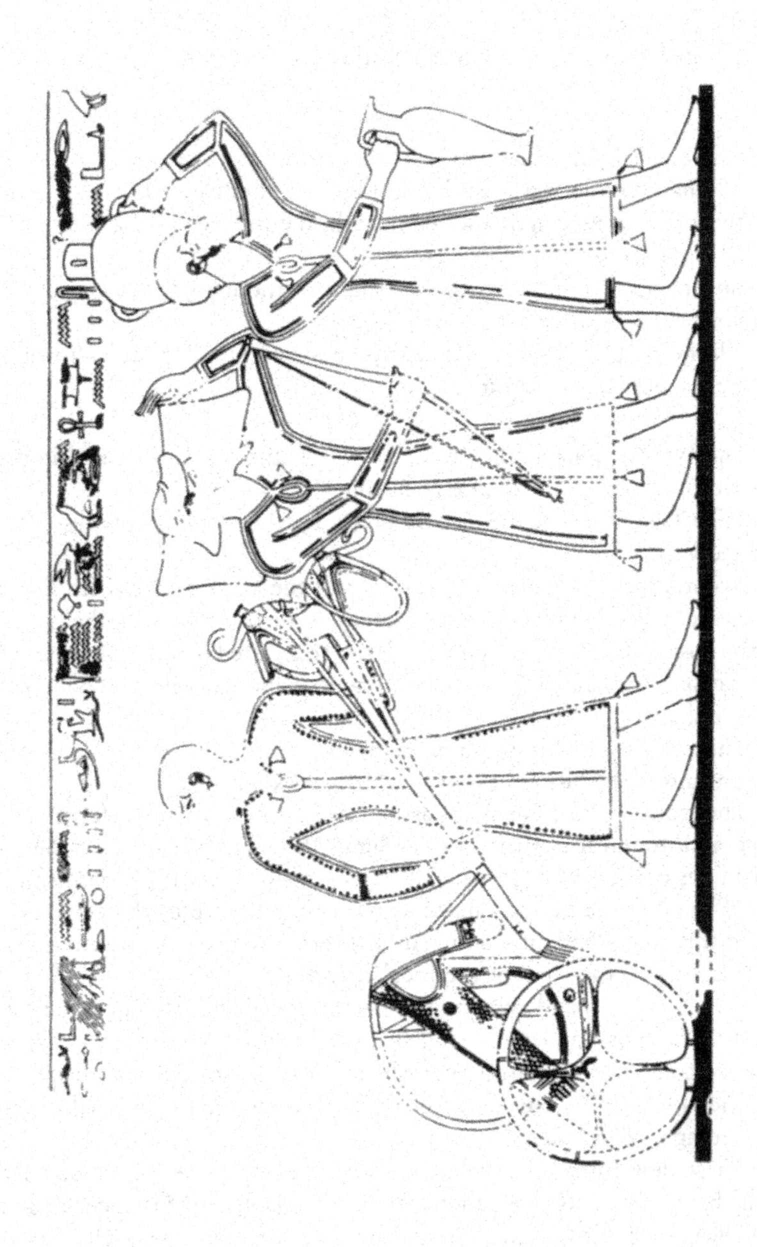

Figures 24, 25: Egyptian XVIIIth Dynasty: Syrian subjects bringing their annual tribute to Pharaoh Thutmose III. Frescoes of the tomb of Rekhmira at Thebes. (Fig. 24: Norman de Garis Davies: *Tomb of Rekh-Mi-Rè at Thebes*, vol. II. Fig. 25: from Gaston Maspero: *Histoire ancienne des peuples de l'Orient*, p. 221.)

The character of the sovereignty was juridically different depending on whether the Pharaoh received it from the local gods or from the sun-god: in the latter case, it was more frequently direct and absolute; in the former, the Pharaoh was the national king of the city, because he held the power of the national divinities.

For the "republican" (already at that date) towns like Tunip and Irgata, it was the established authorities of the city that pledged allegiance. For example:

"To the king of Egypt; my lord. The inhabitants of Tunip, your servant nation. . . . At the feet of my lord, I bow down."

"This is a letter from the city of Irgata to our lord the king. Irgata and her elders bow down seven and seven times at the feet of our lord the king. To our lord the sun." The formulas were still more humble when the vassals spoke for themselves instead of writing in the name of their cities. The vassal of Byblos, for instance, wrote: "To my lord, the king, the sun of the countries, Rib-Addi, your servant, your footstool. At the feet of the sun, my lord, seven and seven times I bow down."

The king of the Amorites writes: "[I am] the dust of your feet . . ."; others say: ". . . the ground you walk on."

In contrast, the Pharaoh always spoke in haughty terms to the Asian vassals: "To the prince of the Amorites, the king, your lord . . .; know that the king, the sun in the sky is in good health; and that his warriors and his chariots are numerous. . . ."

Amenophis III wrote to the vassal of the town of Gezer, in Palestine, a letter in which he asked for the delivery of forty women, "very beautiful women who must have no blemish," and he sent a commander of his troops to this end. Here is the preamble:

> To Milkili, the chief of the city of Gezer. . . . The king your master who gives you life . . . know that the king is as well as the sun and that his troops, his chariots, his horses are [also] very well. Hence, the God Amon has put the upper country, the lower country, the East, the West, under the feet of the king.

One cannot insist strongly enough that interbreeding in Egypt took place from the lower classes to the upper, especially beginning with the XVIIIth and the XIXth Dynasties.

Vassals were always very honored to give their daughters for the Pharaoh's harem without reciprocation ever being conceivable, as is testified to in the correspondence of Amenophis III and the king of Babylon.

No queen of Egyptian stock ever married an outsider, not even during the time of Solomon, despite the famous verse of the Songs of Songs, in which the Egyptian woman says: "I am Black but I am comely." The verse could not, even at this period of the lower epoch, have referred to a true daughter of the Pharaoh.

Egyptian queens were always considered to be depositories of "divine blood," the female perpetuators of the divine royal lineage according to African matriarchal tradition.

In order to have legitimate rights to the Egyptian throne, all usurpation aside, one had to be the son of an authentic Egyptian princess.

Thus the Egyptian conquest of Asia Minor and the islands of the eastern Mediterranean was effective; not even the continental states, much less the islands great and small, could resist the Egyptian might.

> If one were to believe the Egyptians, Crete and the Cyclades paid tribute to Pharaoh. We know that Thutmose III offered a golden cup to General Thuty for having filled his coffers with gold, silver and lapis lazuli paid as tribute by the Aegean islands.[6]

The conquest of the Cyclades goes back to Thutmose I, according to Sethe. In the tomb of Rekhmira, vizier of Thutmose III, precisely, the Cretans, called *Keftiu* (pirates?), are represented, as mentioned above, paying their annual tribute, consisting of "vases in the form of the heads of bulls and lions, goblets, daggers, needles, all of these in gold and silver."[7] We must say that in the presence of so many facts, not to mention those yet to be told, the arguments that Jacques Pirenne advances on the importance of Egypto-Cretan commerce, in order to timidly raise doubts about the reality of these conquests, are very weak.

According to the Egyptian annals of Tel al-Amarna, cited by Pirenne, the king of Asia (of the island of Cyprus) in the year 34 of the reign of Amenophis III, paid to Egypt a tribute of 108 salmons of copper, weighing 2,040 *deben*, or 3,468 tons, of copper, 1,200 salmons of lead, 100 *deben* of lapis lazuli, a piece of ivory, and 2 pieces of wood.[8]

Likewise in the year 24, ambassadors of Assur brought to Thutmose III 50 *deben* and 9 *kedet* of lapis lazuli, vases and gems.[9] A second delegation brought to the Pharaoh, the same year, 190 chariots loaded with precious wood, 343 pieces of lumber, 50 pieces of carob wood, etc.[10]

In the year 33, Babylonian ambassadors brought to the Pharaoh, in the countryside, 30 *deben* of lapis lazuli; Hittite ambassadors brought silver rings weighing 401 *deben*.[11]

In all cases, this is purely and simply tribute paid to the Pharaoh by vassals, according to the Egyptian annals.

In the same manner the annual net tribute from Syria, in the year 38 of the reign of Thutmose III, was: 328 horses, 522 slaves (generally women), 9 chariots decorated in gold and silver, 61 painted chariots, 2,821 *deben* and 3.5 *kedet* of copper objects, 276 salmons of copper, 26 salmons of lead, 650 jars of incense, 1,752 jars of fine oil, 156 jars of wine, 13 bulls,

46 asses, 5 elephant tusks, a table made of wood and ivory, 68 *deben* of bronze, the best lumber. . . .[12]

As for Phoenicia, it furnished the materials necessary for the maintenance of Egyptian ports: Lebanon gave the lumber necessary for the construction of ships, while the agricultural region of the plains supplied food to the permanently established garrisons of the Pharaoh.[13] This is the Phoenicia of the time of Sidon and Tyre (later) that the historians usually present as a political entity independent of the Egyptian empire, whereas it was an integral part of this empire, as proven by the annual obligations actually paid to the Egyptian treasury.

Retenpu (a Syrian district) paid in the year 24: the chief's daughter to the Pharaoh's harem, with jewelry and 30 slaves for her, 65 slaves, 103 horses, 5 golden chariots, 5 chariots plated with electrum, 45 calves, 749 cows, 5,703 heads of small livestock, gold dishes, 104 *deben* and 5 *kedet* of silver, armor, 823 jars of incense, 1,718 jars of honey, etc.,[14] and so on year after year.

In the year 33, Naharin supplied 513 slaves, 260 horses, 45 *deben*, and a *kedet* of gold . . . silver tableware from Djahi (Phoenicia) craftsmen, 28 bulls, 564 cows, 5,323 heads of small livestock, 828 jars of incense, etc.[15]

The Greek legends are illuminated by a particularly bright light when projected against the chronological table of Egyptian history.

Indeed, the XVIIIth Dynasty was contemporaneous with Mycenaean Greece; even Athens was founded by a colony of Black Egyptians led by Cecrops, who introduced agriculture and metallurgy to continental Greece around the sixteenth century B.C., according to Greek tradition itself.

Erechtheus, who unified Attica, also came from Egypt, according to Diodorus of Sicily, while the Egyptian Danaus founded at Argos the first royal dynasty in Greece. It was the same time that the Phoenician Cadmus, an Egyptian subject, founded the city of Thebes in Boeotia and the royalty of that country. Finally, Orpheus, the mythic ancestor of the Hellenic race, became initiated into the Egyptian mysteries, during this same Mycenaean epoch. Therefore, no wonder that on the Mycenaean tablets, in *Linear B*, one should read the name of Dionysus in the genitive: Dionysus, as we know, is none other than a replica of Osiris in Greece and the northern Mediterranean in general. Thus his arrival, in other words the introduction of Egyptian religion in Greece, is much more ancient than Herodotus believed it to be: so many facts underscore the preponderance of Egyptian influence at the birth of the Greek world, the age of heroes.

Thutmose III, son of God, meaning son of Amon-Ra, was guided by his father during all of his conquests: he held the sword of the faith and of divine truth. All the allied leaders of the principal states of western Asia retreated to Megiddo after having been routed by the Pharaoh; the besieged town soon capitulated and the Egyptian army reaped fabulous spoils: 2,132 horses, 994 chariots, etc. The region was subjugated:

> The chiefs of Syria rushed to pay tribute and to take the oath of loyalty. . . . Gold, silver, bronze, lapis lazuli, all that constituted the treasury of the Hittite princes passed into the coffers of God (Amon). The leaders had to give their sons as hostages. . . . Besides the annual tribute, the leaders of the *Rutennu* agreed to contribute by supplying food to all stations where the Pharaoh and his army arrived.[16]

Two years after the defeat and the submission of the principalities of Arwad, Nisrona, Kodshe, Simyra, Djahi (northern Phoenicia), Naharin was attacked. The leader of the Hittites, defeated, fled as fast as he could with his army: "Without any of them daring to look back, for all they thought of was running away, jumping like a herd of wild goats (according to the Egyptian annals).[17]

In order to perpetuate this victory, Thutmose III built stelae, perhaps near Carchemish, one to the east of the river, the other next to the *cippe*[18] that his father, Thutmose I, had consecrated almost half a century before.[19]

We will now give a detailed description of these stelae via Herodotus, whose testimony the ideological historians of today try to question.

> All the peoples of Syria, one after the other, had to bow down before the irresistible power of Pharaoh, the Lamnanu, the Hatti (Hittites), the people of Singra, those of Asia (Cyprus): their repeated revolts resulted in nothing but making even heavier the yoke that was imposed on them.[20]

> The Syrian petty kings, formerly so assertive, resigned themselves to their fate and were offering their daughters to Pharaoh so that he might adorn his harem with them. The conquest seemed finished, at least in Asia, and the correspondence between the vassal princes and the Egyptian governors contained only protestations of devotion.[21]

Consequently, the triumphal hymn of Thutmose III, on the poetic stela at Karnak, is rigorously faithful to the historical truth concerning the enumeration of the countries actually conquered and placed under the political authority of the Black Pharaoh, by the will of his father, the God Amon-Ra.

> I have come [god Amon told him], I am allowing you to crush the princes of Djahi [Phoenicia]; I am throwing them under your feet throughout their territory; I am making them behold your majesty, bedecked in your ornaments of war, when you take up the weapons on your chariot,
>
> I have come, I am allowing you to crush the land of the East; Kefti [Crete] and Asia [Cyprus] are under your terror; I am making

them behold your majesty as a young bull, firm of heart, equipped with horns, that nobody can resist,

I have come, I am allowing you to crush the peoples who are resisting in the ports, and the regions of Mittanni tremble under your terror; I am making them behold your majesty as a hippopotamus, lord of terror, in the waters, and whom none can approach,

I have come, I am allowing you to crush the peoples who are resisting in their islands; those who live amid the sea are under your roar; I am making them behold your majesty as an avenger who stands on the back of his victim,

I have come, I am enabling you to crush the Tahenu [Libyans]; the islands of the Danaens are under the power of your spirit; I am making them behold your majesty as a furious lion who lies down on their corpses throughout their valleys,

I have come, I am allowing you to crush the coastal regions, the entire periphery of the great zone of the waters [eastern Mediterranean] is bound to your fist; I am making them behold your majesty as the master of the wing [hawk] who catches in the wink of an eye whatever pleases him,

I have come, I am allowing you to crush the peoples who reside in their lagoons, to bind the masters of the sands [Hironshaitu or the desert Bedouins] in captivity; I am making them behold your majesty as of the jackal of the South, lord of speed, runner who prowls through the two regions,

I have come, I am allowing you to crush all of the barbarians of Nubia; all the way to the people of Put, all is in your hand; I am making them behold your majesty similar to that of your two brothers, Horus and Seth, whom I have joined hands to insure your power.[22]

Even the Blacks of Palestine, these Biblical cousins of the Egyptians, the Canaanites of the Bible, descendants of the Natufians of the Mesolithic period, opposed a fierce resistance in their different cities, which were all conquered and annexed to the Egyptian Empire.

Among the vassal peoples of the Near East,

> . . . the Phoenicians were those who best profited from the Egyptian conquest. The group from the center and the one from the South, Gebal (Byblos) and Berouth (Beirut), Sidon and Tyre, showed themselves more resigned to their fate, from the time of Thutmose I to that of Ramses II (1500–1300 B.C.), and their resignation gave them serious advantages. Their sailors engaged in commissioned trade in Egypt on behalf of foreigners, and abroad on behalf of Egypt. . . .

> The Phoenicians estimated that a voluntary tribute cost less than a war against the pharaohs, and amply compensated themselves for the dimunition of their liberty by monopolizing the maritime trade of the Delta.[23]

From the above, one can measure how historically improper it is to speak, in the absolute, of Cretan or Phoenician supremacy in the Mediterranean of this period, by ignoring Egyptian colonization and presenting these nations as independent political entities.

The so-called Minoan thalassocracy was under the political domination of the Black Pharaohs of the XVIIIth Dynasty, as was Phoenicia in the time of the Sidonian navigations: neither one of these peoples were inventors; they were doing nothing but transmitting Egyptian cultural values, even in the domain of writing and navigation (figs. 26, 27).

These great military feats made a legend of Thutmose III. The capture of the rebel town of Joppa by his general Thuty (in which five hundred soldiers inside of jars were sneaked into town by a strategem) served as a pristine model for Homer, in the episode of the Trojan horse in the *Iliad*, and later for the storyteller of *Ali Baba and the Forty Thieves*.

The Trojan War took place two centuries later under Ramses II, around 1280 B.C., and the precision of Egyptian chronology can help locate in time the legendary history of Greece.

All of the conquered countries were covered with commemorative stelae, and even statues of Pharaohs of the XIXth Dynasty (Ramses II) and perhaps also of the XVIIIth Dynasty.

> Herodotus had seen several in Syria and Ionia. Travelers have noted, in fact, not far from Beirut, at the mouth of the Nahr el-Kelb, three stelae engraved in the rock and dated as of the years II and IV of Ramses II.
>
> The two figures that Herodotus said existed in his time in Asia Minor still stand today near Ninfi, between Sardis and Smyrna. At first sight, they seem really to have the character of Pharaonic works. . . .
>
> They are, as the inscription proves, the work of an Asian artist, and not that of an Egyptian sculptor.[24]

It would be impossible to underscore more strongly the depth of Egyptian cultural and political influence on the whole of Asia Minor, especially when we know that the writing in question is in hieroglyphics: it was indeed under Egyptian suzerainty (XVIIIth and XIXth Dynasties) that the Hittites adopted hieroglyphic writing and constituted their own archives in the Egyptian manner, which contain precious information about the beginnings of Greek history. The Hittites would thus be the only Indo-

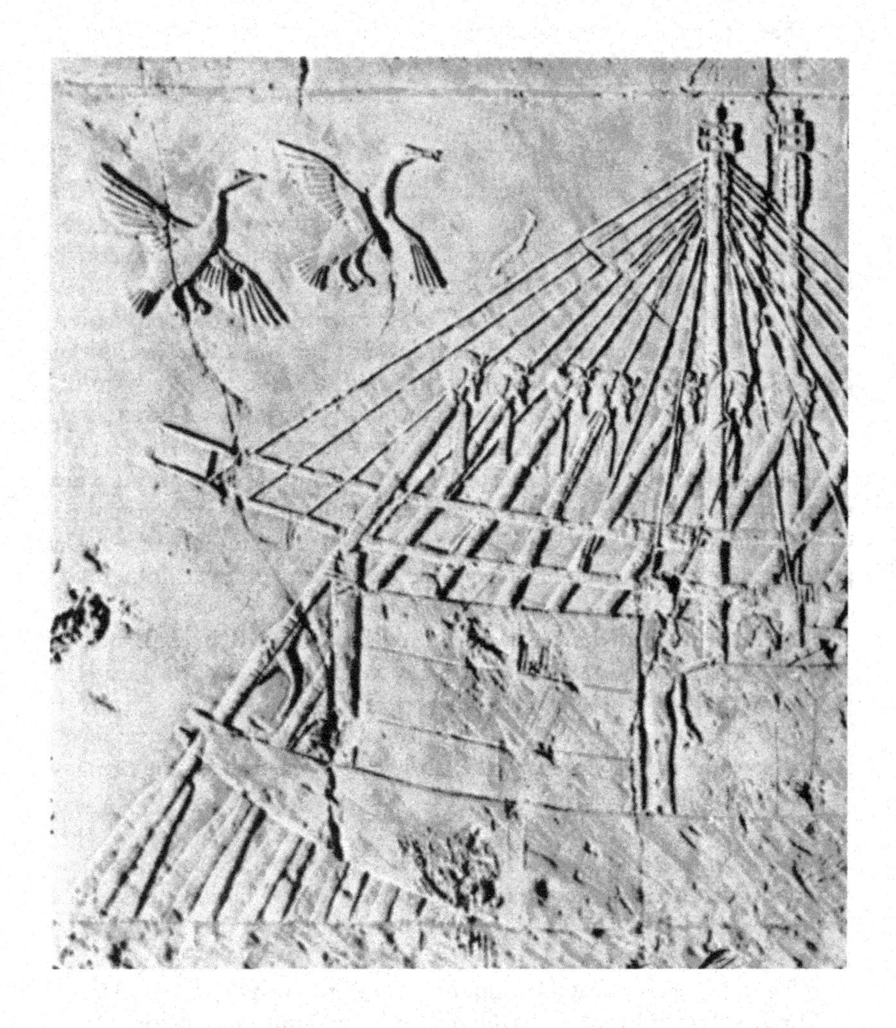

Figures 26, 27: Note on these two figures the axial position of the paddles used as the helm; this is certainly the ancestor of the axial helm fitted with a second stick in order to reduce the movement and to maneuver comfortably. The individual standing up in the back in figure 27 is manipulating this stick.

Figure 26: Bas-relief of the tomb of Khaemhat, 1500 B.C., in Jacques Pirenne, *Histoire de la civilisation de l'Égypte ancienne*, vol. II, fig. 55.

Figure 27: "A boat that could be half for cargo, half for passengers," (in B. Landström: *Ships of the Pharaohs*, London: Allen and Unwin, 1970, fig. 401)

European people to have adopted the hieroglyphic system and this was not by chance; it stems from Egyptian colonization, the indelible mark of which was still visible during the time of Ramses II, whom the Hittite king, Hattusil III, addresses in terms of humility that leave no doubt about his vassalage:

> The great chief of Hatti [Hittite country] informs the chief of Qidi: "Ready yourself that we may go to Egypt. The word of the king [Ramses II] has manifested itself, let us obey Sesostris [Ramses II]. He gives the breaths of life to those who love him: the whole world loves him, and Khati is but one with him."[25]

Hattusil III gave his eldest daughter to Ramses II without the reverse situation being imaginable.

So many facts, after a long war from which Ramses II, after Thutmose III, constantly emerged victorious, illustrate the supremacy of the black Pharaohs in Western Asia.

The often quoted passage by Herodotus relative to the stelae and the engraved figures deserves to be cited: Pharaoh Sesostris (Thutmose III or Ramses II as the case may be), for whom bravery was the supreme virtue, particularly despised peoples who were conquered without a fight:

> In those whose cities he had annexed without combat and without effort, he engraved on the stelae inscriptions of the same meaning as those in the cities of the peoples who had fought valiantly, and moreover, he engraved the image of female sexual organs; he wanted to make it clear that these people had no bravery. In doing this, he crossed the continent from one end to the other, going from Asia to Europe, until he advanced to the countries of the Scythians and the Thracians, whom he subjugated. This is, it seems to me, the farthest point that the Egytian armies reached. In these two countries, in fact, were erected the stelae that I was talking about.[26]

Herodotus thus explains the presence of the Colchians, a Black Egyptian colony, on the banks of the Phasis River in Asia Minor: Was it an advancing garrison intended to occupy permanently a strategic point, in order to prevent the invasion by the northern peoples, after the kings of Thebes, from the South, had driven out the Hyksos and founded the XVIIIth Dynasty?

In any case, Herodotus does not doubt that these were ancient Egyptians, because, like the Egyptians, they had black skin and woolly hair, but above all they spoke a language related to Egyptian; they were circumcised, and worked flax like the Egyptians.[27]

Archaeological excavations have now revealed an unsuspected extension of the influence of Egyptian civilization in Asia and Europe: a sphinx was recently found in Southern Russia.[28]

Herodotus offers some specifics that should not be minimized:

> Of the stelae that the Egyptian king erected in different countries, most are no longer visible and no longer remain; nevertheless, in Syria, I have seen myself some that still exist, bearing the inscriptions that I spoke about and the sexual organs of women. There are also in Ionia two images of this man carved in bas-relief in the rocks along the route that goes from Ephesus to Phocis and on the one that goes from Sardis to Smyrna. On both sides is sculpted a man four-and-a-half cubits tall; he holds in his right hand a spear and in his left hand a bow; the rest of his equipment is, accordingly, part Egyptian and part Ethiopian. From one shoulder to the other across his chest runs an inscription engraved in Egyptian sacred letters, which says this: "I, by the strength of my shoulders, have conquered this country."[29]

Herodotus affirms having seen these stelae with female sexual organs in Phoenicia. The fact seems likely enough because, according to all of the above, this region is one of those that offered no resistance to Egyptian conquest.[30]

On the other hand, modern erudition protests weakly and affirms that these are Hittite monuments of the first half of the thirteenth century B.C., in other words, precisely the period of Ramses II and Khatousil III, during which the Hittite country was effectively under the political and cultural domination of Egypt. A strange Hittite monument one might confuse, "at first," in Maspero's words, "with Egyptian figures." Since when did Hittites dress in the *calasiris*, the Egyptian national dress? They assert that it is a Hittite god. But based on what is given above, the Pharaoh was deified in all the conquered regions of western Asia: he was regarded everywhere as the son of God, fifteen hundred years before the coming of Christ, in the whole empire and even in Egypt from the time of the pyramids, 2600 B.C., when the Pharaohs had for the first time taken the title of the son of God, beginning with the IVth Dynasty.

At the time these monuments were built, the Hittite king, Hattusil III, deified the Egyptian Pharaoh Ramses II, who was in fact his master and suzerain, as shown by the letter from Hattusil III quoted above. Therefore, there is nothing surprising about the fact that divinized Pharaoh is presented by a local artist as the god of the Hittite country for which he was the eminent master. This would explain the fact that this Hittite god is represented with the features proper to an Egyptian or an Ethiopian, with the few misconceptions and errors cited by Maspero and other authors. We have a similar situation during the Hellenistic epoch, when, after the conquest of Egypt, Alexander the Great tried to have himself deified, and, following him, so all the Ptolemaic and Roman kings.

So it was the XVIIIth Egyptian Dynasty which, by colonization and the introduction of writing, brought out of protohistory Crete, Cyprus, continental or Mycenaean Greece, and Asia Minor (Ionia, Hittite country, etc.).

In fact, we know that the XVIIIth Dynasty had restored to use the syllabic writing invented during the XIth Dynasty in order to transcribe correctly the numerous foreign names of the conquered peoples of the 110 states that made up the empire: *Linear A*, used precisely in the sixteenth century B.C. to write the Cretan language, is not an accidental invention independent of its political and cultural Egyptian context. It was necessary for the new administration of the XVIIIth Dynasty, and it would give birth to *Linear B*, in continental Greece (fig. 28), after the volcanic eruption of Santorini Island destroyed Minoan civilization in Crete, as we have seen above.

Linear A and *Linear B* are both syllabic systems, and it is known that *Linear B* was not initially adapted to the Greek language: it was a writing system initially invented for a non-Greek language (Cretan) and adapted later, for better or for worse, to Greek phonetics.

As we have just seen, it was during the XVIIIth Dynasty that syllabic writing would develop in Egypt, under the exigency of vast conquests necessitating transcription into Egyptian of numerous foreign words and names.

> Syllabic writing appears during the XIth Dynasty, but does not come into frequent use until the XVIIIth Dynasty. . . . The purpose of this form of writing is to render in Egyptian, with their approximate phonetic value, foreign names of places and persons, as well as Egyptian names of foreign origin.[31]

Under the same circumstances and for the same reasons, hieroglyphic writing was introduced into Hittite country. Likewise, Phoenician writing, which would give birth to the Greek alphabet in the eighth century B.C., returns via its prior prototypes to the multiple forms of alphabetical writing practiced in Egypt by the secret societies, from the time of the Ancient Empire, and which are almost never mentioned. The Egyptian scribes were in the habit of inventing alphabets, in the strict sense, for various reasons.[32]

The Ras Shamra texts, in other words the texts from Ugarit, in northern Phoenicia, reveal, against any expectation of the Western ideologues, that the ancestors of the primitive Phoenician nation came from the South (Egypt, Africa) and not from the North.

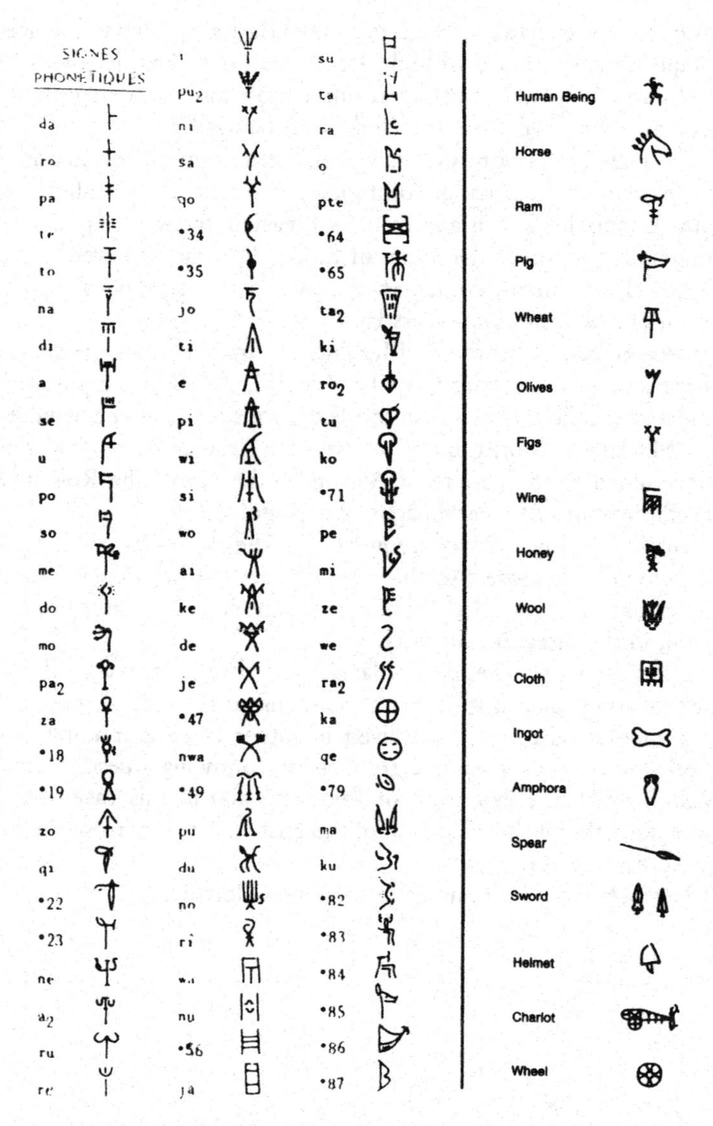

Figure 28: Table of *Linear B*. One sees that from its birth this writing is syllabic, which would be impossible without a foreign influence, which, in this case, is obviously Egyptian. Writing always begins with ideograms before becoming phonetic. *Linears A* and *B* are spontaneously phonetic from their birth, because Crete, colonized by Egypt, learned writing through this contact. On the other hand, if the Cretans were of Greek origin, the language of *Linear A* would have been Greek. However, we know that this is not the case. (J. A. Sakellarakis, University of Athens, in *Musée d'Hérakleion*)

On the other hand, we see that universalism is a consequence of the conquest of Thutmose III and of the creation of the first world empire. It predates the eruption of Santorini: Amon was already speaking before Aton as a universal God, the God of all beings.[33]

The messianism born of this volcanic eruption is a distinct aspect that may have given a particular coloration to Egyptian universalism beginning with Amenophis IV; in any case, as Breasted and so many authors have pointed out, it was at the origin of Judeo-Christian and even Islamic messianism. Everything is comparable, down to the style, when it is not pure repetition, two thousand years later.

It was equally under the XVIIIth Dynasty, by colonizing the quasi-totality of the known and relatively civilized world, that Egypt imposed the state model later called AMP (Asian Mode of Production) on the Minoan (Crete) and Mycenaean world, on all of western Asia—a model that was to be reincarnated in the empire of Alexander the Great, the Roman Empire, and the empires of Charlemagne and Napoleon.[34]

Finally, the migratory consequences of the explosion of Santorini must be studied more closely so that we may see whether the explosion might not explain the so-called "Aryan" migration, at the same time (around 1450), in the direction of India.

It is certain, as Fustel de Coulanges had already shown by the study of their customs, and in spite of the thinking of Georges Dumezil, that the later Indo-Aryans must have lived in rather close community with the Greeks before they separated from them, following a deadly event which might well be the explosion of Santorini; and in this case, it would be quite normal that they fled toward the East to get away from the epicenter of the earthquake.

Research should be pursued in this new domain.

4

LATEST DISCOVERIES ON THE ORIGIN OF EGYPTIAN CIVILIZATION

ANTERIORITY OF NUBIAN CIVILIZATION

We have written in *Nations nègres et culture* and in our later publications that, according to the quasi-unanimous testimony of the ancients, Nubian civilization preceded and might even have given birth to that of Egypt. This is quite logical if one considers the likelihood that the Nile Valley was peopled by a progressive descent of the Black peoples from the region of the Great Lakes, the cradle of *Homo sapiens sapiens*. But conclusive archaeological facts to demonstrate this hypothesis were missing. The gap, it seems, has been filled, thanks to the excavations by Keith Seele, of the University of Chicago, conducted at the Qostul cemetery in Nubia, under the auspices of UNESCO's international campaign of 1963–64, before the construction of the Aswân dam, and the flooding of the region by the filling of the resevoir. The cemetery in question is of *Group A*, a Nubian culture contemporaneous with the recent predynastic period. It was called Cemetery L, and tombs L.23 and L.24, of a special form, contained very rich material, now conserved at the Oriental Institute of the University of Chicago.

It was an associate researcher, Bruce Williams, who, studying these objects in 1978, drew the attention of the scholarly world to the peculiarity of the patterns engraved on the cylindrical censer (fig. 29). Even though the object was damaged, the parts that remained clearly showed a king

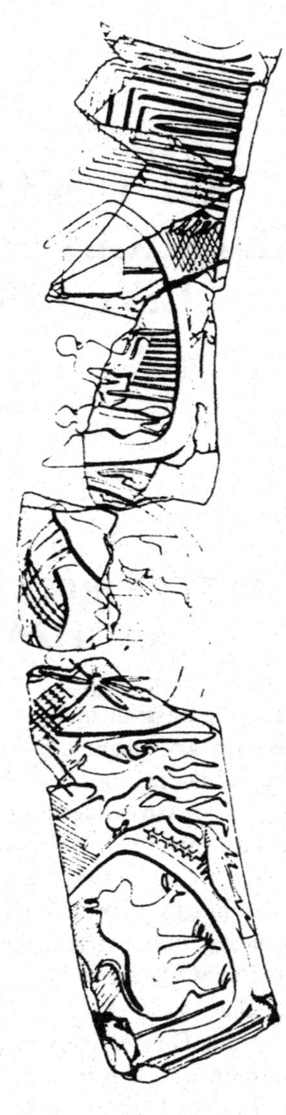

Figure 29: Development of engraved images on the censer studied by Bruce Williams of the Oriental Institute of the University of Chicago. Compare the architecture of the palace, on the left, with that of the funerary domain of Zoser, 2778 B.C. (fig. 30). Near the middle someone is seated wearing the white crown of Upper Egypt. Just above him, we see the falcon-god Horus. (Cemetery of Qostul, Nubia. Photo from the Oriental Institute, University of Chicago)

sitting in a "royal" boat, wearing the long (white) crown of Upper Egypt; in front of him, the royal banner and the falcon-god Horus. One could also observe the wall of a palace, the style of which was reminiscent of the wall of the funereal domain of Pharoah Zoser at Saqqara. The architecture, in cut stones of the IIIrd Dynasty, could not have been created *ex nihilo* (figs. 30, 31).

According to the inventor, this Nubian royalty, which appears to us with the future essential attributes of the Egyptian monarchy, had preceded it by at least three generations. The censer is the most ancient figure of a king found in the Nile Valley. Indecipherable signs of hieroglyphic form presaging the writing of the period close to the end of the fourth millenium also were noted.

The comparison of the Nubian ceramics found in the tombs with clearly dated predynastic Egyptian ceramics allowed precise determination of its period.

The author estimates that proof is now established that Nubian monarchy is the oldest in the history of humanity.[1]

We thus better understand the matriarchal essence of Egyptian royalty and the importance of the role of the queen-mother in Nubia, Egypt, and the rest of Black Africa (see p. 181).

The woman, the queen, was the true sovereign, the keeper of the royalty and guardian of the purity of the lineage. To this end, it often happened that she married her brother or her half-brother by the same father: it was she who transmitted the crown to her husband, who was only her executive agent.

> We have few details about the manner in which the transition was made from the Third to the Fourth Dynasty; we know only that here again it was a queen who maintained the royal tradition by bringing the crown to her husband. This one was named Snofru (father of Cheops), and he founded the Fourth Dynasty.[2]

Osiris, the first legendary king of Egypt, had married his sister Isis.

> This severe law, still in effect at the time of the New Empire, caused Thutmose I to turn his throne over to his daughter and son-in-law after the death of his wife Ahmes (to whom he owed the throne), and to abdicate. It was equally severe for Unas, last king of the IIIrd Memphite Dynasty: as he apparently had no male heir, his daughter Hetephras had to marry a noble of a different bloodline; this put an end to the Fifth Dynasty.[3]

In Wolof, a Senegalese language, the word *sat* (grandson, descent) is an ancient forgotten feminine form. Indeed, *sat* = daughter in Egyptian;

Figure 30: An ancient gate leading into the funerary domain of Zoser. (Photo by Jacques Pirenne)

Figure 31: Details of figures 29 and 30 that allow one to better appreciate the stylistic resemblance of the initial royal architecture of Nubia (fourth millenium) and of that of the IIIrd Dynasty, under Zoser (2778 B.C.).

thus, originally, the Wolof word, it seems, exclusively designated uterine descent through daughters.[4]

More precisely, in ancient Egyptian, *sent* = sister; in Wolof, *sant* = the proper name of a clan, which perpetuates the family line and is that of the mother, in other words, the sister of the uncle in a matrilineal system: it is through the sister that rights are transmitted and the "race" is perpetuated. According to Ibn Battuta, in the fourteenth century in Mali, men were not named after their fathers: "None of them [the men] is named after his father, but each traces his genealogy through that of his maternal uncle. Inheritance is collected by the sons of the sister of the deceased, to the exclusion of his own children."[5]

> It happened, during my stay in Mali, that the sultan became angry with his principal wife, the daughter of his mother's brother [not his father's, according to the text, cf. Legend of Sundiata], who was called *Kàcà*; the meaning of this word, for blacks, is queen. In the

government she is the associate of the sovereign, according to the custom of the people, and her name is uttered on the throne, jointly with the king's.[6]

We also understand better now why the Egyptian term designating royalty etymologically means: (the man) "who comes from the South" = *nsw* < *n y swt* = who belongs to the South = who is a native of the South = the king of Egypt, not only the king of Upper Egypt. Whereas *Biti* = king of Lower Egypt, and has never meant just king, in other words king of Lower and Upper Egypt, king of all Egypt.

A faulty reading that takes the hieroglyphic signs in the visible order above, which must have occurred at one time or another, would give: *Suten* > Sudan (?).

Now we understand better why the Egyptian turns toward the South, the heart of Africa, land of his origins, land of his ancestors, "land of the Gods," just as the Moslem today turns toward Mecca. This is why the right hand designates the West and the left hand the East. It is not, as Edouard Naville assumed, due to a march toward the South, supposing a northern origin of the ancient Egyptians. The Egyptian gods themselves, the god Min in particular, were making this symbolic return to the South: the god was taken out and carried for some time toward the South, and then he was returned to his sanctuary.[7]

The texts on the pyramids preserve the memory of the terrible storms of Equatorial Africa, at the time when the tribes that were to make up the Egyptian people had not yet penetrated deeply into the Nile Valley. "The sky melts into water, where the heavens speak and the earth trembles," says the pyramid of Unas.[8]

The Egyptians supposed that thunder was the voice of heaven. Whence, in the Coptic language:

δρσογ μ πε = the voice of heaven
δρογ σσαη = the voice of the iron ceiling, meaning, heaven[9] (Memphite dialect)

Note that in Serer, a Senegalese language, *Rog* = the celestial God, whose voice is thunder. In Egypt, it almost never rains.

EGYPTIAN		WOLOF	
= *djett*	= desert[10]	*Diatti*	= wilderness (uninhabited by humanity)
šm	= to go toward, to follow	*dëm*	= to go toward, s → d

PART 2

LAWS GOVERNING THE EVOLUTION OF SOCIETIES: MOTOR OF HISTORY IN SOCIETIES OF AMP AND THE GREEK CITY-STATE

5

CLANIC AND TRIBAL ORGANIZATION

Clanic organization, in that it is founded on the taboo of incest, marks the beginning of civilization: the human being is no longer a simply biological animal. His sexual relations are henceforth dependent on very strict social regulations.

The clan is also and above all a social organization whose purpose is to meet economic needs and to challenge nature. It is founded on a deliberate choice of a unilateral type of kinship (patrilineal or matrilineal, according to the economic context), of a private or collective type of ownership, of a mode of inheritance, etc.

Therefore, at the moment of clanic formation, humanity already knew the respective roles of both spouses in the physical conception of the child; it had a clear notion of physical kinship, ownership of goods and inheritance, and the possible relationships between individuals.

Clanic organization only socialized these notions, for its convenience, by giving them a particular structure and content that might correspond to the demands of this phase of human evolution.

Hypotheses about the forms of human existence prior to the clan need not be dealt with here: promiscuity, primitive communism, etc.

Nevertheless it is our opinion that clan and tribe were born simultaneously, because, since clanic exogamy stems from the taboo of incest, clanic organization, in order to be viable, requires the existence of neighboring clans (organized into villages or not) which, by dint of contracting exogamic marriages, end up becoming a monolingual tribe, a nationality: thus there exists a dialectical link between clan and tribe. The clan is merely a blood-related, extended family exclusively founded on either matrilineal or patrilineal kinship. It was to avoid consanguineous marriages that clanic endogamy was prohibited and that clanic exogamy was established as a rule. The nuclear family (man, woman, children) thus preceded the clan, which sought only to regulate its development to the greatest advantage of the group.

The clan, whether patrilineal or matrilineal, has always been a male creation, to the exclusion of women. The same is true for all later forms of political and social human organizations: tribal confederations, monarchies, and republics.

The man was the one who, in nomadic state, in the Eurasian steppes, chose to organize the social cell on the basis of the patrilineal clan, supposedly the best possible form of adaptation to the physical environment. Likewise, in the African agricultural sedentary milieu, it was again the male who decided to found the matrilineal clan.[1]

In order better to project the irreducibility of these two forms of adaptation to different environments, we will now, in brief review, compare their specific traits point by point:

AFRICAN CLAN	INDO-ARYAN CLAN
Matrilineal	**Patrilineal**
Created by man	Created by man
Sedentary	Nomadic
Exogamous sedentary	Exogamous nomadic
Clan exogamy	Clan exogamy (Rape of the Sabine Women)
Subsistence based on agriculture, essentially	Subsistence based on raising cattle, essentially
Religion: ancestor worship[2]	Religion: ancestor worship
Funeral rites: burial of the dead	Funeral rites: cremation of the dead, whose ashes can thus be transported in urns: fire cult
The husband brings the dowry.	The wife brings the dowry.
Matrilineal filiation and succession.	Patrilineal filiation and succession
Matrilocal marriage	Patrilocal marriage
Kinship through men: impossible	Kinship through women: impossible
The wife keeps her totem, meaning her domestic god, therefore her natural family name, her legal identity, after marriage.	The wife abjures her domestic gods before the altar of her husband's gods, therefore loses her family name, her legal identity.
The husband has no rights over his wife and children.	The husband has the right of life and death over his wife and children: he may sell them.
The children have no social kinship with their father and therefore do not inherit from him. They inherit from their maternal uncle, who has the right of life and death over them: the uncle is the social father.	The children inherit from their father: avuncular inheritance is unknown.[3] Until the reforms of Solon (590 B.C.), the children of two sisters had no social kinship.

AFRICAN CLAN	INDO-ARYAN CLAN
Matrilineal	**Patrilineal**
The wife may divorce her husband. The natural family always remains the social security milieu in case of necessity: the bond can never be broken.	The wife is the property of the husband; she may be sold like an object or killed; she cannot divorce; her own family no longer exists for her, socially speaking.
The land is an indivisible collective property: the notion of private property is marginal, but it is far from being ignored.	Land is private property, made divine by the local religion of the ancestors: terminal gods.
The sense of community is highly developed. Solitude is prohibited: all women must be married; polygamy becomes a social necessity due to the fact that there are fewer men.[4]	Individualism is the supreme virtue: even after the clan becomes sedentary; joint ownership is sacrilege: families may not come in contact with each other, even in the afterlife.
All children born are raised.	Malthusian practices Daughters are buried alive.[5] Excess babies, even though normal, are thrown away as garbage, even after the clan becomes sedentary. Eugenicism, the myth of Ganymede, homophyly
Matriarchal society: optimistic cosmogony; no notion of original sin.	Patriarchal society: pessimistic cosmogony; with notion of original sin: Prometheus; Eve's sin
Evil is introduced by men: Seth murders Osiris, as opposed to Isis, female inventor of agriculture.	Evil is introduced by women: Eve and the forbidden fruit are used to tempt Adam.
Pacifistic morality	Warrior morality: warriors fallen on the battlefield alone enter the Germanic paradise, Valhalla.

All the social revolutions that have intervened since the age of polished stone (Neolithic), no matter how radical, have not succeeded in completely wiping out the original clanic structures, which still remain embedded in our respective societies and are recognizable by numerous characteristics.

A modern European language like French reflects, in its deep structure, the nomadic Indo-European institutions unfavorable to women: there is no proper word in French to express the murder of mother or sister; the terms relative to the murder of father or brother respectively are used: *parricide* = murder of one's father, or one's mother by extension; *fratricide* = murder of one's brother, one's sister by extension.

6

STRUCTURE OF KINSHIP AT THE CLANIC AND TRIBAL STAGE

PROCESS BY WHICH THE NAME PASSES FROM THE CLANIC COLLECTIVITY TO THE INDIVIDUAL

The structure of kinship depends strictly on the material conditions of life; it evolves or changes with them in a way that Lévi-Strauss's structuralism would be incapable of foreseeing. A Nuer explained to Edward Evans-Pritchard that the child bears the name of his mother's clan as long as the marriage is matrilocal; filiation then is matrilineal. But, if the situation is reversed during the lifetime of this same child, with the woman rejoining the clan of her husband, the marriage becomes patrilocal, and filiation becomes patrilineal: the child changes his or her name and henceforth bears the name of the father's clan.[1]

The situation is the same with the Ouêhi people of the Ivory Coast: "In the father's clan, the Ouêhi is known by his *nenangnéné*.[2] But when he lives in or arrives at his mother's village, he automatically loses his patronym in favor of the *nenangnéné* of his mother. This custom naturally confers some rights and obligations."[3]

Among the Hupa Indians, who follow patrilineal filiation, Robert Lowie notes:

> Nevertheless, this paternal line, though objectively distinguishing itself from the other by a communal residence, was not specifically

> recognized by the Hupa people as a distinct unity. It could thus happen that a man, when he could not pay the price of his fiancée, was obliged to enter into service in the village of his father-in-law, and the children of this marriage then belonged to the family of the wife.[4]

Further on he writes:

> The Pueblo Indians are matriarchal in the full sense of the term; it is not the same with most of the peoples classified under this heading. We commonly find that a husband begins his conjugal life with his parents-in-law, holding in all areas the functions of a servant, but that he later establishes, often after the birth of his children, an independent household. This is the case with the Hidatsa, the Owambo of South Africa, the Khasi of Assam. The influence of maternal kinship is therefore less pronounced than in permanent matrilocal associations.[5]

This transitional phase, the passage from matriarchy to patriarchy, is rich in information for sociology. We see at work the very historical and material conditions that have given rise to both the matrilineal and patrilineal systems and the avuncular relationship.

Kinship, filiation, inheritance, all derive essentially from the privileged social situation of the spouse who remains in his or her clan and therefore hosts the other. We might cite the example of the blue blood of Ireland: the husband who migrated from the Continent had no rights over his children by the island mother.

Therefore, the two systems are not the result of a racial factor; ethnicity is not involved. If the respective cradles of civilization had been reversed, Blacks and Whites would have left to history social models opposite to the ones we received from them.

The Taboo of Incest and the Formation of Tribes, Nationalities, and Nations

The passage from clan to monolingual tribe, i.e., to ethnic group, to nationality, is a consequence of clan exogamy; biological and material reasons, the nature of which is still being discussed by specialists, very early led archaic society to practice the prohibition of incest, which marked the starting point of civilization. Clan endogamy being prohibited, several neighboring clans contracted marriage ties that with time became bonds of kinship by alliance. All these clans that occupied the same territory ended up speaking the same language even if their idioms were originally different. The number of clans that can gather together to form a more or less powerful tribe does not follow any rule and depends, at the most, on the fertility and extent of the land occupied by the group. Thus was born nationality. The individual would bear the clanic name, especially after detribalization.

Dominant Structure in Clan and Tribe

The dominant structure in the clan and to a lesser degree in the tribe was the blood tie. The law of retaliation governed clanic "stateless" societies, and weakened only gradually as a supraclanic authority, in the first instance tribal, emerged and became a counterweight to individual justice.

The idea of kinship was founded on the sacred, on the local religion, which required two relatives to have a common mythical ancestor, whether or not it was identified with a totem. The solidarity that this requirement implied was the best guarantee of individual security as long as society maintained its elementary clanic or tribal structure. It diminished when society expanded inordinately, under the pressure of productive forces and the division of labor, taking on forms of increasing complexity, obliging individuals to cooperate in the social labor necessary for the development of all.

The blood ties remained very strong in the monarchial form of the state, despite the complexity of the social organization and sometimes the size of the kingdom. Indeed, too many material interests remained attached to the blood ties, and great efforts were made to maintain them at the initial sacred level of the clanic stage; the inheritance of public offices and responsibilities reinforced kinship ties. Monarchial Europe of the *Ancien Régime* and precolonial Black Africa were in this category.

Thus the secularizing of thought and the development of social structures are the two factors that contributed to the attenuation of the blood ties; the latter actually were reduced to the minimum only in the phase corresponding to a republican and secular form of the state.

Division of Labor and Inheritance of Public Offices at the Clanic Stage Process of Social Stratification, Primitive Accumulation, and Passage to the Monarchial Phase

The division of labor and inheritance of public offices in African societies go back to the clanic stage; this very important fact must be considered by the sociologist. The clanic name is also the name of an inherited calling, and the same evolution applies all the more strongly to African societies not using family names.

Through an obvious concern for social and political equilibrium, one Nuer clan provided hereditarily the priest of grain, another the rainmaker, the "king," the (specialist) tamer of lions or leopards, the healer, etc.

The division of labor inherent in the tribal structure engendered a cumulative process, a first development of productive forces (agricultural surpluses), allowing a qualitative leap, in other words, the passage to the monarchial phase.

If such a clanic and tribal society had to defend itself at home against an exterior enemy, the most valiant warriors very quickly arrogated to themselves rights and powers legitimized by the circumstances; hence the emergence of a military and semitribal aristocracy.

The preexisting division of labor engendered a system of "castes," or at least a social stratification, for, progressively, there developed a striking disdain for manual labor as compared to the risks of military functions. However, a true system of African castes implied, at the most, the prohibitions to which the blacksmith, manual worker par excellence, was subjected. It could be that this particular case was a direct inheritance from Pharaonic Egypt where, until the low epoch, great superstition surrounded working with iron. In the temple, priests who touched iron instruments had to purify themselves.

Thus, there are two types of stratified societies in Black Africa: the one, without the idea of castes, includes South and Central Africa, and the other, with castes, includes West Africa, the ancient kingdoms of Ghana, Mali, Songhai, the Upper Nile, etc., rather generally corresponding to the area of the taboo of the blacksmith.[6] This Sahelian zone, without the tsetse fly, was also that of the noble war horse, the instrument of conquest, extension, and consolidation of these empires where a military aristocracy headed a rigorous caste system: thus there was a trilogy of horse, caste, and griot. The latter category of African society seems to have derived more directly or later from Pharaonic Egyptian society than the first category. This issue will be reexamined later.[7]

In reaction to the various calamities and social upheavals (shortage of men due to wars, epidemics, genocide, etc.), the African communitarian system adapted by applying the communitarian principle to perversion with frightening logical rigor: thus, in certain cases, a son might marry a wife of his deceased father, excluding, of course, his own mother.

These are the same communitarian principles that require polygamy, so that the individual, and every woman, may be spared social solitude: this was a deliberate choice of precolonial African society, a choice that was the opposite of the material and moral solitude necessary to individualistic Western societies.

The result is that, as great as the sphere of private life in the latter societies is, it is as much reduced in the former, where society invades all available private personal space: thus, the neuroses of Western societies are due to an excess of solitude, whereas those of African societies or communities in general are to be found in the very excess of communal life.

Different Phases of Evolution

Absolute matriarchy, in its pure state, is characterized by avuncular inheritance. This system was conceived only at the truly elementary stage of the first emergence of the matriarchal clan. The mistakes in analysis have come from the fact that most of the clans and tribes studied had already undergone a very complex evolution. This was the case for African societies that had lived under a monarchy and that retribalized to different degrees during the period of the slave trade. There was then a coexistence of tribal and monarchial elements as well as varied systems of filiation that misleads the observer who is not perspicacious.

When, for different reasons (except in the monarchial phase) marriage ceased to be matrilocal, the male regained his rights, and filiation became or tended to become patrilineal (patrilocal marriage), or bilateral in the case of an evolution leading to the extended and complex society that is monarchy.

Thus in the case of the Cayorian royalty, where the woman could not reign in place of the damel (king), the matriarchal system was subjacent; but only an inside observer could be aware of this. Maternal kinship remained predominant.

Likewise, if the initial stage was the Indo-European patriarchal clan, at the "final" monarchial stage, the system changed and filiation became bilateral, always with the predominance of paternal kinship.

Thus, no matter what the clanic structure was at the start, at the monarchial or pseudo-monarchial (evolved tribe) stage the kinship became bilateral, for the interests of the men and the degree of evolution of productive forces required it; but the structure of kinship always retained, in the fossil state, even at this stage, the primary structure (matriarchal or patriarchal) recognizable by the observer in many details.

Note I

We have previously had the occasion to classify all the "etymons" and toponyms below both ethnically and regionally (Wolof, Peul, Tuculor, Serer, etc.).[8] Within the great Wolof ethnic group, one can isolate the Lebu subgroup characterized by the following "etymons," all of them present in Nuer country:

NUER	LEBOU
Bor	*MBor*
Pot	*Pot*
Dial or *Dil* or *Diel* (aristocratic title)	*Dial* (aristocratic title)
Jikul	*Jokul* (toponym)

According to Nuer genealogy, Duob was the son of Nyajaani (Evans-Pritchard, *op. cit.*, p. 278). Likewise, according to Senegalese tradition, Diop was an ancient son of NDiadiane NDiaye, who supposedly changed his name following a familial incident. One also encounters the following Senegalese names:

NUER	WOLOF (Senegal)
Gaa-jok	*Gaajo* (Tukculor)
Gaa-jak	*Gajaga* (Laobe)
Ma-Thiang } *Ma-Nyang*	*Ma-Nyang*
War	*Waar* (Demba Waar)
Gaa-war (aristocratic clan)	*Gawar* (horseman, knight, lord, lover)
Jaa-logh	*Diallo* (Peul)
Lem (p. 274)	*Lem-Lem* (ancient tribe, on the Faleme River)
Baal (p. 274)	*Baal* (Tukulor ethnicity)
Pilual (p. 285)	*Peul* (?)
Juong (p. 285)	*Jong*
Lak	*Lag* (legendary order knights)
Ghaak	*Gak*
Dup	*Diop*
Thul (p. 277)	*Tul* (toponym)
Ger (p. 274)	*Ger* (clan, "casteless man")
Nyam nyam (p. 285)	
Ma-Jaam (p.285)	*Ma-jaane*
Gaa-liek	*Ngalik* (toponym)
Jaang (p. 248)	*Dieng*
Dinka-Balak	*Balla*
Nyayan (p. 238)	*Nyaanang* (toponym)
Kraal (Nuer camp)	*Daral* (animal enclosure)
Tut bura	*Bur* (king)
Jara-nyen (p. 237)	*Jaane*

The Jaang-Naths or Jaang-Nas (Evans-Pritchard, p. 253) are Dinka-Nuers, meaning Dinkas who became Nuers and, because of this, are called:

Caa-Nath } names of the same structure as *Tia-NDella*
Caa-Nas } (Wolof) or *Ca-NDella*.

The Anuak of the Sobat River (Evans-Pritchard, p. 253) recall the protohistoric tribe of the Anu (of Osiris ethnicity), who originally occupied the Nile Valley.

Lastly, we see that Baal is also a name that might explain Belianke (see chapter 12, p. 182); that is to say actual ethnic facts are very difficult to interpret, and complementary research alone will enable us to reach a decision.

A *dil* (*dial*) or *Tut bura* is an aristocrat of the Bor tribe (Evans-Pritchard, p. 244), a *dil* (dial) or *Tut laka* is an aristocrat of the Lak tribe (p. 244).

The Dinka-Nuer worship a god in heaven, named *Deng* (rain), to whom they built a great pyramid. The prophet of this god, probably of Dinka origin, is Ngundeng (Evans-Pritchard, p. 216) = *Ngunda*? (Wolof).

Let us note that *Simba* = the game of "lion" (a man disguised as a lion) in Senegal, and that *Simba* = lion, in Zaire.

Note II

For Emile Benveniste, one indication of the diminishing juridical role played by the mother, in Indo-European societies, is the absence of a *matrius* opposite a *patrius*. He notes that Greek vocabulary retains quite different social structures, probably not of Indo-European origin.[9]

We have seen that the Greek Mycenaean world came out of protohistory, following the Egyptian colonization of the XVIIIth Dynasty. It was during this period that Greece probably adopted the foreign social structures alluded to by Benveniste and Dumezil.

The ancient Indo-European structures have survived the longest among the southern Slavs, who still preserve the extended patriarchal family system called *Zadruga*, comprising several couples or nuclear families, totaling sixty members.

A stranger can enter this type of patriarchal family by marrying the chief's daughter; but he then loses even his own last name, and it is the daughter, who remains with her own "clan," who continues the lineage by giving her name to her progeny.[10]

This again is a singular confirmation of the conditions, cited above, that gave rise to matriarchy. It sufficed that a patriarchal family became sedentary and no longer found it necessary to bury its daughters alive, and that these daughters, owing to a change in economic conditions, remained in their "clans," so that marriage became matrilocal, and the foreign man found himself in an inferior position and lost all his rights.

According to Benveniste, only the custom of marriage between cross cousins can explain the fact that the Latin *avunculus*, derived from *avus* (paternal grandfather), means "maternal uncle."[11] In any case, this remark clearly shows the anteriority, in Indo-European society, of the patriarchal conceptual system of designating kinship: matrilineal kinship here clearly appears to be a later institution, so much so that the language lacks terms to designate it and employs inappropriate concepts, as we have seen.

The tripartition of functions[12] (priest, warrior, farmer), also pointed out by Georges Dumezil, returns us to the Mycenaean structures contemporaneous with the eruption of Santorini and allows us to narrow down the time of the immigration toward the East of the Indo-Iranian branch.

In all of Siberia, where nomadism reigned, there was not a single matrilineal tribe.

7

RACE AND SOCIAL CLASSES

THE LAWS OF ETHNIC RELATIONS IN HISTORY

1. The Law of Percentage

An Eskimo in Copenhagen or a few Blacks in Paris trigger an amused curiosity and the outpouring of very sincere sympathy on the part of the population of either of these cities.

But just inject immigrant workers up to the fateful threshold of 4–8 percent, and you will have a racial situation comparable to that of New York City: the nature of social relationships changes, engendering ethnic tensions, global reflexes painful to describe. The more the percentage increases, the more the class struggle transforms itself into racial confrontation. In the nineteenth century in Denmark, the gypsies were hunted down like foxes. Today, with the economic crisis, racial discrimination vis-à-vis immigrant workers appears, of all places, in Sweden. We now see that Sweden, the champion of antiracism, was ignoring the true nature of the racial problem and its implications in everyday life. The appearance of a small percentage of foreign workers disclosed this; for it was sufficient to make racial discrimination appear spontaneously in this people who previously believed itself wholesome and devoid of any racist sentiment. "Sweden first" could be heard in a line of passengers waiting for the bus (from the Swedish correspondent for the French newspaper *Le Monde*).

2. The Law of Assimilability

If the majority and the minority belong to the same large ethnic group, and thus share the same culture, assimilation occurs progressively: the Spanish and Portuguese workers despised today in France will integrate themselves into the population within the space of one generation, as did the descendants of the Corsicans and the Poles in the Napoleonic era; the same would be true of the Bambara minority (from Mali) living in Senegal, after one generation.

In cases where the ethnic and cultural gap is too great, tensions are exacerbated with time: Africans—Blacks and Arabs—find themselves in this situation in Europe. Coexistence then becomes possible only in a truly Socialist state, or a state that has adopted a high moral philosophy.

3. The Law of Distance

Two ethnic groups that are not fighting over the same living space or the same market, and that, instead of cohabiting in the same territory, occupy different territories separated by space, can enter into normal relations; thus the alliance might be explained, during World War II, between Hitler's Germany and Japan, between "pure Aryans" and Yellows. Today, Pretoria is counting on this factor to try to fool the Black states with which it is trying to establish normal diplomatic relations, forgetting that the whole African continent is our native land. Pretoria's relations with Israel fall into this same category.

4. The Law of the Phenotype

In the historical and social relations among peoples, the only intervening factor at the outset is the phenotype, i.e., the physical appearance, and consequently, differences that may exist at this level. It would matter little that Botha and a Zulu have the same genotype, i.e., the same genes in their chromosomes; this would have no influence on their daily lives since their external physical features are so different.

The laws of class struggle according to historical materialism apply only to a society previously made ethnically homogeneous by violence. Historical materialism, in its analyses, practically ignores the phase of bestial, Darwinian struggles that came before; this is all the more regrettable because it is one stage that most of the nations of today have gone through. This is the most general case, and not the exception, as Engels thought: "These few exceptions are isolated cases of conquests, in which the more barbarous conquerors exterminated or drove out the population of a country and either devastated or abandoned the productive forces that they did not know how to use."[1]

Indeed, this category includes the Americas (North, South, and Central), Australia, Tasmania, New Zealand, a good part of Asia, the Pacific Islands, Greenland, Iceland, Scandinavia, and many others. The Blacks of the Americas were brought over to work the land, while the indigenous races were being destroyed. Today they present particular problems that have not yet been resolved. The strenuous annual training of Western officers in the Amazon, to be ready to destroy an (Asiatic) enemy who might come there to settle, is, to say the least, strange.

All the authors who deal with violence without daring to descend to this primary level, where bestial violence is practiced on a collective basis, where a whole group of people organize not to subdue another group, but to annihilate it, all of them, consciously or not, are engaged in metaphysics, in sublimating the theme in order to retain only its philosophical aspects.

In the course of history, when two groups of human beings have argued over a vital economic space, the slightest ethnic difference can be magnified, temporarily serving as a pretext for social and political cleavage: differences in physical appearance, language, religions, morals, and customs.

In the course of history, conquerors often misused these arguments to enforce their domination on ethnic bases: man's exploitation of man then assumes an ethnic modality; social class, in an economic sense, for an indefinite period of time fits the outlines of the ethnic group of the conquered race.

Sparta. The Sparta of antiquity offers the most complete model of this form of economic exploitation founded exclusively on ethnic difference. The Spartiates, who probably were of Dorian origin, conquered Laconia during the period of Greek history called "the dark ages" (twelfth to eighth centuries B.C.), and they subjugated the inhabitants of this region, the Helots. Before the repeated revolts by the latter, the Spartiates established the most ferocious military regime in history, living in entrenched military camps, centering the education of the citizens on the military arts from birth, and organizing periodic pogroms against the Helots in order to maintain the numerical relationship of the two ethnic groups, conquerors/conquered, within the limits of security.

However, Sparta, which had no more than nine thousand citizens, could not exercise absolute control over a large territory. Thus Messenia, conquered later, was less integrated than Laconia: its communities remained inviolate and merely paid tribute. The Perioeci were Spartan subjects, without the status of citizens, but subject to military service, which was an important distinction in relation to the Helots; thus the fact of participating in the defense of the territory gave them the right to some not insignificant privileges.

In spite of all the precautions taken, Spartan domination ended by crumbling, particularly because of the great numerical weakness of its real citizens. The class of the conquerors, the "equals," advanced through corruption. In spite of the initial vow of purity and sobriety, it ended up having within itself rich and poor; the same thing happened in the social strata of the subjugated and the exploited.

This social osmosis would increase and would be accentuated. Because the Spartan conquerors and conquered Helots belonged to the same large white-skinned race, the ethnic differences became blurred, allowing class differences to appear only in an economic sense. But it would be historically false to deny the ethnic origin of this class struggle and the forms of Darwinian bestial violence that it initially took.

Rwandans—Burundians. The relations between Tutsi and Hutu in Rwanda and in Burundi seem to belong to the ancient type of relations between Spartiates and Helots, whatever the role of the former colonial power had been in the deterioration of these relations.

Rome and Carthage. The rivalry between Rome and Carthage for supremacy in the Mediterranean and domination of the world markets in antiquity led to the physical destruction of the Carthaginian people, who perished in flames; in this case also, the ethnic opposition was manifest: apparently the two peoples did not live on the same land; but Carthage tried several times to conquer Sicily, where it had succeeded in getting a small site for a port.

Rome did not wish to colonize Carthage, the danger being too great and at its doorstep. It pronounced a curse on the ancient site of Carthage and ritually sowed it with salt to sterilize it forever.

Such rites of expiation and cursing, one might say, were commonplace after the destruction of an ethnic group in a Darwinian type of struggle. The brutal destruction of an entire ethnic group could not indemnify the conscience of the conqueror, which was, after all, the seat of a diffuse feeling of guilt.

The destroyed people then became the scapegoat; they deserved their fate because they were impious, sinister, lustful, and addicted to Dionysiac orgies, in short, incapable of promoting progress. Purification rites had to be performed before the founding of a new city on the ashes of the barbarian victims. These are the echoes that we find here and there in the legends and the various tales evoking the fate of the ethnic groups that were thus destroyed: the descendants of the race of Cadmus in Boeotia (Greece), worshipers of earthly divinities in the form of snakes; the Etruscans and the Umbrians in Italy, the Canaanites, etc.

Future generations must forget these dead so that the conquering people can undergo a rebirth with an angelic conscience.

Franks and Gallo-Romans. After the conquest of Gaul, the victorious Franks established a domination founded solely on race and having nothing to do with what is called the "personality" of laws, i.e., that Burgundians, Visigoths, Romans, and Gauls be judged according to their respective customary codes, when they committed common offenses.

In Visigoth countries, intermarriage with conquered Romans was officially forbidden.[2]

Frankish legislation went so far as to oppose "Barbarians" and "Romans," stipulating stronger (generally doubled) penalties whenever the victim of an aggression or even simply a petty offense belonged to the race of the Frankish conquerors.[3]

Because of the quasi-identical ethnic origins, assimilation progressed, even in the laws, and the Frankish/Germanic racial domination over the Romans and the Romanized Gauls gradually became a domination based on class. It was this right of conquest of the Frankish nobility, ancestors of the French nobility at the time of the 1789 revolution, that the royalists, adversaries of the liberals, such as Augustin Thierry, invoked to legitimize the monarchy.

The nobles were descendants of the Frankish conquerors and the commoners were descendants of the conquered Gauls and Romans. That these were different ethnic groups is historically true. What is false and irrational are the racist considerations that the elite classes ultimately derived from this situation: namely, that the so-called commoners (and later, the industrial workers) belonged to the brachycephalic Alpine race, who were submissive, born to be dominated, a degenerate race, physically and intellectually inferior; a race whose members are little or not at all prone to suicide, because they have only a pusillanimous soul, incapable of the great moral sentiments that ground human courage.

Whereas, from this perspective, the nobles who descended from the Franks and the Germans belong to a superior race, born to command and dominate, called *Europaeus* or *Nordic European*. They are big, dolichocephalic, blond with blue eyes, the "blond beast" of Count Joseph de Gobineau[4] (the precursor of the Nazi theoreticians), the race whose members willingly commit suicide whenever life's trials justify such an extreme act. This intra-European racism, reducing social class to ethnicity, flourished in Europe throughout the nineteenth century, following the French Revolution, and went into temporary eclipse only after World War II, with the defeat of Nazism. In 1789, the cry went out that what had taken place was the victory of the "Gauls" over the "Franks."

For social anthropology, all sociological phenomena, class relations, wealth, distribution of cities, political events, are explained by biological considerations, by the presence or absence (the degeneration) of the characteristic traits of the superior race, the *Homo europaeus*.

G. Vacher de Lapouge developed Gobineau's racist theory at the end of the nineteenth century. In an article published in 1897, he did not hesitate to formulate the "law of the distribution of wealth," which stipulated that in the mixed *Europaeus-Alpinus* countries wealth grows in inverse ratio to the cephalic indicator; the "law of urban indicators," which proclaimed that inhabitants of cities are much more dolichocephalic than those of the surrounding countrysides; and, according to the "law of stratification," the cephalic indicator decreases and the proportion of dolichocephalics increases from the inferior to the superior classes in each locality.[5]

According to A. Rosenberg, the French Revolution was only a revolt of the brachycephalics of the Alpine race against the dolichocephalics of the Nordic race, and Bolshevism was nothing but an insurrection of Mongoloids.[6]

An American immigration law (not yet repealed, I believe) aims at limiting the influx of the Alpine race, by singularly curtailing the admission to America of Europeans from the regions south of the Loire River.

Likewise in antiquity, the plebeian class, after its victory over the aristocracy, at first imitated the aristocracy in all domains before acquiring enough autonomy of thought to find its own way. This was also true after the French Revolution. The modern bourgeoisie, as if it would make them forget the racism they had suffered under the *Ancien Régime*, became guilty of racism in the strict sense toward the working class and people of humble origin.

In May 1849, a professor at the Sorbonne wrote in a propaganda brochure against the "Reds," i.e., the Socialists:

> A red is not a man, he is a red . . . he is not a moral being, intelligent and free like you and me. . . . He is a fallen and degenerate being. Besides, he wears on his face the sign of this degradation. A despondent, besotted physiognomy, without expression, dull eyes, mobile and evasive like those of a pig, gross features, without harmony, a low forehead . . . his mouth mute and insignificant like that of an ass.

Dr. Alexis Carrel, in *Man, the Unknown* (1936), maintained that workers owed their situation to the hereditary defects of their bodies and their minds, and that peasants had ancestors who, by virtue of the weakness of their organic and mental constitutions, were born serfs, while their lords were born masters.[7]

Progressively, since the sixteenth century, this intra-European racism has moved outward, serving sometimes as support and justification for colonial expansion.

"Bishop Quevedo and the historian Sepulveda, chaplain to Charles V, base the 'civilizing mission' of Spain in America on the inferiority and natural perversity of the Indians."[8]

8

BIRTH OF THE DIFFERENT TYPES OF STATES

There are at least four types of states.

I. The state known as the "Asian" type—or "of the Asian mode of production" (AMP) was born as a result of the great hydraulic works, described by Marx and Engels, the most perfected model of which is the Pharaonic Egyptian state. It should therefore be called, with utmost precision, the "African type of state."[1] In our opinion, one of the distinctive traits of this category is the weight of civilian power as compared to military power; military aristocracy is practically absent, and in normal times, the soldiers play only an unobtrusive, if not nonexistent, political role. The military aristocracy is not the focal point of society. War has rather a defensive function. The entire ideological substructure is only an apologetic for moral and human values, excluding the values of warfare.

The privileged physical situation of Egypt (abundance of resources, a valley protected by two mountainous deserts with only two access roads, at the north and south) ensured the quasi-permanence of these characteristics of the Egyptian state. Egypt had to be invaded by the Hyksos in order to embark, in reaction, on the conquest of western Asia beginning with the XVIIIth Dynasty, under Thutmose III (1470 B.C.).

Elsewhere, where conditions were less favorable to the defense of states born by this same process, from major works, the transition was much faster; the military aristocracy progressively took over from the other social institutions; the pacifist ideological superstructure of the beginning underwent a mutation: a warlike morality appeared; militaristic values were established: this might have been the case of the ancient Sabaean states of the Arabian Peninsula, of the states of Mesopotamia, mainly after

Sargon I of Akkad, and of the Aegean and Etruscan states. In all these cases, the state, born as a result of heavy public works and then forced to adapt to warlike conditions, modified its social and political philosophy.

Be that as it may, this type of state, as shown above, is founded on a collectivistic basis, which was accepted and defended by all the citizens of the nation as the only way of survival for the collectivity.

The suddenness and volume of the flooding of the Nile obliged the first African populations, whom chance had brought to this valley, either to rise above individual, clannish, and tribal egoisms or to disappear. Thus emerged a supratribal authority, a national authority, accepted by all, invested with the powers necessary to conduct and coordinate irrigation and water distribution, works essential to the general activity. Thus was born a whole hierarchic body of functionaries whose abuses and privileges would neither shock nor become unbearable until much later.

Such inequalities are not imposed overnight by a group of foreign invaders coming from the outside after unification. They are the result of the on-the-spot development of internal contradictions in the system; therefore, they are often seen through the extenuating lens of tradition, a tradition that blends with the original foundations of the nation.

We are dealing with a state whose contours exactly match those of the nation. The institutions were not knowingly created to isolate and subjugate a foreign group rightly or wrongly considered to be ethnically different from the conquering group; they are, so to speak, for internal, national consumption, and consequently present a less abrupt aspect. For this reason they are prone to engender a more or less casted social stratification "accepted" by the people, provided the system foreswears outright abuses.

In this sense, these structures are less inclined to lead to political or social revolutions than others that we will describe. (We will return to these questions in the analysis of constitutions, in chapter 12.)

Therefore, a confederation of tribes molds itself into a nation and creates a state, to the degree that it organizes itself to take up a challenge presented by nature, in Toynbee's sense, to overcome an obstacle, the elimination of which necessitates a collective effort that exceeds the means of a small group.

II. State born out of resistance to the enemy. This second type of state is akin to the preceding one, as only the nature of the obstacle to be overcome changes.

A homogeneous ethnic group (a confederation of exogamous tribes) organizes, not for conquest, but to drive off a danger, an outside enemy. With the help of the embryonic division of labor at the level of the clan, a military aristocracy appears and progressively arrogates to itself political rights that rapidly become hereditary. The ideological superstructure will give privilege, in this case, to the military profession, which outclasses all others, because of the risks involved; the protector of society ends up commanding it, governing it, given the circumstances that engender this protective activity.

But it is still a nation-state. The contours of the state exactly match those of the nation, which, in collective resistance to the enemy, under the direction of a military caste of quality, becomes singularly conscious of its individuality: this applies on different levels to the Gauls of Vercingetorix; to the French nation under Charles Martel, who stopped the Arab invasion in 732 A.D.;[2] or again, to the same nation galvanized by the humble and heroic example of Joan of Arc, during the Hundred Years War. It was during the latter period that the French nation was really formed. One might say as much of the Greeks against the Persians, during the Median wars in the fifth century B.C.; the Nubia of antiquity under Queen Kandaka (Candace) against the armies of Augustus Caesar, commanded by General Petrone; the Mossi against the emperors of Mali and Songhai, in the Middle Ages and in the sixteenth century; the ancient Chinese building the Great Wall of China, the most colossal military defensive work ever built by humanity in the past.

Even though the military function is given privilege in the ideological superstructure of such a state, it is no less true that, as in the preceding case, it is used, so to speak, for internal purposes, and is not essentially conceived for the domination of one ethnic group by another.

The existence of a military aristocracy at the top of the society makes abuses and social and political perversions more frequent; however, the social organization has an indigenous, national character, and is sanctified by tradition: it can easily assume the structure of a "caste," in the African, not the Hindu, sense.

The two types of states that we have discussed can therefore be distinguished at the level of their ideological superstructures, provided that the later political evolution has not radically transformed the initial superstructure; in fact, even though born under comparable circumstances and presenting several similar features, the two types of states diverge at one fundamental point: the one gives privilege to the "social," the other to the military, and this remark can be useful in many analyses.

Military feudalism is a degraded, anarchistic, and perverted form of this second type of state with a military character.

Indeed, a "feudal regime" is often the transition between the disappearance of a central power and the appearance of a new one in AMP states.

The case presented itself three times in Egyptian history and once in the Middle Ages in Europe. This regime appears with an endemic insecurity, against which it temporarily protects isolated individuals and families.

III. The third type of state is represented by the ancient Athenian model, a result of the dissolution of the mode of production of antiquity; the state is only the legal instrument of domination of one class over another.

The first occupants of the land are the only citizens and landowners, to the exclusion of the masses or Metics, immigrants in ancient Greece, who peacefully entered the country by infiltration and not through war, and gradually turned into a homeless proletariat reduced to selling its labor. Cleisthenes's reform completed the formation of this class on a purely economic basis, through the elimination of the earlier ethnic divisions, which had long remained subjacent.

One must never lose sight of the initial structure that made possible the emergence of this type of state: namely, the existence, at the beginning, of a class of citizen landowners who long controlled the situation, which allowed it to proletarianize the newcomers to whom the rights of citizenship were long denied; the conditions of the immigrants' arrival and settlement did not allow them to dramatically reverse the situation, or even to change it; however, the Dorian conquest preceded this state of affairs.

At the time this type of state was being formed, human struggles were of course constantly subtended by economic interests (occupying fertile soil, disputing vital resources), but the victories were always those of one ethnic group over another. The victorious ethnic group dictated its laws, which governed relationships between the conquerors and the conquered, between the Eupatridae ("of noble birth") and the Thetes in Athens, from the collapse of Mycenaean society after the arrival of the Dorians, in the twelfth century B.C.

This new society was already present in Athens and Sparta in the eighth century B.C., as is shown in Hesiod's great poem, *Works and Days*.

In this type of situation, if, for reasons examined above, ethnic assimilation of the conquered by the conqueror or the reverse is possible, ethnic opposition used in support of economic exploitation progressively becomes a class opposition. This is the kind of evolution that occurred in Athens between the eighth and fourth centuries B.C. and in the Gaul that was conquered by the Germanic Franks from whom the France of today gets its name (see pp. 126–28).

IV. The Spartan and Tutsi type of state. If, for whatever reason, the conquering ethnic group refuses to mix with the indigenous conquered element and bases its domination on this absolute separation, the opposition is essentially ethnic and will always be resolved, in ancient and modern history, by genocide.

This category includes: the Spartan state of antiquity (equals against inferior Helots); the opposition of Tutsi and Hutu in Rwanda and Burundi, whatever the causes of their antagonism; the three Americas, including

Canada, in varying degrees; Australia, New Zealand, Tasmania, Scandinavia up to a point; Greenland, South Africa, a large part of Asia; and still others. Consequently, most of the present states of the modern world belong to the model of the state founded on genocide; it is not the exception, but rather the general rule, which today encompasses three-quarters of all dry land, including virtually all of Antarctica.

The European ethnic group has thus confiscated the quasi-totality of the habitable land of this planet, in only four centuries, and it categorically refuses the reintroduction of ethnic heterogeneity in all countries in which it physically destroyed the former "native" inhabitants.

In types 3 and 4 (Athens and Sparta), the state does not recover the nation: a minority of conquerors subordinate to its law the conquered or proletarian majority by means of coercive state institutions conceived toward this end.

When the process of eliminating the native population is completed, like a snake that has finished swallowing its victim, a feeling of collective guilt, which is hard to suppress, grips the conscience of the conquerors and gives rise to an expiatory literature, in the form of legends of the founding of the cities in which the conquered people are charged with all the sins. This was the fate of the forgotten Etruscan people destroyed by the Romans, the Canaanites of the Bible destroyed by the Hebrews, etc. The mystery grows deeper with time and encourages the obliteration of painful memories.

The murderous people in this way regain a pristine conscience, a childlike purity in some cases; at times expiatory rites recall the acts of violence through which the states of this category were built.

When a minority ethnic group conquers a vast space, peopled by many ethnicities, the empire becomes a political necessity, because the numerical ratio between conquerors and conquered is too unfavorable for a solution of the Spartan type to be considered; a universalist ideological superstructure is then born and develops in order to assimilate the divergent peoples who cannot be destroyed; all the great conquerors have entertained the illusory ambition to govern the entire world: Thutmose III, the first in history, Alexander the Great, Julius Caesar, Napoleon, etc. It may be a paradox, but imperial philosophy always has universalist pretensions and is almost never racist; this is true for all the conquerors just mentioned. All of them sought, in their own ways, to be the intermediary between God and humanity.

There is another path that leads to the empire: when a national state is invaded and repulses the enemy in a defensive-offensive dialectic, as Egypt did after the departure of the Hyksos, it becomes an empire through the conquest of safe borders that are as remote as possible. This, moreover, was the case with the first true empire in history, under Thutmose III. The Egyptian state became imperial in the XVIIIth Dynasty: Amon, the father of Thutmose III, was also the god of all his subjects, of all the world. This tendency was confirmed under Amenophis IV with the solar cult of Aton (see pp. 85–87).

Marx was amazed by the ephemeral character of Asian formations. This is an error that theoreticians unthinkingly repeat after him, for, if the incongruous, polyglot empire is ephemeral, the monolingual national state of the "Asian" type, of which the Egyptian state was the finest model, is quasi-permanent, having existed nearly three thousand years: from 3300 to 525 B.C.

9

REVOLUTIONS IN HISTORY: CAUSES AND CONDITIONS FOR SUCCESS AND FAILURE

We will study successively the revolutions in ancient and modern AMP states in the slave and individualistic Greco-Latin city-states, the Roman Empire, and Europe of both the Middle Ages and modern times.

The study of the AMP (Asian or African mode of production[1]) analyzes:

1. The economic functions of the state and its relations with village communities
2. The characteristics of village production
3. The fundamental contradiction in societies defined by this mode of production
4. The administration of land in these societies
5. The role of commerce and urban life in these societies

1. The economic functions of the state have a direct relation to the conditions and reasons of its creation. It will be remembered that a whole community must accept a supraclannish authority transcending tribal self-interests. It must be able to act, at the beginning at least, for the greater good of all, for the survival of all "citizens" of the state without exception and not only in the interests of a small minority group of "Eupatridae," i.e., those of noble birth, or the "conquerors."

The public, economic, social, and military usefulness of the AMP state is therefore an indisputable, tangible fact in the eyes of the entire community. As long as the state does not betray its mission, it may ask much without fear of being disobeyed or encountering resistance. Because the ideological, religious, and social superstructure has been intensely experienced by the group, it does not feel alienated when the state requires work from it. This is how tasks were accomplished that today amaze us, from the great pyramids of the Incas to the Celtic megaliths.

But Marx calls this type of work "generalized slavery," as opposed to the private slavery that was practiced in the individualistic societies of the Greco-Latin city-states. Does this concept really explain the unique and complex relations that existed between states of the AMP type and their citizens? Does it not misrepresent the reality of things to a certain extent by its Eurocentrism? By definition, is not the slave the individual who has the feeling of having lost his freedom? The slave becomes an actor in history only to the extent that he is fully conscious of his alienation and actively tries to change his condition. A slave who is unaware of having lost his freedom will play no revolutionary role, even though a theoretician might have no trouble demonstrating his status as a slave; such would be the case of the citizen in a society of the AMP. We will examine the circumstances under which this citizen came to change his attitude historically.

Besides, slaves have never been responsible for any historical revolution, except perhaps the one that took place in Bagdad in the eleventh century A.D.; revolutions have always been made by free men of humble station.

Only a free man, made a slave, rebels; the slave born into the second generation (*diam njudu* in Wolof) already has the outlook of a lumpenproletarian, who is less inclined to revolt. This is an error that almost all theoreticians continue to make: the theoretical agent of revolution has never, or almost never, carried it out anywhere.

In conclusion, the public role of the AMP state is more obvious than that of the individualistic Greco-Roman city-state. The people of the first type of state are, with all due allowances, less revolutionary, having less desire for change than those of the second type of state.

2. According to Marx, village communities live in a closed economic system, and Marx sees in this economic autarchy, this "immutability," one of the reasons for the "stagnation of the AMP state."

The divorce between work and working conditions does not materialize; agriculture and local industry are part of village activity. Now, for Marx, the condition of capitalist production lies in the divorce between work and working conditions; the village peasant masses must be expropriated in order for them to become alienated workers, no longer owning any means of production and having only their labor to sell, either to the country farmer or to the boss of the urban enterprise: this wage-earning labor force is the necessary and sufficient condition for the birth and functioning of the capitalist system that must lead to revolution, by the uprising of the exploited masses.

We will see (pp. 141–44) that this principal condition will be met in the Egyptian and Chinese AMP societies, that revolutions will break out without the resulting revolutionary movements ever leading to victory: the study of the causes of these failures is what will furnish truly new elements to sociological or revolutionary theory.

3. What is called the fundamental contradiction of AMP societies is the fact that "state capitalist" production develops on community bases characterized by the collective appropriation of the land. The AMP society does not appear to have enough internal forces to carry this contradiction to its conclusion, i.e., the dissolution of collective ownership and the appearance of individual private ownership of land.

4. We will see that the facts are more complex and that AMP societies (Egypt and China), during periods of anarchy and social decomposition, had a regime of private alienable ownership of the land.

5. The role of commerce and urban life: The average density of the population, the greatest in antiquity, reached two hundred inhabitants per square kilometer in the Nile Valley. Ancient Egypt was par excellence the country whose towns bulged with multitudes of completely detribalized individuals and in which commerce with all known regions of the time flourished: "Ulysses carried cargo to Egypt." Business people from all over the Mediterranean coasts could settle in Egypt and open shops under certain conditions. From the time of Psamtik I, the seventh century B.C., Greeks were authorized to settle in the port of Naucratis, in the Nile delta, to do business. A Greek vase of the fifth century B.C. (among other objects) representing an Amazon, found in a pyramid in Nubia, gives an idea of the extent of this commerce, which was already active in the Neolithic period all along the shores of the Mediterranean, as shown by the pottery unearthed and the chemical analysis of amber beads.

So many facts show that the ideas that were held about the singularity of commerce in the individualistic slave regimes of the city-states were wrong and must be corrected. Cities and commerce were not peculiarities of these regimes. They were also found in West Africa of the Middle Ages, as we will see below (p. 154). Commerce occupied so important a place in the economic life of Mali and Songhai that the emperor used to name a head of the market. It is erroneous to attribute such commerce to the state, in order to make one's point, and to decree that only private ownership of the land can bring forth private commerce: in Greece, after the victory of the aristocracy over the royalty, with the feudalization of the system, private commerce regressed. The lords, descended from the Dorians, lived in the country on large private properties where they were served by a mass of slaves and clients working on their estates; the multitude of all these landowners excluded any notion of collective or state ownership of the land, or of commerce for the profit of the state.

Ownership of the land can *ipso facto* engender private commerce only when the land is exclusively reserved for the Eupatridae and the plebeians must resort to commerce in order to make a living; and this is indeed what happened in Greece before the peoples' revolutions, at the time when the domestic religion of the Eupatridae forbade ownership of the land by the homeless. This individualistic, patriarchal religion, inherited from nomadic life, had indexed all possible and imaginable goods, as in Aryan India, and had stamped them with its seal, in order to forbid their possession by the plebs: it overlooked only money, which did not yet exist, and secular commerce, unworthy of a great lord. In order to survive and live outside the cities that were so long forbidden to them, the common people did not have any choice: they were forced to turn to commerce and usurious lending; in fact, they accumulated wealth in the same proportion that the landowning nobility became poorer, pauperized to the point that very often, between the sixth and fourth centuries, the nobility, in order to rebuild its fortunes, had to marry plebeians. A famous quip of the times ran: "Of what birth is this man?"—"Wealthy!"

From then on, the money of those who originally did not have the right to own land, those plebs who had now become bourgeois, opened the doors of the great noble landowners who were now in need; those are the very special, even exceptional, reasons that explain the development of commerce in the individualistic regimes of Greece and its city-states. Therefore, there is no necessary and sufficient, logical relationship between private ownership of land and the development of commerce, not even to increase the value of land, as Maurice Godelier believes.

To sum up, the distinctive elements cited above, namely, "generalized slavery," the administration of land ownership and the fundamental contradiction of the AMP societies, the domestic type of village economy, the importance of urban life, and individual as opposed to state-owned commerce, all these factors developed sufficiently here and there in the AMP societies to engender germs of dissolution leading to true revolutions, which indeed broke out but later failed.

That being the case, the specificity of the AMP state, as heretofore discussed, no longer matters.

Indeed, whatever the virtues or failings of the AMP societies, they ended up being questioned by the people, who attempted to overthrow them through authentic revolutionary movements, as in the individualistic societies of the Greco-Latin city-states. Once more, why did revolution succeed in the individualistic city-states and fail without exception in the community AMP states, or even in individualistic states (but Asian in form due to the vastness and complexity of the state machinery, as in Rome)?

That is the big question that cannot be evaded. Not knowing how to answer the question, the theoreticians have avoided asking it up to now; they have pretended to believe that there never were any revolutions or revolutionary movements in the AMP states and that the social convulsions that arose and developed there were only vulgar jacqueries that could not be taken for revolutions. It is against this erroneous manner of seeing the problems, which almost amounts to a Eurocentric attitude, that we speak out. It is as if those holding this position elevate to the dignity of revolution only those movements that "succeeded." However, the Paris Commune and the Russian Revolution of 1905 show that not all revolutions are successful and that sometimes the cases that fail are more instructive.

We will now undertake to demonstrate that there were authentic revolutionary movements in the AMP societies and that the study of the causes of their failures alone might renew the theory in this area.

We will successively review: the Osirian revolution in Egypt, sometimes referred to as "proletarian," the first in the history of the universe, which marked the end of the Ancient Empire (2100 B.C.); and the Chinese revolution of An Lu-shan during the T'ang period, in the ninth century A.D.

10

THE DIFFERENT REVOLUTIONS IN HISTORY

THE "OSIRIAN" EGYPTIAN REVOLUTION (VIth Dynasty, 2100 B.C.)

The contemporaneous document that describes the event and its episodes is the text known as: "Admonitions of a Sage."[1] Consequently, the facts recounted, although very ancient, are neither imaginary nor reconstructed. Concerning some of the revolutions of the Greek cities (reforms of Codrus and Lycurgus), there is not as much information as is contained in the above-mentioned document.

The "feudal" regime (anarchy) of the Vth Dynasty reached its highest point during the VIth Dynasty; a general paralysis of the state's economy and administration resulted in the cities as well as in the countryside. Thus, the end of the VIth Dynasty saw the first people's uprising of certain date in universal history. The destitute of Memphis, the capital and sanctuary of Egyptian royalty, sacked the town, robbed the rich, and drove them into the streets. There was a true reversal of the social conditions and the financial situations. The movement rapidly spread to other cities. It appears that the city of Sais was temporarily governed by a group of ten notables. The situation that reigned throughout the country is depicted in a striking manner in the above-mentioned text written by Ipuwer, a malcontent conservative who belonged to the overthrown noble, or bourgeois, class.[2]

The sacking of Memphis showed that the monarchy would have been conquered and swept away permanently if the Egyptian kingdom had been reduced to the dimensions of a simple city comparable to the Greek city-state.

Two facts stand out: discontent was strong enough to provoke a complete upheaval of Egyptian society from one end of the country to the other; but what was lacking was the strength of modern movements—direction and coordination. The same was true of the Greek revolutions until the time of the tyrants. The disclosure of administrative and religious secrets; the dispersion of tribunal archives; the numerous attempts to destroy the bureaucratic machine that was crushing the people; the proletarianization of religion, which extended the Pharaonic privilege of immortality of the soul to all the people;[3] the profaning of religion itself; and the extent and violence of the social upheaval as they are recounted in the text cited in our note are the many facts that leave no doubt as to the profoundly revolutionary character of the movement.

During the whole period of turmoil, most of the Egyptian cities secured governmental autonomy, which later disappeared with the resurrection of the royalty. Indeed, the same quoted document tells of the suppression of royalty, the profaning of its symbols, and the kidnaping of the "king." It is therefore clear that the goal of the revolution was the democratization of the empire, if not the creation of a republic.

In history, with the exception of the Soviet Socialist revolution, no revolutionary movement, including that of 1789 in France, has had as a goal from birth the creation of a republic; that has always been the unexpected, unforeseen, and sometimes perilous result of a lengthy revolution. We will return to this aspect of the problem.

During the reforms of Codrus, Draco, Lycurgus, and even Solon, there could have been no question of a republic in Athens or Sparta, and yet, this was a full-blown revolutionary period.

The Third Republic in France was hastily voted in as part of an amendment, which passed by one vote (that of a priest), and only because the Count of Chambord, who had been chosen to reign, stubbornly refused to accept the tricolored flag. This did not prevent the republic from lasting until the middle of the twentieth century. The vote concerned the Wallon Amendment, which was adopted on January 30, 1875 by 353 votes against 352.

Throughout all of history, until education and technical progress made possible a better coordination of insurrectional action (1789, 1917, 1949—France, USSR, China), the peoples of the AMP countries were always overcome by the complexity of the state machinery and the size of the kingdoms whose social systems they wanted to transform through authentic revolutionary movements.

The study of the failures of revolutions in the AMP countries is, to a great degree, the study of the historical economic factors that gave rise to "precocious" territorial unification here (Egypt, China) or opposed it there (Greece).

By creating state machinery (that of the AMP) allowing the coordination of social, military, and political action on a large scale over a vast territory including several cities, the peoples had unwittingly forged chains that could be broken only by the progress of modern times, which made possible the education, instruction, information, and coordination of the struggle of the working classes on an equally large scale. We might cite by way of illustration of this idea, the turns taken by the French Revolution of 1789 in Paris and the provinces. That is why revolution became impossible in ancient times as soon as a state took the Asian form, whether in Greece, Rome, Persia, or elsewhere. This is a law, and perhaps the most general one in the domain of human sciences, because there is no exception in the whole world, during the five thousand years of the written history of humanity. This must not be taken for the absence of revolution, for it was everywhere present in those states, but it failed irremediably. Thus, those theories are erroneous that pretend that the AMP states are incapable of developing the fundamental contradiction that they harbor until their dissolution, that is, up to the outbreak of revolution. It breaks out everywhere, but theory, being unable to explain its failures, has chosen to ignore it by refusing to take into account the authentic unsuccessful revolutions in history.

THE CHINESE REVOLUTION IN THE NINTH CENTURY A.D.

In China of the T'ang Dynasty, after the revolt by An Lu-shan, the process of primitive accumulation assumed clearly capitalistic forms.

The revolt had as a direct consequence a demographic drop and a social crisis during which the imperial regime almost collapsed.

During the T'ang period, the state no longer enjoyed anything other than the eminent domain of land. In fact, the state had become merely the distributor of it. Each peasant automatically received a lifetime concession of three to six hectares on the land of his village, and the "ownership" of one-and-a-half hectares that he could pass on to his descendants.[4] These two types of concessions that the peasant received from the state remained inalienable. In return, he paid a land tax, served in the militia, and did statute labor. At his death, the land returned to the village community for redistribution.

But high officeholders had the possibility of acquiring large hereditary estates, which they leased to country farmers or hired agricultural workers to cultivate.

However, following An Lu-shan's revolt, the small peasant lifetime concession suddenly disappeared. Indeed, in order to replenish the imperial coffers depleted during the revolt, heavy taxation was imposed on the people, who went into debt, sold their lifetime concessions, even though this was forbidden, and turned into a true agricultural proletariat. Landowning families no longer represented more than 5 percent of the population. The peasantry's limited ownership of land had practically disappeared. There were now only agricultural workers ready to sell their labor.

The split between labor and working conditions had occurred, it seems, on a sufficiently large scale and to a sufficiently deep degree that a revolution of the capitalist bourgeois type might break out.

Taxation triggered riots. The revolutionary movement found a brain in the person of Huang Ch'ao, a well-read, energetic, and intelligent person embittered by social injustices. This special condition for the revolutions of antiquity and the Middle Ages was thus met. All the conditions for a capitalist type of revolution seemed in place.

The revolt began in the overpopulated region bordering Hopeh and Shantung. However, at first it took only the form of a jacquerie. It spread when the government made the mistake of arming the peasants so that they might organize their own defense. Huang Ch'ao devastated Shantung and the Kaitung plains of Honan. He descended on South China and "sacked" the ports of Fuchou in 878 A.D. and of Canton in 879. He returned north and captured the imperial capital cities of Loyang and Schangnan. The royal court then fled to Szechwan from where it asked the Turkish horde of the sand desert (*Chöl*) to come to its rescue. The chief of the horde, Li K'o Yong, succeeded in saving the T'ang dynasty by exterminating the peasant masses in revolt and recalling the emperor to the capital. When he entered the imperial capital city, it had already turned into a desert. "Grass and brush grew in the deserted streets where hares and foxes had made their dens."[5]

The episodes of this struggle show perfectly that if the empire had been reduced to the size of a Greek city, the revolution would have succeeded, because the capital had been taken and become a desert; this revolution from the bottom up would not have been a mere reinstatement of the old order.

The revolution was therefore put down by outside intervention, the complexity of the state apparatus, and the size of the territory, which allowed the dynasty to flee to the outlying provinces and call for outside help from vassals, or allies who had remained faithful. All these conditions were unthinkable, or at any rate impossible, in Greece of the eighth to the fourth centuries B.C., in other words, Greece of the period of successful revolutions and of "absolute" individualism, when even if a city were conquered, it would never have occurred to the conqueror to annex it so as to expand his kingdom; the religious superstructure opposed this. The conqueror considered himself a stranger vis-à-vis the gods of the conquered city and thought that he would not be accepted by them as king; therefore he could only kill all the inhabitants or sell all of them as slaves. After the fall of the city of Plataea, all the men were slaughtered, and the women sold.[6]

Once the influence of meridional Egyptian thought and philosophy had destroyed this superstructure,[7] nothing more kept Greece from adopting the AMP state model. Alexander the Great integrated all of the ancient Greek city-states into the vast empire he conquered in "opposition" to the Persians. He was so fascinated with the model of the civilization and the state of Egypt that he built the capital of his empire, not in Macedonia, his native country, or in continental Greece, Athens or Sparta, but in the new town of Alexandria, which bears his name, in Egypt, the conquered country. There is therefore no doubt about the fact that Alexander's empire is a replica of the empire of the "Fari" of Egypt from the VIIIth Dynasty onward. He had thus inherited from it at least the large territorial framework, grouping several cities.

What is interesting to note is that this single feature in common with the AMP states, it seems, was enough to make revolution impossible. It must be pointed out that even in the cities of the northern Mediterranean, which had already had their revolutions and known republican regimes, the republican spirit faded away without coming back during all of antiquity.

Alexander's empire was ephemeral, but its Roman replica inaugurated by Caesar lasted five hundred years. The Roman empire was built on the ruins of the republic founded five hundred years earlier, after the partial unification of the Italian peninsula: Brutus, the last defender of the republic, died tragically at Epirus by throwing himself on his sword planted in the ground—an act of despair confirming the failure of a noble and just cause.

Before him, the slave revolt led by Spartacus had already failed, because the territorial context had changed with the conquest of the other Italian cities. Caesar at thirty-three painfully noted that at his age Alexander the Great had already conquered the world, thereby showing that Alexander was his favorite hero, as he himself would be to Charlemagne, who tried in vain to rebuild the Holy Roman Empire.

The great dream of Napoleon Bonaparte was also to repeat the examples of Alexander and Caesar.

It is therefore evident that the Egyptian model of the state, which had fascinated Alexander, survived through all these attempts.

In order to get back to antiquity, let us make an important observation: in Alexander's empire (especially in the northern Mediterranean) and in the Roman Empire in particular, the fundamental contradiction of AMP societies was completely developed. The land was an absolutely alienable good and its private ownership was a tangible fact on which the empire itself was founded. On the other hand, Roman society was a slave-holding one in the strict sense; Rome, for five hundred years, would remain the citadel of slavery; therefore all the conditions required by classical theory were effectively met, including those concerning commerce and urban life, and yet the revolution would never take place, or more precisely, all attempts from then on would be defeated, after the territorial unification, as in the other AMP societies. It would fall every time due to the complexity of the new state machinery and the vast expanse of the territory, which compounded the possibilities of reaction by those in power. It would take five hundred years before this regime, corroded on the inside by social injustice, collapsed, not due to a revolution, but as the result of an almost mechanical external cause, the barbarian invasions.

The accidental survival of the Eastern empire of Byzantium shows that the fate of Rome might have been different: the emperor of the East had the good sense to influence the path of the barbarians, by negotiating with them to move on and settle farther away.

In modern times, one might say the same about the regime of Francisco Franco in Spain that lasted forty years, and that of Antonio Salazar in Portugal. The fall of Salazar's replacement, Marcello Caetano, in 1974, was a direct consequence of the colonial war; it was therefore an outside cause and not an internal development.

This manner of presenting the facts is all the more valid in that the Spanish regime, which decolonized in time, not only maintains itself, but is "quietly" proceeding toward the restoration of the monarchy.

If a revolution that was ripe in 1936 was postponed more than forty years for all the known reasons, one must admit that it failed, at least in its initial phase. However, the Spanish example is not obvious, for the failure of the revolution was due to the intervention of the Axis powers (Germany, Italy) and the hands-off policy of the French Socialists. Even the Soviet Socialist revolution of 1917 was furthered by outside circumstances: the weakening of czarist Russia, following its participation in World War I.

We may equally note the failure of the revolution in Germany and the crushing of progressive movements in that country after the armistice of 1918 and under Hitler.

Similarly, the extension of socialism to the Eastern countries and the formation of popular democracies were not the result of an internal maturation of the revolutionary conditions and action by the masses, but the result of World War II and a courageous and voluntary act by Stalin. The division of Germany into two parts forcibly toppled the Prussian stronghold overnight into the Socialist camp, providing the most amazing case of the exportation of revolution. Contrary to theory, revolution was exported under our very eyes, as of thirty-five years ago, to half of the most conservative and warlike nations of Europe, while the other half remains in the capitalist camp!

It is not by chance that revolution, at the end of the Middle Ages and at the beginning of modern times, began on a religious level, with the Protestant Reformation in Germany, following the invention of the printing press and the translation of the Bible into the vernacular, particularly into German by Luther.

The educational conditions thus radically change as we pass from antiquity to modern times, following the development of technology. The failure of the German jacqueries of the sixteenth and seventeenth centuries can be explained in similar fashion.

Because of the use of ideograms, the invention of Chinese printing could not have the same far-reaching results in regard to the rapid dissemination of knowledge. The mastering of more than three thousand characters is necessary in order just to begin the study of Chinese.

The creation of AMP states is in no way linked to ethnic considerations. Blacks (Egyptians, Sabaeans), Yellows (Chinese, pre-Columbian Amerindians), Whites (Etruscans, Aegeans, Persians, or proto-Iranians), placed by chance in geographical conditions requiring "great public works," have all invariably had to come very quickly out of their nomadic tribal egoism in order to create this same type of state. But it was Egypt that inaugurated the cycle and initiated most of the peoples.

REVOLUTION IN THE GREEK CITY-STATES OF THE NORTHERN MEDITERRANEAN (Athens, Sparta)

We have already stated—a remarkable fact, the significance of which we cannot stress too strongly—that revolution was possible in these cities only from the eighth to the fourth centuries B.C., that is to say, during the period exactly corresponding to political disintegration. Before and after that period, the state having taken the form and dimensions of an AMP state, revolution always failed, until modern times when technical conditions changed.

The present state of Greece is certainly a subject for meditation!

THE EMPIRE AS AN EXTENSION OF AMP STATES

The empire is a perversion of the model of the AMP state: the first empires in history are extensions of these states (XVIIIth Egyptian Dynasty, 1500 B.C.). This is not by chance; we will see how difficult it was for the individualistic Greek city-state to break out of its narrow framework.

As paradoxical as it may appear, the empire was always to have universalist ambitions: the ideological superstructure of the empire would always be the opposite of the individualistic superstructure of the city-state. Xenophobia would give way to cosmopolitanism.

The dimensions of the empire a priori exclude any possibility of genocide practiced by a small ethnic group of conquerors within the scale of the country. It must turn toward other methods of domination, which necessarily include cosmopolitanism.

THE ISLAMIC REVOLUTION IN AFRICA: CAUSES OF FAILURE IN THE SPECIAL CASE OF BLACK AFRICA

As Islam triumphed from the Middle Ages onward, the Moslem clergy undertook a social and political revolution by way of their religion. The terrain was eminently favorable. The traditional religion was dead in the people's hearts, it had withered away. Heaven was no vain promise to converts to the new faith, which alone galvanized the masses. Holy war was the dreamed of opportunity that assured entrance into paradise: it meant volunteering for glorious death. The Tieddos of Cayor saw this at the battle of Samba Sadio against the fanatic soldiers of Ahmadu Cheikhu of Senegal.

Islam, in Black Africa, finally became superimposed on the caste system, but in its essence, Islam ignored caste; therefore, no barrier of birth could prevent anyone from becoming a respected religious chief, if he were virtuous. Better yet, only the halo of holiness stemming from Islamic practice could erase and make meaningless a humble extraction and thus eliminate the social hindrances it might entail: in this, Islam was socially revolutionary. It could, for these various reasons, mobilize the masses from all social strata who were ready to sweep away the supporters of traditional power, now considered completely desacralized heathens, because the traditional religion was dead. The fact that Islam was propagated by the nationals themselves radicalized the action: therefore, the revolution was able to succeed, but it came too late.

The revolt of the marabouts of Koki, in Senegal, under the Damel Amari Ngone Ndella, the help they received from the Almamy Abdul Qadir of Futa, the formation of the Lebu theocracy of Cape Verde, governed by Koranic law allied to custom, are so many facts that show the movement's self-awareness and that it was to reach unusual size under the leadership of men such as Ousmane Dan Fodio and El Hadj-Omar.

Islam might have eliminated castes and started a social revolution, the basis of all progress; but the religious dignitaries of common origin preferred to become "ennobled," in a way, by marrying princesses, so that their children would be nobles through their mothers and marabouts through their fathers. Thus, outwardly, the model of the conquered aristocratic society continued to be conveyed, in some manner, by the subconscious of those whose mission had been to eradicate it from the mental universe of the people. The failure of the social revolution was painful. However, some religious chiefs did at times put the nobility back in its place. This was the case with "Lamp Fall" (Cheikh Ibra Fall), creator of the Muride subsect of the Baye Fall. He had a calabash full of sun-dried "turds" given to all of his princess wives who were demanding the privilege of having their meals separately, apart from the other wives of popular or slave origin, and exclaimed indignantly: "Try to tell your 'turds' from those of the common women!"

Another specific feature of the aristocratic society survived. "Asking" is a normal act, not a humiliating one. From the bottom to the top of the social hierarchy, everyone, casted or not, may ask his social superior for various things. Even the marabout making a series of requests of God, after having sung his glory in beautiful poetry, is only transposing to the divine order the social reality of everyday life.

Be that as it may, aristocratic ideas, even after the destruction of the nobility as a class, survive in everyone's consciousness; the proletarian is often an aristocrat without knowing it.

The religious conceptual apparatus, essentially forged during the monarchial phase of human evolution, bears the imprint of that period. Thus, in the language of the revealed religions, the relationship between God and humanity is one of master and slave: "Lord, we are your slaves." The idea of God on his throne is a symbol. Osiris was the first god in the history of religions to sit on a throne on Judgment Day, to judge the souls of men.

11

REVOLUTION IN THE GREEK CITY-STATES: COMPARISON WITH AMP STATES

How was the Greek city-state born? Why was revolution possible there, when it was not in earlier sociopolitical structures, and would cease to be after the decline of the city, until modern times?

Because these two questions have already been dealt with in chapter 8 of our book entitled *Antériorité des civilisations nègres: Mythe ou vérité historique?*, we will limit ourselves here to the essential.

We have already seen (chapter 3) that in the sixteenth century B.C., the XVIIIth Egyptian Dynasty had effectively colonized all of the Aegean Sea and, consequently, brought this region of the world out of protohistory into the historical cycle of humanity, by the introduction of writing (*Linears A* and *B*) and a body of agrarian and metallurgical techniques too long to enumerate. This was the period when, according to Greek tradition itself, which had remained mysterious for a long time, Cecrops, Egyptos, and Danaus, all Egyptians, introduced metallurgy, agriculture, etc. It was the period of Erechtheus, the Egyptian hero and founder of the unity of Attica. According to this same Greek tradition, it was these Egyptian Blacks who founded the first dynasties in continental Greece, at Thebes (Boeotia) with Cadmus the Negroid who had come from Canaan, in Phoenicia, or in Athens itself, as we have just seen.

The first form of government was therefore that of the colonizer: Mycenaean Greece first had the African model of state, meaning the Egyptian or AMP state, with its elaborate bureaucratic apparatus; this was the period of palace royalty that was described by Homer eight centuries later in the *Iliad* and the *Odyssey*; this foreign state apparatus was, in many aspects, very advanced compared to the structures that had been there before; this is the reason why Greece, after the Dorian invasion, was quite naturally to lose the artificial use of writing for four centuries (from the twelfth to the eighth centuries B.C.), and to rediscover it only in the eighth century, this time as a real need for development, in perfect accord with the forms of organizations of the time.

Because Egypt was the quasi-exclusive teacher of Greece in all periods on the road to civilization, there is a historical solidarity between the two civilizations of which the researcher should not lose sight, if he or she wants to be scientific. We have already said that projection of the archaic and semilegendary period of Greece on the parallel Egyptian historical chronology is often of great comparative interest: thus, the destruction of Troy in the middle of the thirteenth century effectively took place under the reign of Ramses II, at the zenith of the Black civilization of Egypt, whereas Greece was still at the stage of human sacrifice: it was Agamemnon who sacrificed Iphigenia to the gods in Aulis.

It is believed that the Egyptians, who had adopted the chariot as a means of warfare as early as the sixteenth century B.C., after having driven out the Hyksos, introduced chariots into Mycenaean Greece, where they met the same fate as writing had after the Dorian invasion and the modification of battle techniques.

The chariot was the principal vehicle of war during the siege of Troy. We can say that Agamemnon's tomb, the monument referred to as "the treasure of the Atridae," is nothing but a rudimentary Egyptian mastaba.

In terms of religion, the cult of Osiris, i.e., of Dionysus, was already known in Mycenaean Greece, for the name of Dionysus in the genitive has been found on a *Linear B* tablet.

This cult of Osiris-Dionysus was probably also eclipsed during the "dark period" (twelfth to eighth centuries B.C.), and Greek religious consciousness remained closed to any idea of the hereafter until the sixth century B.C., the time when the cult of Isis/Osiris-Dionysus, a religion of mystery and salvation of the soul, was reintroduced into the northern Mediterranean, and Greece in particular. As for mythology, the gods of Olympus, like the Egyptian gods four thousand years before, substituted their reign for that of the Titans, after a victorious battle, during which all of the latter were massacred;[1] here also the Egyptian influence remains apparent: the ubiquity of the structures of myths, the diverse forms of religious, social, and political organization would be tenable only if the demonstration could be based on the contemporaneity of comparative facts. But this fundamental condition is radically lacking among all authors, without exception; and they seem not to be aware of this contradiction, which nullifies the scientific value of all their demonstrations: Claude Lévi-Strauss, Mircea Eliade.

All the ideological superstructures at issue above, and many others, were present in Egypt at clearly dated times, thousands of years before their appearance through diffusion (in Elliot Smith's sense) in other regions of the planet, which had remained in the darkness of history during this whole period. That is why it is fallacious to compare superstructures of the fifth century B.C., or more recent periods, to those of King Narmer's Egypt, 3300 B.C., without emphasizing the notion of the diffusion of Egyptian culture. This is the mistake made by those who use as a chronological base the erroneous method of glottochronology.[2] All the anachronisms of the Homeric poems, pointed out by M. I. Fineley,[3] might be explained by using Egypt as a reference: the sumptuous palaces, bearing no relationship to the rudimentary Mycenaean "palaces," rather remind one of those of the city of "Thebes of the hundred gates," and it is now known that this verse of Homer refers to the city of Thebes at the time of Ramses III. If Homer visited Egypt—and this fact is attested to by Greek tradition—it was probably during the time of the XXVth Sudanese Dynasty, under Piankhi or Shabaka, around 750 B.C.

In a pertinent study, Victor Bérard has demonstrated that Homer, far from having created *ex nihilo*, relied heavily on models, particularly Egyptian ones.[4] We know that eight hundred years before Homer, under the XVIIIth Dynasty, and even before that, Egypt had already invented the art of poetry. It was also during the "dark period" of Greek history, to which Homer belongs, that the use of iron spread throughout the northern Mediterranean, probably from Napata, from this same Sudanese dynasty which had then conquered Egypt and brought about a rebirth of Egyptian civilization, coinciding with the development of a new form of Egyptian language and writing known as demotic. The piety of these Sudanese Pharaohs corresponds in all respects to Homer's testimony in the *Iliad*; Homer is mistaken when he attributes iron weapons to the Mycenaeans of the Bronze Age.

The society described by Homer is one of "Oriental despotism," with a king who is priest, judge, legislator, and military chief, subject to no control by the people, who as yet had no political power. Such was the condition of the people of Ithaca, or those who participated in the Trojan expedition but not in the war, which was the business of princes and, moreover, the occasion of individual battles.

After the destruction of the Mycenaean society, the Dorians formed an aristocracy at the head of the conquered peoples, grouped in small formations, which were the embryos of the future independent city-states of classical Greece of the fifth and sixth centuries B.C.

Social struggle, extremely violent in these new states, is first known in a documented way through the poet, a small farmer and slave owner,

Hesiod: his *Works and Days* was written between the end of the eighth and the beginning of the seventh century B.C., therefore clearly after Homer's time. Hesiod belongs to the properly historic period of archaic Greece, which he in a way introduces with his work. He gives valuable information on farm work, from which can be deduced precise information on political and social organization (see p. 204). Society was already composed of kings (unjust and greedy), nobles, small freeholders, landless wage earners, and slaves.

Private ownership of the land was already an established fact. However, commerce, especially maritime commerce, was still abhorred and remained in the hands of foreigners: according to theory, those who practiced commerce were not the ones one would expect; they were not the landowners increasing their profits through slavery and commerce, they were the homeless, constituting the embryo of the future plebs who were progressively to awaken to commerce. This was the only economic activity that they were allowed to practice, and they also progressively replaced the Phoenicians, who had reintroduced (alphabetic) writing in the eighth century B.C. The merchants were the "landless."

The new cities mainly had a wall around them and a temple on an elevated place, where the citizens alone could go for common worship. In all, there were about fifteen hundred cities, according to Fineley,[5] divided into three types:

1. *citadel*, like Smyrna, living off the spoils of war;
2. *group of villages*, like Sparta (revenues from a sanctuary);
3. *town and countryside*, like Athens and its suburbs (commerce and handicrafts).

In fact, after the conquest had been achieved, the Dorian aristocracy lost no time casting the royalty out in order to govern itself directly: it left the priesthood to the royalty and took over political power, according to Fustel de Coulanges.

Although Athens boasted and congratulated itself on having avoided the turmoil of the Dorian invasion, this first purely political revolution did affect it, according to tradition, through the reforms of Codrus in the eleventh century B.C., about which almost nothing is known.

THE REVOLUTION IN SPARTA

In Sparta, there was the reform of Lycurgus (ninth and eighth centuries), if he indeed ever existed. That being as it may, the *Rhetra*, which is attributed to him, preserved the three Homeric powers: royalty, council, and assembly. Royalty became double, hereditary, and belonged to two families, the Agides and the Eurypontides.

The two kings were only simple magistrates, not even the most important ones. They had mainly religious functions and were controlled by the *gerousia*, an assembly of thirty members, the twenty-eight others of whom were elected for life from among the citizens over sixty years of age, in other words, those no longer subject to military service. It was this advisory body which held the real judicial and executive power.

The people's assembly, or *apella*, met regularly to vote by acclamation on the laws submitted to it by the *gerousia*; it could not amend them; but its prerogatives, as well as those of the two kings, although already very much reduced, would continue to dwindle with time. The two kings had authority only when they acted together; after the first Messenian war, an amendment to the *Rhetra* reinforced the authority of the *gerousia* and gave it the power to nullify assembly votes of which it disapproved.

Later, a fourth power even more sweeping than that of the *gerousia* was created: an annual college of five magistrates, the ephors, who were placed over all the magistrates of the *gerousia*, including the two kings. They were in charge of all the activities of the state, and particularly the upbringing of the children.[6]

Spartan education illustrates the saying according to which one who suppresses the liberty of others becomes a slave himself. For it to be possible that a handful of nine thousand individuals (the number of citizens of Dorian origin in the Spartan state) could make slaves of all the conquered Helots, they had to renounce their own individual liberty and organize the whole state under the strictest military discipline of all time.

Newborns belonged to the state, which ordered that they be fed to predators if they had any physical malformation making them unfit for military service in defense of the state. Otherwise they were returned to their parents until the age of seven; the state then took them back and enrolled them in the *agogy*, where they underwent a training of inhumane severity that disregarded any intellectual development: endurance, courage, and blind obedience were the Spartan ideals. The child was taught to steal to feed himself; he had to catch a Helot by surprise at night and kill him: this is the *crypty*. The same moral situation exactly was to be found among the Germanics in the process of their moving from a nomadic to a sedentary way of life. Tacitus described their customs: theft and murder, the killing of an enemy, were moral ideals and part of the tests imposed on the young German before he could enter the circle of adults.

In Sparta, all male adults were career soldiers until the age of sixty. They spent their lives in military camps, separated from their wives and children. Family life did not exist, and the existence of the couple was of marginal importance; the proverbial perversion of morals, the extraversion of masculine habits raised to the level of an institution in all of Greece, especially in Athens (over which the modern West always throws a veil of modesty), had their origin in the particular style of life, which, long after settlement, still carried the stigmata of the prior period of nomadism. Decency forbids the detailed discussion of the moral decay of Greek society, even and especially at the level of its greatest men: Aristotle, Plato, the family of Pisistratus, the tryant of Athens, etc. The moral license of Spartan women was legendary. Until he was thirty, the male Spartan slept in barracks and could see his wife only furtively. His "family" life did not begin until he was thirty, but until he was sixty years old he had to dine every evening at the mess (*syssition*) of his military unit, and he became theoretically independent only after he had reached the age of sixty.

In fact, the land itself belonged to the state, which ceded to each of the Equals (about nine thousand of them), that is, only the citizens, a plot of ground as well as the number of Helots necessary to cultivate it.[7]

It is instructive to analyze the process by which the lordly individualism of the twelfth-century Dorians led in the seventh century B.C. to a state collectivism, no less lordly, and the most draconian in history.

The initial numerical ratio between the Dorian conquerors and the conquered Helots as well as their ethnic separation imposed the singular path of evolution that Sparta followed. When nine thousand individuals organize on an ethnic, racial basis to attempt to dominate forever a whole people momentarily conquered, they do not have much to chose from: there is only one way to do it, that of genocide, with all its daily consequences. All the Spartan politico-military laws and organization therefore stem, of necessity, from those initial absurd and primitive principles. The logical rigor of this system leads to the total suppression of freedom for the "conquerors," for whom hell is now on earth, if one closely examines their situation.

Spartan life was a perpetual preparation for war; the Equals were haunted by the fear of Helot revolts throughout Messenia, which they tried in vain to reduce in number by cowardly assassinations, institutionalized as educational principles of Dorian youth. Life was no longer anything but perpetual torment, and inhumane measures imposed on the entire society did not prevent the frequency of Helot revolts; Sparta was thus progressively to decline, for if the city-state in general was no longer viable, that of Sparta was, because of its political foundations, the most vulnerable of all.

Spartan collectivism was not proletarian, and we should not be mistaken about its nature, which was lordly. We need only underline the irony of history and fate. These individualistic nomads cherishing freedom above all else, it seems, were condemned to lose even the memory of it, due to the mere fact that the foundations on which they chose to build a state that would guarantee them that freedom were nonviable and unsound: the Spartan state controlled even the wearing of beards and might dictate the type of feelings that citizens must display in exceptional circumstances.

After the disaster inflicted on it by the city of Thebes (in Boeotia) at Leuctra in 371 B.C., Sparta ordered the reversal of feelings: women whose sons had died in battle had to smile and show joy, whereas those whose children had escaped death were to be sad and to weep; and so it was done. It should be pointed out that the surrounding communities that Sparta annexed were not completely formed cities with their own gods and institutional apparatuses; otherwise annexation would not even have been thinkable. The conquered city would have been destroyed, its inhabitants either sold or dispersed; or it would have become an ally in what are incorrectly called *leagues* in modern vocabulary: *The Peloponnesian League*, whereas in its time it was referred to as Sparta and her allies; *the Athenian League*, made up of Athens and one hundred fifty (out of a total of fifteen hundred) city-states, scattered haphazardly, sometimes separated by enemy states; and *the Boeotian League*, with Thebes at its head.

However, in the sixth century, Sparta had become the principal military force of Greece and was able, with the support of Persian gold, to conquer and dislocate the Athenian League.

These "leagues" were not even the beginnings of a political unification as we understand that concept today.

The amphyctions are only religious associations whose member cities together exploit the sanctuary of a divinity and share the revenues among themselves.

Fustel de Coulanges has shown that the idea of a real integration of several cities in the setting of a centralized state, governed by one law, was absolutely alien to the Greek mentality and religion, until the triumph of the universalist philosophy that came from abroad. Theirs were ephemeral and fragile coalitions against an interior enemy: Sparta and her allies against Athens and hers; or the Boeotian League that inflicted on Sparta the defeat of Leuctra, which allowed the liberation of the Helot people and began the decline of the Spartan state, which would fall apart in the third century B.C. during the civil war.

Sparta had never wanted to extend citizenship to foreigners, who, as a result, had no reason to sacrifice themselves for her survival. Furthermore, corruption and greed ended up taking over the ranks of the Equals: social inequalities were introduced; Spartan citizens lost their plots of land and, consequently, their rights as citizens.

Sparta had never known an artistic flowering comparable to that of Athens of the fifth and fourth centuries. The artists who built her monuments were almost all foreigners: Bathycles of Magnesia directed the works of the "throne" of Apollo at Amyklai;[8] her ceramics cannot compare with either those of Attica, or even those of Corinth.

Let us insist on the fact that the term *slave*, often applied to the conquered Helots who still remained on their own national land, is improper: more appropriately, they were people dominated and colonized momentarily, so to speak, in their own motherland; these people were neither uprooted nor dispersed. Their culture was intact, they did not lose their national pride, and their unceasing revolts, which would end by overcoming the descendants of the Dorian conquerors, prove it. There were two great revolts, corresponding to what are called the first and the second wars of Messenia, homeland of the Helot people; the last one lasted for seventeen years; it was a veritable war of national liberation, momentarily lost. Sparta was compelled to transform the state into a truly entrenched camp constantly on the alert.

Sparta was, therefore, not liberated by slaves in the strict sense of the term, but by the uprising of the autochthons.

THE REVOLUTION IN ATHENS

Athens would go from the individualism of the Eupatridae ("of noble birth") to end up also with the imperialism of the all-powerful state, following a parallel evolution but with notorious differences that we will not fail to stress.

In Sparta, in the sixth century, the much diminished royalty still continued to struggle against the ephoralty, the Lacedemonian institution of five magistrates installed each year as a check on regal power, but in Athens, the royalty had long been conquered and the power was entirely in the hands of the aristocracy which, from the sixth century onward, was confronted only by the people: the reforms of Draco, Solon, and Cleisthenes were going to blaze the trail for the period of popular struggles that were about to take place.

The reform of Draco corresponds to a period when Athens was almost mired in murder and anarchy.

The feeling of anxiety and the climate of pessimism that overwhelmed Greece at the turn of the sixth century clearly reflected the rise of the popular forces, which would no longer stop acting to dethrone the aristocracy and to modify profoundly the structures of the state, in order to subordinate them to the public welfare. If one takes into consideration the declarations of Athens according to which she was spared by the Dorian invasion, this might explain to a large extent the evolutionary peculiarities of the Athenian state.

In fact, this would mean that the different *genos* that reigned over the primitive populations of Attica between the twelfth and the eighth centuries B.C. constituted an indigenous nobility of some kind, because it stemmed from previous, perhaps Mycenaean migrations. The land originally belonged to these nobles and to the free peasantry who were the first occupants of the land, all of them forming a pseudonational complex, a city in gestation, whose structure corresponds perfectly to Marx's "antique mode of production," even if the institution of the Roman *Ager publicus* is not clearly attested to: for this reason, one could more correctly speak of the antique mode of ownership.

This Athenian nobility was already lulled by time and the sedentary life; even though retracing its origins back to the gods, in the manner of the

Pharaohs of Egypt, it was much less bellicose than the Dorian hordes who, coming out of nomadic life, conquered Messenia and Laconia in the Peloponnesus. But these different *genos*, or *génè*, had not yet accepted a rigorous common law: the conflicts between clans were settled by customary law, the *dike*, and vendetta was the rule; murder was avenged, not by society, but by the family, the *genos*; similarly, each *genos* was sovereign over its own territory, and we will see that the fusion of the *genos* into a single, true Athenian people will not be accomplished until the reform of Cleisthenes in the fourth century B.C.

What is going to occur in Attica between the eighth and the fourth centuries B.C.?

The destruction of the Mycenaean civilization, it seems, had left in place a pseudoroyalty: the "dark period" did have a "king" called Basileus, eliminated by the first aristocratic revolution at the end of the eighth century B.C., in Athens, when he was replaced by a decennial archontate, then annual, group of archons, the list of which began in A.D. 683–82.[9] What is going to happen when foreigners, Greeks mostly, "metics," arrive in such a society not in waves of conquering armies, but through infiltrations, in a rhythm that the receiving milieu can contain and condition? Athens established an immigration code of sorts: the Eupatridae were at the top of society, after the elimination of royalty; they were the chiefs of the *genos*; only they and the first occupants of the land, the free peasantry, could own land in the ritual sense and were, as a result, the only citizens: the person who lost his plot of land ceased to be a citizen; the foreigner, the metic, could not own land; if he became a dependent, if he became a domestic slave of one of the Eupatridae who protected him, he could receive the usufruct, but from the sixth century onward he could, if he were rich, buy himself the military equipment of a hoplite and participate in the defense of the state, which increased his rights.

It did not take long for the Eupatridae to dispossess the peasantry, while the metics and the true "plebs," the Thetes, meaning the homeless, showed a trend toward commerce and usurious lending.

Such a situation leads to favoring class struggle to the detriment of the initial ethnic domination which, we have already said, will completely disappear under the reform of Cleisthenes; the Athenian state will tend more and more to become, not the domination of one ethnic group over another, but the instrument of the domination of one class over another. Thus, Athens deviates from the Spartan path, even though there were originally many common points: the Eupatridae were, or considered themselves, an indigenous nobility of Attica; they were not strangers who arrived just yesterday, like the Dorians in Sparta. Thus the ethnic separation was less brutal and less humiliating in Athens than in Sparta, and from this fact it grew blurred with time, in order to give way to a true class struggle among the same people. But aristocrats of all countries resemble each other in some ways. From Homer to Pericles, the Eupatridae and other Greek nobles loved to trace their family trees, back to a divinity. The generosity of Simon, the rival of Pericles, was as legendary as that of today's Africans who cannot rid themselves of the monarchial state model.

Athens, which was the largest of the Greek city-states, during the classical period had a surface area equal to that of the Duchy of Luxembourg: 2,600 km^2, town and countryside included. It had 250,000 inhabitants, men, women, children, and slaves. It was by far the most populated of the Greek cities—Corinth: 90,000 inhabitants; Thebes, Argos, Corcyra: 40 to 60,000 inhabitants—and the other cities decreased to 5,000 inhabitants and even fewer.[10]

Among this Athenian population, the number of citizens was only 40,000 as opposed to 80,000 slaves, because, from the sixth century B.C. onward, Athens showed a trend toward massive buying of slave laborers, imported from the south of today's "Russia."

The ancient kings were military and religious chiefs. In Athens, these two functions were dissociated during the seventh century with the decline of royalty and were entrusted to two persons: a simple magistrate was named king of Athens, without doubt to sacrifice according to custom, as it is very difficult to wipe out the past; the waging of war was entrusted to the polemarch. The Eupatridae held the real power in the Areopagus, a tribunal composed of magistrates who held office for life and were in charge as custodians of the law.

The citizens together formed the assembly of the people that elected the magistrates, but this assembly could only designate the Eupatridae, to the exclusion of those who came from its own body.

With the rise of popular forces, represented by the former disinherited who enriched themselves through commerce, Athens was literally about to fall into anarchy on several occasions; in addition, the legislation of Draco was essentially devoted to the problem of murder. The legislator attempted to "substitute the justice of the state with individual vengeance."[11]

The legislation of Solon introduced for the first time *habeas corpus* in Greece, abolished slavery for indebtedness, and made a compromise that increased the rights of the people without the aristocracy losing face; the legislation of Cleisthenes brought the people together. It first chose its tyrants, meaning the lay political chiefs, from among the Eupatridae, and later from within its own group.

The popular forces triumphed. Athens knew direct government without bureaucracy.

The decrees of the Athenian assembly were promulgated by the *demos*, bringing together four times every thirty-six days the male citizens of at least eighteen years of age. Those present, from among the 40,000 citizens, made decisions valid for the whole population. It was the same way for the courts, made up through a drawing of lots from a list of 6,000 volunteers. There was neither representation, nor civil service, nor bureaucracy of any importance.

The *boule*, a council of five hundred citizens chosen for terms of one year (maximum eligibility: two terms) by drawing lots drew up the many issues: war, peace, budget of public works, on which everybody could speak, propose amendments, and vote.

The person responsible for each task was directly responsible to the *demos* and not to a senior in the hierarchy. Only the ten strategists (*strategoi*, or generals) were indefinitely eligible, as were the special commissions for diplomatic negotiations.[12]

The drawing of lots, the compensation allocated for work accomplished allowed the poor to sit on the council or on the tribunals and to fulfill whatever duty fell on them. The drawing of lots and the obligatory rotation multiplied the opportunities for participation. The compensation was not a source of wealth, but it offered a living wage.

The power belonged to the assembly, which explains the importance of the orators. The assembly met outside in the open, on a hill called the Pnyx, near the Acropolis. There was no political party nor governmental body. The president, for the day, was chosen by drawing lots from among the members of the council of five hundred, according to the principle of rotation: proposals were made, discussed, amended, and voted on in one day. Whoever wanted to make the assembly change a course of action had to appear on the Pnyx and explain his reasons, even if he was a member of the council; the assembly could immediately put an end to the assigned task of anyone, no matter who he was.

After Pericles came the era of the demagogues who pandered to the people. Pericles himself went out of public favor and was made to pay a heavy fine at the beginning of the Peloponnesian War, ostracism being the custom.[13]

Athens thus passed, in three centuries, from an exacerbated individualism to the omnipotent state, to which all citizens were subject without distinction, the Eupatridae as well as the lower classes; if it were so, it was because the people and the plebs, composed of the Thetes, victims of glaring injustices and of the high-handedness of the Eupatridae, directed all of their protests toward the adoption of one law for all people.

For the lower classes, the written and respected laws, which were the same for everybody, were the best guarantee of security against the extortions of the Eupatridae: from the sixth century B.C. onward, when the Eupatridae were calling for a well-ordered, well-governed state, "eunomy" (we know what that meant), to which the disinherited of the plebs retorted: isonomy, the same political rights for all, and their triumph established the advent of democracy in Athens.

It is, therefore, an evolution parallel but not identical to the one that took place in Sparta: the omnipotence of the Spartan state was wanted and accomplished by the Dorian nobility, in order to contain the popular pressure of the Helot ethnic group. Thus the state was an instrument of domination of one ethnicity over another, while the omnipotence of the Athenian state was the result of victorious battles of the people against the Eupatridae. Here, the state having been conceived as the guarantor of liberty of the weak, they henceforth accorded the state all powers.

In the first case, individualism leads to "collectivism" (a very specific collectivism, it should be stressed) from the top down, from the social strata of the dominant ethnicity; in the second case, individualism leads to state imperialism, caused by pressure from below. Modern society has not yet finished pondering the heritage of these two experiences of antiquity.

COMPARISON WITH THE AMP STATE

In each case, the authentically Indo-European model of the state, the city-state, was not viable. Condemned by its multiple insufficiencies, it declined and was replaced by the model of the African state, particularly the Egyptian model, known as the AMP state, beginning with the conquests of Philip II of Macedon, and especially of his son, Alexander the Great.

After the battle of Chaeronea in 338 B.C., Philip II of Macedonia became the master of Greece. He created, at Corinth, the league of the Hellenes which intended to invade Persia, and which had profaned, let us remember, Greek sanctuaries one hundred fifty years earlier!

The second goal of this league was to guarantee that in no city-state would there be any execution or any banishment contrary to the laws established in the cities, nor would there be any confiscation of goods, any redistribution of the land, any abolition of debts, or any liberation of slaves in order to achieve a revolutionary goal (anonymous author of the third century B.C.[14]). All that had been attained from the reforms of Solon was annulled with one stroke; this was a veritable counterrevolutionary reaction led by the monarchy, which would be carried into modern times—thanks to the changing of the framework of sociopolitical struggle—that is, for more than two thousand years, and this to a large extent because revolutions were accomplished in nonviable sociopolitical settings that would all disappear with the city-states. The more the city had to pay its armed forces, the more it was incapable of satisfying its citizens economically (whence migrations to settle other colonies as the population increased). The problem of foreigners became insolvable. Some cities sold, in vain, citizenship to a few foreigners.

The polis had a past, a fugitive present, and no future.[15] The fact that, even during the epoch of Thucydides (II, 5), all of the interior and particularly the northern part of Greece remained at the ethnographic age, shows clearly that civilization had come from the South.

Philip of Macedonia was a semibarbarian. Alexander, imitating the Egyptian Pharaohs, had himself called son of Zeus-Amon in the famous sanctuary of the oracle of Amon in Lybia.

The new Greek kings of the Hellenistic epoch, after the short-lived empire of Alexander, endeavored to be absolute monarchs, in the setting of states that comprised several cities; they adopted the state model of the conquered countries: the Ptolemy in Egypt, the Seleucids in Syria and Mesopotamia, and the Antigonids in Macedon on the Greek continent. The latter had to face, for some time, resistance from the Greek cities.

Some elements of the Greek polis were transposed to the structures of the new states, but only on a cultural and administrative level: the agora, the temples, the gymnasia and the stoa, the assemblies, the councils, and the magistrates. But henceforth, the new sovereigns claimed to be king-gods like their Egyptian or Mesopotamian predecessors; an important bureaucracy asserted itself; it was therefore the AMP state that was perpetuated, by integrating some elements of the bygone city of antiquity. The cult of the sovereign was instituted, which took on a divine character, as in Egypt; even in continental Greece, with the Antigonids, there were sanctuaries where the cult of the king was assured, in the ancient city-states, even though it is also said that Demosthenes sneered when, in 324, Alexander the Great ordered the Greeks to recognize him as the son of God.

The ideological superstructure of the city died with it because of the new economic necessities; the Indo-European religion of the city, too individualistic and xenophobic, died; it was vanquished by the new Oriental cults and, in particular, by the cult of Isis, which introduced universalism, the notions of the immortality of the soul and of individual salvation in the northern Mediterranean. Individual religion replaced the public and communal cult of the city, conducted by lay priests appointed by the state, even if they came hereditarily from certain families, before the popular revolutions.

In terms of philosophy, stoicism preached the brotherhood of men subject to a unique (why not Pharaonic?) divine law, the indifference to fate, to misforture, to pleasure, to wealth, to poverty, to slavery, or to civil rights. Indifference to social position, and, consequently, acceptance of one's social status, no matter what it was, became a doctrine and a duty: it was really the ideal philosophy, the new ideological superstructure adequate to peacefully govern the new universe, conquered with its own consent.

We have already explained how the structure of the city made revolution possible and why it became impossible in the larger AMP states up to modern times (chapters 9 and 10). The narrow framework of the city, allied with its isolationist philosophy, made possible the victory of an oppressed social class over the dominant one.

We have seen that the revolution was the act of the disinherited, free lower classes in those cities, and not the act of slaves; so much so that at Corcyra, when the revolution broke out, in 427 B.C., the two parties each sought help from the slaves, according to Thucydides.

The present difficulties, encountered by world revolution, are to a great extent linked to the AMP character of the modern states, on the double plane of the size and complexity of the wheels and structures of organized intervention (United States, Europe, etc.): hence the defeatism of many revolutionary movements and the appearance of a new class of theoreticians of this special situation: Herbert Marcuse and others.

Revolution, progress, and democracy disappeared from continental Greece, from the unification by Philip of Macedon until our time. Strictly speaking, the revolutions of modern times should have broken out first in Greece where, all things considered, the cumulative effect ought to have been much more intense. But the first revolution of modern times would explode on the outlying island that inherited the least from Greece and Rome in Europe. What would lead one, in the late Middle Ages, when all factors born from the Greco-Roman heritage were already in place, to guess at the singular role that little England would play in modern times? This even when taking into account the cultural role of the monks, such as the Englishman Alcuin, who was the moving spirit of the Carolingian Renaissance.

The history of England illustrates the role of human will in the grappling with economic factors, in order to forge the destiny of a people: Kipling surely exaggerated when he wrote: "Nature held council with herself and said, my Romans are gone; to build a new empire, I shall choose a rude race, all masculine with British strength."[16] But he still expressed the willpower of a people small in number, who, after the Egyptians and the Greeks, shaped the face of the Earth in modern times.

Why did the revolution not take place in the African city-states that have existed in history? As an initial response, one could point to the difference in agrarian conditions; nowhere in Africa was land a possession, a property reserved for the nobility and inaccessible to the disinherited lower classes and to foreigners. On the contrary, everywhere, the stranger who arrives "in the evening" will find "the next day," a community that welcomes him and guarantees him the usufruct of a plot of land, as long as he needs it; therefore, the principal reason for the revolution in the Greek cities is absent from the African cities, which, moreover, do not know xenophobia and the corollary isolation of the foreigner that derives from it. Thus, the customs and practices did not allow the establishment of a plebeian class made up of disinherited, homeless foreigners on the outskirts of African cities.[17] In addition, all African states, even the city-states, are interventionist in both the economic and political sense.

12

CHARACTERISTICS OF POLITICAL AND SOCIAL AFRICAN STRUCTURES AND THEIR EFFECT ON HISTORICAL MOVEMENT

These questions have already been the subject of an in-depth study in our works entitled *Antériorité des civilisations nègres*, *L'Unité culturelle de l'Afrique Noire*, and *L'Afrique Noire précoloniale*,[1] and we will not come back to them here. We could well refer to the above-mentioned works for the study of the primitive accumulation process, of the divorce of work from working conditions, of the internal contradictions, and therefore of the driving force behind the history of African societies.

The latter publication has a methodological character and should demonstrate the possibility of writing a nonfactual history of Africa. Suffice it that I recall here some traits common to African political and social institutions.

ROYALTY

If the royal function had obvious advantages, it was also regulated by a ritual so exacting that at times, everything considered, the king's fate was not enviable at all. In fact, the act of physically putting the king to death after he had reigned for a certain number of years (eight, in general), depending upon the region, was not an exceptional event: it persisted, here and there, throughout time and space, in precolonial Black Africa. Most recently, in 1967, a young Nigerian "prince," a college graduate who had accepted the "royal" duty of his tribe, became a victim of this practice.[2] He was almost killed at the end of his reign as established by rite.[3]

Everywhere that this custom survived, becoming king was a task that aroused little desire and few intrigues. In Nigeria, where the crown's secret council, presided over by the high priest, could decide on the king's death according to this rite, it happened that there was a shortage of candidates for the throne.[4] It is fair to say that the king's fate was not envied by the people at all.

The council's decision was conveyed to the king by presenting him with a parrot's eggs; he then knew that he had to kill himself, or others would not delay in carrying out the sentence for him.

The competition for the throne existed mainly in countries where the "eligible class" had succeeded in bypassing the tradition by substituting ritual symbolic death for the real, physical one, as in Egypt, from the IIIrd Dynasty onward: one can see at Saqqara, in the funeral domain of Zoser (2778 B.C.), the rounded pathway made for this purpose, which the Fari (Pharaoh) had to travel to demonstrate his vigor, his regeneration; he was not to be caught by those in pursuit of him. African vitalist concepts form the basis for these practices.

The ascent of Pharoah Unas of the Vth Dynasty, to his *Ka(w)* or *Ka(u)*, after death, illustrates clearly these vitalist concepts that underlie African life.[5]

In the neo-Sudanese states, Ghana, Mali, Songhai, where the actual physical killing had disappeared, traces of vitalism are noticeable in the fact that a king cannot, under any circumstances, be physically handicapped (one-eyed, one-armed, etc.). Even if wounded in battle, he must leave the throne until he is healed, and he has to either designate an intermediary or have one designated; this often creates complications; this happened in Cayor with the Damel Lat-Sukabé (1967);[6] for Sundiata Keita (see p. 324).

Thus the vitalism and the symbolic or real death that is a part of it are traits common to African royalty from the Egypt of the Fari (Pharaoh) to today's Africa.[7]

In the same way, the importance of the priests' role and the government by oracle (Pythia), which Egypt seems to have exported to Greece as well, probably constitute another Egyptian heritage, or at least another trait common to the two types of royalty and of government.

All the traditional African kings are designated by the clergy or the sacerdotal caste, because their legitimacy comes from the indigenous religion. This is particularly true for the Nubia of antiquity, Egypt, Nigeria (Yoruba, etc.).

Still today, great African university graduates consult these oracles, put their political or other destinies in the hands of the masters of the occult, and pay them bewildering amounts of money: a primitive act that one would believe to be of another age, but which does not exclude a discourse on rationalism!

Jean Pierre Vernant, who noted this anomaly among the Greeks, tried with difficulty to place it in a rational framework.[8]

Another common trait of African political institutions is the particular importance of the role played by the queen-mother, ever since Nubia and Egypt. It is obviously a matter of the survival of the African matriarch of the clan and tribal stage. Matriarchy is a tribal institution, and, as such, should disappear with the decline of tribal authority and the appearance of the monarchy; but its deep-seated vestiges still remain in the whole society: this applies to Nubia, Egypt, and to all the other regions of Africa.[9]

Another common trait is the important place reserved for the castes and the slaves, even in the neo-Sudanese societies where the taboo of the blacksmith reigns. The three authentic documents received from the Senegalese archives, thanks to the kindness of Oumar Ba, and analyzed below, clearly illustrate this idea.

The council in charge of electing the Damel[10] is composed as follows:

1. President: the representative of free men without caste. This is the *Diawerigne Mboul Ndiâmbur* or *Ndiâmbur*.
2. Three representatives of free men, each hereditarily administering one region: they are the *Lamane*, who administers the Djamatil region, the *Botal*, who administers the region of Ndiob, the *Badié*, who administers that of Gatagne.
3. The two representatives of the Muslim clergy: the imam of the village of Mbal and the marabout of the village of Kab.
4. The representatives of the slaves of the crown, and of the Tieddos, meaning all sorts of courtiers: the *Diawerigne Mboul Gallo* or the *Djarâf Bunt-Ker*.[11]

The *Badié Gatagne* originally had to belong to the craft-related group of the "girdle makers," the *Badié*, as his name seems to indicate. But this modest origin quickly became blurred, because of the fact that all those closest to the king become, with time, pseudoprinces. The *Badié Gatagne* was certainly the "girdle maker" of the king. There were also the *Fara Tögg*, the *Fara Wundé*, the *Fara Laobé*, etc., who represented the blacksmiths, the shoemakers, and the Laobés, etc., respectively.

It follows from the analysis of these documents that men of castes as well as the captives of the crown had an interest in the conservation of power and the established order.

An examination of the second and third lists of the second document of the archives shows that the free men, casted or not, and the slaves were also associated with power, not in a factitious or symbolic manner, but on a very broad base. This gives an idea of the specificity of African slavery of the precolonial period: slaves who administered free men.

However, the political systems were far from being perfect. We have shown, in *L'Afrique Noire précoloniale*, that to look for the driving force of African history amounted to finding the social categories that did not resign themselves to their fate, because they were exploited without compensation; these were the truly alienated of society: those who produced for society, but received almost nothing in return. In the particular case of the Cayor, and with minor differences in the case of all the neo-Sudanese societies, they were made up of the peasantry, the Badolo; and of the third category of private slaves, called captives of the Father's hut.[12]

The social order based on castes is probably at the same time a heritage of Egypt and a consequence of the introduction of the war horse. If the case of the blacksmith is hypothetical, enough facts are available to demonstrate that the caste of the griots is a direct inheritance from the Egypt of the Fari (Pharaonic society). In fact, during the time of Diodorus of Sicily, that is, under Caesar Augustus (30 B.C.), Egyptian society, which had lost its independence five hundred years earlier, was still casted.

This author tells us that an Egyptian never taught his son music, even though the musicians' caste in Egypt enjoyed great respect. This is also the situation in all of the precolonial neo-Sudanese region. Added to this, there is the identity of the shape of the West African griot's guitar and that of the Egyptian guitar.[13]

Finally, the griots of the neo-Sudanese region, without knowing it, always begin their songs by praising the Fari, meaning the Pharoah, who is represented by today's district sovereign: no matter what the people's language is, the song begins with the following intonations: *Farii Farii Fari yo*.

The region of the blacksmith's taboo, that of the griots, of the casted societies and of the war horse, "conqueror" of vast empires, covers and corresponds roughly to the savannah zone that reaches to the Upper Nile, and where the tse-tse fly does not exist; whereas the region where the blacksmith enjoys a high degree of esteem, is feared, respected as principal magician, and can even reign as king, corresponds to the rest of Africa, where there are no horses (because of the tse-tse fly's presence), and where there is social stratification but no caste system.[14] It is our idea that these two parts of Africa have been to different degrees or at different times in contact with Egypt and were, therefore, equally marked by the Pharoanic society. It can be observed that even the political and administrative functions of Pharaonic society have survived in the neo-Sudanese region, under their proper Egyptian names.

In Senegalese society, the king par excellence is the *Bur Fari*, meaning the supreme king. This was the most glorious title that one could attribute "gratuitously" to the Damel of Cayor or to any other king or lesser sovereign that one wanted to flatter. There are also in Wolof (the language of the Damel): *Fara*, *Farba*, which are political and administrative functions; one need only refer to the above-cited archival documents to notice the frequency of the use of these titles. In the Mande language of Mali and of Upper Guinea, one again finds the terms: *Fari, Farima, Farma,* designating political functions; in Songhai: *Faran*; in Hausa: *Fara*, etc.[15]

Stratified African society, without caste,[16] would have been more susceptible to evolving into a capitalist type of society with industrial development. And, in fact, this evolution had a start in the Gulf of Benin, in Yoruba country, in Dahomey, where the power of money was great: a rich merchant could marry a princess, or the daughter of the king of Dahomey; according to Leo Frobenius, money opened all doors in Yoruba country. Such circumstances must be put in perspective with the existence of a semi-industrial commercial form of production. Here we have in mind the corporation of glassmakers of the precolonial epoch, among others. There were embryonic social classes, in the economic sense of the term.

Similarly, in order to explain the greatest development of the plastic arts in Benin, we must recall the absence of the caste, this defect in the neo-Sudanese societies. In fact, in casted societies, a great number of individuals, by the sole fact of their birth, are excluded from the category of artists for reasons similar to those that Diodorus of Sicily spoke of with respect to Egyptian society.

In the People's Republic of Benin, members of the royal family, that of Glélé, for instance, are weavers by birth: here is something beyond the understanding of a Cayorian from the Sahel. Similarly, when the father is a prince, the mother must almost always be a commoner, which stems from a concern to create political and social equilibrium.

Finally, in Rwanda and Burundi, the proud Tutsi also ignore caste: the musician is not despised; the king can enoble his subject, even if he is a Pygmy, a case unique in Black Africa where the social situation is generally hereditary. The queen-mother, very influential at the court, is sacrificed as soon as she has some gray hair: new traces of African vitalism.

Thus there were in Africa at least two types of kings:

> the warrior king, riding the war horse, despising manual labor, and reigning over a closed, casted society;
>
> the artisan king, the blacksmith in particular, having no reason to devalue manual labor and reigning over a hardworking, merchant, noncasted society, open to development.

Figures 32 and 33 show that this latter society is much more extensive than the former. In other words, the casted blacksmith of the Sahelian district is the authentic prince of the vast equatorial forest region, among the Mayombe, the Bayaka, the Bambala, the Badinga, the Balesa, the Basoko, the Baholoholo, the Balamba, the Akela, the Mongo, the Wanande, and the Basonge.[17] Even in the societies of the Sahelian type, the legacy of his Promethean function (the hero who stole the secret from the gods for the good of humanity) before the climatic change and the introduction

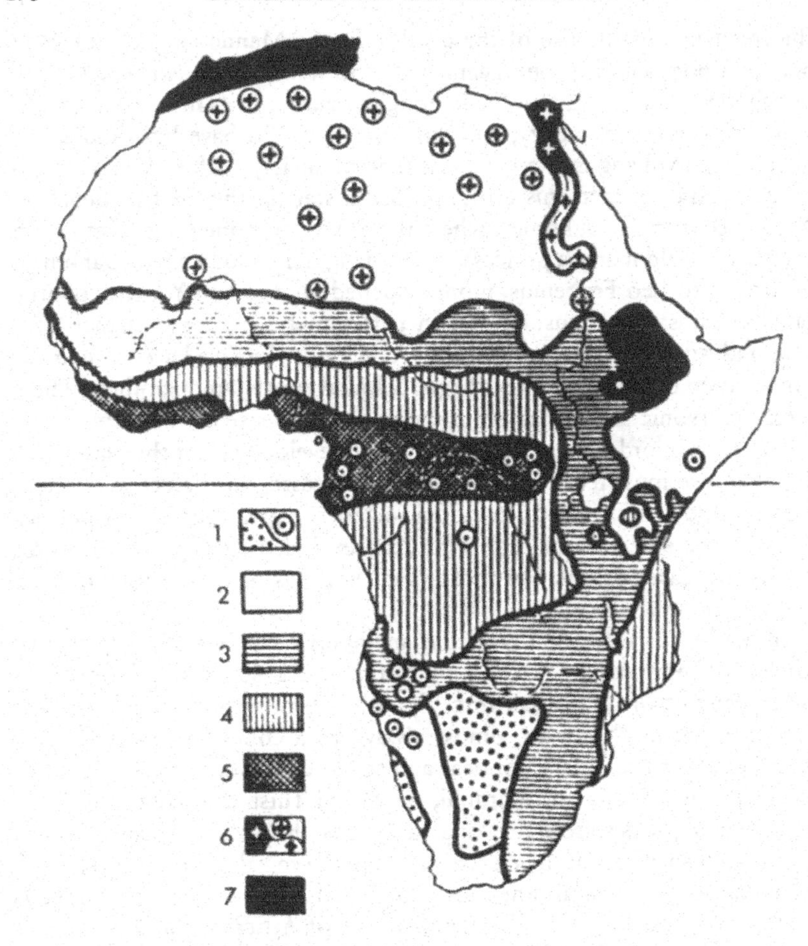

Figure 32: Economic Systems in Africa:
Zone 1 Gatherers
Zone 2 Nomad shepherds practicing cattle raising
Zone 3 Farming during the rainy season with cattle raising
Zone 4 Farming during the rainy season without cattle raising
Zone 5 Permanent farming
Zone 6 Oasis farming with artificial irrigation
Zone 7 Plow farming

By comparing this map to the next one, one realizes that the forest zone without cattle raising and, particularly, without horses is the noncasted zone, where the taboo of the blacksmith not only does not exist, but where he often is a part of the nobility and can become king; whereas the zone of the Sahel, that of the horsemen of the conquering empires, is the zone of the castes. (Hermann Baumann and D. Westermann, *Les Peuples et les Civilisations de l'Afrique*, Paris: Payot, 1948, fig. 24)

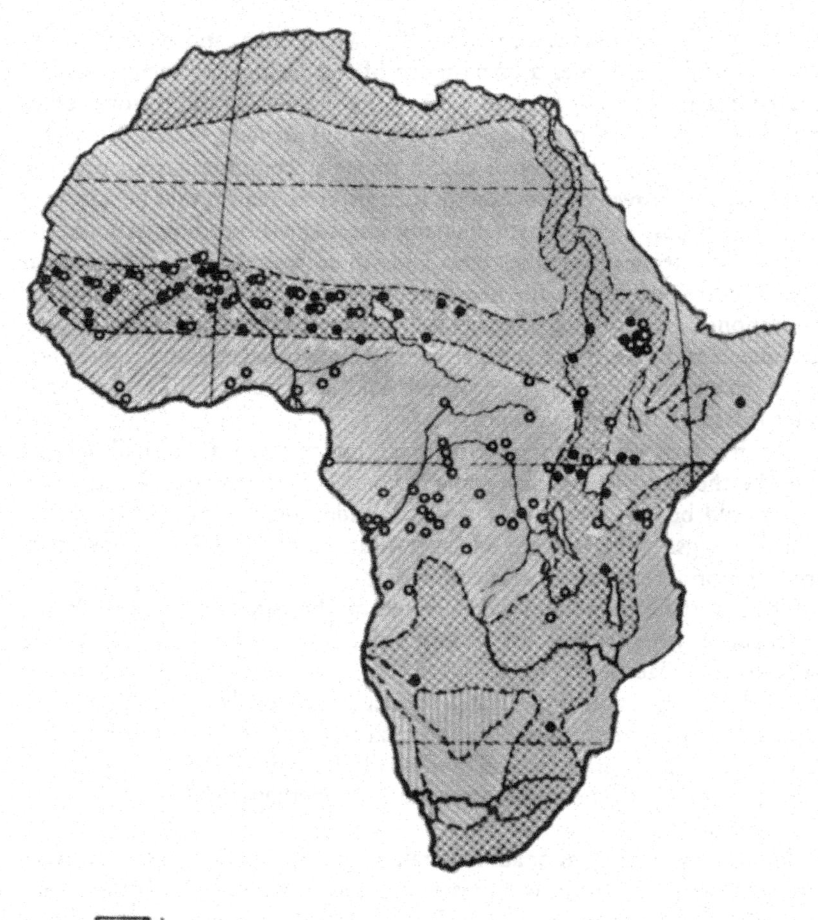

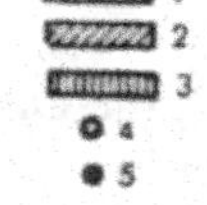

Figure 33:
1 Pastures, cattle raising
2 Agriculture
3 Hunting
4 Respect for the blacksmith
5 Contempt for the blacksmith

Relationships between the dominant economy of a region or of a given group and the attitude of that group toward the blacksmith. (Pierre Clément, "Le forgeron en Afrique Noire," in *Revue de Géographie humaine et d'Ethnologie*, no. 2, April–June 1948, p. 51) of the war horse, subsisted; thus in that whole area, and particularly in Mali, there is sometimes a coexistence of the feelings of ancient respect and of recent contempt for him. One of the superstructural reasons sometimes given, in order to try to justify a scornful attitude, is that the blacksmith had violated, in days of old, a divine prohibition, by sharing the gods' secrets. However, it is exactly for this same reason that he can be a king in the forest societies, which do not know cattle breeding, as possessor of the most technological secrets. Thus there would be a technological royalty corresponding to the noncasted societies and a war-horse royalty corresponding to the casted societies. In this way, if a Sahelian prince was accompanied by his blacksmith servant to Equatorial Africa, upon arrival the roles would be reversed; he would yield his saddle to his servant until their return to their native land.

The relativity of our social structures, thus put forward, could help us free the theoretical bases for going beyond our casted societies, a move that would be irreversible only if it is founded on the knowledge of the why of things. Is that not the social revolution, or, in any case, one of its most important aspects in our countries?

The fact that many states were created on the banks of rivers favorable to irrigation works argues for an origin due to the great works (loop and delta of the Niger River, etc.).

On the other hand, those states founded on the edge of a desert have always suffered its devastating and sterilizing effects: they had to resist, to disappear, or to migrate, which is what the legends of the destruction of Ghana teach us.[18] Therefore, some authors, perhaps mistakenly, discard this possibility.

Among the ministerial or administrative functions in Songhai, there were those of the *Lari-Farma*, or minister of water resources; the *Dao-Farma*, or minister of forestry; the *Guimi-Koï*, or chief of boats or canoes, functions that all attest to the importance attached to rural hydraulics.

Similarly, the functions of *Yobu-Koï* (chief of the market); the *Ouassei Farma*, or minister of property; the *Korei-Farma*, or minister in charge of the white minorities living in the country[19] show that we are dealing with a type of economy or commerce already much developed.

In *L'Afrique noire précoloniale*, we also described the level of the productive forces for the whole neo-Sudanese area, meaning the degree of technical progress that determines the new relations of production.

The model of the Egyptian AMP state was thus adopted from the Ancient Empire onward, the period of the pyramids, almost everywhere in the rest of Black Africa. But it is perhaps in the neo-Sudanese zone and in the region of the Upper Nile that one finds a quasi-complete replica of Egyptian civilization:

1. Same type of royalty with the surviving of names, titles, and administrative functions.

2. Same state model
3. Same social structure in castes[20]
4. Caste of griots in particular
5. Same architecture[21]
6. Almost the same language, in the case of Wolof, a Senegalese language related to the Serer, the Diola, and the Peul languages.[22]

While the model of the most organized Black state has been exported almost everywhere in the world, particularly around the Mediterranean basin, and this from the megalithic epoch[23] onward, some misinformed ideologues did not hesitate to wonder if all models of the Black African state were not of foreign import. Authors were asking themselves whether all African states had not been formed at the level of the contact zones—thus alluding to Ghana's proximity to the desert—whether it was not with the help of commerce with the outside, in this case the Mediterranean, that this state was born? Finally, they answered their own question negatively, by considering the example of the Mossi state, to which we could add that of Benin, which lie outside all of the central road systems.

The analysis of the Cayorian constitution contained in the archival document below shows that the AMP state model of Black Africa, with its flaws and its peculiarities, is a purely indigenous creation related only to Pharaonic Egypt.

Still one must possess a model before exporting it, and this basic condition, in the present case, is not met by the countries that could be exporters of these institutions.

I pointed out in February 1975 in Fez, at the many receptions organized in honor of the UNESCO delegation, that among the singers and the musicians, there were authentic sherifs (descendants of Muhammad), and of the highest rank—the president of the Supreme Court, a member of the royal family, a very close relative of his majesty, King Hassan II—and each time they would join, voluntarily and spontaneously, the group of musicians and play the role of orchestra conductor with simplicity and joviality.

During the reception given by the president of the Chamber of Craftsmen, the lead singer was a sherif.

Consequently, Arab society in general and the Moroccan one in particular, unfamiliar with the defects of the Senegalese society, did not bequeath the griots' caste to it, as some have seen fit to postulate.

DESIGNATION OF THE NEW DAMEL

The Council of the Crown, having the authority to "elect" or to designate the new Damel, was composed as follows:

The Lamane Diamatil The Botal ub Ndiob	Representatives of the free men, with or without caste, of *gor, gér, or ñéño*
The Badié Gateigne The Eliman of MBalle The Serigne of the village of Kab	Representatives of the Muslim clergy
The Diawerigne MBoul Gallo The Diaraf Bunt Ker	Representatives of the Tieddos and of the crown's prisoners

The Council was called and presided over by the Diawerigne MBoul Diambur, hereditary representative of the free men.

The Damel was chosen from among the pretenders to the throne of the seven dynasties of Cayor:

1. Ouagadou = 1 Damel totaling 30 years' reign
2. Muyôy = 5 Damels totaling 47 years' + one day's reign
3. Sogno = 3 Damels totaling 99 years' reign
4. Gelwar = 2 Damels totaling 29 years' reign
5. Dorobé = 5 Damels totaling 15 years' + 7 months' + 10 days' reign
6. Beye = 1 Damel totaling 6 years' reign
7. Guedj = 13 Damels totaling 221 years' + 6 months' reign

As a reminder, the names of two families are added to this list, Djauje, or Diose, and Tejek, who have each provided one Damel; respectively: Mafaly Coumba Ndama, tenth Damel, one day of reign, and Khaly Ndiaye Sall, eleventh Damel, seven days of reign; therefore these two families would not be considered as dynasties.

The Council of the Crown took its task very seriously; thus the discussions were long and laborious before the nomination of the Damel; rights to the throne, in other words the degree of legitimacy of each candidate, individual virtues, all the facts that had to be taken into account in choosing the prince, were carefully examined. The mother had to be a "princess of the royal race." The Damel had to be chosen from among the three following categories of princes: Diambor, chief of the nobles; Boumi, viceroy; Bédienne.

The system thus appears as a specific type of constitutional monarchy.

The Damel "elect," or the one chosen by the Council of the Crown, is enthroned by the hereditary representative of the people, the Diawerigne MBoul Diambur. For this occasion, a mound of sand about one meter high is erected. The Damel sits on it; the Diawerigne MBoul then offers him solemnly a vase containing the seeds of all Cayor's plants, a symbolic offering that has old agrarian origins, as in Egypt where the Pharaoh was also the first agriculturist, and as such, had to inaugurate the farm work so that nature would be fertile.

Then the Diawerigne puts the ancestral crown on the Damel's head; this crown is a turban "adorned" with scarlet and with golden and silver amulets, and it contains other amulets for the mystical protection of the king. He then addresses the king with these words: "Hail Damel. You must govern us with wisdom and safeguard the independence of your country." The Damel sits there for some time in order to be seen by the people; then on Diawerigne MBoul Gallo's orders, certain strong men lift him onto an open palanquin and take him to a sacred forest, outside of the capital city, where he will dwell for eight days. Only upon his return will he be able to reign.

In Ghana also, the ritual of enthronement includes a stay in the sacred woods.

The Damel distributes traditional, generous gifts in line with the different social classes; he must give ten units of everything to those who elected him, including horses, captives, etc.

He then appoints the dignitaries or, more precisely, he swears them in, because all these functions are hereditary; he collects a fee attached to each function on this occasion; and here, in the social sense, it is the picture of true feudality that imposes and reinforces itself as one goes through the three lists of the hereditary functions.

First he names the *Fara Seuf*, commander of the royal elite guard, who in turn proposes the other names to the king.

All the kingdom's princes are guarded by their slaves, in whom they put more trust than in their peers; this explains the improvement in the conditions of the princes' or the crown's prisoners. Those who are in charge of the princes' security deserve not to be annoyed too much. They are the ones who terrorize, by their frequent inspection of the princes' domains, the poor and free peasants, the Badolo; we fear these captives, they say, because "they have the ear of the princes." This is an expression that could well have been inherited from Egypt.[24]

Only the *Fara Seuf* or *Diaraf Seuf* and the *Diawerigne MBoul Diambur* can freely enter the Damel's home.

Then comes the *Diaraf Bunt Keur*, who is the superintendent of the royal court, and as such, is in charge of guarding the main gate, as opposed to the *Diaraf pôt*, who guards the secret back door, reserved for secret agents and other personalities whose comings and goings must be kept from the general public.

The *Diaraf Ndiambur*, the *Diaraf Ramane*, and the *Diaraf Ngourane* are in charge of collecting contributions and paying some of the Damel's expenses.

Following the enthronement of the Damel, the free men were expected to furnish, for one year, the palace's food and an ox a day. Each village of the kingdom, in turn, made the same contribution, and also sent fifteen young men and fifteen young women in order to serve at the court.

Each village was administered by its chief, who, at times, acted as the conciliatory magistrate; the important matters were brought before the Diaraf for his judgment. If the parties did not agree, the provincial chief convened a seven-member council to deal with the issue. The more serious matters that called into question the integrity of the provincial chiefs were judged by the Damel, who summoned the high council, composed of Diawerigne MBoul Diambour (the president), Botal ub NDiobe, Lamane Diamatil, Lamane Palmèv, Badiè Gateigne, Bourgade Gnollé, Djaraf Khandane, Bessigue de Saté, and the Fara Seuf representing the Damel. Once judgment was rendered, the president instructed the Fara Seuf to transmit it to the Damel for execution.

The institution of the *cadi* in the Cayor did not begin until the Lat Dior's conversion to Islam.

The death of the Damel is kept secret for eight days, the time necessary for his burial in the greatest secrecy in order to prevent pretenders to the throne, from rival dynasties, from conducting any magical practices on the Damel's remains. According to some, a talisman made from the shoulder blade of the deceased Damel would destroy his dynasty forever, or in any case would guarantee his throne to the prince who would have the talisman made for him by an expert in the science of the occult.

The funeral ceremonies are held by displaying a clothed mannequin who is buried conspicuously in order to deceive the rivals.

I
DIGNITARIES CHOSEN FROM THE CLASS OF THE PRINCES OF THE BLOOD AND THE KINGS' SONS AND THE PRINCESSES

Diamboor	Prince of the blood, in command of Diadj, Khamenane, NGagne, and the different villages of Diander.
Bédienne	Was chosen by the Damel from among the princes of the blood who had rights to the throne. He commanded the Mbandé, Ndaldagou, Mbédiène, Selko.
Boumi NGourane	Was chosen by the Damel from among the princes of the blood who had rights to the throne. He commanded Rètè country, the Ngouyou, the Bakaya.
Beudj NDenère	
Beur Get	In order to be appointed Beur Get one had to be the son of a princess of the blood and a Diambour. He commanded a part of the Get.
Diawerigne NDjinguène	Was a prince of the blood with full rights to the throne, but who had lost all chances of being elected. He commanded Keur Mandoubé Khary country, that of Coki Kadde, Ndialba, Ndigne, Tiolane, Ndiarga Mbakol, Keur Matar Ndague, Keur Khali Ngone, Ndikne, Gueidj (all these countries are in the Mbakol).

Thiéme	Was directly appointed by the Damel and commanded Gandiole country. He had the right to steal from everybody.
Diawar	Commanded Guemboul (southeast of the Mbakol). Belgor Commanded the Belgor.
Gantakhé	Was chief of the Niayes around Mboro.
Thialaw Dembagnane	
Dialiguey	
NDienguenne	
MBeudj Toubé	Was named by the Damel. He commanded the Toubé and the population of the country between Toubé and Ker.
Barlaffe	
Gankale	The Gankale had to be the son of a Damel or a Beur Guet; his mother could even be a prisoner. He commanded Ouarakh country.
Guemboul	Commanded Guemboul (southeast of the Mbakol).
Fara Ndoute	Was chosen by the Damel from among the princes of the blood on either their mother's or their father's side, meaning that they had no right to the throne. He commanded the Serer country of the Ndoute.
Beudj Solo	
Bérine	Notable of the country, commanded the Mbérine.
Beur Eum Halle	
Beudj Nar	
Guoune	
Dianéka	
Beur Khoupaye (or Beur)	Was the chief of the Niayes of Gelkouye.
Diarno Dieng	
Lamane Massar	
Bour Andale	Commanded the Andal.
Beur Ngaye	
Beurlape	
Fara Ngnollé	
Linguère (woman)	
Awa (woman)	
Dié-Soughère (woman)	Princess of the blood (father and mother); commanded the Niakhen, Amb, Soa, Ndiemel, and Mber (Poular country).
Dié-Mekhé (woman)	
Dié-Khandane (woman)	
Dié-Khanté (woman)	
Dié-Sen (woman)	
Dié-Botolo (woman)	
Dié-Mboursino (woman)	

We see that noble women, under the title "die," also administered districts.

II
DIGNITARIES CHOSEN FROM THE CLASS OF FREE MEN AND MARABOUTS CASTED AND NONCASTED MEN

Diawerigne MBoul Ndiambour	The DiaoudineMBoul[25] was one of the greatest chiefs of Cayor; he is the one who summoned the free men of the country in order to elect the Damel. He commanded the Sab, Robnane, and Diakoul countries, the Touhbé, Ndat, the Dembagniane land, the Ndioulki, Ndabbé, Médheyé, Ndande, Ndiakher, Ga NDiole, Khoupaye, Kabbe. He is the one who led free men to war.
Lamane Ndande	
Lamane Diamatil	Was appointed by the Damel, on the Diaoudine Mboul's recommendation. He commanded Diamatil country.
Baraloupe NDiobe	Commanded the Ndiokb (between the Mboul and Ndioulki).
Batié Gateigne	
Lamane Palèle	
Diawarigne MBoul Mekhé	
Diarno MBaouar	
Dieleuck	
Tibar	
Sérigne Gueidj	
Sérigne Diob	Commanded the Ndiob.
Sérigne Kandji	
Sérigne Merina	
Sérigne Mérina Yocoum Babu	Commanded Mérina Yocoum Babu country (between the Guignéne and the Guet) where dwelled the Babu Moors of Cayor. He had under his command Sérigne Diouar, who lived in Mérina Yocoum Babou and who replaced him.
Sérigne Seck	
Sérigne NGuidiane	Commanded the Guiguédiane (southwest of the Guet).
Sérigne Mbolakhe	
Sérigne Ndob	Commanded the Ndob (southwest of the Ndiob).
Sérigne Dambligouye	
Sérigne Pire Goureye	
Sérigne Walalane	Free Tiédo; commanded the Walalane country (between the Guet and the Baol).
Sérigne Varé	
Sérigne NGagnaka	Commanded Gagnakh country (Ndiambour). He was independent from the Diaraf Ndiambour.

Sérigne NDiang
Diarno NDiasse
Lamane Gale
Lamane Guèye
Lamane Votoffo
Lamane Thiothiou
Lamane Loyène
Lamane Taby

III
DIGNITARIES CHOSEN FROM THE CLASS OF THE CROWN'S PRISONERS

Diawerigne MBoul Gallo	There were two Diaoudine Mboul. The Diaoudine Mboul of the free men (the one we just mentioned) and the one of the prisoners. The latter led the "Diam Gallo" to war, after Fara Seuf. Within the Crown, he followed the orders of the free men's Diaoudine Mboul.
Fara Seuf	Was a "Diam Gallo." He was the commander-in-chief of the "Diam Gallo" of the whole country, and during wartime had under his command the prisoners' Diaoudine Mboul. He had Djeraf Seuf directly under him.
Djaraff Bountou-Keur	Was directly appointed by the Damel. He commanded the countries of Tabbi, Nianedoul, Pire, Yandounane, Mbaba, Keur Ndiobo Binta, Sin or Damécane, Diari, Sirale, Diokoul (behind Tabbi, Khayeguenen, Gadou Kébé, Diémoul).
Diawereigne Khatta	
Djaraff Thiaye	Was a "Diam Gallo" chosen by the Damel; he commanded the Keur Bi Ndao, Mbidjem, Tiaye.
Diawerigne Mékhé	
Djaraff MDiambour	Was a "Diam Gallo." He resided at Geoul and commanded the Diambour with the exception of some small regions.
Fara Bir Keur	Was chosen by the Damel from among his own prisoners. He was his personal envoy, who carried his orders to all the provinces and made sure they were carried out. He collected the taxes and was in charge of listening to the people who brought complaints to the sovereign.
Djaraff Get	"Diam Gallo," appointed by the Damel. Commanded the other part of the Get.
Djaraff MBaouar	Commanded the Mbaouar and collected taxes for the Diambor, who was a prince of the blood with rights to the throne.
Dieguédj	Was chosen by the Damel from among the "Diam Gallo." He commanded the Serer country of Dièguène, Mbao, Deen-y-Dak, Gorom, Bargny, Ber or Tiélane (half Serer, half Lebu), of Rap, Deni Biram Dao, Kounoune Niakoul.

Fara Laobé	Was a "Diam Gallo" who was in command of all of the country's Laobe.
Fara NDérioute	
Fara NDiafougne	
Fara Gnakhibe	
Djaraff Mékhé	Commanded the Niayes of Tiendi and of Touffagne.
Djaraff Bour	
Diawerigne NGuiguis	Was the Damel's cup-bearer. He was a "Diam Gallo."
Diawerigne Khandane	Was directly appointed by the Damel, and commanded the Tialkhêan, Nguéyguèye, Keur Ndianga-Mbaye, Ndekou, the country of the Diombos.
Diawerigne MBousine	
Diawerigne Soughère	
Diawerigne Kandié	
Diawerigne NDiahene	
Djaraff Khandane	
Djaraff Soughère	
Djaraff Kautiè	
Djaraff MBoursine	

The last Damel (king) of Cayor, Lat Dior Diop, died at Dekele in 1886.

The total reign of the Damels, according to tradition, as the above-cited documents show, was 455 years. If this is correct, the origin of the kingdom would date back to around 1886 − 455 = 1431, in other words, about twenty-four years before Cadamosto moved to Cayor (1455).[26] This journey would have occurred under the reign of Damel Amari Ngone Fall.

Thus the founder of the Damels's kingship, Amari Ngone Fall, who came from Ouagadou (in Ghana?), reigned for thirty years, from 1431 to 1461. His successor, Masamba Tako, founder of the Muyoy dynasty, reigned for twenty-seven years, from 1461 to 1488, and would have been a contemporary of Sunni Ali, whose reign began around 1464–65; then Makhouredia Kouly, founder of the Sogno dynasty, would have reigned for thirty-six years, from 1488 to 1525, etc.

Seen from the outside, the precolonial African institutions were fine in principle, but the way they operated was often defective.

If the workers and the slaves are "represented" in the Council of the Crown, their representatives were not tribunes from the masses, nor leaders who took to heart the needs of a well-defined stratum of the people, of a class. They did not gather the masses to hear their complaints before they would sit in judgment. Rather, they became pseudo-princes reigning over entire regions, cut off from their original social milieu.

NOTE I

Concerning the ceremony of the "sed" or of the regeneration of the king, Charles G. Seligman writes:

> That the sed was associated in proto-dynastic times with the marriage of the princess, the "royal child," who brought with her the crown of Egypt, seems certain; that the ceremony, at any rate in later times, had become a reinvestiture ceremony is also clear.[27]

This passage also shows that the Egyptian matriarchy was evident during the protodynastic epoch. According to Flinders Petrie, in that epoch, only women were landowners.[28]

Seligman reports that the act of putting to death the "divine kings" existed among the Shilluk and the Dinka of the Upper Nile, as well as among numerous other tribes of all the regions of East, West, South, and Central Africa, too many to enumerate here.[29] He concludes "that Egyptian influence did in fact penetrate to the very heart of Negro Africa."

Seligman continues: "Turning now to West Africa, we find Divine Kings in their typical form in a group of tribes (Jukun, etc.) with sun-worships, and a ceremony corresponding to sed."[30]

He also cites the Nuer, who present a great many traits in common with the Wolof of Senegal. In fact, their true name is not Nuer, but Naas or Nahas, which is the term by which the Egyptians designated the Nubians and other Blacks of Africa (singular: Nahas; plural: Nahasiou).

In the tombs of the Vth Dynasty, 2500 B.C., one finds representations of oxen with artificially deformed horns, as practiced by the present-day Nuer.[31]

Kerma civilization, which was already in existence during the VIth Dynasty (Reisner's excavations) and which persisted until the XXth Dynasty, presents traits common to the protohistoric civilization of the Tumuli of Senegal and of ancient Ghana: collective burial in a "royal" grave. The Nuer live next to a tribe called the Golo: this term means monkey in Wolof, and could explain the loss of the Egyptian root *gef*; such pejorative usage of proper names among neighboring tribes occurs frequently.

Lastly, Senegalese proper names still keep their meaning in the Upper Nile region, which they have completely lost in Wolof country: *Nyang* = cayman, in Nuer language: *Dieng* = rain in Dinka language, etc. Some are, in the Upper Nile regions, compound names, which we can barely detect today in Wolof country. So many facts show their true Nilotic origin. Examples:

NUER		WOLOF
Gaa-jok	→	*Gaajo* (Tukulor)
Gaa-war	→	*Gawar* (?)
Jaa-logh	→	*Jallo*
Caa-Nath / *Caa-Naas*	→	would explain *ca-Ndela* → Tia-Ndella
Anuak	→	Anu=protohistoric tribe (Egypt)
Nyajaani	→	*Njaajaan* (?) (p. 278)
Ladjor	→	*Latjor* (p. 210)
Jaanyen	→	*Nâani*?[32]

Thus there are still today, in Nuer country, Njaajaans, and Ladjors; a certain Ladjor man is reported to have led an expedition to the East.

An expedition to the Upper Nile would shed some unexpected light on the famous tradition of the Njaajaan Njaay. If it were not for what we know about the antiquity of these names in the Upper Nile region, we would have asserted that these were survivors of the Marchand mission's column to Fashoda.

There was therefore, at a relatively recent period, a migration from east to west originating from the Upper Nile, which came to superimpose itself in the West African Sudano-Senegalese region on a more ancient north-south migration, whose first waves arrived around 7000 B.C., with the beginning of the drying up of the Sahara. The last ones, during the protohistoric epoch, might have consisted of the proto-Wangara of the Mande language, whereas the tribes coming from the east brought the neo-Bantu languages.

Finally, let us interpret a Senegalese oral tradition to which no attention has ever been paid, and which, in our opinion, would militate for a Carthaginian presence in antiquity on the Senegalese shores: this would be a strong confirmation of Hanno's expedition.

It is said that Barka was Ndiadjan Ndiaye's brother and that his mother, Farimata Sall, Lam Toro's daughter, was of the Peul race of the Belianke. It is from his name, Barka, that came the word "Barka," or "Barak," designating the king of Walo, a region of the Senegal River's estuary, which the Carthaginians sailed (according to the very controversial interpretation of some Roman historical documents) to Bambuk, near Kaarta. There is in this story a constellation of Carthaginian names that may not be a matter of chance; but only well-conducted excavations all along the Senegal River up to the Kaarta country could one day confirm this hypothesis, with the discovery of characteristically Punic objects.

In fact, Barka is not of Arabic origin; it is Carthaginian and it designates the royalty there where the Carthaginians had landed, if they ever came to Senegal. Belianke is a compound term which, in the Peul or even the Soninke languages, breaks down as follows: Bel + nke = the men of Bel or Bal (Punic god). And we know that Bal is still today a proper name of the Tukulors, the ethnic group that lives in the river region above.

Kaarta is practically the exact term that the Carthaginians used to designate their town, which the Romans called *Carthago*, or Carthage.

According to the controversial text of Hanno's long and complicated journey, the Carthaginians supposedly left a colony (sixty persons or thirty couples) on Cerne Island, which is a strip of land near the Senegal River's estuary. The term Belianke, formed in the same manner as Soninke, Malinke, Foutanke, etc., necessarily precedes Islam and goes back to the sixth century B.C. during the time when the cult of Baal was still in force.

The oral tradition almost always conceals part of the truth, but it is very difficult to place it correctly in its chronological context: a story from *Tarikh es-Sudan* is attributed today to contemporaries in Senegal. It concerns a religious personage who, having arrived late at Mecca for the pilgrimage, is supposed to have seen the Kaaba gates open by themselves miraculously before him, after he had recited a verse from the Koran and touched the portal.

It will be noticed that it is Seligman, the inventor of the Hamitic theory, which we attacked in *Nations nègres et culture*, who detects the Egyptian influence all over Black Africa; he even indicates the areas of penetration: the White Nile all the way to the Congo, the Blue Nile and the coastal regions of North Africa all the way to Senegal, passing through Mauritania. But the idea of a Black Egypt was alien to him; it was to escape from this that he invented Hamitism.

NOTE II "THE SENTENCE OF THE CANNIBALS"

or the ascent of King Unas in order to attain his *ka(w)*, in heaven.

The sky is heavy with clouds
Stars are hidden
The celestial vault quakes
The bones of the earth tremble
All movement is stopped,
Because they have seen king Unas
Like a mighty and shining god,
Who lives off his fathers
And feeds upon his mother
King Unas is well provided for,
He has incorporated their force.
Whomever he finds in his path,
He devours piece by piece,

He first bit into the backbone
Of his victim, as he had wanted it,
He tore out the heart of the Gods.
King Unas feeds upon the livers of the Gods
That contain wisdom.
His high rank will never be removed from him
For he has swallowed the power of each God
It is King Unas who eats men
And lives off the Gods,
Who has messengers
And gives orders.
They seize men by the tip of the skull for him.
Head raised, the serpent guards them for him.
He who is enthroned red with blood ties them up for him.
Khonsu, who bleeds the lords,
Cuts their throats for King Unas.
And slaughters them for him,
The God of the wine presses cuts them for King Unas
And has them cooked on the hearth for his evening meal.
It is King Unas,
Who has incorporated their magical powers
And has swallowed their strength
The great ones among them are for his breakfast
The average ones for his dinner
And the least among them for his supper.
He fuels his fireplace with old men and women.
The stars of the night sky stir the fire
Where the thighs of his ancestors cook in the caldrons
The Gods serve King Unas.[33]

Unas is the last king of the Vth Dynasty. This text is the most ancient written document that makes the study of vitalistic practices possible that would lead to the myth of the man-eating sorcerer, in today's Black Africa. They are to be compared with the Osirian rites (see p. 312) and with the Christian Eucharist.

13

CRITICAL REVIEW OF THE LATEST THESES ON THE AMP[1]

The various approaches to the AMP, in the collective work cited below, are remarkable in many ways, but the authors all seem to have missed the essential point: in fact, in order to demonstrate the dynamism of the Western or slave societies as opposed to the stagnation of the AMP societies, whose internal force was not strong enough to develop their fundamental contradiction to its dissolution, an edifying method would have been preferable. A more or less exhaustive description of the AMP is not enough. Here, the comparative method is a must; whatever is comparable should be compared.

By comparing the sociopolitical evolution of a simple city (city-state) to that of a territorial state, grouping hundreds or even thousands of towns, the fundamental factor, i.e., the difference between the contexts, is neglected from the very start, without realizing it. It is not difficult to see what is wrong with such an attitude; because of the great difference in scale, the realities studied are no longer of the same nature.

The ancient city had an ephemeral, sociopolitical form, essentially non-viable, which disappeared after a brief existence of just four centuries, and was replaced by the Roman state, Asiatic in exterior form and dimension.

The Roman state inherited the cumulative effect of the slave system of the ancient city; it gave its classical legal forms to private property, to the merchant monetary economy, and to private slavery.

Thus, all of the conditions theoretically predicted were present, so that revolutionary transformations could take place starting from endogenous factors. However, for half a millennium the revolution did not take place.

As soon as the state takes the Asiatic form, whatever the tenor of its institutions, revolution becomes impossible, as in the other authentic AMP states. This general law has no exceptions from the beginning of history, 3300 B.C., in Egypt, up to modern times, in the seventeenth century, in Holland and in England.

This total failure of revolution in antiquity, from the moment that the state takes on the Asiatic form, obliges us to reevaluate the relative importance of the factors in the theory of revolutions.

Yet, none of the authors cited below has formulated the problem in such clear terms; they were not moved by the failure of the Roman revolution that continued for five hundred years, despite the existence of the most ferocious slave system that man has ever invented. They have thrown a discreet veil over the Roman stagnation instead of comparing it to the "stagnation" of the AMP states, in order to try to develop the sociology of revolutions on more objective, more scientific, and less ethnocentric foundations. On the way they forgot the essential purpose of their theories: to show in what way a slave society of the Roman type was more revolutionary than the AMP societies, and then to explain the fundamental contradiction of Roman society; namely, why antiquity's most dynamic society, and its most revolutionary one because it was a slave society, did not make revolution. Why were all the attempts at revolt easily suppressed as soon as the society adopted the Asiatic model?

It is important to point out the specific traits of the AMP states, which allow them to constantly dominate the revolutionary situations that they have bequeathed to the modern states. For it must also be asked why it is more and more difficult to make revolution in the contemporary states, all of which have the AMP's form and structure.

The *size* of the territory comprising several cities, even thousands, the *complexity* of the state machinery and the centers of decision making are two traits common to the AMP states and the present states, which allow them to adapt to varied and perilous situations.

The idea of an AMP state, without revolution, without social convulsion, is an error to which theory has accustomed us. Ion Banu shows that peasant revolt was quasi-endemic in China,[2] and that in Egypt the decay of the ideological superstructure from the Ancient Empire onward, as imposing as it was, is reflected in the dialogue of a desperate man with his soul, where it is said that "the gods are interested only in the rich; they let evil go unpunished, therefore sacrifices are of no use."

In the literary text "Truth and Lie," dated from the New Empire, the man who is stripped of his property has to take the law into his own hands without relying on judges, king, or gods. The adventure of Horus and Seth (New Empire) deals with the problem of justice in the state.[3]

Elsewhere, in the legend of "Horus of Behutet," he promises the Pharaoh that he will be by his side in case of rebellion.[4] Consequently, at a very early stage, the divine order and the cosmic order ceased to be reunited, to be one with the state, in the mind of the exploited and insurgent people.

The history of all the AMP states is therefore marked by restrained and in the end subdued revolts. Thus, it is important to study the different ways state intervention was used to repress the discontent and to reestablish order, if not peace, every time: this also is a trait common among the modern states. Economic intervention is a common means by which modern states reestablish social harmony, one completely alien to the feudal and slave states, founded on private production. The cumulative process, for the increase of production, by the very fact of its collective base and the free nature of labor, is infinitely more important than the private production, quantitatively mediocre, of the feudal and slave states, which *a priori* allows no increase, no less any technical progress: it would be nonsense to speak of a cumulative increase of the production in Sparta, which is still the most confirmed slave state of all time.

The notions of the capacity for the broadening of production in the AMP states and in the slave states have to be reviewed on a more objective basis.

Let us add that the formulation of the fundamental contradiction of the AMP states is erroneous and ethnocentric: namely "exploitation of a tribal communal property on a class basis." In fact, it is not scientific to confuse, in the same definition, the notion of property during the protohistoric epoch of the Hawk and the Crocodile Clans with the idea that the Egyptians of Ramses II's epoch had about collective ownership of the land, after 2,500 years of an integrated national life, among the people who presented the strongest cohesion in the history of antiquity. A qualitative leap has taken place, which is not taken into account in the analyses, when there is a transition from tribe to nation.

The AMP state is born every time that tribes integrate to become a nation, in order to survive, by taking up a challenge of nature, thanks to a rational organization and a division of labor. Hence, the concepts characterizing the original situation become inappropriate when it is a question of analyzing national institutions. It is also the necessity of survival for the whole community that explains the relative speed with which national unity is accomplished in such a precocious manner, in order to allow the creation of a territorial state bringing together all of the old nomes (tribal territory), out of which thousands of cities will spring up where individuals live completely cut off from the umbilical cord of their former tribes, whose memory they may even forget.

Property is thus just collective, but it is no longer tribal, for those who work on it are simply individuals who can come from any area of the country.

The AMP state, like the modern states, combines public and private interests on a national, not a tribal, basis, in order to blunt the tip of the revolutionary spirit, and this is particularly true for Pharaonic Egypt. But the AMP state, or its administrative machinery, is not to be confused with its leadership class, as has been postulated: the terrible practice of the king actually being put to death, so widespread in Black Africa (and probably in protohistoric Egypt), shows that early on the Africans made a very clear distinction between the state, abstract concept of the public entity, and its servants, to such an extent that the most eminent of them, the king himself, was sacrificed to this state, generally every eight years.

Thus, traditional royalty was conceived as a priesthood that permitted one to be useful to the community, without having the time to serve personal ambitions. Even today, eight years represent the duration of two presidential terms in the United States.

In order for the gods to lavish gifts and for nature to be fertile, the king has to be the legitimate man for the throne, just long enough to ensure the perpetuity of the state: of course, here and there, difficulties were circumvented, but this does not change anything in the essence of the AMP state, even if its form becomes monarchial.

All these various "feedbacks," which often caused a shortage of candidates for the royalty in Black Africa, testify to the perfectly clear concept of the state that the Africans had: the state, born out of the group's need to survive, precedes class antagonism; class opposition presupposes an embryo of state power, even if only tribal, that forces individuals to obey. Therefore, Engels's views on this subject are not very accurate. Moreover, it could be said that a simultaneity exists, that a dialectic bond exists between the exploitation of man by man and the appearance of the state, if only in embryonic form, which would exclude any notion of the anteriority of one form with regard to the other.

Consequently, instead of the absence of revolution, it brews all the time in the countryside and at the city gates, in the AMP states, from China to Egypt, passing through India and western Asia, and if it is suppressed each time, it is thanks to the ultrasophisticated interventionist machinery that has allowed the prevention of revolutions, a permanent concern of kings, to be elevated to a Machiavellian level prematurely, as in Kautilya's India in the sixth century B.C.

This interventionism, in relation to social unrest, is one of the heaviest legacies that the AMP state has bequeathed to the modern state, and one which explains the enormous difficulties that the world revolutionary process encounters today in different countries.

MAURICE GODELIER

The Notion of the "Asiatic Mode of Production" and the Marxist Schema of the Evolution of Societies[5]

Maurice Godelier's text is brilliant, rich, well documented, and reflects a great breadth of view in its analysis, but it does not deal with the one topic mentioned above, which seems fundamental to us: why did Rome, Imperial Rome, behave so pitifully vis-à-vis the revolution, as a stagnant AMP society would, for half a millennium? A theoretician of the caliber of Godelier should not have dodged such a difficulty, of which he could not have been unaware. All the necessary theoretical conditions, apparently sufficient for triggering the revolutionary process, were present, but Rome would meet the fate of the AMP societies, based on the fact alone that she adopted their framework, with all of its resulting implications.

Thus the author's text is mainly descriptive. He recalls the metamorphoses of the notion of the AMP in Marxist literature, then sums up the successive phases of evolution of the societies as they are envisaged in historical materialism:

Primitive community
AMP (Asiatic mode of production)
Ancient, Germanic, feudal, then capitalistic modes of production

Concerning the AMP, he deems that "commerce is here not the expression of a merchant production inside the communities' life, but the transformation of the surplus in merchandise. . . . The merchant appears as a state official" (*op. cit.*, p. 65). This idea that they wished to create of commerce in the AMP societies is completely erroneous and calls for revision: it is applicable neither to Pharaonic Egypt, nor to Kautilya's India, nor to the medieval states of Black Africa.

On the other hand, the official of the AMP states in charge of commerce, who, in fact, had the rank and the title of minister, is, in every respect, comparable to the minister of commerce (exterior) of the modern states, whether capitalist or socialist: this is a new institution that the AMP state bequeathed to the modern states.

Godelier continues his analysis:

> The productive use of slaves cannot become the dominant relation of production. . . . But a genuine development of productive slavery assumes the private ownership of the land within the rural communities and this, in Europe, was accomplished through what Marx calls "the antique mode of production."[6]

This was the case with Rome (as Godelier shows), where revolution was not made; for the purpose of the analysis was to show the revolutionary virtues of a slave system; this is true in itself, but all depends on territorial context, as we have said so often.

But what is most serious is that the most important phase of the analysis is summarized in one neutral phrase: "The slave mode of production evolves and decomposes in a long agony where its place is taken by the

Germanic forms of ownership, one of the bases of the feudal mode of production."[7]

It should be remembered that this agony of the slave system lasted for five hundred years and that its disappearance in 476 A.D. was due quite by chance to a quasi-mechanical external cause, the barbarian invasions—so much so that the Oriental half of the Roman Empire, spared from these invasions (after negotiation), continued for another thousand years, until the conquest of Constantinople by Muhammad II, the Conqueror, in 1453.

Between 476, the end of the Roman Empire, and the year 800, the time of the coronation of Charlemagne and the Carolingian renaissance, there was a veritable regression in all fields of knowledge; even the architectural techniques of antiquity were lost. New scientific progress was to come from Arab contributions and from the role played by the Catholic Church, which, during the whole period of the high Middle Ages, contained the historic memory of the West, thus making any cumulative process possible.

With the English monk Alcuin, cultural and technical advisor to Charlemagne, knowledge began to come out of the monasteries after an eclipse of five hundred years. The cumulative process that developed with the landowning nobility and the villages of the eleventh century would not have been conceivable without the special role of the Church: it is thus important to emphasize this when describing the singularity of the Western evolutionary path. Therefore, this evolution was not due to racial factors, as Marx himself tended to believe: "The Greeks were normal children, while many of the ancient nations belonged to the category of ill-bred and old-looking children."[8] If it were otherwise, the Persians, the Medes, the Aryans of India, etc., should have followed the same evolutionary path as the Greeks of the same race. However, nothing of the sort happened. Consequently, as a good Marxist, one must purify sociological theory of tendencies to racial hierarchization, tendencies that are sometimes implicit among the best disciples or even in Marx himself. Given the aim of sociology to find the objective historical factors responsible for this Western evolution, it is not scientific to omit the role played by the Church in the formation of the Western sociopolitical structures.

The taking into consideration of the numerous common points between the AMP and the modern state, which we have indicated throughout this account, must have led Wittfogel, an adversary of Marxism, to affirm that "the structure of the AMP state is the proof that a bureaucratic class, having despotic power, could edify itself based on the socialist collective forms of ownership."[9] Godelier rightly criticizes and rejects this idea.[10] In another connection, he points out, against the supporters of the thesis of the universal evolutionary path of societies—primitive community, slavery, feudalism, capitalism, socialism—that the hypothesis of a plurality of the forms of passage to the class society slipped more and more into obscurity, as Engels's analysis relative to the Germanic social formations was forgotten.[11]

The AMP state can evolve toward the antique mode of production and end up as a slave system (the singular Greco-Roman path), but the most frequent evolution leads to feudalism, with the transformation of collective and communal property into individual private property by the aristocracy; this happened in China, Vietnam, Japan, India, and Tibet, where class societies developed.

However, the feudality that developed from the AMP would be specific in more than one way and would delay the development of commercial production and the appearance of capitalism. The specific traits of the AMP would subsist through feudality because of the permanent need for heavy construction.[12]

Even though it was not a question of feudality in Rome, it should be remembered that the mercantile production did not engender a revolutionary dynamism exceeding that of the AMP societies, as soon as the managerial systems became comparable.

Also, the major productive enterprises, in the sense meant by both Marx and Engels, did not exist in many AMP states, such as Kautilya's India, some medieval African states, etc. On the other hand, certain public utility works are common to the AMP and the modern states, and are to a great extent even their theoretical raison d'être. Godelier's reasoning, then, leads to the statement that revolution is not possible in states with major productive enterprises.

Godelier writes:

> If Egypt . . . belongs to the AMP, it belongs to the most brilliant civilizations of the Metal Age, during the time when man definitively breaks away from the economy of the soil, passes to dominating nature, and invents new forms of agriculture, architecture, mathematics, writing, commerce, currency, law, religions, etc.
>
> The AMP therefore does not mean stagnation, but rather the greatest progress accomplished on the basis of communal forms of production.[13]

But the author continues:

> The Western way is universal because it is unique, because it is not found anywhere else. . . .
>
> Only the Western path of development has created the conditions for its own betterment. . . .
>
> The universality of this uniqueness! . . . This contradiction is in life and not in thought. If it is not perceived, one ends up with theoretical powerlessness.[14]

JEAN SURET-CANALE

Traditional Societies in Tropical Africa and the Concept of the Asiatic Mode of Production

Jean Suret-Canale in a way recalls the fact that the African institutions have a semifeudal structure with the exception of the mode of production, a point of view that we supported in our work *L'Afrique Noire précoloniale.*

Suret-Canale holds that:

> The state is not the cause of exploitation but its consequence. . . . Element of the superstructure, the State could not fit into the definition of a mode of production.
>
> In the Asiatic State, a ruling class, freed from immediate productive work, appears and merges with the State machinery. As such, the latter has not yet dissociated itself from the society that gave rise to it. . . . Merged with the ruling class, the machinery still belongs to the grass roots.[15]

We have already shown above (p. 188) that the Africans made a clear distinction between the state and its machinery on the one hand, and the servants of the state, the king in particular, on the other hand. Consequently, the idea of a state machinery merged with the grass roots, as defended by Suret-Canale, is untenable. Similarly, the AMP state, obviously born out of a need for the survival of an entire and as yet undifferentiated collectivity, precedes class antagonism and could not be its consequence. It is correct that once the danger that menaced the collectivity's survival was removed, with time, even the economical interventions of the state also mask relations of exploitation.

Lastly, there is an obvious relationship between a given type of state and its mode of production.

Suret-Canale deems that "the internal contradiction proper to the AMP—class exploitation and maintaining the collective ownership of the land—cannot be resolved in a progressive sense by its own development, because the arrangement of class exploitation, far from destroying the structures founded on the collective ownership of the land, reinforces them." (*op. cit.*, p. 127). And, we have already seen above (pp. 143 and 191) that the opposite did happen in many AMP societies: China, Japan, Vietnam, India, Tibet, etc.

The AMP society is constantly fraught with a revolution that erupts here and there, but which is constantly brought under control and crushed, for the reasons explained above. Nothing is more erroneous than the idea of an AMP society lacking revolutionary content and dynamism.

G. A. MELEKECHVILI

Slavery, Feudalism, and the Asiatic Mode of Production in the Ancient Orient[16]

G. A. Melekechvili shows that free labor was predominant in the Oriental AMP societies: Mesopotamia, China, India.

Contrary to the theoretical prognostications, for reasons of profitability itself, the slave owners preferred the small, undersized operation (thus orienting themselves toward the transformation of slaves into serfs) to the large rural enterprise.[17]

Similarly, slavery as a result of indebtedness was marginal (see Toumenev) because of the very fact that it is an endogenous factor of disintegration: Hammurabi's code sets the limits thereof.[18]

Melekechvili points out, quite rightly, that the notion of generalized slavery must not be taken literally, because there is a difference that cannot be totally erased between the free man in the countryside, endowed with a civic personality, and the individual outside of society like the slave.

But in the East, in Mesopotamia as well as in Egypt, even in Assyria, the slaves that are settled on the land are protected by law: thus there is the onset of feudalization.

For Melekechvili, the fundamental stages of social development are: the classless primitive society, the society with classes, and the classless developed society.[19]

The exception is the slavery stage, not the general rule, and it is not even a necessary stage.

History does not contain cases in which a developed slave society was formed by the simple socioeconomic differentiation within a given society.[20] There is no correlation between generalized slave labor and an increase in the material productive forces; it is rather the reverse that one notes, with the mediocrity of the productivity of slave labor.

Similarly, for Melekechvili, there is no demonstrable relationship between the passage from one mode of production to another and the technical level, or more precisely, the development of tools.[21]

In Europe, the passage from slavery to feudalism occurred under conditions of decadence rather than from a rise in production: one and the same instrument of work can form the basis of the slave structure as well as that of the feudal structure; it is the same today, where the same technique can form the basis for capitalism in one case, for socialism in the other.[22]

Criticizing the original thesis upheld by Melekechvili, Charles Parrain makes the remark that each passage from one mode of production to another is accompanied by an acceleration of historical time.

Melekechvili considers the Roman slave system to be a momentary deviation, and that after the fall of Rome, Western society again took the normal, universal path toward feudalism.

But Parrain rejects this "pan-feudalism" which does not take into account the level of the productive forces, in the study of the diverse varieties of "feudalism":

> In order to really be qualified as a progressive epoch (universal by nature and not fact) in Marx's sense, it is indispensable for the ancient slave stage to have contained the seed of the next stage of a feudalism which itself contained also the seed of the stage of capitalism.
>
> There is feudalism only if agriculture (fundamental to this stage) has the technical acquisitions of ancient slavery and if the conditions of the exploitation of direct producers allow increased reproduction and, as a result, the maturation of the new productive forces necessary for the constitution of capitalism.

It is only in contempt of these considerations, says Parrain, that one can reject the Marxist series of progressive epochs or stages without which all logic seems to be eliminated from human history. "If the capacity of society's adaptation to the changes caused by the development of the productive forces were absolute, there would not have been a revolution: society could pass from one mode of production to another without revolution."

It might be observed that here Parrain merely poses the inverse problem, without critically examining the idea that today's American capitalism and Soviet socialism have the same technical basis and that this clearly illustrates the idea of a revolution without a qualitative leap in the productive forces.

One can even say that American technology is more sophisticated, that with the appearance of multinational companies we are witnessing a progressive change in the mode of production and a globalization of the relationships of production that could trigger a planetary revolution.

ION BANU

The "Asiatic" Social Formation in the Perspective of Ancient Oriental Philosophy[23]

Ion Banu denies having deduced ideological economy, or having "sociologized" thought.

For him, absolute rigid relations between superstructure and social structure, social determination of classes, do not exist.

There is even a certain "permanence" in a society's thinking throughout several and even all of the social formations that it went through: perhaps this is cultural identity.

It is probably the ideological superstructure identifying divine order, cosmic order, and that of the state, which better portrays the perfecting of the AMP state.

According to Banu, "the intervention of the monarch in hydraulic works is beneficial and sacred. The State fulfills a beneficial technical and economic function. There is an association of social and cosmic significance in the conception of the State."

In the *Book of the Dead* (Egypt) the obligation of not damaging irrigation works is considered an ethical duty, next to that of not killing, and not committing adultery or sodomy.[24] This is a good example of a utilitarian origin of morals; one could almost speak of ecology elevated to the level of morality.[25] "In the universe, the same vital force maintains, through the intermediary of the royalty, the fertility of the soil as well as that of the human species" (*Book of the Dead*).

According to Diodorus, Isis invented agriculture and the laws.[26] The divinity from whom all these functions would emanate, both royal and terrestrial, will be venerated as the condition of their constant realization. Everybody is interested in seeing that the economical and the techno-scientific tasks are well done.[27]

Thus, the divinity helps the king, here the Pharaoh, to surmount the popular riots, which, at this time, were far from rare.

One understands why the cosmic order is supposed to be troubled during revolutions and interregna. According to Ipuwer, women and nature had become sterile following the Osirian revolution of the Ancient Empire, a revolution that had profamed the kingdom and its institutions.[28]

The Chinese philosopher Xun-Zi (third century B.C.) had even imagined a system allowing the evaluation of the economic needs of the subjects, the numerical estimate of production in order to improve it, and the sending of people to different sectors of production according to what was needed.

To be a statesman, said he, is to possess the mechanism of the economic differentiation of the people.[29]

Thus the AMP state had already elaborated, all things considered, a veritable economic science designed to maintain social equilibrium.

These types of calculation and economic speculations were already common among the Egyptian scribes of the Ancient Empire, and the quasi-totality of the mathematical exercises of the *Rhind Papyrus* deal with economic calculations of this type, the evaluation of quantities of commodities and of raw materials.

Therefore, the AMP state, instead of corresponding to one faltering phase in the sociopolitical order, responds to the most complete theory of state ever designed by humanity, until the dawn of modern times. This explains the paradox of the resurgent dissolution of the Greco-Roman city-state, in spite of the revolution that took place in this city-state; because it was stricken by an original defect, it was not capable of survival.

Thereby, one of the paradoxical traits of the evolution of societies is explained: namely, the revolution's regression and eclipse, from antiquity to modern times, from the fourth century B.C. to the seventeenth century (Cromwell and Jan de Witt).[30]

All of the present types of states, revolutionary or capitalist, have sprung in different degrees from the AMP state, of which they are only modernized and secularized replicas; the AMP state's legacy is visible at all levels: varied ideologies, foundation of the state's ontology, interventionist socioeconomic structures, "branches" of activities, territorial setting, etc. There is thus a certain permanence of the AMP state, even throughout the institutions of the modern Socialist states that have made their revolution.

One of the constant concerns of the AMP state was the augmentation, the enlargening of production (the creation of overproduction, also) for the establishment of food reserves, in order to prevent mass starvation: it has to be said that these good intentions were not always successful; nevertheless, they are alien to slave and feudal states.

Ion Banu notes that in the slave state, the slave is silent; even the opposition between patricians and plebeians, between aristocrats and democrats, takes place within the social category of free men.

The materialist Democritus was as much in favor of slavery as was the idealist Plato, and also Aristotle; no voice speaks out against the exploitation of man by man, contrary to the rule in the AMP societies, where this claim is strongly advocated by the free men themselves: thus the contradiction emphasized by Banu is that in the slave regimes, it is the free man who makes demands on behalf of the slave, who never has a voice, while in the AMP states, it is the free and exploited peasant who makes demands, always to the exclusion of the almost silent slave.[31] It is therefore only in the AMP societies that the ideological opposition translates into a real class antagonism.

The presence of social protest against man's oppression by man occurs frequently in Oriental texts. While Greek and Roman history is marked by slave riots, the revolutionary figure that dominates in the East is that of the peasant.[32]

"Throughout the thousands of years of the history of pre-Hellenistic Egypt, documents prove the anxiety of those who governed, provoked by the spirit of revolt of the peasants."[33]

The agents of the so-called Osirian revolution[34] described by Ipuwer, and which put an end to the Ancient Empire, were free men, peasants, who momentarily profaned, desacralized, and threw down the royalty and its repressive state machinery.

> In regard to China, the sinologist Edward Erkes affirms that throughout its history "riots by slaves are unknown," the driving element being "the peasant revolt."

> This long string of facts would hardly agree with a social scheme in which the slaves are in the forefront, overshadowing the exploited peasantry.[35]

In China, criticism of social injustices constitutes a permanent part of ancient philosophical thought: it concerns always the peasants' sufferings and not that of the slaves.

According to the Chinese Marxist Yen Zi Yi, the precocious discovery of dialectics[36] by the Chinese is linked to the breadth of the peasants' social movements, without equivalent in history.

The criticism is never of social relations, but of the manner in which the leadership fulfills its obligations to the people, due to the existence of these relations. The sovereign is simply menaced with replacement by another more human one.[37] It is the opposite of what happened in Egypt, where social relations were actually questioned by the people, who destroyed the "divine" laws during the Osirian revolution, thus conferring a character of singular authenticity on this revolution.

MARINETTE DAMBUYANT

A State with a "Higher Economical Command": Kautilya's India[38]

"He will always go toward that which makes a profit, and he will avoid that which does not."[39]

The Arthashastra (the teaching of economic profit) is Kautilya's political treatise in the fourth to third centuries B.C.; a political theory aware of itself, Machiavellianism before its time, this treatise, according to Marinette Dambuyant, radically questions the affirmation according to which the Greeks invented politics.

The cynically pursued aim is the prosperity and the aggrandizement of the kingdom, whereby no rational or efficacious means was excluded. Everything that can increase public finances, without which nothing is possible, is good.

The creation of this empire, in the Asia of monsoons, probably did not require any major enterprises, according to Dambuyant. Power is autocratic and secular; the king is not deified.

The method of government is based on the systematic use of statistics, as in Egypt: surveys, integral census of the country's people and goods.

Everybody must be well paid; officials who provoke discontent in one region are moved to other areas, or the revolt is crushed.

Various techniques, all the way to "religious swindling" (false miracles), are used to fill the state coffers; the king is a usurer and practices lending with interest. This is not a pure AMP state in the traditional sense.

In all the branches of economy, of agriculture, and of commerce, there exists a state sector and a private sector: labor is wage-paid, even that of the slaves in the royal workshops, who can buy their freedom by saving money to do so; the economy is based on money.

There is a clear-cut difference in classes. There is a true merchant class instead of the state controlling all commerce. The cities are functional and in no way superfluous, as theory would have it; each section of the town is occupied by a given social class. The economic level is very high; production is abundant and is even based on a sector of heavy industry, of metals and mining. Currency is used, and the division of labor is very much developed. The line is drawn between domestic activities and productive work, and agriculture itself is treated as a trade. There is a separation between rural agriculture and urban industry.

In addition, Dambuyant judges it difficult, if not absurd, to consider the AMP as anterior and inferior to the slave system. It would appear rather as parallel to other pre-capitalist systems.

The society was not based on slavery. The state was not the representative of the slave owners, as in Athens or in Rome. The slaves did not constitute a separate class.

Only the Sudra, representing the aboriginal population conquered by the newly arrived Aryans, were treated like the Helots in Sparta: one could do with them whatever one pleased. During Kautilya's epoch, the killing of a Sudra was no more punishable than the killing of a frog. The "Helotism" culminated during Brahma's time and continues, in attenuated form, during the Maurya epoch.

It is forbidden, except in special cases, to send a Sudra child into slavery, which (later) means that it makes of him or her an Aryan (III-13).

We can see, in the case of India's Sudra, a striking example of how man's exploitation by man, the antagonism between classes, espouses the ethnic contour of the group of the first occupants of the land, conquered by invaders, like the Helots of Sparta vis-à-vis the Dorian lords.

The India of the Maurya empire is thus a highly evolved AMP society, driven by an extraordinary dynamism; and if the system does not fall apart, it is not for lack of internal pressure, but because of its keen awareness of the pressure, which causes it to be always on guard and to defend itself daily through spying, swindling, assassination, and the most rational, possible economic and financial organization.

HÉLÈNE ANTONIADIS-BIBICOU

Byzantium and the Asiatic Mode of Production[40]

For Hélène Antoniadis-Bibicou, the AMP can only be considered in prefeudal Byzantium. Byzantium is not a hydraulic or even a marginally hydraulic society. Private property came first, and that of the state, second.

The rural community is characterized by fiscal solidarity, as in India; but it is difficult to establish the relationship between private property—a relationship that here defines the mode of production—and socioeconomic structures. The existence of small properties allowed the emergence of big landowners and feudalization: therefore, from a legal point of view, Byzantium does not depend on the AMP.

In the AMP systems, where commerce was state-controlled, commercial exchanges could not act as a dissolvent of the rural community.

The Byzantine rural community, instead of being endowed with immutability, is fragile: commerce is largely private; the economy is a monetary one, as in Rome, and it does not belong to the AMP.

The society is also a class society and differs from that of the AMP. The great legal division between slaves and free men is, by itself, a proof of the above. The nobility is palatine.

The Church, like the temples of ancient Egypt, owned a great deal of land that greatly absorbed the temporal occupations of the clergymen. There was a genuine pre-bourgeoisie.

Power was centralized and by divine right. Even the Church, so powerful and so well organized, could not detach itself and become independent, like the Roman branch after the fall of the Western Roman Empire.

The emperor is the commander in chief of the army, the supreme judge and the only legislator, on the ruins of the ancient city; he is the defender of the Church and of the orthodox faith. He is king by divine investiture and no longer a magistrate exercising rule as the delegate of the people: he is an "Oriental despot" who relies on a highly developed bureaucratic machine in order to govern. There is no feudalization of power.

Byzantium is an autocracy, tempered by palace revolution and assassination, concludes Antoniadis-Bibicou.

We can observe that Marxism did not create the theory of historical regressions and of the shifting of areas of sociopolitical evolution.

Byzantium had to be the sociopolitical area where the accumulative process was the most intense, and, as such, the continually smoldering hotbed of all the revolutions.

If the theory were rigorously true, the Industrial Revolution should not have started in England, but in Byzantium, which accumulated the heritage of Hellenism, of the ancient city in particular, of Rome, and of Christianity. Only the spirit of adventure and the will for power explain England's rise, from the high Middle Ages to the period of industrialization of the British Isles, in the eighteenth century! Kipling's poem cited on page 164 illustrates this quite well.

CHARLES PARRAIN

Mediterranean Protohistory and the Asiatic Mode of Production[41]

Charles Parrain remarks that in 2800 B.C. the Egyptian state structure was already very solid. But the slave mode of production was not to be fully established in Greece until the twelfth century B.C. and in Rome until the fourth century B.C. For Parrain, this hiatus of two thousand years shows that, once the primitive community was dissolved, the slave mode of production did not easily form itself.

We have shown that the latter system could not and should not be formed within the framework of the structures of the Pharaonic state, as Parrain would have it, and that the question is wrongly posed. In any case, we agree with Parrain in saying that these two millennia could not have constituted a period of indefinite transition toward the slave mode of production, a period of slow maturation.

But Parrain himself reminds us that brilliant civilizations in the Near East did develop and then declined without ever going through the slave mode of production.

He considers that megalithic, Creto-Mycenaean and Etruscan civilizations developed, at different levels, following the path of the AMP.

Parrain writes:

> Now, these three entities were not formed somewhat spontaneously following a so-called regular passage from the primitive to the "Asiatic" society. Each one of them got its momentum, with varied intensity and luck, from the models offered by the great civilizations of the Near East, all of the "Asiatic" type, and particularly from Egypt, the most successful model.[42]

Need it be recalled, in passing, that this is the point of view that we defended in 1954 in *Nations nègres et Culture*, and which now seems to be accepted more and more? From the beginning of the second millennium B.C., the Egyptian meridional state model and that of Black Africa had adapted to the Northern Mediterranean, to Crete, to Greece, to Brittany, which will not prevent certain ideologies from asking themselves how the concept of the state was introduced in Africa.[43]

But Parrain makes a distinction between the concepts of generalized slavery, slavery itself, and feudal statute labor, before analyzing the above-cited three civilizations.

The AMP is not just a combination of village communities and a despotic regime. The important trait, according to Marx, is generalized slavery, which allows it to be considered as progress after the dissolution of the primitive community: it is the dynamic element of the system.

The economic use of this factor is the most important, but the political (military defense) or religious use is possible; it necessitates a society in which man's exploitation by man is done through the intermediary of collectivities, i.e., village communities, a despotic centralized power: thus generalized slavery, by itself, would explain the whole AMP system.

Manpower is quasi-free; one does not have to buy or to support the worker. The abundance of manpower will engender waste, of which the most typical case will be that of the Egyptian pyramids. Unskilled manpower will only be fit for heavy work. There will be, on the side, a small number of artists dependent on the despot.

> Generalized slavery would have had, as a direct consequence, the mastering of water, an improvement in the general conditions of agricultural production, and, as an indirect consequence, the flourishing of culture and art. But it would not have favored the progress of the techniques of agricultural production, whence a kind of impasse in the ensemble movement ahead of the productive forces.

Parrain cites *Das Kapital*,[44] where Marx writes:

> It is always the direct relationship of the owners of the conditions of production to the direct producers—a relation always naturally corresponding to a definite stage in the development of the methods of work and thereby its social productivity—which reveals the innermost secret, the hidden basis of the entire social edifice, and consequently the political form of the relation of sovereignty and dependence, in short, the corresponding specific form of the state in a given period.

We think that the process put forth by Marx should, for once, be reversed: it is the material cause that is at the basis of the birth of the state and that determines the process of its appearance, the type of state, and its specific political form. Therefore, the form of the relations of production is determined by the type of state thus created; consequently, the relations of production of the slave type are excluded by the AMP.

Man's exploitation by man cannot be conceived of outside of the framework of a state, no matter how embryonic it is. In spite of Engels's expositions in *Anti-Dühring*, this phenomenon did not exist before the state did. This form changes when one goes from the slave states to the nonslave states, called the "AMP."

On the other hand, it would be difficult to distinguish generalized slavery, defined above, from general wartime mobilization in the modern states.

In the true slave system, the slave is private property, merchandise, which in turn has to produce saleable goods, while "the despot's subject" produces only usable values, sometimes in the interest of the whole society,[45] sometimes to satisfy the exigencies and the whims of the despot and his entourage. The difference between the two types of slavery is striking, remarks Parrain.

For Parrain, Egypt served as the model for the megalithic civilizations of Western Europe, in the period from 2000 to 1400 B.C.

The dolmen of La Ferté-Bernard weighs ninety tons; similarly, the king of the Breton megaliths, the Men er Roeck menhir, was twenty-three-meters high, five-meters wide at its base, and weighed around 350 tons. It is estimated that fifteen thousand individuals were needed to move it on wooden wheels. Parrain writes:

> The general opinion is that the early model of similar monuments should be searched for in the Near East, and that we are dealing with an indirect and a necessarily degenerate imitation of the funeral or religious monuments of the mastaba or obelisk type. It is clear that there was no organized expansion, but rather imitation by degrees.[46]

According to Parrain, the principal centers of this megalithic diffusion from the Egyptian model would be southern Spain and Malta, in the Copper and Bronze Ages, from 2500 to 1500 B.C., and 1400 B.C. for Stonehenge, in England.

The paths of diffusion are the Rhone Valley and the Atlantic coasts in Europe: Brittany, the British Isles, Denmark, the northern coast of Germany with penetration in the Elbe Valley, meridional Scandinavia, and also the Caucasus.

The Egyptian influences in the northern Mediterranean during this epoch is equally attested to in the domain of pottery. In the Neolithic pottery from Liguria to Malta and in Northern Italy, one finds the decoration of a type of square-necked vase, characteristic of predynastic Amratian Egypt, with a gap of five hundred years.

Parrain is amazed that the megalithic period was not followed by a true slave phase, as was the case in Mycenae and in Etruria, after the stage of generalized slavery corresponding to the AMP.

The Creto-Mycenaean Civilization

The palatial type of civilization of Crete served as the model for Mycenae, better known thanks to the deciphering of *Linear B*.[47] It concerns, as shown by J. P. Vernant, a replica of the Egyptian model:

> The king concentrates and unifies in himself all the elements of power, all the aspects of sovereignty. Through the intermediary of scribes, who constitute a professional class rooted in tradition, and thanks to a complex hierarchy of palace dignitaries and royal inspectors, he controls and regulates in minute detail all the sectors of economic life, every domain of social activity.[48]

Vernant notes that this state model was obviously borrowed from the Near East, from Egypt in particular.

With this type of palatial economy used during the time of the *damos*, which is the equivalent of the AMP's village economy, there was no private commerce, therefore no development of private property.

According to Parrain, "the *damos* owns land of which one part is separated out and given in usufruct to individual beneficiaries, but another part remains undivided for the community. This undivided part had to be collectively exploited."[49] Exchanges were made through bartering. The *damos* was subjected to diverse fees by the palace, of which a functionary seems to preside over the college of operators that manages it.

The slaves and cattle of the *damos* were collective property; thus the slave existed, but only marginally and patriarchally: this was not a question of an actual slave regime.

Parrain underscores again how belatedly Greece imitates the Egyptian model through the Cretan one, which most probably came forth from it, as we will see. The first Cretan palaces, Cnossus, Phaestos, Mallia, date back to 2000–1700 B.C. The epoch of the second palaces begins around 1700 B.C. However, at Mycenae, he says, the underground tombs are dated between 1580 and 1500 B.C., and the Mycenaean civilization really begins in 1450 B.C. Therefore, Mycenae also is separated by a five-hundred-year time lag from Crete.

There is the same time lag for the Hittites, who would have arrived in Asis Minor in 2000 B.C., at the time when the first Greeks reached Greece. But it is only around 1600 B.C. that the first Hittite empire is built, which will last until around 1450.

The second Hittite empire is contemporaneous with the apogee of Mycenae: 1450–1200 B.C.

A fact that did not catch Parrain's attention must be pointed out here: 1580 B.C. marks the year that the Hyksos were thrown out of Egypt, and the beginning of Egyptian imperialism, which will reach its apogee under Thutmose III, around 1470 B.C.

According to the poetic stele (text in verse) of this Pharaoh, more than 119 states and principalities of Western Asia actually fell under Egyptian rule: all the islands of the Aegean Sea, Crete in particular, were conquered and paid tribute to Egypt. The Cretans, called *Keftiu*, figure fully among the conquered nations that came to pay taxes to Egypt, and who are precisely represented in the tomb of Rekhmira, vizier and tutor of Thutmose III himself (XVIIIth Dynasty) (figs. 22, 23).

Therefore, the facts are there; this is not legend. Even the name of a general named Houry is known; Thutmose III sent Houry, in the same period, to the Cyclades to collect taxes, and after he had accomplished his mission, he was given a golden cup as a reward.

Thus, it is probably in the course of these precise historical contacts that Egypt would have introduced its governmental and administrative model in the previously cited countries of the northern Mediterranean.

In spite of the Assyrian colonies of Cappadocia, dated 1850 B.C. in Hittite country, the AMP will not become implanted in this region for a period of five hundred years.

The organization for defense (The Great Wall of China, Cyclopean constructions of the protohistoric Mediterranean, the fortifications of Mycenae and Tirynth) imply generalized slavery and the appearance of the AMP, based on Parrain.

The Hittite and the Mycenaean states were essentially warrior states. But according to Parrain, the Mycenaeans would have also built major works in order to control water, according to certain indirect evidence.

The Dorian invasions then destroyed the Mycenaean civilization. The AMP societies were particularly vulnerable, in spite of their imposing character: thus there were three destructions followed by reconstructions, of the Pharaonic state. In Greece, this was not the case, for the development of private property had destroyed the cohesion of the village communities and the corollary social equilibrium, notes Parrain.

Hesiod's book, *Works and Days*, written around 750 B.C., gives precious information on this period of transition.

The centralized power of the *wanax*, during the Mycenaean epoch, breaks apart in the hands of the *basileis* of Hesiod's epoch, "great landowners, unjust and monopolizers at the expense of the small landowners who eke out a living." The children of the latter had to make a living from a small plot of land. According to Hesiod, "in order to fill the void between gods and men, there is only one way, agricultural work as religious practice and as a form of justice."

The solidarity and interdependence typical of the AMP make a place for the reinforcement of private property and for the ravages of calculating individualism:

Hesiod writes:

> In the house prepare all tools needed, so that you will not have to ask someone else for them; if he refuses, you remain in trouble, the season passes and your work is lost. (verses 407–409)
>
> Easy to say: Give me your oxen and your wagon . . .
> Easy also to answer: My oxen are busy. (verses 453–454)

Henceforth, wealth is the supreme goal:

> Wealth is always followed by merit and glory. (verse 313)
>
> It is a terrible shame that follows in the footsteps of the poor. (verse 318)

The slave becomes the instrument of enrichment: Hesiod cynically gives advice on how to exploit slave labor to the maximum.

The Etruscans

Greece was already behind Crete, but Etruria was even further behind, because the AMP society there was contemporaneous with the Iron and not the Bronze Age. These people had a particular development in the seventh century B.C. characterized by: a privileged position of women as opposed to later in Rome and; traces of major works to master the water in one of the badly drained regions (canals that were dug in the lower valley of the Po River, in the vicinity of Spina, played an economic role of the highest order in the sixth and fifth centuries B.C., during the era of huts with funerary urns, characteristic of the previous period!).

According to Parrain, "These works imply the AMP, for the slave mode of production implies private entrepreneurs whose aim is to satisfy personal interests and not, as in this instance, collective interests."[50]

Thus, there was no authentic slave system during the royal epoch; otherwise one cannot explain the regression of the two centuries that followed the expulsion of the Etruscan kings.

According to Titus Livy, there was generalized slavery (Book I, chapter 39, Tarquinius the Elder, beginning of the sixth century): the drying out of Rome's low-lying ground, construction of Jupiter's temple on the Capitoline Hill (a vow made during the war with the Sabines), *cloaca maxima*, etc. Workers coming from all the Etruscan regions were used, as well as public funds and the plebeian work force. Tarquinius fought against Ardea, town of the Rutulies, a very rich people, in order to capture their wealth, to restore the finances ruined by the great public works, and to reduce popular discontent.

Having seized power by force, without mandate from the people or the "Senate," Tarquinius protected himself with bodyguards.

Parrain writes:

> Between 700 and 600 B.C., an Orientalizing period, Greek influence progressively outmatches that of Phoenicia and Cyprus (Corinthian vases). Between 600 and 475 B.C., the Ionian and the Attic influence becomes overwhelming: the appearance of the Etruscan temple, based on the model of the Greek sanctuaries, in the sixth century B.C., with a wooden skeleton and a coating of baked earth.[51]

The statuary of Vêtes reminds one of Greece's archaic art. Why the regression, after this artistic boom parallel to that of Greece?

The Roman republican state perpetuated the custom of the great works of the despotic epoch, just like today's modern states, which from this point of view, are of the Asiatic type.

The Latins in revolt won a victory with the help of Cumes, a Greek city in Italy; the latter, defended in turn by Syracuse in 474 B.C., won a decisive naval victory over the Etruscans, in Campania. Parrain would see the reasons for the Etruscans' decline in the absence of a slave system, contrary to Greece!

"Perhaps Greece's great fortune is that the Dorian invasions had given the last blow to the Asiatic mode of production there."[52]

One could compare this to the barbarian invasions that led to the destruction of Rome, while the Roman Empire of the East continues and prevents the appearance of a feudal stage.

Thus, following an external accident, on could say that this unitary Roman Empire, governed according to one unique law, is going to split into two parts that will evolve in a divergent manner, one leading to modern capitalism and the other to the conservation of the same imperial structures, frozen up to the dawn of modern times, if not up to our days.

According to Giacomo Devoto:

> . . . the linguistic considerations allow us to verify that two profoundly different modes of production marked on the one hand classical Rome, with, in the interval, a period of decomposition and of slow maturation, not only by a new socioeconomic structure, but also by a new state of the language.[53]

In order to characterize the Latin language, one must start with rare and obscure texts prior to the fourth century in order to speak of the "protohistory of Latin."

According to Parrain, Devoto distinguishes three periods:

> **1.** The Etruscan royal period that corresponds to archaic Latin, already stabilized, a commonly written language, even though there are no texts.
>
> **2.** and **3.** The obscure period of the republic (500–350 B.C.), a phase of crisis during which Latin underwent more changes than it would undergo from 350 B.C. to our times, meaning that today's Italian is closer to Plautus's Latin than Plautus's Latin is to what can be reconstructed as having been the Latin of the sixth century B.C.

This mutation between 500 and 350 B.C. corresponds to the cessation of the political and cultural coordination exercised by the Etruscan kings and to the class struggles between plebeians and patricians. This is an evolution comparable to that which took place in the transition from the Latin of the Imperial Roman epoch to the French of the eleventh century, after the destruction of the Roman Empire by barbarian invasions. This last evolution corresponds to the passage from the Roman slave mode of production, at the beginning of the fifth century A.D., to the feudal mode of production in the eleventh century.[54]

In *German Ideology*,[55] Marx, cited by Parrain, says that it is necessary to calculate the periods of the flooding of the Nile, which created Egyptian astronomy, and, at the same time, the domination of the sacerdotal caste, in order to organize agriculture.

The external natural conditions break down into two classes:

> the natural resources for a means of subsistence: soil fertility, waters abundant with fish, etc.
>
> the natural resources for a means of work: waterfalls, navigable rivers, metals, coal, etc.

At the beginning of the civilization, it is the first category of resources that prevails; at the end, it is the second.

Marx applies these considerations to Egypt: it is to the power of utilizing a considerable part of the population for unproductive works that ancient Egypt owes its great architectural works. But the use of generalized slavery for the development of the Nile Valley had a greater historical importance.

CONCLUSION

We have just reviewed the most recent studies of the AMP. They all contain valuable information on the AMP societies. But none of them, in our opinion, has tackled the fundamental question, namely: Why, every time that a state took the AMP form in antiquity, did revolution become impossible? Following this line of thought, why did Roman society have to wait in vain for the revolution for half a millennium, while all the conditions predicted in theory were present from the beginning?

The idea developed by certain theoreticians like Godelier, according to which Roman society did not know a bourgeoisie that could make the revolution, is untenable. In fact, the tax collectors formed the richest class of businessmen, and its members belonged to the fortunate class of "knights." They constituted societies of the modern type with the Roman state's blessing; these societies had the equivalent of a president-general manager, a council of administration, and were composed of shareholders. The state could put them in charge of the exploitation of a mine or the collection of taxes from a province. The auditors kept the financial books. Only the senators and their sons were forbidden to do business, but this difficulty was easily bypassed: the free man was used as a figurehead, mainly in the business of equipping ships for the great maritime trade. These societies also conducted the banking business: currency exchange, transfer of funds, and usurious lending.[56]

PART 3

CULTURAL IDENTITY

14

HOW TO DEFINE CULTURAL IDENTITY?

For every individual his or her own cultural identity is a function of that of his or her people. Consequently, one must define the cultural identity of a people. This means, to a great extent, one must analyze the components of the collective personality. We know that three factors contribute to its formation:

1. An historical factor
2. A linguistic factor
3. A psychological factor

Every attempt to reinforce or to modify the cultural personality must consist of carefully studying the appropriate mode of action on these three factors. Perfect cultural identity corresponds to the full simultaneous presence of these factors in the individual. But that is the ideal case. In reality, one finds all types of transitions, from the normal to the extreme case of an identity crisis following a lessening of the distinct factors cited above. Their specific combinations offer all possible cases, individual or collective: where one factor functions fully, another has a very weak effect or even none at all, as we will see when linguistic expression of the mother tongue is lost in the diaspora.

One could ask oneself which of the three is the most important, in other words, which one would suffice to characterize cultural personality in the absence of the other two. Does this question make sense; is such a case possible?

To answer this question we must review the relative importance of each of these factors in a brief analysis.

HISTORICAL FACTOR

The historical factor is the cultural cement that unifies the disparate elements of a people to make them into a whole, by the particular slant of the feeling of historical continuity lived by the totality of the collective.

It is the historical conscience thus engendered that allows a people to distinguish itself from a population, whose elements, by definition, are foreign, one from the other: the population of a large city market is composed of foreign tourists who come from the five continents and who do not have any cultural bond with each other.

The historical conscience, through the feeling of cohesion that it creates, constitutes the safest and the most solid shield of cultural security for a people. This is why every people seeks only to know and to live their true history well, to transmit its memory to their descendants.

The essential thing, for people, is to rediscover the thread that connects them to their most remote ancestral past. In the face of cultural aggression of all sorts, in the face of all disintegrating factors of the outside world, the most efficient cultural weapon with which a people can arm itself is this feeling of historical continuity.

The erasing, the destruction of the historical conscience also has been since time began part of the techniques of colonization, enslavement, and debasement of peoples. The passage below by M. Peyronnet, cited by Georges Hardy, is proof of this:

> There is a subject I would see disappearing without regret [from the program of our African schools] declares M. Peyronnet, senator from Allier, in a recent article in the *Annales Coloniales*: it is history. A few readings during the French course would be enough to give them the notion of our country's power. . . .
>
> There is an even simpler way to give a clear idea of our strength to the native youth, which is to decorate the classroom with the intertwined manigolos and to set a miniature 75mm cannon on the teacher's desk. This, by itself, in some measure and for a given period of time, can replace history; but one should not forget that people very quickly get used to scarecrows: the sparrows end up making their nests in the pockets of the gentlemen who gesticulate in the cherry trees.[1]

It is these possibilities of cultural aggression, linked to the vital importance of this subject matter, that have led the developing nations coming out of the colonial night, such as Morocco, Algeria, etc., to make the teaching of history a national activity. In any case, the teaching of this material must particularly hold the attention of the state.

One sees that what is important for a given people is not the fact of being able to claim a more or less grandiose historical past, but rather to be simply pervaded by this sense of continuity so characteristic of the historical conscience. It could never occur to the working-class people of Albania to envy the brilliant historical past of the British. The knowledge of their own history, no matter what it is, is what is important. This presupposes a research activity that unfolds itself entirely in the scientific field, away from any ideological interference. UNESCO is well placed today to know that the Africans are capable of devoting themselves to this type of activity. Indeed, it has in its own archives convincing documents on this subject.

We have said earlier that a people without an historical conscience is a population. The loss of national sovereignty and of historical conscience following a prolonged foreign occupation engenders stagnation, or even sometimes regression, disintegration, and the partial return to barbarism: this was the case with Egypt under the Romans, if we can believe Juvenal. Because of the continuing loss of national sovereignty from the time of the arrival of the Persians in 525 B.C., Egypt, which had civilized the world, and from 1600 B.C. onward under Queen Hatshepsut was cruising the seas with tall ships towards the country of Punt, only knew how to build clay barges under the Romans in the second century A.D.

Worse, she fell back into superstition and barbarism. Juvenal describes tribal wars between two groups, Denderah and Hombos, whose totems are inimical and who are supposed to have destroyed each other through cannibalism. This event is to have taken place under the consulate of Iuncus, in A.D. 127 [2]

Even if one makes allowances, and takes into account the fact that Juvenal was not an impartial author and did not like the "Orientals," one must admit that as a whole, there occurred a genuine regression of the Egyptian civilization. This regression strikes the Egyptian people in their own birthplace before any emigration, and this, let us repeat, was due to the simple fact of foreign occupation. A great enigma of history is seen in a new light; namely, how did it happen that a people who built great civilizations fell so low afterward, and particularly the African people? It is clear that the exhaustive development of this idea would take far too much space here; we are only sketching a brief overview in passing, but enough to provide some elements for an answer. In any case, recalling so many facts is but a manner of emphasizing the importance of the historical factor in the definition of the cultural personality of a people.

But then, what would we call an African history? We need to distinguish two levels: The immediate one, of local histories, so dear, deeply lived, in which the African peoples, segmented by diverse exterior forces the principal one of which is colonization, are shriveled up, find themselves trapped, and are vegetating today.

A second level, more general, further off in time and space and including the totality of our peoples, comprises the general history of Black Africa, insofar as research permits restoring it today from a purely scientific approach: each history is thus pinpointed and correctly situated in relation to general historical coordinates. Thus all of the continent's history is reevaluated according to a new unitary standard suited to revive and to cement, on the basis of established fact, all of the inert elements of the ancient historical mosaic.

It becomes obvious that the feeling of historical unity, and consequently of cultural identity that scientific research is capable of providing at this time to the African cultural consciousness, is not only qualitatively superior to all those known up to now, but also plays a protective role of the first order in this world characterized by the generalization of cultural aggression. Thus emerges a direction of commendable research for the reinforcement of the cultural identity of the Negro African peoples. It is by engaging in this type of investigative activity that our people will discover, one day, that the Egypto-Nubian civilization played the same role vis-à-vis African culture as did Greco-Latin antiquity in regard to Western civilization.

Definition

One can say that a people has left prehistory behind from the moment that it becomes conscious of the importance of the historical event to the point where it invents a technique—oral or written—for its memorization and accumulation.

LINGUISTIC FACTOR

Let us move to the linguistic factor as a constituent element of cultural personality and, consequently, of cultural identity. It would be difficult to say, between the historical and the linguistic factors, which of the two is the most important from our angle of interest; Montesquieu would very probably lean toward the linguistic factor, he who wrote that "as long as a conquered people has not lost its language, it can have hope," hereby stressing that language is the unique common denominator, the characteristic of cultural identity par excellence.

But what does African linguistic unity mean? Africa is a Tower of Babel, it will be said. Not more so than Europe, which also has more than 360 languages and dialects.

The apparent linguistic unity does not exist on any continent: languages follow the migratory currents, the particular destinies of peoples, and fragmentation is the rule until an official effort, a political will, tries to expand a mode of expression to the detriment of others: thus the speech of the Ile-de-France, that of the kings of France, was privileged in relation to the other dialects, Picard, Provençal, Breton, etc.

However, everyone knows today, thanks to linguistic research, that this superficial heterogeneity in Europe hides a kinship, a profound linguistic unity that becomes more and more obvious as one goes back to the Indo-European language, which is the "mother tongue," the ancestor from which all of the present and the past branches derive, following a very complex evolution.

If we speak today of a European linguistic unity, it is only at this profound level, released and restored to science by linguistic archaeology. Otherwise the French, the English, the Germans, the Italians, the Rumanians, the Lithuanians, the Russians, etc., do not understand each other any more than the Wolof, the Bambara, the Hausa, etc., do.

But African linguistic research of the past few years has helped reach a level at which the kinship, the African linguistic unity in a genetic sense, is as obvious as that of the great Indo-European linguistic family. And we see the avenues that are open to an affirmation and a strengthening of the African cultural identity.

Similarly, it is linguistic research, and only that, which very recently allowed the twentieth-century Europeans to experience the feeling of their linguistic unity. Before the research on comparative grammar of the German Franz Bopp in the nineteenth century, no feeling of a European linguistic unity existed.

Africa has had a delay of only a little more than a century compared to Europe.

It is therefore a necessity that a duly conducted African linguistic research bring our people to experience deeply their linguistic unity, in the same way as Europeans have, in spite of the apparent superficial heterogeneity. The results obtained already allow us to undertake the cultural education of the African consciousness in that sense.

Africans would quickly discover, to their great surprise, that it is a typically Negro African language that has been the oldest written language in the history of humanity. It began 5,300 years ago, in Egypt; whereas the most ancient testimony to an Indo-European language (Hittite) goes back to the XVIIIth Egyptian Dynasty (1470 B.C.) and this, probably under the influence of the political and cultural domination of Asia Minor by Egypt. But this would take us too far. Let us only say that, all of a sudden, African linguistic research offers breathtaking possibilities to comparative linguistics and is about to reverse the traditional roles in this field. Be that as it may, it is through the study of the Egypto-Nubian languages that the historical dimension, up to now missing, is introduced in African studies; the comparison that derives from it allows, with each passing day, reinforcement of the feeling of linguistic unity of the Africans, therefore the feeling of cultural identity.

The review of the historical and linguistic factors as constituent elements of cultural personality brings to light the necessity for a total recasting of the African program of education in the fields discussed above, and for a radical centering of these on Egypto-Nubian antiquity, in the same way that the Western educational system has its foundation in Greco-Latin antiquity: there is no way more certain, more radical, more scientific, more sane and salutary to reinforce the African cultural personality and, consequently, the cultural identity of Africans.

PSYCHOLOGICAL FACTOR

Continuing with the analysis of the three factors mentioned at the beginning of our account, we arrive now at the third and last constituent factor of the cultural personality: the psychic factor, recognizable from the outset by everybody, if it exists at all. The Greek physician Galen, who lived in the second century A.D., reduced the characteristic traits of the Black person to two, which appeared fundamental to him: 1) inordinate length of his penis, 2) hilarity, strong propensity for laughter. The Black person is an hilarious human being with oversized genitalia.

For Galen, these two traits, one physical and one moral, were enough to characterize the generic type of Black. Even though Galen regularly visited the library of the temple at Memphis, where he was the last Greek scholar, six centuries after Hippocrates, to consult Imhotep's annals, the brilliance of Egyptian civilization was about to be forgotten and Rome was dominating the world. Galen was born three years after the death of Juvenal. We are witnessing the birth of the portrayal of the Black in Western literature. The caricatured identifications of Blacks starting from some psychological traits, more or less wrongly construed, will be pursued up to our days by authors badly in need of definitions, via Count Arthur Joseph Gobineau, the ideological ancestor of the Nazis. For him, all art is a result of the marriage between the vegetative sensibility of the Black, an inferior quality, and the Apollonian rationality of the White, a superior quality. He writes:

> Whence this rigorous conclusion, that the source from which the arts have sprung is alien to the civilizing instincts. It is hidden in the blood of Blacks. This, one may say, is a beautiful crown that I put on the deformed head of the Black, and it is a great honor that I give him to gather around him the harmonious choir of Muses. The honor is not so great. I did not say that all the Muses were gathered there. The noblest ones are missing, those who use thought, those who prefer beauty to passion. . . . Let someone translate the *Odyssey* for him, and particularly the meeting between Ulysses and Naucisaa, the sublime example of thoughtful inspiration: he will go to sleep. In all human beings, in order for sympathy to be expressed, the intellect must first have understood, and this is where the difficulty lies with the Black. . . . The artistic sensibility of this being, in itself powerful beyond all expression, will thus remain necessarily limited to the most miserable uses. . . . Also, among all the art forms that

the dark-skinned creature prefers, music holds first place, because it caresses his ear with a succession of sounds and requires nothing of the thinking part of his brain. . . . How foreign he remains to the delicate conventions for which the European imagination has learned to ennoble its senses. . . . The White's illuminated sensuality, directed by science and thought, with the first notes, as they say, begins to create a picture. . . .

The Black sees none of that. He does not understand any part of it; and yet, let us succeed in awakening his instincts: the enthusiasm, the emotion will have an intensity different from our contained delight and the satisfaction of decent people.

I can see a Bambara listening to the performance of a tune that he likes. His face lights up, his eyes shine. He laughs and his wide mouth shows, flashing in the midst of his dark face, his wide and sharp teeth. Enjoyment comes. . . . Inarticulate sounds make an effort to come out of his throat that is restrained by passion: big tears run down his prominent cheeks, a little longer and he is going to shout, the music stops, he is overcome by fatigue. . . .

Thus the Black possesses to the highest degree the sensual faculty without which art is not possible; and, on the other hand, the absence of intellectual aptitudes renders him completely unfit for the culture of the arts, even for the appreciation of what this noble application of the human intelligence can produce of significance. In order to develop his faculties, he must ally himself with a differently gifted race. . . .

The artistic genius, equally foreign to the three great types, has manifested itself only after the marriage of Blacks and Whites.[3]

The Egyptian civilization, with its grandiose art, entirely due to a Black people, is the most categorical refutation of Gobineau's "scholarly" inanity, and we will not even bother to criticize this constellation of errors.

We only want to stress the fact that the intellectual and psychological climate created by all the writings of this type strongly conditioned the first definitions that the Negro-African thinkers of the period between the two World Wars had tried to give to their culture.

The "Negritude" poets did not, at that time, have the scientific means to refute or to question these types of errors. Scientific truth had been White for such a long time that, with the help and writings of Lucien Lévy-Bruhl, all these affirmations made under the scientific banner had to be accepted as such by our submissive peoples. Therefore the "Negritude" movement accepted this so-called inferiority and boldly assumed it in full view of the world. Aimé Césaire shouted: "Those who explored neither the seas nor the sky," and Leopold S. Senghor: "Emotion is Negro and reason is Greek."

Thus everybody was led, step by step, to specify too much, to maybe grant privilege to this psychic, constituent, third factor of the personality, which everybody else simply calls national temperament, and which varies from the Slav to the German, from the Latin to the Papua. The slope was too slippery and everybody followed it. This is due to the fact that this last factor is traditionally grasped in a qualitative way through literature, particularly through poetry: all peoples have sung their own virtues; whereas the other two factors, historical and linguistic, are susceptible only to a rigorously scientific approach.

But today, in order to better grasp peoples' cultural identity, a scientific approach to the psychic factor can equally be tried. For this, in the context of a sociohistorical approach, one should try to answer the following question: What are the *psychological and cultural invariants* that political and social revolutions, even the most radical ones, leave intact, not only among the people, but among the very leaders of the revolution? If one tries to answer such a question from the analysis of the historical conditioning of a given people and of the African peoples in general, one then already arrives at some results relatively better elaborated than before. One realizes that this communicative gaiety, which goes back to Galen's epoch, instead of being a permanent trait due solely to the sun, is a result of the reassuring communally securing social structures that bog down our people in the present and in a lack of concern for tomorrow, in optimism, etc., whereas the individualistic social structures of the Indo-Europeans engender anxiety, pessimism, uncertainty about tomorrow, moral solitude, tension regarding the future, and all its beneficial effects on the material life, etc.

Today, with the explosion everywhere in the world of these structures inherited from the past, we are witnessing a new moral and spiritual birth among peoples: a new African moral consciousness and a new national temperament are developing before our eyes, and unless the structures resist—and how could they?—this phenomenon of spiritual transformation of the people will become greater.

Until now, the cultural traits that we inherited from the past are the very ones that we analyzed in *L'Unité culturelle de l'Afrique Noire*: goodness, gaiety, optimism, social sense, etc., and this brief account shows that there is nothing fixed or permanent about them, but that they change with the conditions: Africa is beginning to experience some strongly individualistic consciousnesses, with all of the usual consequences. How can one, then, explain the feeling of cultural identity throughout this permanent change? What are the cultural invariants that we were talking about earlier? We cannot answer this question in detail here, but we can at least recall that the historical and linguistic factors constitute coordinates, quasi-absolute reference points in relation to the permanent flux of psychic changes.

And the Blacks of the diaspora? The linguistic bond is broken, but the historic bond remains stronger than ever, perpetuated by memory; just as the cultural heritage of Africa, which is evident in the three Americas, attests to the continuity of cultural customs: it has even been said, I believe, that the difference between the White American and his English, or in any event European, ancestor is the Negro laugh, so pleasant, inherited from the household slave who raised his children.

15

TOWARD A METHOD FOR AN APPROACH TO INTERCULTURAL RELATIONS

An approach suitable for explaining the difficulties and the failures in intercultural relations would consist of recalling the process according to which two given cultures are born, develop, make contact with each other, and come to influence each other in space and time.

Let us take as an example to study, on the one hand, the European geographic area, located in a temperate climate with its specific fauna and flora; its own history; its social and political structures; its morals and customs, born of the milieu indicated and on the other hand, the diametrically opposed tropical geographic area.

In order to limit ourselves to objective facts that everyone can observe, let us analyze the limitations imposed by the historicogeographic coordinates on the superimposition of the semantic fields of the concepts, in the general domain of linguistic expression, as one passes from one area to the other.

All the European languages (English, German, Spanish, French, Portuguese, Russian, etc.) have come from the same birthplace, whose literary expressions and richest poetic images are woven together, fabricated with the same elements of the real, drawn from the same milieu. Thus the terms: oak tree, cypress, fir tree, primrose, snowdrop, ivy, rose, wolf, bear, snow, etc., enter into the fabric of literary images that do not generally have their equivalent in all of the African languages of the tropics.

This fortunate example is suited to bringing to light the peculiarities of the problem of intercultural relations. It thus appears that in the domain of linguistic expression, which is the fundamental means of "total" communication, the Europeans would encounter only minor difficulties in communicating among themselves. A literary piece written in any European language can be translated into another European language with a minimal impoverishment; the identity of the fauna, the flora, of history, guarantee the existence of expressions rigorously equivalent in all the languages of the geographic-cultural area under consideration.

For this reason also, the phenomena of inter-European acculturation and cultural alienation are more attenuated, because they occur within the same great civilization.

The situation is different when a translator tries to translate the literary message of a written work, of a poem, from a European language into an African language or vice-versa. Three cases are possible:

> **1.** The concepts and images that carry the message are, according to the above, of a specific type, and a literal translation is therefore impossible in a language that does not participate in the same culture. For example: "white as snow," "bear one's cross."
>
> **2.** Images and expressions are of a universal type in the sense that they are sufficiently detached from all sociogeographic and climatic coordinates, so that the terms that designate them in one language can be translated without distortion into any other language no matter what its climatic zone. For instance: "great hardship," "to burn one's boats," "to be doubled up with laughter," "to smell disaster."
>
> **3.** There is a third category, made up of specific images that are susceptible to an adapted translation in the languages of different climatic zones. Thus, the French expression "*attendre sous l'orme*" (to wait until the cows come home) can be compared to its equivalent in Wolof, a Senegalese language, with the following adapted translation: "*Neg ci ron dahaar gi,*" which literally means "to wait until the tamarind tree grows," but which retains practically all the flavor of the original French expression.

Thus it can be shown in passing that the systematic translation of the expressions under (2) and (3) above into the African languages would be one way to enrich these without their losing their own genius. Besides, the reverse is possible, meaning that there can be introduced into European languages (or others) the types of expressions under (2) and (3) from the African languages. Though a language is, at each stage of its evolution, a closed system that is sufficient unto itself to express the whole universe as perceived by the thinking subject, similar integrations of new and fresh images would incontestably enrich the language under consideration, be it European or African, and would not duplicate the stock of already existing expressions. Translations of entire and diverse works, on a global level, would be thereby facilitated.

The European linguistic consciousness, or the foreign one in general, would more easily accept these perfectly intelligible and delectable expressions, encountered in the translations of many works, than the neologisms that are nothing but sounds that absorb the meaning of the sentence, because they cannot evoke any precise image in the mind of the reader. This fact will be more clear in what follows.

It is evident from the above that the Italian or the Rumanian who is condemned to speak Spanish would be less alienated, less in need of acculturation than the African who finds himself in the same situation. Let us suppose that the latter is a poet. Every time that he mentally conceives and elaborates an original image from the cultural elements of his own native tongue, and he tries to express it adequately in French, English, or Spanish, the poetic rhythm will be broken by the "barbarous" neologisms that litter the poetic field like rubble: the proper terms are radically, desperately nonexistent; the baobab is not the equivalent of the oak tree. The European linguistic and aesthetic consciousness (the foreign one in general) has not yet assimilated these terms which only represent sounds.

Unless the process of acculturation has been achieved, if the African poet proceeds and speaks of roses, of the lily of the valley that he has never "picked in the woods of Chaville," he is simply ridiculous and he no longer produces any effect. Nor will he give it the true cachet of exotic and savage nature in a language that is truly his own. Even Charles Marie Leconte de Lisle in his *Poémes barbares* would succeed better than he. It is this failure that Jean-Paul Sartre points out in *Orphée Noir*, as an irony of fate. He writes:

> [The Black] is perfectly at ease in it [French] when he thinks as a technician, as a scholar, or as a politician. It is necessary rather to speak of the slight but constant gap that separates what he says, when he speaks of himself, from what he wishes to say. It seems to him that a septentrional spirit steals his ideas from him, that it softly bends them to signify more or less that which *it* wishes, that the white words lap up his thought as the sand absorbs blood.[1]
>
> It is impossible for him to express his negritude with precise words which efficiently hit the mark at every blow. He can scarcely express his negritude in prose. Yet it is common knowledge that this feeling of failure before the language when considered as a means of direct expression is at the source of all poetic experience.[2]

Sartre goes further in his analysis and writes:

> The specific traits of a Society correspond exactly to the untranslatable locutions of its language. Now, that which dangerously

> threatens to curb the effort of the Blacks to reject our tutelage is that the harbingers of the new negritude are constrained to compose their gospel in French.[3]
>
> And since French lacks the terms and concepts to define negritude, since negritude is silence, to evoke it they employ "allusive words, never direct ones, reducing themselves to an equal silence."[4]

Sartre, one of the better-intentioned men among the Western intellectuals with regard to Africa, was not speaking for the average Negro intellectual. The failure he describes is that of the African poets, the very ones whose poems he analyzes. In any case, for him, the African poets express themselves in a language that is not the French language of the French people. These authors, says he, are going to de-Frenchify French before writing in it.[5]

> It is only when they [the words] have disgorged their whiteness that he [the Black herald] adopts them, making of this language in ruins a solemn and sacred super language, in short, Poetry.[6]

He adds:

> ...among the colonized the colonist manages to be the eternal mediator; he is there, always there, even though absent, all the way to the most secret meetings. And because words derive from ideas, when the Negro declares in French that he rejects French culture, he takes in one hand that which he has pushed away with the other. He installs in himself, as a brake, the thinking apparatus of the enemy.[7]

Naturally, Sartre shows that an allusive poetic language, bordering on silence, in a de-Frenchified French, remains possible. That amounts to saying the poetic images that you are expressing in our language are opaque to our French spirit. We would need a Biblical exegesis in order for us to understand their meaning: but then all of the poetic savor has already evaporated.

From the above it follows that for the African who borrows a European expression, the only literature that remains immediately and wholly possible is a scholarly one, an ideological, a militant one, or a poetry that uses universal images of type 2 above, or is adaptable to type 3.

One could cite very beautiful verses, even of an admirable beauty, written by Negro Africans and belonging to this category, that is to say, using universal images:

"Emotion is Negro and reason is Greek." (Leopold S. Senghor)

"... those who explored neither the seas nor the sky." (Aimé Césaire)

It is these types of successes that create the illusion that a foreigner can also penetrate the specific cultural nucleus elaborated by another people, in order to exploit its riches and treasures.

But an exhaustive review, author by author, would reveal the relative poverty of the constituent vocabulary of the African writers' poetic images in foreign, European languages: a very short list of epithets, mainly "moral," would give the most frequent terms: valorous, noble, fiery, langorous, etc.

Picturesque terms painting the nuances of colors, taste, of smell, of hearing, and of touch are forbidden to Negro-African poetry, in the proportion that they belong to the stock of specific vocabulary tied to geographical coordinates.

This is the manner in which the limits that are imposed on the originality of an African literature in a foreign Western language must be shown, as long as the process of acculturation or of alienation is not achieved.

This brief comparative study allows us to clearly distinguish three conceptual levels from the analysis of the specificity of linguistic expression. The observation is a general one and could be applied to the comparative study of any two foreign cultures, provided that both of them are sufficiently different.

To these three levels correspond three types of conceptual apparatuses, which have to be isolated with care, at least, while keeping in mind their intercultural relations, if one wants to deepen their analysis while methodically examining the difficulties one by one.

In fact, to continue our analysis, we will bring these levels back to two principal stages of the specific cultural fact (the incommunicable), and of the universal cultural fact: specific concepts and universal concepts.

THE ARTS

After having examined the specificity of linguistic expression and the constraints that it imposes on intercultural relations, let us see if the other modes of expression are privileged, those that are exclusively plastic, such as sculpture, painting, music, dance. These art forms are *a priori* universal languages because they have the authority to create plastic forms or rhythms that our senses can grasp directly without aid of the spoken language. Therefore, one has the impression that in the case of the plastic arts, there does not exist, in the domain of intercultural relations, an irreducible, impermeable nucleus where the specific elements of a given culture would be concentrated.

Let us consider Negro sculpture, which without doubt has strongly influenced Western modern art of the twentieth century. In studying this phenomenon, one realizes that the Western artist has borrowed from his anonymous African colleague less a canon of beauty than the right to free himself from the classical canon of gold work and of anatomical rigor, so many factors that, under various forms, have governed European art from Phidias to Rodin, from antiquity to modern times. The creative freedom of plastic forms and rhythms is the greatest lesson that modern art has learned from Negro art. Obviously, this feeling of liberty is difficult to separate from the plastic inventions that it engenders, and almost all modern artists create forms related to those of Negro art; the filiation, the influence are obvious, even among the artists who would deny it.

This does not prevent, all snobbery aside, the average Westerner, without any experience or artistic education, from being generally very ill prepared to appreciate the aesthetic value of a piece of Negro art. And did not André Malraux, who was a great connoisseur of Western art, go so far as to purely and simply deny the existence of a Negro art, in spite of its obvious influence on the Western art that he adored?[8]

In the same vein, Japanese and Chinese painting is diversely appreciated in the West, even though it involves a universal language whose meaning is obvious from the start.

Because of this very fact, the details, the whole painting, or the sculpture (Negro art) end up revealing a universe in which the incomprehensible particularities triumph over the universal traits common to all of humanity, and in which the human message that the work of art carries is not appreciated because of lack of education.

Thus, in the present state of artistic education in the world, even in the realm of the plastic arts, cultural customs tend to favor the existence of residual cultural centers whose (cultural) substance cannot be grasped and appreciated except from the inside.

If we take African music or dance, the findings are similar, even if, by our imagination, we strip our ballets of all their ethnographic and brutally erotic character. A Western musicologist, with the best intentions, after many efforts at adaption, confesses to have heard only cacophony, after listening to the religious music and songs of the Murides in Senegal. Other Westerners say the same thing about the griots' songs, which are among the most beautiful epic solos of the precolonial epoch.

I heard a great Western intellectual describe a part of Hindu music where all the Hindu listeners fell into ecstasy while he remained completely cold and indifferent, not being able to appreciate said music.

One can thus say that, in every culture, there are two domains:

A *specific* level to which, in fact, corresponds a specific conceptual apparatus. It is the most dense level, where the fundamental elements of the culture are elaborated, which maintain it as a center from which its effects will radiate. This nucleus can explode or perish as a cell; then there is no longer any cultural radiance. And yet, all the phenomena that occur are practically impossible to express through universal concepts, in accordance with the above. If one who is foreign to this culture tries to penetrate it, he runs into a psychological barrier, one could almost say a barrier of potential.

A second cultural level would correspond to the *universal* concepts. If we had the right to use the atomic image for the convenience of this account, we would say that cultures interfere with each other especially at the level of their radiance outside of their specific nuclei, at the level of their electronic charges, and that this domain is surely that of universal relations.

But this atomistic conception could very rapidly lead to dangerous and erroneous mechanistic views.

Factors that can be called *cultural invariants* must also be studied, meaning elements left untouched by the revolutionary cultural transformations, even by the radical ones, the deep aesthetic sentiment, for instance. The grace of the dancer and of the athlete of Western and Socialist countries. The cultural and social invariants, typically Western, that can be found after the Bolshevik revolution, in Lenin, Stalin, and Trotsky?

Finally, one can see that no matter what the mode of knowledge with which the problems are viewed, the conclusions of this account remain the same.

PART 4

AFRICA'S CONTRIBUTION TO HUMANITY IN SCIENCES AND IN PHILOSOPHY

16

AFRICA'S CONTRIBUTION: SCIENCES

EGYPTIAN MATHEMATICS: GEOMETRY

It would be very edifying to underscore, as a matter of introduction to this chapter, the undeniable connections that exist between Egyptian mathematics and the so-called discoveries that made celebrities out of Greek scholars, such as Archimedes and Pythagoras, just to cite these two.

As for his method of investigation, Archimedes, the greatest representative of Greek intellectualism in antiquity, does not hesitate to reveal in a letter to his friend Eratosthenes, that he proceeds by weighing, first empirically, in order to confirm the equality of the surface of two geometrical figures before undertaking a demonstration of a theoretical character *a posteriori*; and he even recommends his method to Eratosthenes: it is precisely the same method that he used in the quadrature of the parabola.

According to Paul Ver Eecke, "Archimedes dedicates his treatise *The Method* to his friend, the geometrician Eratosthenes, and he reveals to him his mechanical method (of weighing geometrical figures) as the hidden source of his principal discoveries."[1] But Ver Eecke adds further, as if in his inward self he was accusing Archimedes of intellectual dishonesty:

> In fact, if the treatise on the mechanical method, recently brought to light, has come to reveal to us the secret of some of the most beautiful discoveries of the great geometrician, he has, however, raised only a corner of the veil that covers the genesis of the great number of propositions, which, demonstrated by a double reductio *ad absurdum*, presuppose in spite of everything a previous notion,

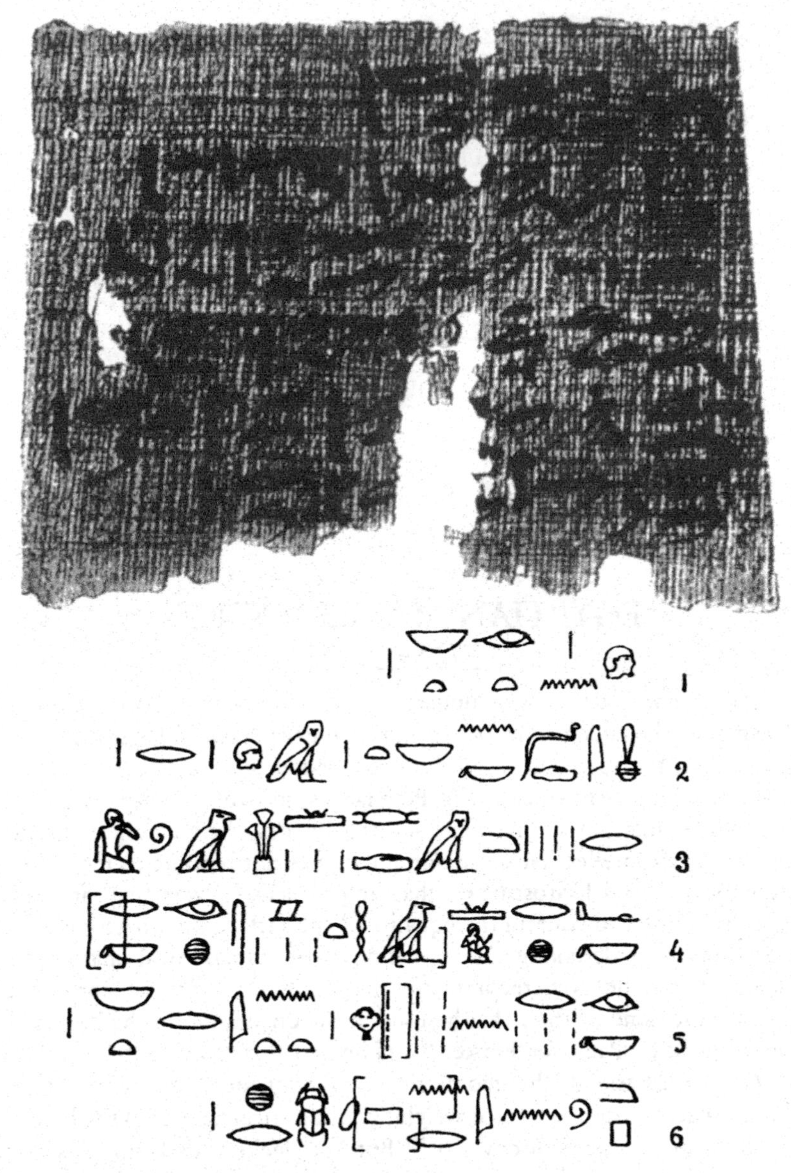

Figure 34: Hieratic text of problem 10 of the *Papyrus of Moscow* and a partial transcription of the first six lines in hieroglyphic writing, according to Struve. One will notice that the last line (6) contains the expression that is the object of controversy: "*ges pw n inr*" = "half of an egg." (Otto Neugebauer, *Vorlesungen über Geschichte der antiken mathematischen Wissenschaften*, Berlin: Julius Springer, 1934, vol. I, p. 129)

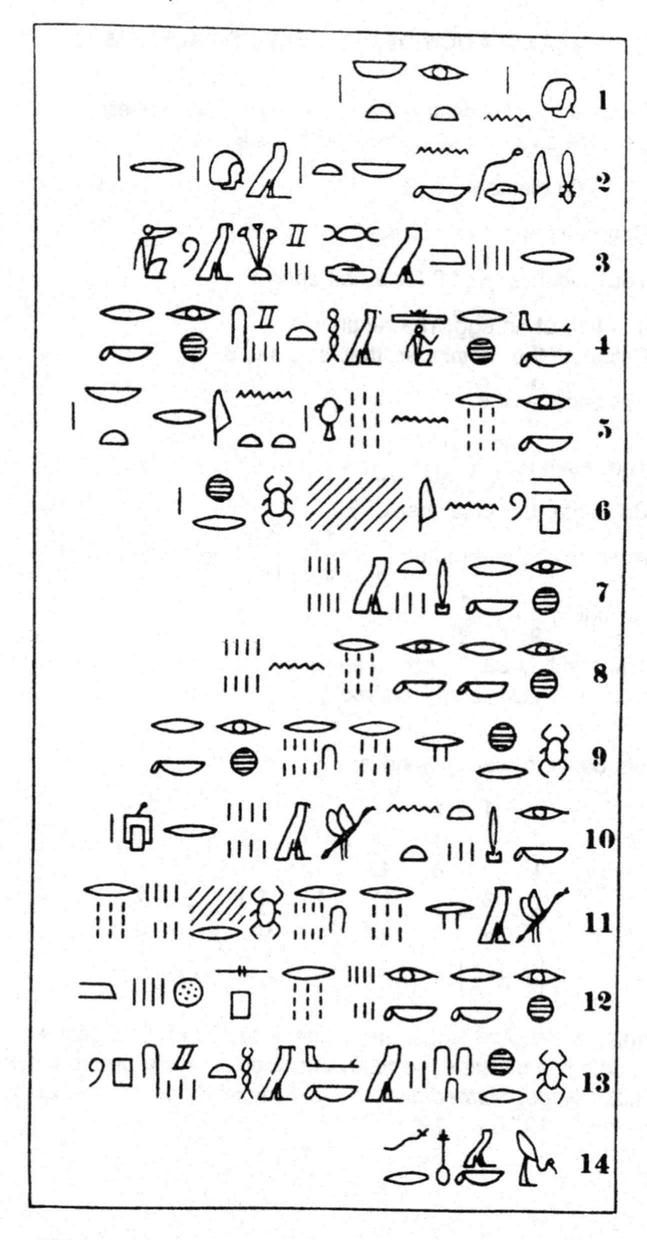

Figure 35: Complete text of problem 10 of the *Papyrus of Moscow*, from T. Eric Peet. (T. Eric Peet: "A Problem in Egyptian Geometry," in *Journal of Egyptian Archeology*, vol. 17, 1931, pp. 100–106, fig. XII)

TRANSLATION OF THE TEXT OF PROBLEM 10

1. Method for calculating (the surface) of a half sphere
2. You are given a half sphere (with a magnitude)
3. of $4\frac{1}{2}$ (in diameter).
4. Can you tell me its surface?
5. You calculate $\frac{1}{9}$ of 9 for a half sphere.
6. It is half of an egg. The result is 1.
7. Calculate the remainder, that is to say 8.
8. Calculate $\frac{1}{9}$ of 8.
9. The result is $\frac{2}{3} + \frac{1}{6} + \frac{1}{18}$.
10. Calculate the remainder of 8.
11. After having subtracted $\frac{2}{3} + \frac{1}{6} + \frac{1}{18}$. The result is $7 + \frac{1}{9}$.
12. Multiply $7\frac{1}{9}$ by $4\frac{1}{2}$.
13. The result is 32; that is its surface.
14. You have calculated it correctly.

The sequence of calculations is:

$$9 - 1 = 8$$
$$\frac{8}{9} = \frac{2}{3} + \frac{1}{6} + \frac{1}{18}$$
$$8 - \frac{8}{9} = 8 - \left(\frac{2}{3} + \frac{1}{6} + \frac{1}{18}\right) = 7 + \frac{1}{9}$$
$$\left(7 + \frac{1}{9}\right) \times \left(4 + \frac{1}{2}\right) = 32 = \text{the surface}$$

As emphasized by Gillings, the scribe is especially preoccupied with methodology and made the following calculations in problem number 10 (R.J. Gillings, *Mathematics in the Time of the Pharaohs*, London: M.I.T. Press, 1972, p. 199):

He began by doubling the diameter of the half sphere on line 5:

$$\left(4 + \frac{1}{2}\right) \times 2 = 2d$$

On lines 6 and 7, he calculates $\frac{8}{9}$ of $2d$, that is to say $\frac{8}{9} \times 2d$.

On lines 8, 9, 10, and 11, he calculates $\frac{8}{9}$ of the last result, which yields:

$$\frac{8}{9} \times \frac{8}{9} \times 2d$$

On line 12, he multiples the whole by d to obtain the surface (S):

$$S = d \times 2 \times \frac{8}{9} \times \frac{9}{9} \times d = 2 \times \frac{64}{81} \times d^2$$

Hence (r being the radius of the sphere):

$$S = 2 \times \frac{64}{81} \times (2r)^2 \text{ or } S = 2 \times \frac{256}{81} r^2$$

$$S = 2\pi r^2 \text{ with } \pi = \frac{256}{81} = \underline{3.16049}$$

That which precedes is equivalent to the following literal notation from Struve:

$$S = \left[\left(2d - \frac{2d}{9}\right) - \frac{1}{9}\left(2d - \frac{2d}{9}\right)\right] d$$

$$S = 2d^2\left[\left(1 - \frac{1}{9}\right) - \frac{1}{9}\left(1 - \frac{1}{9}\right)\right]$$

$$S = 2d^2\left[\left(\frac{8}{9}\right) - \frac{1}{9}\left(\frac{8}{9}\right)\right] = 2d^2\left[\frac{72-8}{81}\right]$$

$$S = 2d^2 \times \frac{64}{81}$$

$$S = 2 \times \frac{64}{81} \times (2r)^2 = 2 \times 4 \times \frac{64}{81} \times r^2$$

$$S\frac{1}{2} \text{ sphere} = 2 \times \frac{256}{81} \times r^2 = \underline{2\pi r^2}$$

obtained in ways that Archimedes said nothing about or arrived at through methods that we still follow today, but from which he had carefully erased his footprints.[2]

Since V. V. Struve published the *Papyrus of Moscow*[3] (figs. 34, 35, 36) the international scientific community knows with certainty that two thousand years before Archimedes, the Egyptians had already established the rigorous formulae of the area of the sphere: $S = 4\pi R^2$. Struve, who did his utmost to find the approach of the Egyptian mathematicians, thinks that they used an empirical-theoretical method comparable at every point to that of Archimedes; this remains arguable, but the *Rhind Papyrus* published by T. Eric Peet shows us that the Egyptians also knew the exact formula for the volume of the cylinder: $V = \pi R^2 \cdot h$ and the constant ratio between the area of a circle and its diameter. All the more reason that they had to know the area of the cylinder which, cut along a generating line, becomes a rectangle whose area they knew how to calculate. They must have established an elementary basic parallel that is glaringly obvious in comparison to the more difficult formulae that they established, namely: establishing the ratio between the length of the former circumference, that has become the length of the rectangle, and its diameter, to find $\pi = C/D$.

They knew the exact formulae of the area of the circle: $S = \pi R^2$ with a value of $\pi = 3.16$, therefore they very probably knew the length of the circumference $l = 2\pi R$ with the same approximation as Struve shows it: "But exercise 10 has brought us both the formula for the formula for the area of the sphere and that of the length of the circumference."[4]

In a similar vein, it is exercise 14 of the *Papyrus of Moscow* dealing with the calculation of the volume of a truncated pyramid (fig. 36) that has allowed us to know that the Egyptians also knew the exact formula for the volume of the pyramid; otherwise we would still be debating today, in spite of the materiality of the Egyptian pyramids, whether the Egyptians really knew the formula for the volume of the pyramid. But who can do more can do less, and those who have established the formula of the truncated pyramid

$$V = \frac{h}{3}(a^2 + ab + b^2)$$

knew all the more that:

$$V = \frac{h}{3}a^2.$$

As luck would have it, the most complex expression, analytically speak-

Figure 36: Problem 14 of the *Papyrus of Moscow*, dealing with the volume of the truncated pyramid. (Otto Neugebauer, *Vorlesungen über Geschichte der antiken mathematischen Wissenschaften*, p. 127)

the most inaccessible, was rescued from oblivion by the rare papyruses that survived the vandalism of the conquerors. Thus, exercise 14 of the *Papyrus of Moscow* and exercises 56, 57, 58, 59, and 60 of the *Rhind Papyrus* (figs. 37, 38, 39, 40) show us that the Egyptians, two thousand years before the Greeks, studied the mathematics of the pyramid and of the cone, and that they even used the different trigonometric lines, the tangent, the sine, the cosine, the cotangent, in order to calculate their slopes. This would not keep Archimedes from writing to the geometrician Dasitheus that it is "Eudoxus of Cnidus to whom we owe the measurement of the pyramid and of the cone."[5] Furthermore, Eudoxus and Plato were former pupils of the Egyptian priests at Heliopolis,[6] but as the documents prove, the Egyptians had already proceeded, two thousand years before the birth of these two, with the study that is attributed to them. In fact, the cube, the pyramid, etc., are also a part of the basic volumes improperly "baptized" Platonic bodies of work.

Struve shows that the Egyptian mathematicians who established the rigorous formula for the area of the sphere, a formula identical to that

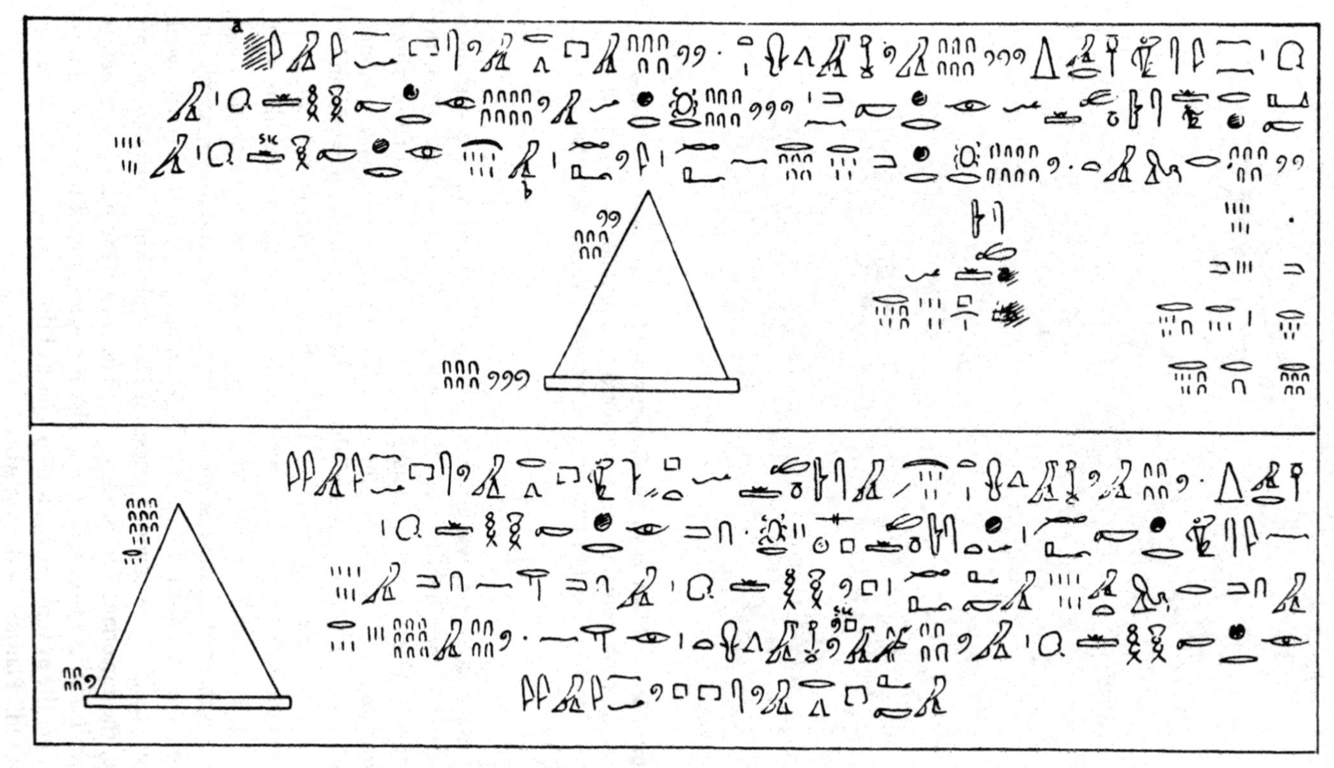

Figure 37: Problems 56 and 57 of the *Rhind Papyrus*.

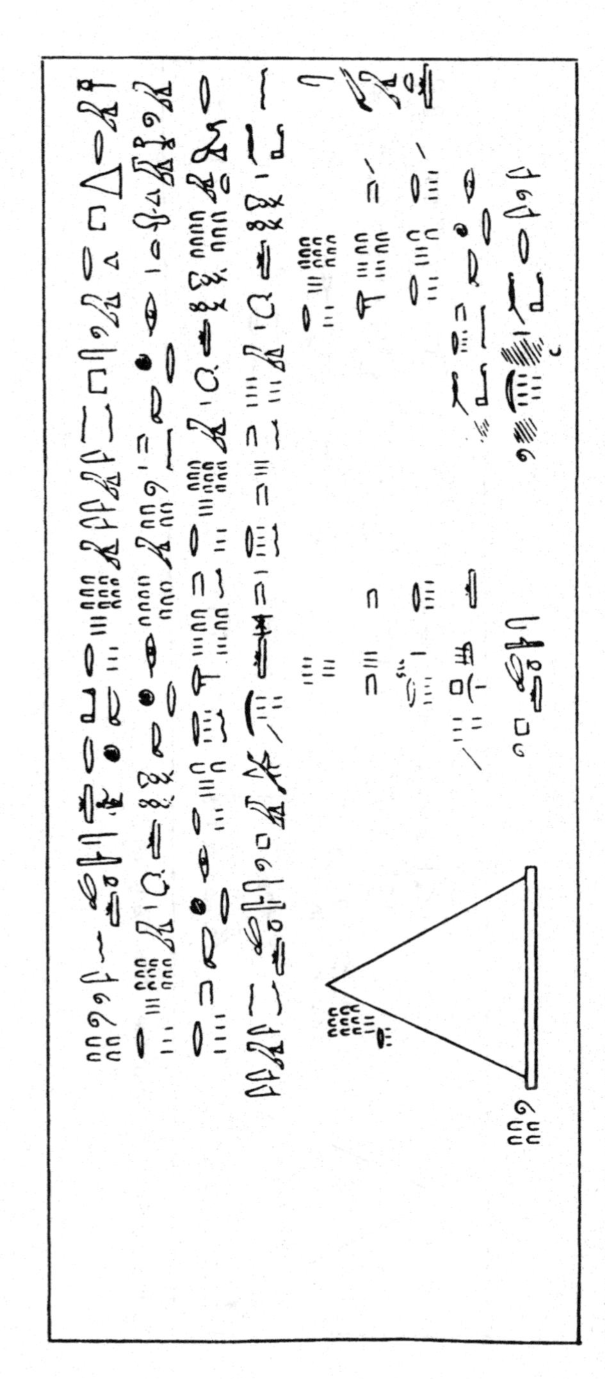

Figure 38: Problem 58 of the *Rhind Papyrus*.
Problems 56 to 60 of the *Rhind Papyrus* deal, for the first time in the history of mathematics, with trigonometry, the slopes of the pyramid, and conic volume. (T. Eric Peet, *The Rhind Mathematical Papyrus*, The University Press of Liverpool, 1923, plates Q, R).

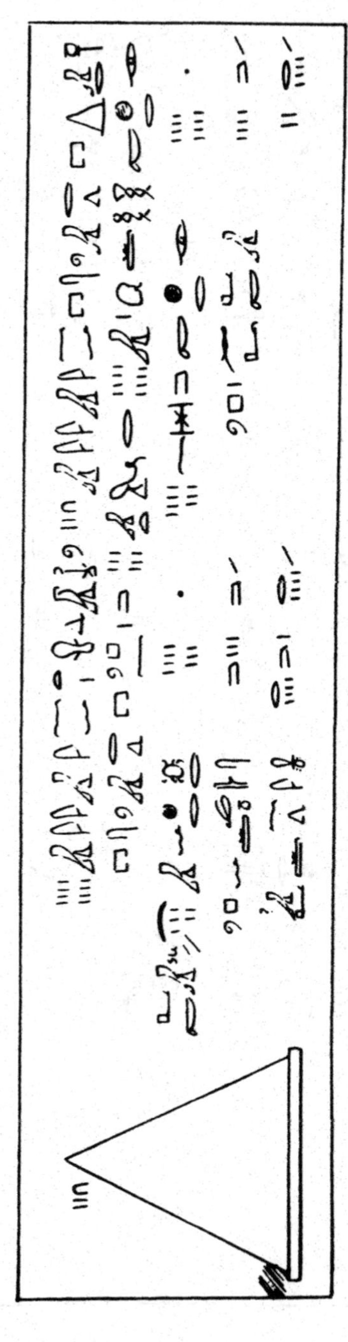

Figure 39: Problem 59 of the *Rhind Papyrus.*

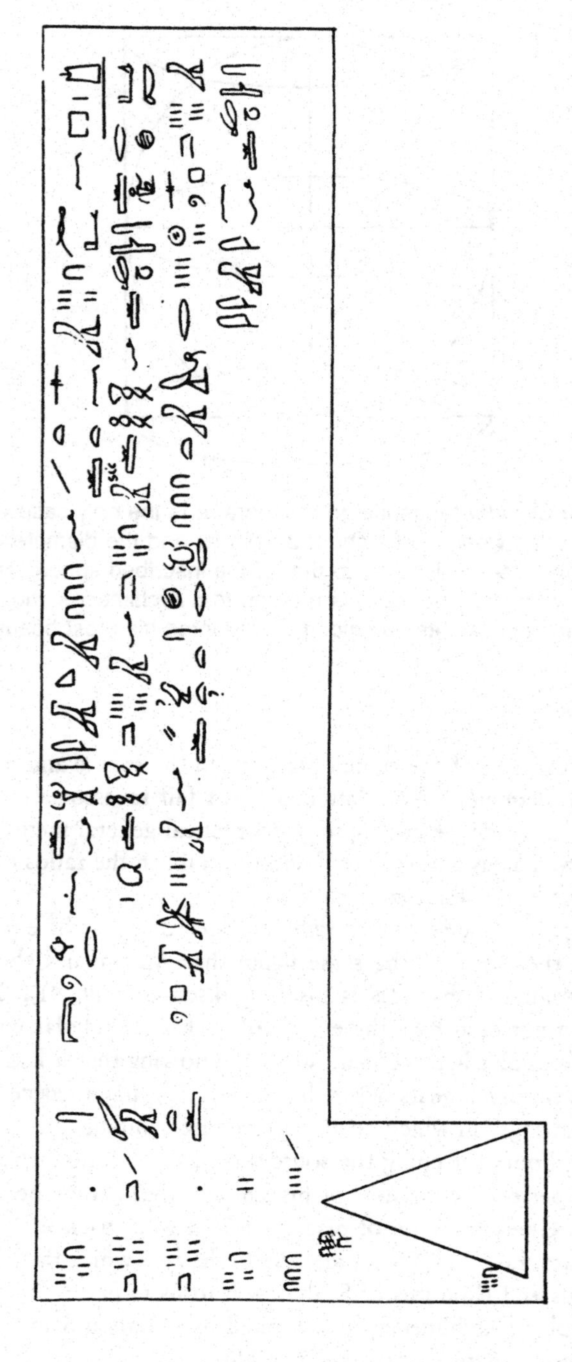

Figure 40: Problem 60 of the *Rhind Papyrus.* One notices the conical pillar (*inw*) at the top right, at the very beginning of the first line.

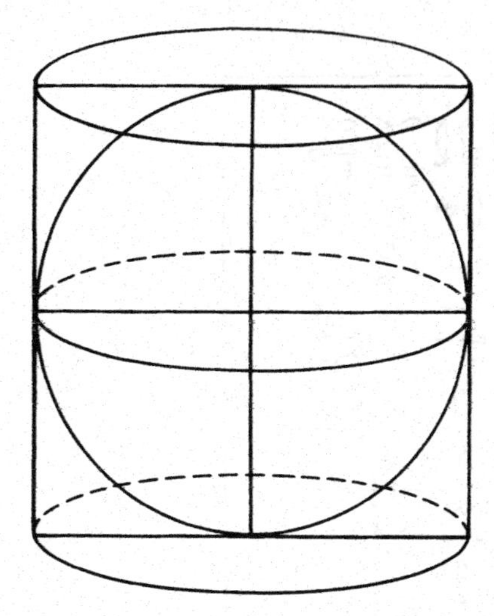

Figure 41: Cylinder tangential to a sphere. It is the only case where the equality between the height of a cylinder and the diameter of the circle at the base, which is also that of the inscribed sphere, is of particular interest. This figure is the one that Archimedes chose as an epitaph, because, as he said, it represented his most beautiful discovery.

which gives the area of the cylinder tangent to the sphere and of a height equal to the diameter of the latter, did not fail to associate these two figures in order to derive an empirical-theoretical general method for the study of curved areas and volumes[7] and to establish the ratios of the area and the volume of these two bodies.

Now, a sphere inscribed in a right cylinder of a height equal to the diameter of the sphere is the same figure that Archimedes chose as his epitaph, considering that this is his best discovery (fig. 41). Thus, Archimedes did not even have the excuse of an honest scholar who would rediscover an established theorem, without knowing that it had been discovered two thousand years before him by his Egyptian predecessors. The other "borrowings" in which he indulged himself during and after his trip to Egypt, without ever citing the sources of his inspiration, show clearly that he was perfectly conscious of his sin, and that hereby he was being faithful to a Greek tradition of plagiarism that went back to Thales, Pythagoras, Plato, Eudoxus, Oenopides, Aristotle, etc., which the testimonies of Herodotus and Diodorus of Sicily reveal to us in part.[8]

The epitaph of Archimedes, rediscovered by Cicero at Syracuse, proves that this is not a myth propagated by tradition.[9]

It is remarkable that the Romans, who had less contact with the Egyptians, have contributed practically nothing to the exact sciences, to geometry in particular.

Therefore, the scientific acquisitions anterior to the ancient Egyptians are for the most part implicated in the books of Archimedes, entitled *On the Sphere and the Cylinder, On the Measurement of a Circle*, to name just a few.

In fact, Archimedes, in the latter book, in calculating the value of $\pi = 3.14$ did not make any reference to the very close value of $\pi = 3.16$ found by the Egyptians two thousand years before him. He did not suspect that an Egyptian papyrus would accidentally reveal the truth to posterity.

As a matter of fact, Archimedes does not explicitly calculate the value 3.1416. He shows that the ratio of the circumference to the diameter lies between 3.1/7 and 3.10/71. We will see that the best approximation found by the Babylonians was 3 (a whole number) or else 3.8!

Archimedes's treatise entitled *On the Equilibrium of Planes or of Their Center of Gravity* deals with the equilibrium of the lever, a problem that the Egyptians had mastered in 2600 B.C., the era of the construction of the pyramids.

In fact, to elevate a five-million-ton stone monument to a 148-meter height and comprised of blocks of several tons, one had to have a solid knowledge of mechanics and above all of statics; the knowledge of the theory of leverage was indispensable,[10] and Struve writes: "Also we must admit that in mechanics the Egyptians had more knowledge than we wanted to believe."[11] He adds: "The Egyptian plans are as correct as those of modern engineers."[12]

The Egyptians are the inventors of the scale. Referring to figure 42 representing a scale from 1500 B.C., one notices that the manipulator acts on slides in an initial position symmetrical to the central support, which is a refined manner of weighing. It is an astute way of playing masterfully on the length of one of the lever's arms that is part of the scale, and of displacing the center of gravity of the system.[13]

The scale is the first rigorous scientific application of the theory of leverage.

The first three propositions of Archimedes' book on the equilibrium of planes consider "a lever, weighty bodies hanging at each of its extremities and a point of support. They then successively establish that, when the arms of the lever are equal, the weights supposedly in balance are also equal, and that unequal weights will balance at unequal distances from the point of support, the heaviest weight corresponding to the shortest distance."[14]

The *shadoof* (1500 B.C.) was already a mechanical application, in Archimedes' sense, of the lever with unequal arms (fig. 43).

Figure 42: Egyptian balance with cursors. Notice the initial symmetry of the position of the ring-shaped cursors that the operator is manipulating in order to adjust the weight. These submultiples of weight, whose displacement caused the changing of the center of gravity of the system, show that the Egyptians had to have mastered the theory of leverage, as confirmed by figure 43, which represents a lever in the most general sense, with two unequal arms and a counterweight at one end, in order to draw water with a minimum amount of effort. The "point of support" of Archimedes was already there, two thousand years before his birth. (The weighing of golden ingots, around 1500 B.C. Taken from Norman de Garis Davies, *Rekhmire*, fig. LIV)

Figure 43: The watering of a garden using the *shadoof*, during the period of the New Kingdom. Application of the lever with unequal arms: the instrument that would allow Archimedes to "lift up the Earth, if he had a point of support" was already invented by the Egyptians a thousand years before his birth. (Norman de Garis Davies, *The Tomb of Two Sculptors at Thebes*, fig. 28)

Similarly, Archimedes would not "invent" the continuous screw, the spiral, in Syracuse, Sicily, but during a trip to Egypt where this screw was invented, evidently, centuries before the birth of Archimedes, as Strabo's account proves.

On the use of this screw in Spain for pumping water out of the mines, Diodorus of Sicily writes: "What is so amazing is that they (the miners) pump the water entirely by means of Egyptian screws that Archimedes of Syracuse invented during his trip to Egypt."[15]

But Ver Eecke adds: "In spite of this account, there still is doubt about the origin of this equipment which perhaps goes back to a much earlier antiquity. In fact, Strabo also mentions the use of this screw in Egypt, without attributing its invention to Archimedes."[16]

Far be it for us to say that Archimedes or the Greeks in general, who came three thousand years after the Egyptians, did not go further than they in the different domains of knowledge; we simply want to say that as honest scholars, they should have, each time, put things straight by clearly indicating what they had inherited from their Egyptian masters and what they themselves contributed. But almost all of them failed to observe this elementary rule of intellectual honesty.

Problem 53 of the *Rhind Papyrus* shows us a figure clearly derived from the so-called theorem "of Thales," seventeen hundred years before the birth of Thales (see p. 256 and fig. 44).

Pythagoras' case is also typical, as we will see below. Regarding the theorem improperly attributed to him, P. H. Michel writes:

> Whether stated or not by Pythagoras himself, . . . the connection . . . had, furthermore, already been known for a long time by the Egyptians and the Babylonians, who had verified it in certain cases. The formula remained to be put into widespread use and to be geometrically demonstrated, without using numbers. This decisive progress was accomplished, in all probability, conjointly with the discovery of the irrationals, when the opportunity presented itself in a problem that did not have a numerical solution, that of the duplication of the square. What had to be demonstrated was both the incommensurability of the diagonal with the side (or of the hypotenuse of the isosceles rectangular triangle with its sides) and the fact that the square constructed on this diagonal was equivalent to double that of the primitive square.[17]

One will find below (p. 258) that the definition of the "double remen" or of the Egyptian "double cubit" answers to these two necessities. Indeed, it concerns the definition of a length equal to the diagonal of a square with a side a, which necessarily presupposes the knowledge of Pythagoras's theorem without numerical data, whence $d = a\sqrt{2}$. This formula as a definition shows that the Egyptians necessarily knew the irrational number *par excellence* $\sqrt{2}$ (in addition to π) and that the finality of the relation that bears his name (double cubit) is the duplication of the square; in fact, one has only to raise it to the square in order to see that it allows the

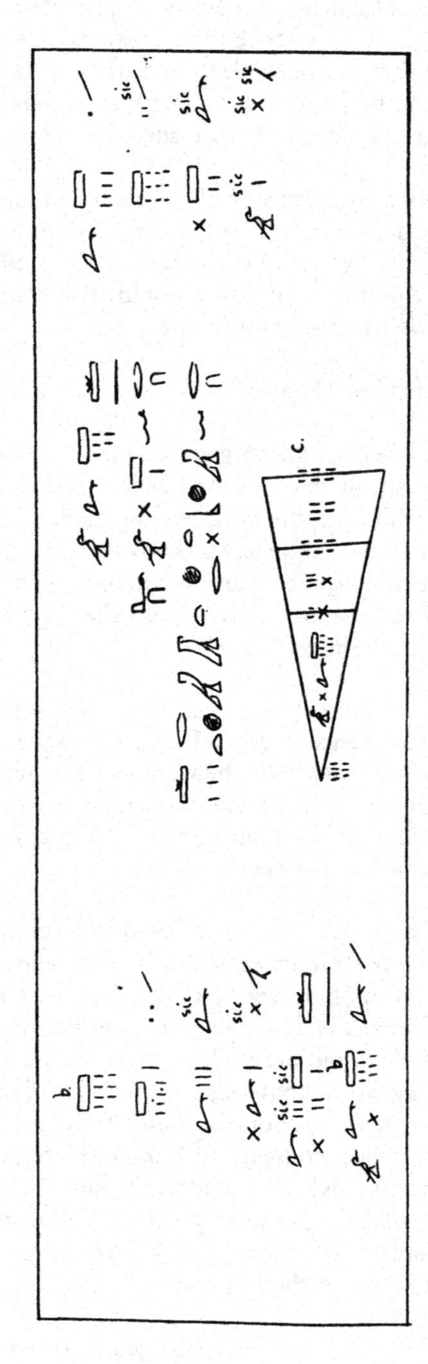

Figure 44: Problem 53 of the *Rhind Papyrus*. The famous figure implying the knowledge of the theorem of Thales. (T. Eric Peet, *The Rhind Mathematical Papyrus*, fig. P)

construction, on the diagonal, of a square double that of the one with side *a*. Richard J. Gillings mentioned this relationship without accompanying it with these few indispensable commentaries.

The remark below, by Struve, shows that many fundamental questions relative to Egyptian science have been evaded. He writes:

> If the interpretation by Borchardt of a drawing on one of the walls of the Temple at Luxor [fig. 45] is correct, then the Egyptians have posed the problem of calculating the surface of an ellipse."[18] Consequently, even Apollonius of Perga would have something to account for vis-à-vis Egyptian mathematics.

But Struve goes further. He adds:

> *The Papyrus of Moscow*, which gives us, among many others, the proof that a famous discovery by Archimedes has to be credited to the Egyptians, confirms in the most striking manner the statements of Greek writers on the mathematical knowledge of Egyptian scholars. We therefore no longer have any reason to reject the affirmations of the Greek writers according to whom the Egyptians were the masters of the Greeks in geometry."[19]

In order to better underscore the already very much advanced theoretical character of Egyptian science in general, Struve insists on the fact that in the *Medical Papyrus Adwin Smith*, the word *brain* is mentioned, and that this term was unknown in all the other (scientific) languages of the East of that period and that the Egyptian author of this papyrus already knew the body's dependency on the brain.

> Thus, it is again a great discovery attributed to Democritus that will have to be pushed back fourteen hundred years before the birth of its presumed inventor. These new facts, by which the *Papyrus Adwin Smith* and the *Papyrus of Moscow* enrich our knowledge, force us into a radical review of our persistent value judgment held up to this moment about Egyptian knowledge. A problem like that of the research on the brain's functions or that [of the determination] of the surface of the sphere no longer belongs to the circle of questions by which empirical knowledge is edified, within a primitive culture. These already are pure theoretical problems, which hereby prove that the Egyptian people as well as the Greek people strove to acquire a pure intellectual vision of the universe.[20]

This fact of the exactness of Egyptian geometry, which causes no other discovery to ever be questioned, was without doubt also the

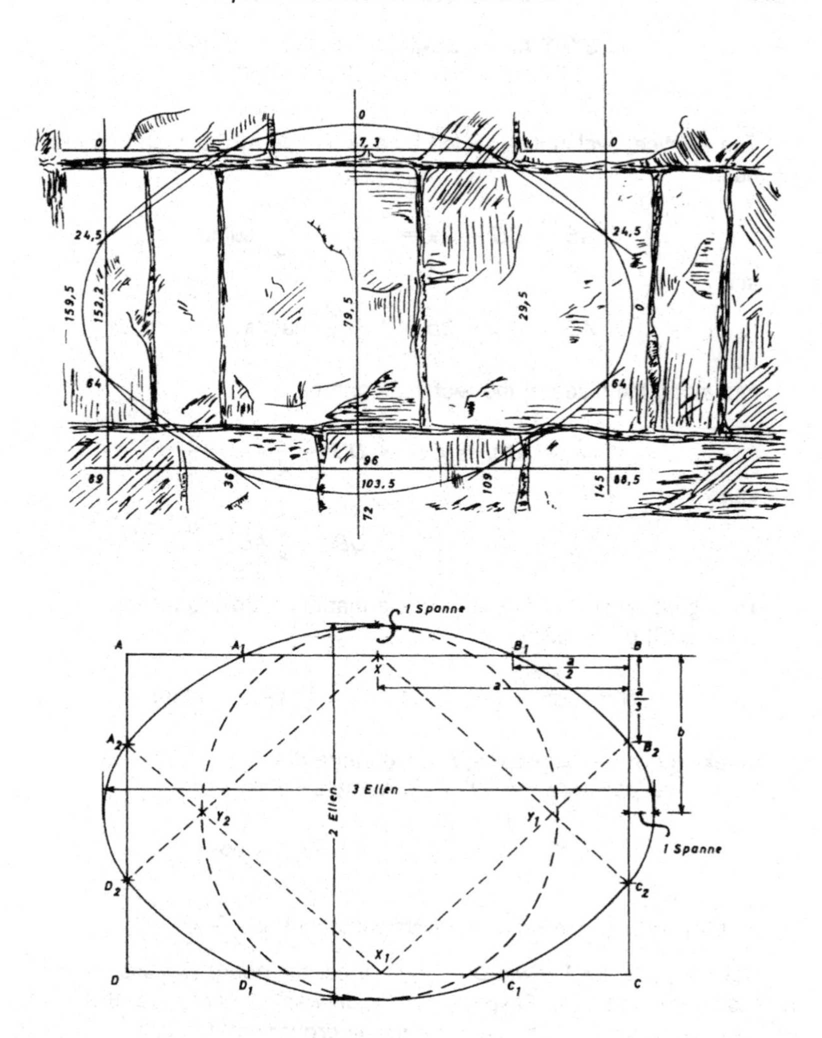

Figure 45: Reproduction of the ellipse drawn on a wall of the Temple of Luxor. This wall was built under Ramses III, around 1200 B.C. (Drawing by Amadou Faye, IFAN, after the original by Ludwig Borchardt, *Zeitschrift für Aegyptischer Sprache*, vol. XXXIV, 1896, fig. VII)

reason why, according to Greek tradition, geometry came to Hellas not from Babylonia, but from Egypt.[21]

From this fact we have every right to suppose that in the Egyptian schools (Houses of Life where they recopied the papyruses), across

EGYPTIAN RESEARCH ON THE ELLIPSE (CALCULATION OF THE SURFACE?)

The elliptical oval is intersected by a rectangle ABCD such that one has:

$$AB = DC = 2a = 2 + \frac{1}{2} = \frac{1}{4} \text{ cubits}$$

and

$$AD = BC = 2b = 1 + \frac{2}{3} \text{ cubits}$$

and along the sides of the rectangle one has:

$$AA_1 = BB_1 = CC_1 = DD_1 = \frac{1}{4} AB = \frac{a}{2}$$

and

$$AA_2 = BB_2 = CC_2 = DD_2 = \frac{1}{6} AB = \frac{a}{3}$$

The figure presents itself as if it is a matter of looking for the surface (S) of the ellipse:

$$S = \pi ab = 1 \times 1\frac{1}{2} \times \pi = 4.71 \text{ (exact value)}$$

In taking not the demi-axes, but the entire diameters, which are 2 and 3 respectively, the following formula yields:

$$S = \left(2 - \frac{2}{7}\right) \times \left(3 - \frac{2}{7}\right) = 4.65$$

and the error of the Egyptian architect would be $\frac{6}{471}$ or $\frac{1}{78}$. Nevertheless, for Ludwig Borchardt, a certain doubt remains as to the problem that the Egyptian technician wanted to resolve. But there is no doubt that it pertains to the property of the ellipse.

> the millennia, very vast mathematical knowledge was accumulated, but which with the great temples and the royal libraries are, for the most part, lost forever.[22]

These are the facts. We will see next how an ideologue like T. Eric Peet is going to fruitlessly try to contest them.

Surface of the Sphere
$S = 4\pi R^2$

T. Eric Peet has made a superhuman and particularly whimsical effort to contest the idea that problem 10 of the *Papyrus of Moscow*, studied by Struve, deals with the curved surface of a half-sphere. He believed that he demonstrated it, using philological considerations and arbitrary modifications of the text.

He wanted to prove that this problem in reality deals with the surface of a semicircle, or a half-cylinder. Therefore, he did not hesitate, with obvious dishonesty, to propose arbitrary modifications of the very text of the problem, using some fragile philological considerations, as we will see.

The text of the *Papyrus of Moscow*, and therefore of problems 10 (surface of the sphere) and 14 (volume of a truncated pyramid), is written in hieratic, a cursive form of writing (2000 B.C.). Struve transcribes it in hieroglyphic signs (figs. 34, 35, 36).

A formal convention exists in Egyptian writing: every sign followed by a vertical bar rigorously represents the shown object; no other interpretation is permitted; thus *nbt* = calabash = half-sphere. No rule of the language permits a different translation. Struve insisted on this fundamental law of hieroglyphic writing in the following terms:

> The word is written with the hieroglyph *nbt*, [accompanied] by the *t* of the feminine gender and a vertical bar. This vertical bar indicates that the hieroglyph that it follows designates in the literal sense the thing that it represents. As the hieroglyph *nbt* represents a basket in the form of a half-sphere, the word *nbt* here signifies, in exercise 10, a basket.[23]

Whereas any honest critique should start by eliminating this fundamental difficulty, Peet, throughout his criticism, resolutely closes his eyes to this observation that forbids him, at the risk of appearing to be an eccentric ideologue, from confusing a half-sphere with a half-cylinder. He writes:

> To this it may be replied that Struve has produced strong etymological evidence to show that the *nbt* is in effect a hemisphere. . . . Struve, who translates it as hemisphere, finds confirmation of this in line 6,

> where he thinks that the *nbt* was stated to be half an *inr* (= egg), which he holds to be the technical term for a sphere.[24]

The dishonesty is obvious; not being able to criticize Struve's first argument cited above (namely: *nbt* followed by a bar must be taken in its literal sense), Peet is completely silent on the subject, for the uninformed reader who does not refer to Struve's analysis; he jumps on Struve's second argument, which Peet considers weaker and easier to criticize, and tries to make it look like the main argument.

Why does he content himself with saying that Struve has given "powerful etymological evidence"? Which evidence? He is careful not to cite the most important piece, which, by itself, constitutes a sledgehammer argument that prohibits relying on any secondary obscurity of the text, or on its classically mathematical laconism in order to cause doubt about the true significance of *nbt* = basket = calabash = half-sphere. It seems as if there is an implicit complacency on the part of some scholars who take into consideration Peet's criticisms, because none of them, Otto Neugebauer in particular, mentions this grave omission by Peet; the latter, by beginning his critique with Struve's second argument, thus makes a monumental confession: in line 6 of the text of problem 10, it is said: "because the *nbt*, meaning the calabash, is half of an egg." But the reading of this last word, *inr*, of the hieratic text of the papyrus is difficult from the outset, because the papyrus is badly damaged in this spot. Nevertheless, the first letter *i* of the word is very clear, likewise the beginning of the *n* and the *r* in hieratic, as well as the determinative of the word: an "egg" entirely drawn in oblique position. Struve reinforces his argument by showing that this is not the only case where the Egyptian scribe compares in a problem a *nbt* (a half-sphere) with half an egg. To this end, he even cites a Greek text of the Ptolemaic epoch, because, as he will say in concluding his study, Greek geometry derives not from Babylonian "geometry," but from that of Egypt, as exercises 10 (surface of a sphere) and 14 (volume of a truncated pyramid) attest, edited two thousand years before the birth of Greek mathematics.[25]

Similarly, the author explains the use of *m* instead of the genitive *n*, in the Egyptian phrase, to indicate the only necessary dimension to know in the case of exercise 10.[26]

Now, it is on these two facts (the debatable term "egg" and *m* instead of the genitive *n*) that Peet tries to play. Therefore, for him, problem 10 deals, not with the surface of a half-sphere, but with that of a half-cylinder: he wants to demonstrate that the term missing in the damaged part of the papyrus is *ipt* and not *inr*. The first pertinent objection that his exegetes or critics refrain from telling him is the following: If, as he claims, the scribe means to speak of a cylinder (*ipt*), and not of a sphere (*nbt*), why did he use three times the term *nbt* with the vertical bar and not once *ipt* in the intact part of the papyrus? One must refuse to see reality, as Peet did, in order not to see an egg in the determinative of the word whose reading is discussed; and this certainty, drawn from the evidence of the determinative, thoroughly confirms the idea that the two signs that are partly extant after the *i* are surely *n* and *r* and not *p* and *t* in hieratic, signs which they do not resemble at all. If, instead of an egg as the determinative, the scribe had wanted to represent a barrel with the usual jet of grain to write the word *ipt*, where did the jet go? And on the other hand, what a difference with the usual forms! But here is another weighty argument that has not been emphasized: if the problem deals with the surface of a sphere, the scribe only needs to give one datum, the diameter of the sphere, and this is exactly what he did. If this concerned a cylinder, two data would be needed: the diameter or the radius and the height of the cylinder; obviously, this latter data are lacking because of all the reasons given above. But Peet does not recoil from this difficulty; he will invent the missing data, adding a phrase of his own making to the scribe's text; but even in this case, things cannot "hold" together, as they say, because, by a miracle, the diameter and the height of the cylinder would have to be equal. Peet arbitrarily postulates this equality of the diameter and the height of his invented cylinder, which he substitutes for the half-sphere of the scribe. He is so unsure of his arbitrary modifications of the problem's text that he adds that, after all, it could also concern a semicircle (what a trite exercise), but more certainly a half-cylinder. All of this because he estimates that if it really dealt with a half-sphere, the idea that one wanted to have about Egyptian mathematics would change completely: ". . . and in this case we should have, as Struve sees, to put Egyptian mathematics on a very much higher level than previously seemed necessary.[27]. . . It would be very flattering to the Egyptians, and very important for the history of mathematics, if we could place this brilliant piece of work to their credit."[28]

Peet lets his imagination run its course to explain to us how, according to him, the copyist-scribe—special agents of the state who were in charge of recopying these papyruses in the "houses of life"—must have made a mistake: "When the copyist, after writing *nbt* in line 2, brought his eye back to the original, he may have skipped from the , (*nt*) which followed it, which he had already vaguely sighted, to the exactly similar (*m*) a few millimeters further on, and so omitted both *nt* and the numeral,"[29] meaning the second missing numerical datum!

Peet claims that the word *inr* (stone) is only a metaphor when it designates the egg, and would not be intelligible without the proximity of the word *swht* = egg in the sentence. He affirms that *inr* used alone, without association to *swht*, cannot designate an egg, and he believes that the scribe would rather use this last word as a technical term to designate a sphere. He disputes the transcription of the word *inr* in hieroglyphics by Struve, because, says he, the order of the determinatives should have been reversed, the most general following the most specific: in the direction of the writing, one should encounter the egg first, then the stone: and not . Peet means to say that in the case that he supposes to be correct, the determinative of the egg preceding that of the stone would be invisible, for it would be found in the damaged part of the papyrus, and therefore the oblique barrel that one sees on the papyrus in hieratic could not represent an egg, but an oblique drum as in the word: . It appears that Peet, in the case of problem 10 of the *Papyrus of Moscow*, has decided to take systematically the opposite course of Struve's analysis, at all costs: thus ideology leads him to fall into the ridiculous and the extravagant.

In fact, everything above is literally false, as we will see. The attested terms invalidate Peet's point of view, for instance:

= *inrty* = the two eggs from whence came, from which was born the god Thoth (*The Book of the Dead*)

This term presents two variants:

and (texts of the pyramids)[30]

The grammatical form common to these three terms is the Egyptian duel. The first one, in spite of the rule articulated by Peet in the arrangement of the determinatives, reproduces the reverse order, in conformity with the restoration by Struve, the stone first and the two eggs second. These two have exactly the form and the same inclined position of the determinative, preserved in the text of problem 10. Thus we see, by its ellipsoidal form and its inclination, that this determinative could not be confused with the determinative of the word *ipt*. On the other hand, this last word is not the technical term for "cylinder" in Egyptian; it designates a measure, a quantity of grain and not a form, a geometric body. "Cylinder" is shown as *šɜ' dbn* in Egyptian.

In the other two variants, of which the one is attested to in the texts of the pyramids, the determinative constituted by the parallelepiped block of stone or of granite is regularly omitted, contrary to Peet's opinion, and only the one represented by the two eggs is extant, reinforced even in one case by the presence of a bird.

Thus, it is false to maintain that *inr* can mean "egg" only when associated with *swht* and that it has only a metaphorical value.

Peet is astonished by the presence of an unexplained nine (9) in line 5 of the text of the problem; Struve had noted that the scribe had multiplied the diameter 4½ by 2 in order to simplify the result following from lines 5 and 6, namely taking 1/9 of 9 = 1, to make 9 − 1 = 8 (line 7). In the same manner, in lines 8 and 9, he found that 1/9 of 8 = 2/3 + 1/6 + 1/18 without making any calculations (Gillings, p. 198).

It follows, from the above, that if Peet did not know how to hide his intentions, his critics, far from weakening Struve's analysis of the *Papyrus of Moscow*, have only confirmed it, by their obvious prejudice, their incoherence, their gratuitousness, and, in short, their falsehood.

More informed and dispassionate authors, like Richard J. Gillings, know this, and that is why they do not doubt the fact that problem 10 of the *Papyrus of Moscow* clearly deals with the surface of a half-sphere, and consequently, of a sphere. In fact, Gillings shows that in any case the evil is identical, because even if it were dealing with the surface of a half-cylinder, one must admit that the Egyptians knew fourteen hundred years before the Greek Dinostratus the formula $C = \pi d$, giving the length of the circumference.

In the case of the sphere, it is an advance of two thousand years on Archimedes.

Of course, in these practical exercises where it was a question of applying known and established formulas by means that could be only theoretical, the scribe was not repeating a demonstration of the formula that he was applying. Modern scholars also get lost in conjectures trying to find again the Egyptian methods. All the scholars who have struggled to demonstrate that the Egyptians used empirical formulas instead of rigorous mathematical demonstrations, ended up with results of a proverbial foolishness. Even a scholar such as Gillings, whose honesty, impartiality, and high competence must be saluted, almost fell into this difficulty.

In fact, after having rejected Peet's idea of a half-cylinder, he supposes that the Egyptians were able to establish the rigorous formula of the surface of a half-sphere $S = 2\pi R^2$ by considering that the quantity of bark used to make a basket is double that needed to make the lid, which is a circle whose surface they knew how to calculate.[31] If this were the case, all the illiterate basket makers of the world would become mathematicians by dint of daily observation. No, formulas like that of the surface of the sphere come only out of lofty mathematical speculations. All those who are even a little familiar with mathematics know that it is absurd to want to draw it from empirical considerations.

This is the place to recall that if this were so, the Greek contemporaries of the Egyptians would have been the first to point it out to us.

If the Egyptians were merely vulgar empiricists who were establishing the properties of figures only through measuring, if the Greeks were the founders of rigorous mathematical demonstration, from Thales onwards, by the systematization of "empirical formulas" from the Egyptians, they would not have failed to boast about such an accomplishment. It would have been important to find in the writing of a biographer of antiquity that the rigorous, theoretical, mathematical demonstration is of Greek origin and that the Egyptians had only been empiricists. There is nothing of the sort; all the statements, unanimously, from the pen of the greatest Greek scholars, philosophers, and writers, glorify the theoretical sciences of the Egyptians—a fact all the more important because these Greek scholars are contemporaries of the ancient Egyptians. One might expect that the Greeks, who had just succeeded the Persians on the throne of Egypt, through national pride, tried to misrepresent the facts on the fundamental point of the origin of theoretical science and particularly of mathematics: the idea could not occur to them, because their emergence was too recent and the reputation of Egyptian science too ancient! Also Egypt, even conquered, remained the venerable home of the sciences that she had kept secret for millennia. Now, the barbarian had broken through the doors of her sanctuaries; she is conquered and will become by force the teacher of young nations, of the Greeks in particular: the "Greek miracle" will begin, as a consequence of the occupation of Egypt by the foreigner, Greek in particular, and therefore of the forced access to the scientific treasures of Egypt, of the plundering of the temple libraries and of the submission of the priests. It must be strongly emphasized that the Greeks never said that they were the students of the Babylonians or of the Chaldeans;[32] their most reputable scholars will always boast about having been the pupils of the Egyptians, as the writings of their biographers reveal: Thales, the semilegendary father of Greek mathematics, Pythagoras of Samos, Eudoxus, etc.

The theorem attributed to Thales is illustrated by the figure of problem 53 of the *Rhind Papyrus*, written thirteen hundred years before the birth of Thales. One will notice that the text corresponding to figure 53 has been lost and that the figure next to it deals with another problem that has nothing to do with this figure representing three similar triangles with the same apex and their parallel bases. The anecdote claiming that Thales discovered "his" theorem by making the end of the shadow cast by a stick, planted vertically, meet exactly the end of the shadow cast by the Great Pyramid, in order to have a figure materialize identical to that of problem 53, would only prove that Thales actually spent time in Egypt, that he truly was a pupil of Egyptian priests and that he could not be the inventor of the theorem attributed to him.

Herodotus calls Pythagoras a simple plagiarist of the Egyptians; Jamblichus, biographer of Pythagoras, writes that all the theorems of lines (geometry) come from Egypt.

According to Proclus, Thales was the first Greek pupil of the Egyptians and that after his return he introduced science in Greece, particularly geometry. After teaching what he knew to his pupil Pythagoras, he advised him to go to Egypt, where he (Pythagoras) remained for twenty-two years in the temples, in order to learn geometry, astronomy, etc. (cf. Jamblichus, *Life of Pythagoras*).

An Egyptian priest told Diodorus of Sicily[33] that all the so-called discoveries that made Greek scholars famous were things that had been taught to them in Egypt and which they called their own, once they went back to their country.

Plato, in the *Phaedrus*, has Socrates say that he learned that the god Thoth was the inventor of arithmetic, calculus, geometry, and astronomy (*Phaedrus*, 274 C).

Aristotle, who greatly profited from the plundering of the libraries of the Egyptian temples, acknowledges the essentially theoretical and speculative character of the Egyptian science and tries to explain its emergence not by land surveying, but by the fact that the Egyptian priests were free from material preoccupations and had all the time necessary to deepen theoretical thought.[34] According to Herodotus, the Egyptians are the exclusive inventors of geometry, which they taught to the Greeks.[35] Democritus boasted that he equalled the Egyptians in geometry.[36]

Therefore, no trace is found anywhere, in the texts of antiquity, of a so-called duality of theoretical Greek science, as opposed to Egyptian empiricism: Egypt, even conquered militarily, remains the uncontested mistress in all scientific domains, particularly in mathematics. The idea of an empirical Egyptian science is an invention of modern ideologues, those same ones who are looking for ways to erase from the memory of humanity the influence of Negro Egypt on Greece.

This brings us to the second fundamental theorem applied by the Egyptian scribe in problem 14 of the *Papyrus of Moscow* (fig. 36). The solution given by the scribe shows that the Egyptians knew the theorem related to the volume of a truncated pyramid:

$$V = \frac{1}{3}h(a^2 + ab + b^2),$$

a formula that, according to Peet and Grün cited by Gillings (p. 189), has not been either surpassed or improved on for four thousand years. In reality, Peet tried, first timidly, to contest this formula and then thought better of it. He also started by saying that the formula was accurate with the reservation that h definitely represents the height of the truncated pyramid and not its side (!), then he concludes that the priests, who amazingly arrived at correctly establishing the analytical expression $(a^2 + ab + b^2)$, could not have confused height and side, and that consequently the term *mryt* clearly designates a height in this problem; thus, this achievement has to be credited to Egyptian mathematics.[37]

It is the certitude of the formula of the volume of the truncated pyramid that proves today that the Egyptians also knew the formula of the pyramid's volume:

$$V = \frac{1}{3}a^2h.$$

Now, this is the most common elementary volume in Egypt; and if it were not for the accident of the *Papyrus of Moscow*'s discovery, it would be doubted that the Egyptians ever knew this formula.

Once more, the empirical processes that one tries to attribute to the Egyptians, in order to arrive at the theorem of the volume of the truncated pyramid, are as foolish as the former ones relative to the surface of the sphere: filling up empty volumes with sand and comparing them by weight, etc. Let us repeat that the theorems relative to the surface of the sphere, to the volume of the truncated pyramid, and to the surface of the circle could not have been established with formulas; for these are certainly unique formulas that the mathematical scholars of the whole world have been trying to rediscover for a century to no avail! The Egyptian recipes are therefore more difficult to put forward than even the theoretical foundations of the theorems concerned: supreme consecration of the Egyptian genius; for once, empiricism would outclass theory! Here is the impasse where the negation of the facts leads.

A formula deduced from empirical considerations is never accurate, even in particular instances, and this every mathematician knows. So, all the Egyptian formulas are rigorously accurate.

Babylonian mathematics offer us the example of a formula established empirically, and related to the same volume of the truncated pyramid; it leads to:

$$V = \frac{1}{2} h (a^2 + b^2)$$

a formula less than approximate: let us say, manifestly false!

Square Root, So-Called Pythagoreum Theorem, and Irrational Numbers

We know that the Egyptians knew how to rigorously extract the square root, even of the most complicated whole or fractional numbers.[38] The term that served to designate the square root in the Pharaonic language is significant in that respect: the right angle of a square, *knbt*; "to make the angle" = to extract the square root. Now, the Egyptians defined a fundamental unit of length called "double remen," which is equal to the diagonal of a square of little side a = one cubit (royal); in other words, if d is that diagonal, then one necessarily has, by definition of this length itself, "double remen,"

$$d = a\sqrt{2} = (\sqrt{2} \times 20.6) = 29.1325 \text{ inches.}$$[39]

The royal cubit = 20.6 inches (fig. 46)

The remen $= \frac{d}{2} = \frac{\sqrt{2}}{2}a = 14.6$ inches

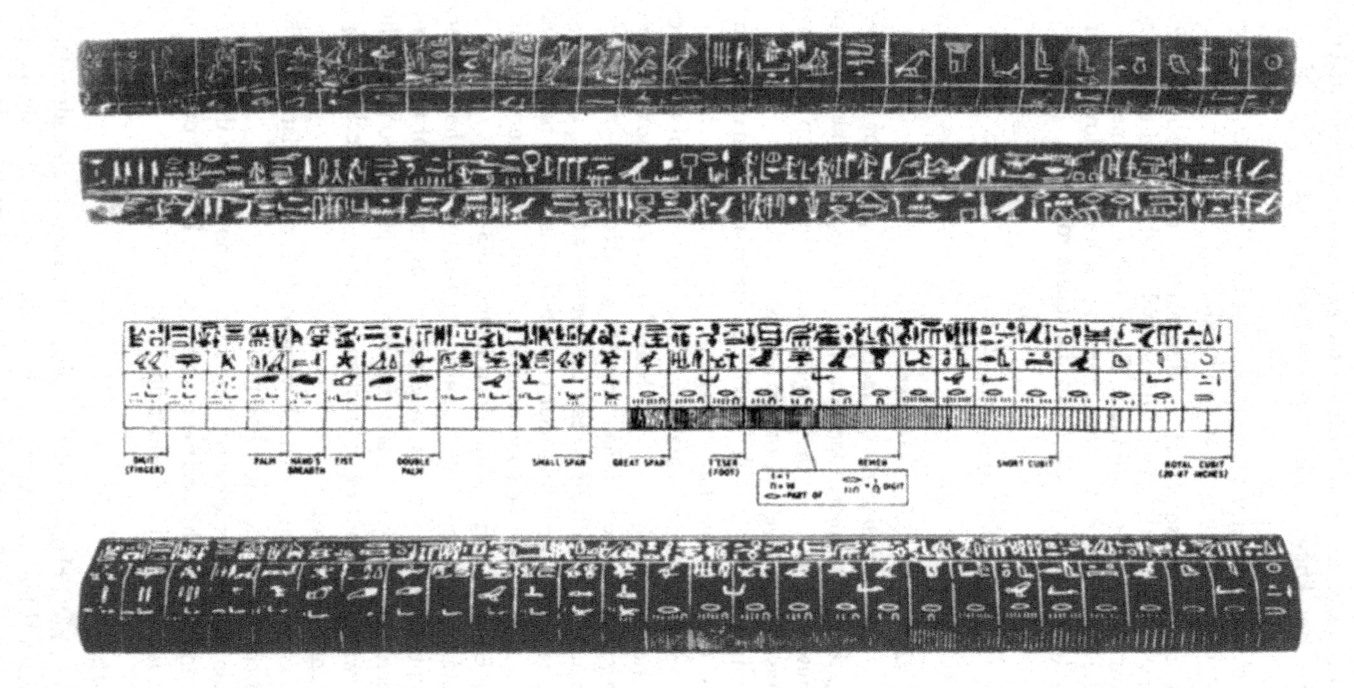

Figure 46: Above: Royal cubit of May, graduated in fractional subunits of measurement, dating from the New Kingdom. Views of the upper side and the bottom, 52.5 cm long. The original is in the Louvre Museum in Paris. (Photo: Louvre Museum) Below: Drawing and view of another Egyptian cubit, probably that of Amenophis I, dating from the sixteenth century B.C. (Museum of Turin, from R. J. Gillings and M. J. Puttock)

The Egyptians, who thus determined the diagonal of the square from the value of the side and who mastered the calculation of the extraction of the square root, knew, as the definition above proves:

> the irrational number par excellence, which is 2, as they also knew the transcendant number (also irrational).
>
> the theorem of the square of the diagonal (falsely attributed to Pythagoras) at least in the case of the isosceles right-angled triangle, to stick just to the undeniable facts. The Egyptians who knew how to calculate the surface of a triangle, certainly wrote the following equation, followed by an extraction of the square root:

$$S = \frac{1}{2}a^2 = \frac{1}{4}d^2 \rightarrow a^2 = \frac{1}{2}d^2 \rightarrow 2\,a^2 = d^2$$

whence: $a\ \sqrt{2} = d = a$ double remen.

It is certain that by bringing these facts of the properties of the sacred triangle (right-angled triangle) together, always dealing with the square of the hypotenuse, one finds that the Egyptians knew the theorem attributed to Pythagoras perfectly well, as others have affirmed.

This definition of the "double remen" by itself, and its mathematical implications, clearly show that Pythagoras was neither the inventor of irrational numbers (incommensurability of the diagonal and of the side of the square) nor of the theorem that bears his name: he took all these elements from Egypt where he had been, as reported by his biographers (cf. Jamblichus), a pupil of the priests for twenty-two years.

Plato thought that the world-soul consisted of isosceles right-angled triangles: an unwarranted and ludicrous idea if one does not take into account the Egyptian origin of his doctrine (pp. 443–44).

The legend attached to the Pythagorean school says that the discovery of the incommensurability of the diagonal and of the side of the square was kept secret for a long time, and that Hippasus of Metapontum, who divulged it, was chased out of the sect and died in a shipwreck as a sign of punishment by the gods.

This is a beautiful legend, which vanishes before the clarity of the Egyptian mathematical facts cited above.

It is certain that the evidence of these facts did not escape the sagacity of the mathematicians who dealt with this question, but they preferred to keep silent, as if they did not notice anything.

Quadrature of the Circle

The Egyptians not only knew the problem of the circle's quadrature, as Struve observes,[40] but they were the first to have posed it in the history of mathematics. In problem 48 (*Rhind Papyrus*), it is a matter of comparing the surface of a square of a side of nine units to that of an inscribed circle with a diameter of nine units, with supporting figure (fig. 47).

Trigonometry

The Egyptians knew how to calculate the slope of a pyramid from the usual trigometric lines: sine, cosine, tangent, cotangent, as shown by exercises 56 to 60 of the *Rhind Papyrus*, (p. 97ff.).

In problem 56 (fig. 37), the height of 250 cubits and the base of 360 cubits are given; what is here called "the base" is the diameter of the circle inscribed in the square of the pyramid's base, which has the same length as the side; the scribe takes the center of this circle as the origin of the "axes," for he divides the length of the "base" or of the square's side, which is the base of the pyramid, by two in order to obtain the radius of this circle; the height of the pyramid is identical to the axis of the sines whose origin is the center of the base's circle (fig. 51). One has then, according to the problem's data:

If α is the angle of inclination of one face of the pyramid,

$$\sin \alpha = 250$$

$$\cos \alpha = \frac{360}{2} = 180$$

$$\mathrm{tg}\ \alpha = \frac{250}{180}$$

The scribe calculates the cotangent:

$$\mathrm{cotg}\ \alpha = \frac{180}{250} = \frac{1}{2} + \frac{1}{5} + \frac{1}{50}$$

He multiplies this result by seven to express the final result in palms, for one cubit = seven palms. Thus:

$$\mathrm{cotg}\ \alpha = 7 \times \left(\frac{1}{2} + \frac{1}{5} + \frac{1}{50}\right) = 5 \text{ palms } \frac{1}{25}$$

For the scribe, this result has the value of an angle, because it allows him to affirm that a horizontal shifting of five palms on the axis of the cosine corresponds to an elevation in height of one cubit on the axis of the sine. One can see that these calculations were necessary in order to obtain the same regular slope on one whole face of the pyramid. The scribe has chosen the cotangent for it is more useful to him here, because of the way he wanted to express the results.

In problem 57 (fig. 38) of the *Rhind Papyrus* (p. 99), the cotg α = 5 palms 1 inch (4 inches = one palm) and the "base" = 140 cubits are given, and the height is asked. Thus:

$$h = \sin \alpha = \cos \alpha \times \frac{1}{\mathrm{cotg}\ \alpha} = 93\frac{1}{3} \text{ (cubits).}$$

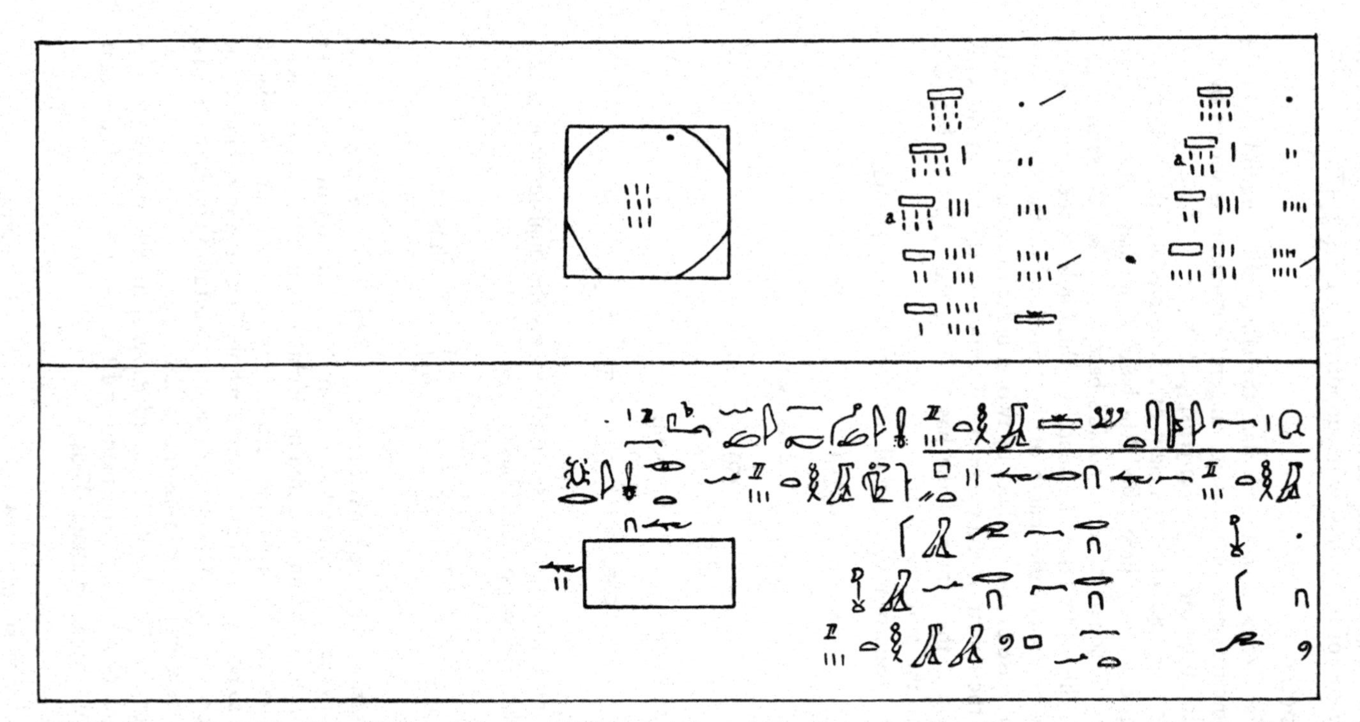

Figure 47: Problem 48 of the *Rhind Papyrus* deals with the squaring of the circle: compare the area of a circle of a diameter 9 to that of a square with a side 9. Problem 49 deals with the area of a rectangle with a length of 10 and a width of 2. (T. Eric Peet, *The Rhind Mathematical Papyrus*, plate O)

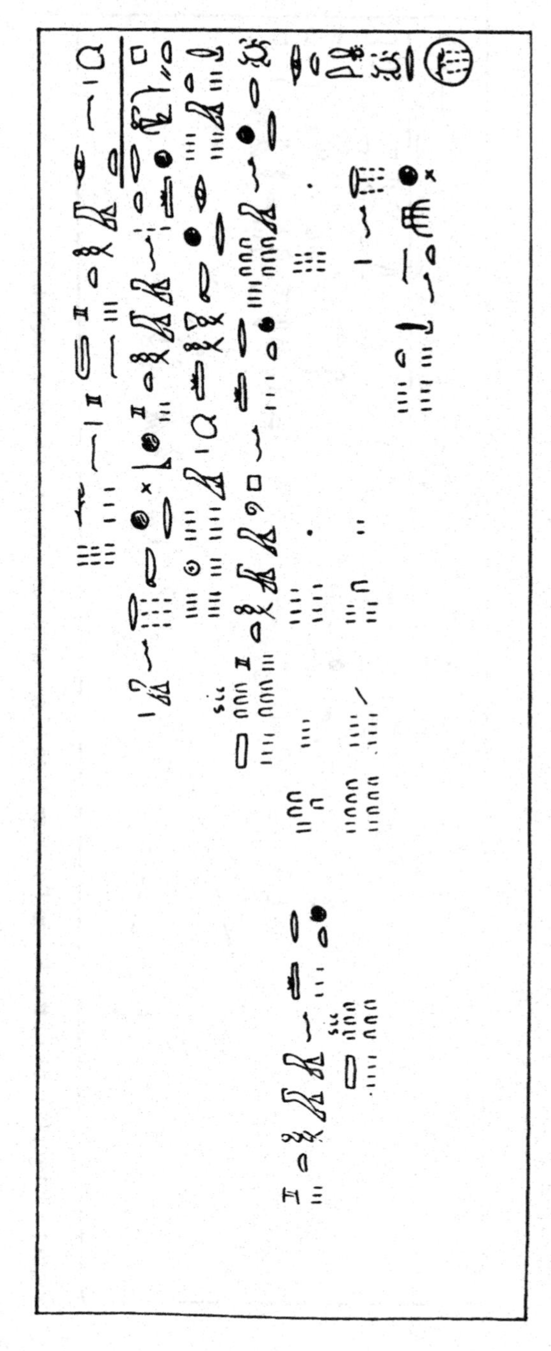

Figure 48: Problem 50 of the *Rhind Papyrus:* Area of a circle of a diameter 9.

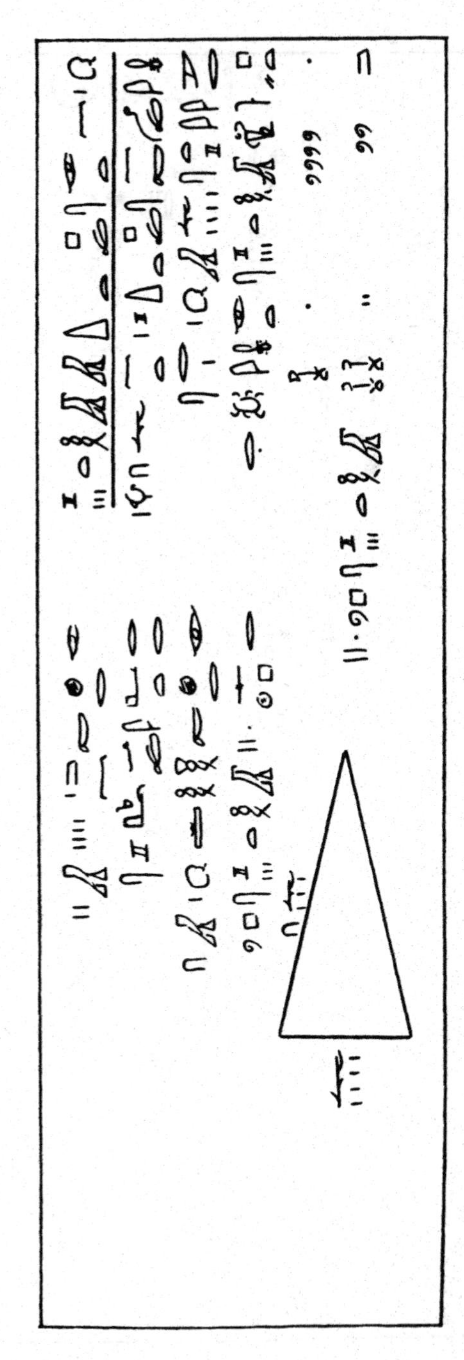

Figure 49: Problem 51 of the *Rhind Papyrus:* Area of a triangle of a height 13 and a base 4.

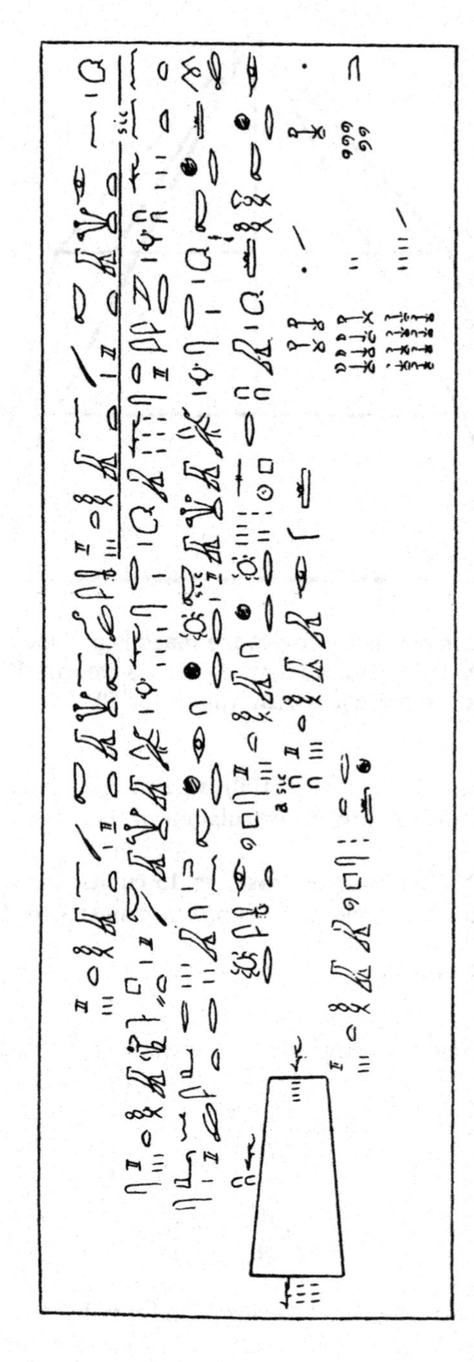

Figure 50: Problem 52 of the *Rhind Papyrus:* Area of a trapezoid of which the large base is 6, the small base is 4, and the height is 20.

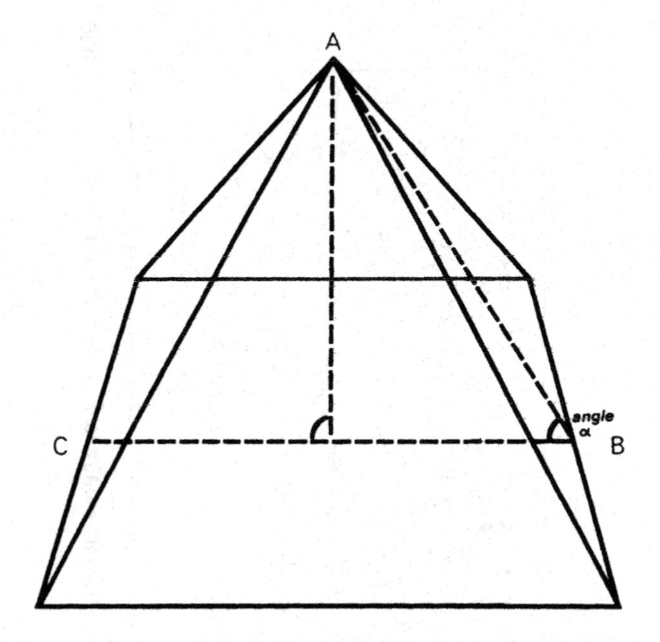

Figure 51: Figure corresponding to the reasoning of the scribe, from T. Eric Peet. On the figure, we have drawn the median *AB* in order to clearly show the angle α = *ABC* (with apex B).

Problem 60 (fig. 40 and *Rh.*, p. 100) is particularly interesting because it concerns, in all probability, the calculation of the slope of a cone or of a conical pillar, *inw*.

Given: h = 30 cubits and the "base" = 15 cubits, find the slope; here, the base is rigorously a circle of 15 cubits in diameter (p. 100).

Surface of the Circle
$S = \pi R^2$

The Egyptians knew the formula of the surface of the circle (fig. 48):

$$S = \left(\frac{8}{9}d\right)^2$$

equivalent to

$$S = \pi\frac{d^2}{4} \text{ or } \pi R^2.$$

The value of π extracted from the Egyptian formula = 3.1605 # 3.1416, which is the correct value. This result is amazing when one compares it to the value adopted by Babylonian mathematics, which modern scholars try to make into a rival of Egyptian mathematics: $\pi = 3$. Consequently, for the Babylonians, was just one whole number among many others, its character as a transcendant, irrational number could not be perceived, because it had not even been calculated to the first decimal; it was a whole number that came out right.

Such rigor in the formulas of Egyptian geometry could not have been the result of formulas added through the centuries to solve practical problems: it was obviously the fruit of a highly theoretical and speculative science—as acknowledged by Aristotle, Democritus, Jamblichus, Plato, Socrates, Strabo, and others whose methods we have lost for now because of the extraordinarily initiatory character of Egyptian science. An empirical-technical mathematics can lead only to grossly erroneous formulas like those of the Babylonians relative to the surface of the circle and to the truncated pyramid. All the graphical methods (Vogel) and others of empirical character that modern authors suggest in order to rediscover the Egyptian processes have no demonstrative value whatsoever. The proof is that they always keep themselves from making a numerical application, because the discrepancy with the results obtained by the Egyptians would show right away the falsehood of the proposed solution.

Surface of the Rectangle
$S = L \times l$

Problem 49 of the *Rhind Papyrus* (fig. 47) and 6 of the *Papyrus of Moscow* deal with the surface of the rectangle from different points of view: in the first case, the two dimensions are given and they ask for the surface, whereas in the second, the surface is given, and the width is expressed in a fraction of the length:

$$S = 12,\ l = \frac{1}{2} + \frac{1}{4} \text{ of } L$$

Calculate L and l? One finds $L = 4$; $l = 3$.

In the modern method, the use of two simultaneous equations is necessary to first determine l, then L. But in the last question, they are asking for the angle of the rectangle, that is, to extract the square root of the sides!

What they do not insist on is that problem 6 of the *Papyrus of Moscow* deals well (is it by pure chance?) with the famous sacred triangle, so much contested, and which the Egyptians had known, according to testimonies by the Greeks themselves:

$$L = 4,\ l = 3 \rightarrow d = 5 \text{ necessarily.}$$

Surface of the Triangle

The formula $S = 1/2\ ah$ was well established. One no longer tries to question this fact by alleging that said formula is accurate only if *meryt* means height and not side. Struve has shown that the Egyptians generally used *k3w* to designate the height of three-dimensional mathematical beings and *meryt* for that of the plane figures. The first meaning of *meryt* is shore, quay. One will notice that its determinative is essentially a line regularly broken at right angles, which implies the idea of the perpendicular.

The Egyptians, who knew the correct formula for the surface of the trapezium, necessarily knew how to calculate that of the triangle, and even Peet finally agrees and rejects Eisenlohr's (translator of the *Rhind Papyrus*) idea, who departed from the approximative formula

$$S = \left(\frac{a + c}{2}\right)\left(\frac{b + d}{2}\right)$$

inscribed in the Temple of Edfu, constructed by Ptolemy XI, in order to say that the Egyptians could not have known the exact formula of the triangle's surface.[41] In fact, this formula generally applies to the quadrilaterals, for the approximate determination of the surface area of fields for land taxation purposes. Obviously, it cannot then be true in the case of the scalene triangle. Furthermore, it is too recent and belongs to the Hellenistic Greek epoch. Is it therefore Greek science or Egyptian science that is in question here?

Anyway, we have already said it: he who has correctly calculated the surface of the trapezium necessarily knows that of the triangle: the inventors of the plumb line could not ignore the height of the figures, and this is why Gillings writes, concerning this discussion about the meaning of *meryt*: "However, these differences of opinion are academic; and modern-day historians agree that perpendicular height is meant by the scribe."[42]

Surface of the Trapezium

The scribe applied the following correct formula:

$$S = \frac{A + B}{2} \times h \text{ (or the half-sum of the bases times the height).}$$

For the calculation of the trapezium's surface: the calculations that he makes amount to the rigorous application of this formula.

Problem 52 (*Rh.*, fig. 50): trapezium (triangle, one of whose apexes is cut parallel to the base) of 20 *khet*, with a large base of 6 *khet* and a small base of 4 *khet*. What is its surface? The scribe proceeds as follows (*Rh.*, p. 94):

$$6 + 4 = 10; \frac{10}{2} = 5; S = 5 \times 20 = 100.$$

Volumes of the Cylinder, of the Parallelepiped, and of the Sphere

Problems 41–43 of the *Rhind Papyrus* deal with the volume of a cylinder, designated by the term šꜣʿ and not *ipt*.[43] These are the two terms that Peet pretended to confuse in this case, when he wanted to reduce the surface of the sphere to that of the cylinder, he thought, in order to disparage Egyptian mathematics!

Problem 44 deals with a cube (square base, *ifd*; three equal sides).

šꜣʿ *dbn* = cylinder

šꜣʿ *ifd* = cube or parallelepiped depending on the case.

Problem 41 deals with the volume of a cylinder of a diameter of 9 and a height of 10 units.

The calculation of the scribe comes down to the application of the exact formula that gives the volume of the cylinder, which is:

$$V = \pi R^2 h = \left(\frac{16}{9}R\right)^2 \times h = \left(\frac{16}{9}\right)^2 \times R^2 \times h = S \times h$$

the surface of the base multiplied by the height, S being calculated with the value of $\pi = 3.1605$ (*Rh.*, p. 81).

Problem 44 concerns the volume of a cube whose sides are each 10 units long:

$$V = a \times a \times a = a^3 \text{ or } 10 \times 10 \times 10 = 1{,}000.$$

Here the scribe purposely elevated the number 10 to the third power, and we will see, with geometrical progressions, that he already had the habit of elevating any number to the power n.

Problem 45 is the reverse of the preceding one: the volume having been given, the side of the cube is asked for (*Rh.*, p. 85). This is equivalent to the extraction of a cubic root.

Problem 46 is relative to a parallelepiped with a square base whose three sides have to be found, knowing the volume.

Volume of the Sphere?

It is probable that the problem of plate VIII of the *Kahun Papyrus* deals with the volume of the sphere, of a hemisphere of 8 units in diameter, as Borchardt speculated.

For Gillings and Peet, it more certainly deals with the volume of a cylindrical silo of 8 units in diameter and 12 units in height.

ALGEBRA

Mathematical Series

The Egyptians had a clear notion of mathematical series and of their particular properties: they very certainly knew the series that are geometric progressions of a ratio r and the arithmetic progressions, and very probably other types of series of much more complex properties.

Problem 79 deals with a geometric progression of ratio seven; it is commonly called the problem on "the inventory of *goods* contained in a house," an obviously inappropriate expression. Here is its wording: there are seven houses; in each house there are seven cats, each cat kills seven mice; each mouse had eaten seven grains; each grain would have produced seven *hekat*. What is the sum of all the enumerated elements? (What is the total of all these things?) This problem deals with a geometric progression of ratio seven, of which the first term is also seven. The reasoning of the scribe leads to the same numerical result as the application of the formula of modern algebra, which gives the sum of a geometric progression:

$$S = a\frac{r^n - 1}{r - 1} = 7 \times \frac{16{,}807 - 1}{7 - 1} = 7 \times \frac{16{,}806}{6} = 7 \times 2801 = 19{,}607$$ [45]

Problem 40 of the *Rhind Papyrus* deals with an arithmetic progression. It consists of dividing one hundred loaves of bread among five persons, so that the shares are in arithmetic progression and so that the sum of the two smallest is one-seventh the sum of the three largest.[46]

Problem 64 deals with a distribution of differences: it is again an arithmetic progression. It consists of dividing ten loaves of bread among ten persons, in such a manner that the difference between two consecutive persons is one-eighth of a *hekat*. One obtains the same result as the scribe by applying the classical formula of an arithmetic progression:

$$l = a + (n - 1)d$$

where l = the last term
a = the first term
d = the common difference: $1/8$ (p. 108).

The *Rhind Papyrus* shows that the Egyptians were the inventors of arithmetic and geometric progressions. Now, the most famous "supposed" discoveries of Pythagoras deal with diverse operations in the arithmetic and geometric series.

The summation of the arithmetic progressions gives polygonal numbers. For instance:

The summation of the terms of the simplest arithmetic progression, corresponding to the series of natural numbers (and whose ratio, or difference of terms, is equal to 1), gives trigonal or triangular numbers.

The one whose difference in terms is 2, meaning that of the odd numbers 1, 3, 5, 7, 9, etc., will give, by summation of its terms, tetragonal or square numbers, such as 1, 4, 9, 16, 25, etc., represented as follows:

1 4 9 16

The one whose difference in terms is 3 gives pentagonal numbers: 1, 5, 12, 22, 35, etc.

The progression 1, 5, 9, 13, 17, etc., having 4 as the difference between the terms, gives the series of hexagonal numbers: 1, 6, 15, 28, etc.

In the same way, one obtains the heptagonal, octagonal, nonagonal, numbers, etc.

Similarly, the *gnomons*, or successive rectangular belts that allow one to obtain all the squares from one unit square, form the arithmetic series of odd numbers:

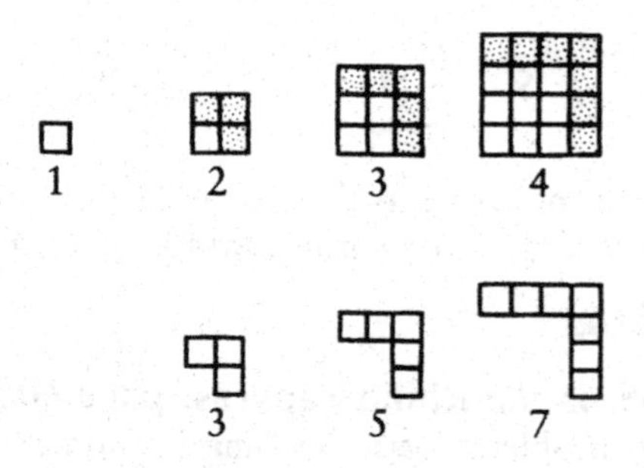

Pythagoras assumed the tetragonal, or square, soul, thus the importance of the tetrad, or *tetractys*, and of the *gnomon*, in his philosophy.

The Egyptian influence on Pythagoras was so strong that he, or in any event his school, in spite of the difference in language and writing, used in his prealgebraic mathematical notation, Egyptian hieroglyphic signs. For example: the sign of water (⁓) symbolized the progressions of numbers. The series of odd numbers was represented by the *gnomon* in the form of a right angle (⅂); the even numbers by the sign (=) of the balance. The circle, the hieroglyph of Ra, the sun, representing perpetual movement (O). The famous sign of the ansate cross of Isis (☥), T-squares or *gnomons* joined back to back and surmounted by a circle, symbolizes the generation of squares by the series of odd numbers, which played a major role in Pythagorean doctrine. And so on.[47]

A passage from Plutarch, quoted by Ferdinand Hoefer, shows that the Greeks knew well that the theorem "of Pythagoras" was an Egytpian discovery:

> The Egyptians appeared to have figured out the world in the form of the most beautiful of triangles, just as Plato, in his *Republic*, seems to have used it as a symbol of matrimonial union. This triangle, the most beautiful of triangles, has its vertical side composed of three, its base of four, and its hypotenuse of five parts, and the square of the latter is equal to the sum of the squares of the two sides. The vertical side symbolizes the male, the base the female, and the hypotenuse the progeny of the two.[48]

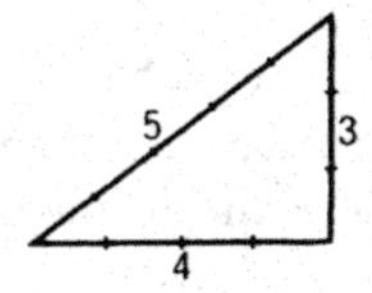

Finally, Gillings shows that the Egyptians knew, without any possible doubt, how to sum up an arithmetic progression, and their reasoning was equivalent to the following modern formula:

$$S = \frac{N}{2}[2a + (n - 1)d]$$ [49]

Consequently, all the elements that could have led to the "discoveries" of Pythagoras were already present in Egyptian mathematics.

Simple Equations

Problems 24–38 of the* Rhind Papyrus, *page 60ff. The Egyptians posed a series of problems corresponding in modern algebra to simple equations; they had a very clear idea of the abstract and symbolic notion of the unknown quantity, but could embody it in hieroglyphic writing only by assimilating the privileged number 1 for X. It is easy to realize that in all of the Egyptian algebraic problems, 1 represents X, and even authors as hostile as Neugebauer acknowledged that the Egyptians knew algebra.

For Eisenlohr, Cantor, and Revillout, the Egyptians reasoned as algebraists, whereas for other authors, like Rodet, it was not algebra because the unknown was not apparent (p. 60).

The problems are divided into three groups:

1. 24–27 belong to the first group and are solved by the method of false supposition. Take for instance problem 24 worded as follows:

A quantity (any) plus 1/7 of it = 19. What is this quantity?

It is clear that one does not betray the spirit of the scribe by wording this problem in modern algebraic terms as follows:

A quantity X plus 1/7 of it = 19; find X

or $X + \frac{1}{7}X = 19$ (simple equation with one unknown quantity)

We see that in this kind of problem, we are dealing with pure numbers in the mathematical sense, and not numbers expressing concrete quantities (measurements of wheat or other cereal).

2. *Type 28 and 29.* Problem 28 belongs to the second type of problem, leading to a simple equation of a more complex form than the preceding one; the wording of the problem is the following (one will notice that it is essentially algebraic): take a number (any number); to it add 2/3 of it, then from this sum subtract 1/3 of it; the remainder is 10. What is this number?

By calling this number X, the corresponding modern expression of this simple equation would be:

$$X + \frac{2x}{3} - \frac{1}{3}\left(x + \frac{2x}{3}\right) = 10$$

3. *The third type of problem, 30–34* (Gillings). The 2/3, plus 1/10 of a number = 10; what is it? Immediately the equation is written:

$$\left(\frac{2}{3} + \frac{1}{10}\right)X = 10 \qquad X = 13\frac{1}{23}$$

Quadratic Equations

Two problems of the *Berlin Papyrus* deal with a system of simultaneous equations, of which one is quadratic.

Written in modern form, they become:

$$\text{I} \quad \begin{cases} X^2 + Y^2 = 100 \\ 4X - 3Y = 0 \end{cases}$$

$$\text{II} \quad \begin{cases} X^2 + Y^2 = 400 \\ 4X - 3Y = 0 \end{cases}$$

Here is an explicit wording of a quadratic problem:

How to divide 100 into two parts, so that the square root of one of them is ¾ that of the other? The solution of the scribe is rigorously correct. In modern symbols, we have:

$$X^2 + Y^2 = 100 \rightarrow Y = \frac{3}{4}X \rightarrow X^2 + \frac{9}{16}X^2 = 100$$

Gillings thinks that problems 28 and 29 of the *Rhind Papyrus* are the most ancient examples of mathematics recorded in history, well before Diophantus of Alexandria, forming a class that can be called "thinking about a number," "finding a number such as . . ." (Diophantus).[50]

Balance of Quantities: "Pesou"[51]

In problems that deal with mass and weight, the mentioned quantities bear coefficients of usage; they are balanced. Example: if the *pesou* of a loaf of bread is 12, it means that this loaf of bread contains 1/12 of a bushel.

All the problems of the algebraic type, in other words those that deal with abstract quantities in the modern sense of algebra, are called precisely *Aha problems.*[52]

The title of the *Rhind Mathematical Papyrus* shows—no matter what one thinks, even if the calculations that follow are elementary, and we know why—that the Egyptians, well before Pythagoras, had an acute sense of the domination of nature by the number, by mathematics: "Laws to study nature, and to understand all that exists, each mystery, each secret." One had to wait for the Renaissance for Francis Bacon to give a new formulation of the "omnipotence of mathematics."

The procedure of the demonstration of the circle's surface shows that the Egyptians had acquired the highly abstract notion of the constancy of the relationship between any circle's surface and its diameter, a relationship of geometric measurements.

According to Democritus and Aristotle, there is no doubt that the Egyptian priests jealously guarded a highly theoretical science behind the thick walls of their temples. Such an affirmation, particularly coming from Aristotle, has colossal significance, for no one was in a better position than he to know where Egyptian science stood.

It is remarkable that Aristotle, who says this, does not explicitly refer anywhere in his writings to any Egyptian work. Yet this influence of the Egyptians shows everywhere in his work. He does not hesitate to acknowledge that if the Egyptian priests were able to reach such a level of speculation in the theoretical sciences, it is because they were free from material worries.

The existence of the sacred right-angled triangle shows that, for the Egyptians, some mathematical proportions had a divine essence in the Pythagorean and Platonic sense.

Richard J. Gillings is assuredly one of the most competent, most honest, and most objective scholars who ever dealt with Egyptian mathematics. Concerning the table of division of the number 2 by the odd numbers from 3 to 101, a table that is found from 2000 B.C. to 600 A.D., Gillings remarks that the Greek, Roman, Arabic, and Byzantian mathematicians have never been able to discover a more efficient technique for dealing with the ordinary fraction P/q.

The Greeks retained in their arithmetic the old Egyptian notation of fractions of 2200 B.C., as a papyrus proves where we find:

$$\frac{1}{17} \text{ of a silver talent} = 352 + \frac{1}{2} + \frac{1}{17} + \frac{1}{34} + \frac{1}{52} \text{ drachmas.}$$

Modern mathematicians, four thousand years later, are searching for the laws and theorems that are the basis of Egyptian arithmetic, and in particular for their procedures for the treatment of fractions, to make up the table $2/n$ without any error. How was the scribe of the *Rhind Papyrus* able to choose from thousands of possible factorizations, each time the simplest and the best one, as Mansion noted in 1888?[53]

In 1967, four thousand years later, an electronic calculator was programmed to calculate all the possible expressions of the fractions with a unitary numerator, of the divisions of 2 by the odd numbers 3, 5, 7, up to 101, in order to compare the breakdowns given by the scribe with the other thousands of possibilities, in all 22,295 possible forms. The result of this experiment was that the twentieth-century machine was not able to beat the scribe of four thousand years ago, or to find any factorizations superior to those given by the scribe of 2000 B.C.[54]

This result is incompatible with the idea of a techno-empirical mathematics proceeding by trial and error: there were reliable theorems that remain to be discovered, and which include those of elementary arithmetic.

ARITHMETIC

We will say almost nothing on this subject. Our friend, Professor Maurice Caveing, has devoted a masterful study to this subject in the form of a thesis for a state doctorate which will mark a milestone in the history of science. One will have to refer to this work that will soon appear.

The originality of Egyptian arithmetic is that it does not require any effort of memory. Multiplication and division are reduced to addition after a series of duplications. Only the multiplication table by 2 needs to be known in order to easily carry out the most complex calculations; by contrast, in Mesopotamian arithmetic, the knowledge of the multiplication tables was necessary in order to be able to calculate.

Operations on the fractions generally deal with fractions whose numerators equal a unit; however, the Egyptians knew and used also the following complimentary fractions: 2/3 (frequently used); 3/4, 4/5, 5/6 (less frequently used). Owing to this fact, the Egyptians had made a table of factorization of the fractions of type $2/n$, including the fractions from 2/5 to 2/101.[55] The method of factorization thus invented by the Egyptians was very complex, very difficult to follow; modern scholars and mathematicians are far from agreeing on the process used to arrive at the result: meanwhile, we still admire today the amazing mastery and the assurance with which the scribes treated fractions; the Greeks and the Romans continued to use the Egyptian methods.

From the third millennium onward, the Egyptians had already invented decimal notation and discovered or portended the zero, as proved by the spaces they left where one would put the zero today.[56] The proportional divisions were known.[57] The examples dealt with in the *Berlin Papyrus* show that the Egyptians knew how to extract, in the most rigorous way, the square root of any number, even fractional ones, and mathematicians still wonder about the path followed by the scribe Ahmes. He obviously was in the same position as a teacher having to explain very complex mathematical notions to students at an intermediate level. Problem 45 shows that they knew how to extract the cube root also.

EGYPTIAN MATHEMATICAL TERMS
THAT HAVE SURVIVED IN WOLOF

Egyptian	Wolof
P(a)mr = *pamer* = the pyramid	*ba-meel* = the tomb
(Other examples found in the Egyptian language confirm this rule of derivation.)	
P(a)cnh = *pa enh* = life	*ba-neeh* = pleasure
P(a)h(a)w = *pa haw* = grass	*ba-haw* = grass[58]

It is known that in the Egyptian language only the articles *pa* (masculine singular) and *ta* (feminine singular) preceded the noun. In Wolof, there is also a derivation of the ancient Egyptian feminine article. For example:

ta-ht = the temple (Egyptian) *tâh* = heavy construction, building (Wolof)

Within the Wolof language itself, this process of forming compound words is frequent. For example:

bw - rëy = a large ancient coin worth 10 cents.
bw - sé bw - sew = small grains of peanut . . .

Egyptian	Wolof
k(a)w = height	*kaw* = height
seked = a slope	*sëgg* = to lean *sëggay* = a slope

Egyptian	**Wolof**
sšd = a slope	*sadd* = a slope (š→d)
nb = basket, a half-sphere	*ndab* = calabash, a half-sphere
inr = egg, sphere (first meaning = stone)	*ina* = enormous[59] *g.inâr=chicken (gallinacean)*
khar = 20 sekat (unit for measuring capacity) = ⅔ of a cube of the side of the royal cubit and consequently = about half of a cube of an ordinary side of a cubit	*khar* = 20 units of the measurement of capacity called *andar* = ½ *mata* < *meh-ta*
= *meh-ta* = a square, with sides equal to the royal cubit	*mata* = 2 *khar*; following some confusion, a cube with each side equal to one cubit came to be called *meh-ta*
hsb or *hsp* = simple cubit	*hasab* = cubit
(double) *rmn* = remen = a unit of a length equal to the diagonal of a square whose side is equal to one cubit	*laman* = the hereditary owner of land (r→l)
dmd = to unify, to reunite	*dadalle* = to reunite, to unify
gs = half, side	*ges* = to look aside
ro = mouth, small portion	*re* = to laugh; *rôh* = *to swallow*
knbt = angle = square root	*kôn* = angle; does not come from the French word "coin," as I had thought in the beginning
hayt = square root[60]	*hay* = to extract, in the surgical sense, to extract a bullet; applies perfectly to the extraction of a square root: in fact, it is more adequate than the synonymous term *duhi*
psš = to divide	*patt* = to divide (š→d or t)
tp n = example	*top* = to follow, in the sense of continuing, exercising, redoing, continuing to do
mi tp pn or *mi tp pw* = just like, like this example	*mi top bw* = which follows this one
sdm-hel or *sdm-hr-k* = has a double meaning: 1. it indicates an order, a politely given command: "you have to . . ." 2. the outcome of an operation	*hel* = is the particle of the Egyptian verbal form that introduces these two nuances expressed by the verb: this is exactly the same in Wolof. Example: *hal-nga-dem* = you have to go (polite command); *hal naa dot* = I will necessarily receive
mitt pw = this one, like = Q.E.D.	*miit bw* or *miit bi* = this one also, like = Q.E.D.
gmk nfr = look (well) that opened is it (*Rh.* p. 22)	*gimmi-nga* . . . = you have your eyes
tp n sity = method of proof (*Rh.* p. 22)	*top seet* = to follow and to verify (math) *seeti* = to go verify *seet* = to prove
išmt < *ššm* = will lead, to guide (*Rh.* p. 22)	*dem* = to go toward

Egyptian	Wolof
tp n sšmt = development (*Rh.* p. 23)	*tp mw dem* = to follow toward, to develop . . .
mi hpr = as it happens (comes)	*mi sopi* = this one changes
hpr→šopi (in Coptic) = transformation, to become	*sopi* = to transform, to change
henu = 1/200 of the khar	*gēnn* = mortar (*h→g*)
khet = 100 cubits	*khet* = wood
wd(a)t = Horus's sacred eye, whose different parts form a decreasing geometric progression of fractions from 1/2 to 1/64 (p. 26) (1/2, 1/4, 1/8, 1/16, 1/32, 1/64)	*da* = to see clearly, distinctly
kite = *kdt* = 1/10 deben = ring (p. 26)	*khet* = a ring
snn pw n = it is a copy	*sanen* = another look alike (of the same kind, similar)
(hel), hr km 2/3 = it must be equal to 2/3 . . . to one 2/3 . . . (*Rh.* p. 54)	*hel kem* = *hala yem* = 2/3 . . . *akl* = must be equal to to one
tp n sity ky = proof other (than) (*Kh.* p. 58)	*top seet ky* = to verify this one
y(a)i = excess, difference (*Kh.* p. 59)	*yaay* = size, width
chw = heap, pile, abstract quantity (*Rh.* p. 61)	*tahaw* = up, standing, that takes the place of something *tahawé* = to take for
twnw = difference of parts (*Rh.* p. 77)	*tolloo* = to be equals *tool* = the remainder of a division, after a division
rht = number ? (*Rh.* p. 86)	*reket* = to come out right
sity = proof (*Rh.* p. 86)	*seety* = to go verify
seked = *skd* = slope	*segg* = bend; in a slope
spdt = pointed = triangle (*Rh.* p. 91)	*pud* = small pointed cone
spdt = Serus the star, pointed	
sti = height (*Moscow Papyrus*, problem 14, cited by Peet, *Rh.* p. 93)	*siit* = vertical trajectory of the drop of water that falls, which could be the technical term for height
hnt = to remove, to subtract (*Rh.* p. 97)	*gente* = action of going out *genn* = to go out *genne* = to subtract
kry p hwi = the last (*Rh.* p. 108)	*pegw* = periphery to be outside (*h→g*)
hsb ni gm. k wi km (= *mak*) = I have calculated while I found that I was complete (*Rh.* p. 111)	*hasab on na, gimi-kw na, (k) emon na* = I have measured, I have discovered, I have reached the limit
sity mw = to pour water (*Rh.* p. 118)	*soty* = to pour (water)
r db = in exchange for . . .	*dab* = to give, to stretch out the hand rapidly, to shake hands, to exchange, to give objects
= *hrt* = to share, portion[61]	*har* = to split, to share

ASTRONOMY

The sources here are the diagonal calendars of the sarcophagi, the orientation of the monuments, the establishment of the astronomic calendar since 4236 B.C., and the *Demotic Papyrus Carlsberg 1 to 9* (A.D. 144).

Phases of the Moon

Even though it came late, the *Carlsberg Papyrus 9* describes a method for the determination of the phases of the moon, deriving from more ancient sources, and without any trace of the influence of Hellenistic science; the same can be said of *Carlsberg 1*; this seems to prove that treatises of the Egyptian astronomy did exist.[62]

Calendar

Just as with geometry, the Egyptians were the exclusive inventors of the calendar, the very one which, barely changed,[63] regulates our life today, and about which Neugebauer says "that it is truly the only intelligent calendar that has ever existed in human history.[64]

They invented the 365-day year, breaking it down as follows: 12 months of 30 days = 360 days, plus the 5 intercalated days, each one corresponding to the birth of one of the following Egyptian gods: Osiris, Isis, Horus, Seth, and Nephthys. These are the same gods who will give birth to the human race and inaugurate the cycle of historic times: Adam and Eve are only belated Biblical replicas of Osiris and Isis.

The year is divided into three seasons of four months, the month into three weeks of ten days that do not overlap the months; the day into 24 hours. The Egyptians knew that this calendar year was too short, that it was lacking a quarter of a day in order for it to correspond to a complete sidereal revolution. Also, in 4236 B.C. (the imagination remains transfixed), they invented a second astronomical calendar founded precisely on this time lag, this delay, of a quarter of a day per year, in the 365-day calendar year as compared to the sidereal, or astronomical, calendar. The time lag thus accumulated at the end of four years is equal to one day. Instead of adding 1 day every 4 years and thus instituting a leap year, the Egyptians preferred the masterful solution that consists of following this time lag for 1,460 years.[65]

Consequently, it is the very cause of the leap year that is at the basis of the Egyptian sidereal calendar; the Egyptians preferred to "rectify" every 1,460 years instead of every 4 years; he who can do more can do less, therefore contrary to popular opinion, they knew the leap year very well. But what is still more amazing is that the Egyptians had equally (observed?) calculated that this period of 1,460 years of the sidereal calendar is the lapse of time that separates two heliacal risings of Sirius, the most brilliant fixed star in the heavens, located in the constellation *Canis Major*; thus is designated the simultaneous appearance of Sirius and of the sun at the latitude of Memphis. Thus, the heliacal rising of Sirius, which takes place every 1,460 years, coinciding with the first day of the year in both calendars, is the absolute chronological reference point that is the basis for the Egyptian astronomical calendar. One gets lost in conjectures in order to figure out *how* the Egyptians were able to arrive at such a result from protohistory, because it is known with certainty that the sidereal calendar was in use from 4236 B.C. onward. Supposing that a celestial phenomenon as fleeting as the heliacal rising of Sirius had accidentally caught the attention of the Egyptians from the fourth millennium onward, how could they have guessed at and verified, within a few minutes, its rigorous periodicity, in a time span of 1,460 years, and thus invented a calendar on this basis? Did they arrive at this result through empirical or theoretical means? Assuredly, the disparagers of Egyptian civilization have their work cut out for them!

The length of the above-mentioned period being in no way comparable to that of a human life, one has to have magic skills to find an empirical solution to such a problem.

When the Romans conquered Egypt, in 47 B.C., Caesar altered the Egyptian calendar by introducing the readjustment every 4 years (leap year), and that was the origin of the present-day calendar. It has been said that Egyptians were ignorant of the notion of an era and that the calendar year was a fluctuating one. This is to forget that the Pharoah had created a national service presided over by the great vizier, the highest official of the Egyptian state, and devoted exclusively to the observation of the rising of Sirius: thus the Egyptian astronomers had made tables that allowed, each year, the monitoring of the gap between the year of the civil and of the astronomical calendars on which historic events were projected, as on an absolutely chronological scale.

All of the historically important events of the calendar year could have a double dating, a double reference; that is why four double dates have been found,[66] each one of them being established to within four years, considering the above.[67]

Here, one clearly has the impression that the last three dates related to Egyptian history correspond well to a fixing on an absolutely chronological scale, to a point of reference on that scale of events as important as the beginning of the reign of this or that Pharoah.

Because of the length of the period of the sidereal calendar, not more than four were needed to cover the duration of the history of Egyptian civilization. Thus it clearly appears that the reference point of absolute chronology, for the Egyptians, was the number of Sirius's heliacal risings.

Therefore, up to our day, with the Egyptian sidereal calendar, which could perfectly well be followed to the letter, humanity, or Africa in any event, has the scale of absolute chronology to which the Christian era, the Hegira, and various other points of reference are all connected.

Besides the civil and the sidereal calendars, the Egyptians used other calendars, the liturgical calendar, for instance, based on lunar cycles and used in determining religious feasts. This is how the method of predicting the lunar phases was invented, described in the *Carlsberg Papyrus* 9, for the setting of the dates for movable feasts.[68]

If a heliacal rising took place in A.D. 139, it can be deduced that others, separated by a period of 1,460 years, had taken place in 1318–21 B.C., 2778–81, 4238–41. These dates have been obtained thanks to the double dates and the knowledge of the curve of Sirius.

The choice of the heliacal rising as an astronomical point of reference for absolute chronology has nothing to do with the specific marking of the beginning of the flooding, for the simple reason that in 4236 B.C. when the calendar was invented, the heliacal rising took place beyond the flooding season and thus could not announce it. Those who support this idea are disparagers who would like to reduce the Egyptian sidereal calendar to the level of an agrarian routine. They are also followers of the "short chronology," who place the invention of the calendar in 2778 B.C. instead of 4236 B.C., which corresponds to the "long chronology," the most ancient date in history (Meyer). They use the fact that the most ancient double date cited by the Egyptian documents that has come down to us is the feast that took place in the year 7 of the reign of Sesostris III, or between 1885 and 1882 B.C. It is known today that the hypothesis of the short chronology is absurd and indefensible for several reasons.

In fact, if the calendar had been invented in 2778, the event would have coincided with the reign of Zoser, the first king of the IIIrd Dynasty. This invention would have very probably been the work of the versatile scholar Imhotep, the architect of Zoser, deified by tradition and by the Greeks in particular. This singularly brilliant invention of a sidereal calendar would have been associated with his legend by tradition. On the other hand, this event would have taken place in the middle of an historic epoch; history would have preserved for us at least one allusion on the subject.

Finally, on a tablet of ivory in a tomb of the Ist Dynasty (3300 B.C.) at Abydos, Sirius is saluted as the star that opens the new year and brings flooding: this shows clearly that the sidereal calendar was already in use and consequently the date of 4236 appears to be a certainty.

It should be pointed out that this date is necessary in order to accommodate the ninety kings who preceded Sesostris III.

An author like Otto Muck,[69] who despises concrete archaeological fact and grants privilege to legend instead of to the most precise historical documents, places Cheops (2600 B.C.) in Zoser's epoch (2783 B.C.) in spite of all historical evidence. This gross twisting of documents, let us remember, is indispensable for him to advance the idea that a primitive decoration without words on a funerary urn's lid, discovered by Dorpfeld (Seligman's successor) at the Troy excavations, represents a solar calendar that was used as a model for the Egyptian one. Philitis, the shepherd, is supposed to have introduced it in Egypt at the time of Cheops (pp. 68–78 and chapter 8 in Muck's book). The same shepherd is to have brought to Egypt even the title of Pharoah (p. 114): consequently, everything came from the North, from Europe; witness Stonehenge in England, where the Nordic

Indo-European calendar, baptized the "Dardanian" calendar, was in use, according to Muck.

These are insipid notions that cannot even provoke laughter, a text unworthy of criticism. The interpretation of the decorative signs on the lid is a pointless tale.

Orientation of the Monuments

The precision of the great architectural monuments, especially the pyramids, defends the existence of a sound astronomical science; in fact, the number of monuments that are oriented in relation to the four cardinal points with an error always below one degree to the true north, eliminates any notion of chance.[70] A method of astronomical observation was surely used to determine the true north, but which one? We know that the method based on the shortest projected shadows is not precise enough. The idea of optical instruments with lenses gains greater credence with the latest discoveries.

The Decans

Furthermore, the Egyptian year was divided into thirty-six decades or ten-day periods, each governed by a constellation. This makes a total of 360 divisions or "degrees" of the circle, the basis of the first dated sexagesimal division in the history of the sciences. *Carlsberg 1* explains the legends that accompany the decans. The ancient text is transcribed in hieratic, then translated word for word into demotic: "In certain cases the usual hieroglyphic signs have been replaced with cryptographic forms,[71] thus hiding the real meaning from the uninitiated reader."

We will come back to this initiatory form of Egyptian education, which has persisted in Black Africa until now.

The decans go back to at least the IIIrd Dynasty, 2800 B.C., and they took on astrological importance during the Greco-Roman epoch. They still survive today in West Africa, in Senegal. Is it an Islamic influence?

The Empirical Character of Mesopotamian Science

The Mesopotamians (Assyro-Babylonians) only knew a grossly inaccurate lunar calendar, sometimes with years of thirteen or fourteen months. When the gap became too flagrant, the king decided to add an extra month. There was nothing similar to the Egyptian calendar. The numerous astronomical observations that were made were empirical, and the attempts at rationalization, accomplished by arbitrarily associating them with arithmetic and geometric progressions in the particular case of the movements of the moon did not correspond to any law: there was juxtaposition pure and simple.

One had to wait until the Seleucid epoch (310 B.C.) for the Mesopotamian astrologists to establish the empirical tablets called "lunar ephemerides," in order to try, in vain, to set the duration of the lunar month according to the factors of visibility of the crescent moon on the horizon (twenty-nine or thirty days).

Thus, compared to the Egyptians, the Mesopotamians were as mediocre as astronomers as they were as geometers:

The cylinder is put into the category of a prism with a value of $\pi = 3$, for the calculation of the surface of the base and of the volume.

The volume of the truncated cone is given in the erroneous formula below:

$$V = \frac{1}{2} h (S + S')$$

Similarly, that of the truncated pyramid, $V = \frac{1}{2} h (a^2 + b^2)$, cited on page 326, is wrong, contrary to that formulated by the Egyptians.

MEDICINE

Theophrastus, Dioscorides, and Galen perpetually cite the prescriptions that they received from the Egyptian physicians, or more specifically, as Galen says, that they had learned by consulting the works conserved in the library of the Temple of Imhotep at Memphis, which was still accessible in the second century A.D., and where, seven centuries before, Hippocrates, the "father of medicine," was taught.

Right or wrong, the method indicated in the *Carlsberg Papyrus 4*, designed to diagnose sterility in a woman, was copied word for word by Hippocrates: "Insert a clove of garlic in the vagina for one night, if the odor comes out of her mouth, she will bear children."

The healing of the possessed was supposed to be accomplished through the simple incantation of magical formulas[72] as in Black Africa. The incantation[73] works of its own accord, without any pharmaceutical treatment: this is the psychological method.

But often, in order for the magical formula to be effective, it had to be supplemented with a drug. The following incantation, which identified the patient with a burned Horus, was used to treat a burn. "My son Horus is in flames on the barren plateau. There is no water there. I am not there. I am bringing water (coming) from the shore of the pool in order to put out the fire." "The formula is to be recited over the milk of a woman who gave birth to a boy." (*Eb.*, 500). One would believe oneself in today's Black Africa. The sick person is healed by the power of the magical words.

In Black Africa, we still witness the combined use of the magical incantatory formula and drugs. But in Egypt, with time, the formula was replaced by medical treatment, and thus medicine was born: the physician replaced the magician; in fact, the rationalization of Egyptian medicine was never complete; some medications were of divine origin, as in Black

Africa; the sting of a scorpion was cured only by reciting magical formulas dedicated to Isis and Thoth.[74]

Medicine was thus practiced at three different levels:

1. There was, besides physicians and magicians, the paramedical body of Sekhmet's priests who guaranteed celestial or miraculous healing as do our marabouts and the saints of the revealed religions, or the water of Lourdes. One could be physician and magician in one. The Egyptian physicians were the ones who first had the idea of taking the pulse[75].

2. There were general practitioners as well as specialists in different diseases.

Medical practice, like the priesthood, was hereditary: just as the priest passed on his knowledge (sacred words, rites, etc.) to the one among his children chosen to succeed him after his death, so did the physician pass his knowledge on to the son who was to succeed him. Is it necessary to say that the situation is the same in Black Africa today?

And it is the poor conditions of the transmission of this hereditary knowledge that bring about the frequent losses and that slow down the development of a true science. However, the physician could complete his training at an educational institution called the "House of Life," where scholars lived who specialized in the different disciplines, as well as directors of workshops in charge of writing or recopying papyruses. That is how the papyruses were composed that have lasted until today.

3. Often, the physicians were officials who, in some cases, gave free treatment: on military expeditions, for instance. There was the court physician, the chief physician of the North, of the South, etc. Clement of Alexandria cites, among other things, the works that the physician had to know.

The *Smith Papyrus* speaks of forty-eight cases of bone surgery and of external pathology. Its scientific conciseness has won the admiration of modern scientists.[76] It is not a collection of prescriptions, but rather a veritable treatise on bone surgery.

The method indicated by the papyrus for the treatment of the dislocation of the lower jaw was copied by Hippocrates and modern scholars. "The clinical observations have great precision and do honor to the surgeons of the Ancient Empire, 2600 B.C., who lived two thousand years before Hippocrates."

They were the first to practice suturing and to use wooden splints for fractures. The African healer proceeds, as in the latter case, to treat a fracture.

"The Egyptian surgeons had reached the peak of their art from the Memphite epoch onward, at least in the domain of bone surgery: everything about them is to be admired, their ingenuity, their good sense."[77]

CHEMISTRY

Etymology of the Word "Chemistry"

The root of the word *chemistry* is of Egyptian origin, as is already known; it comes from *kemit* = "black," alluding to the long cooking process and the distillations that were customary in Egyptian "laboratories," in order to extract this or that desired product.

We know that this root has proliferated in the other Negro languages, where it has retained the same meaning. In Wolof: *hemit* = black, to blacken, etc.

The French chemist Claude Louis Berthollet was struck with such admiration for Egyptian scientific knowledge in chemistry that he devoted a paper to them.

Metallurgy of Iron

The world's oldest voluntary making of steel is, up to now, certified to have taken place only in Egypt, as the text below shows:

Accidentally, a metallographic microscopic examination permits the identification of a "steeled" piece of iron:

> There exists however indisputable proof of a deliberately made cementation: it is the presence in a steel object of successive layers containing different percentages of carbon. A blacksmith would have had no reason to forge an object like this if he had not understood the different properties of the successive layers. The most ancient object of this type is an Egyptian knife, probably made between 900 and 800 B.C.[78]

Archaeological excavations in the southern Sahara are in the process of confirming our ideas on the first Iron Age (2600 to 1500 B.C.), published in the *Bulletin de l'IFAN* and in *Notes africaines*.[79]

Similarly, the late Professor Emery, of Oxford, is supposed to have found, during the salvaging excavations conducted in Nubia under UNESCO sponsorship, traces of iron metallurgy dating back to the Ancient Empire.

ARCHITECTURE

Mathematical Bases of Egyptian Architecture

Egyptian architectural work implies mechanical and technical knowledge that specialists have not yet finished discussing.

The scholars know that nobody is yet capable of giving a satisfactory explanation of the manner in which the Egyptians proceeded with the construction of the Great Pyramid of Khufu (Cheops): the technique used

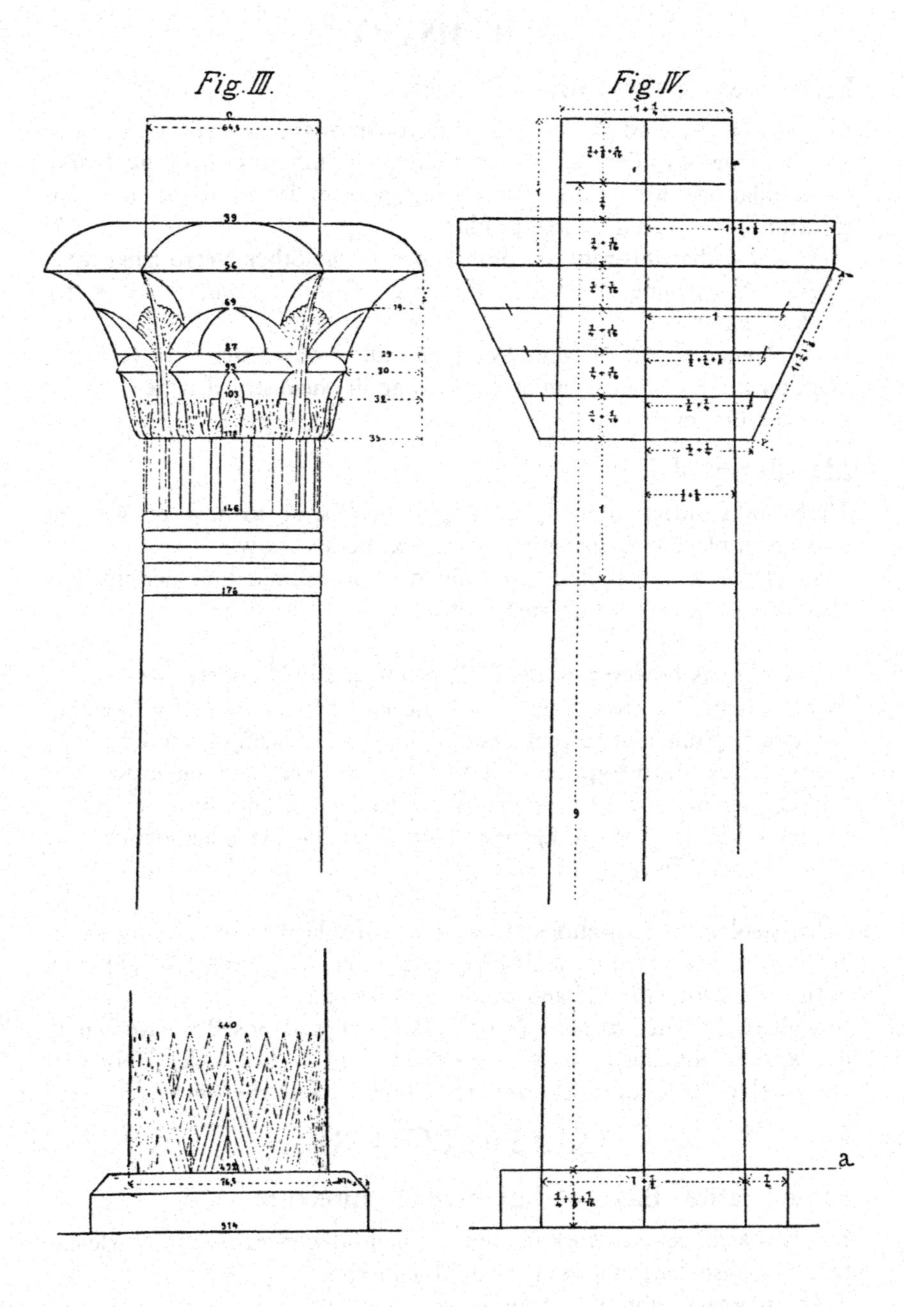
Fig. III.
Fig. IV.
39
56
69
87
146
176
440
514
a

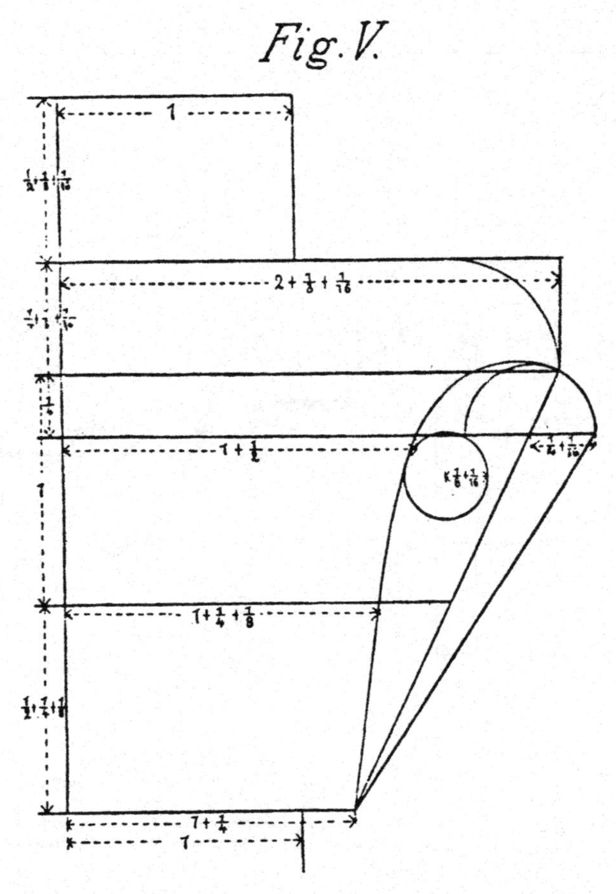

Figures 52, 53: Notice the reduction of the diameter of the column toward the top following the relationships of the geometric series (the eye of Horus), or the narrowing of the capitals toward the bottom following the same geometric proportions, indicated in fractional numbers. (Ludwig Borchardt, in *Zeitschrift für Aegyptischer Sprache*, vol. XXXIV, 1896, pl. IV, figs. III and IV, pl. III, fig. V, the latter taken from W. M. F. Petrie, *Season*, pl. 25)

to assemble 2,300,000 stones, each one weighing two-and-a-half tons on the average, and above all the technique used to polish the surfaces of these stones and to assemble them so perfectly that, even today, one would try in vain to slip a razor blade between the stones. The huge stones that make up the roof of the king's chamber weigh fifty tons each.

The Egyptians used ramps of varying inclines to hoist the stones. Thus Borchardt[80] shows that the Egyptians knew the principle of the inclined plane perfectly, and that they used it, in the full mechanical sense of the

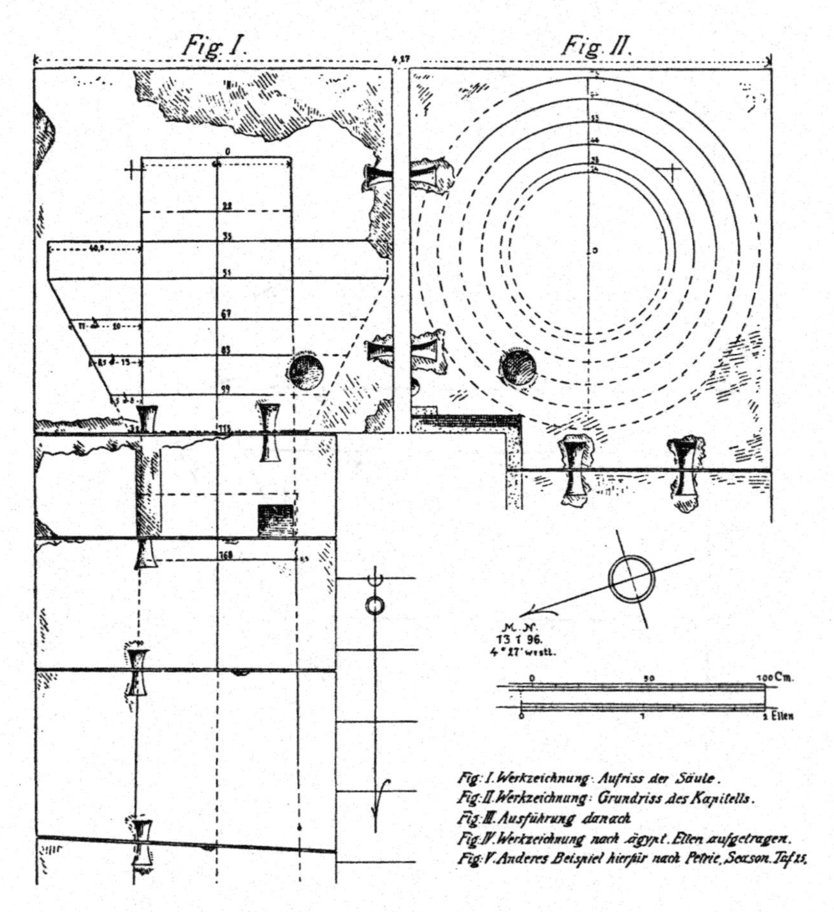

Figure 54: Blueprint of a capital, applying the same remarks as for the two preceding figures. (*Ibid.*, pl. III, figs. I and II)

term, to elevate heavy materials. Remains of these ramps have been found near the pyramids, particularly close to the Snofru pyramid near Meidum; the ramp of Meidum is 65 meters high, 200 meters long, and has a slope of 19°20′, that is, around 20°. Let us not forget that the Egyptians juggled with trigonometric lines (sine, cosine, tangent, and cotangent). They are the true inventors of trigonometry and knew perfectly how to establish the relationship between the angle of an inclined plane, represented by one of these trigonometric lines, and the reduction of the weight of the blocks, observed and measured during traction. The trigonometric exercises of the *Rhind Papyrus* deal with calculating the slope of the pyramids and the conical pillars (see pp. 236–41 and pp. 261; 266–67).

Borchardt has tried to calculate the number of workers and the time necessary for the construction of the pyramids.[81] After having made all

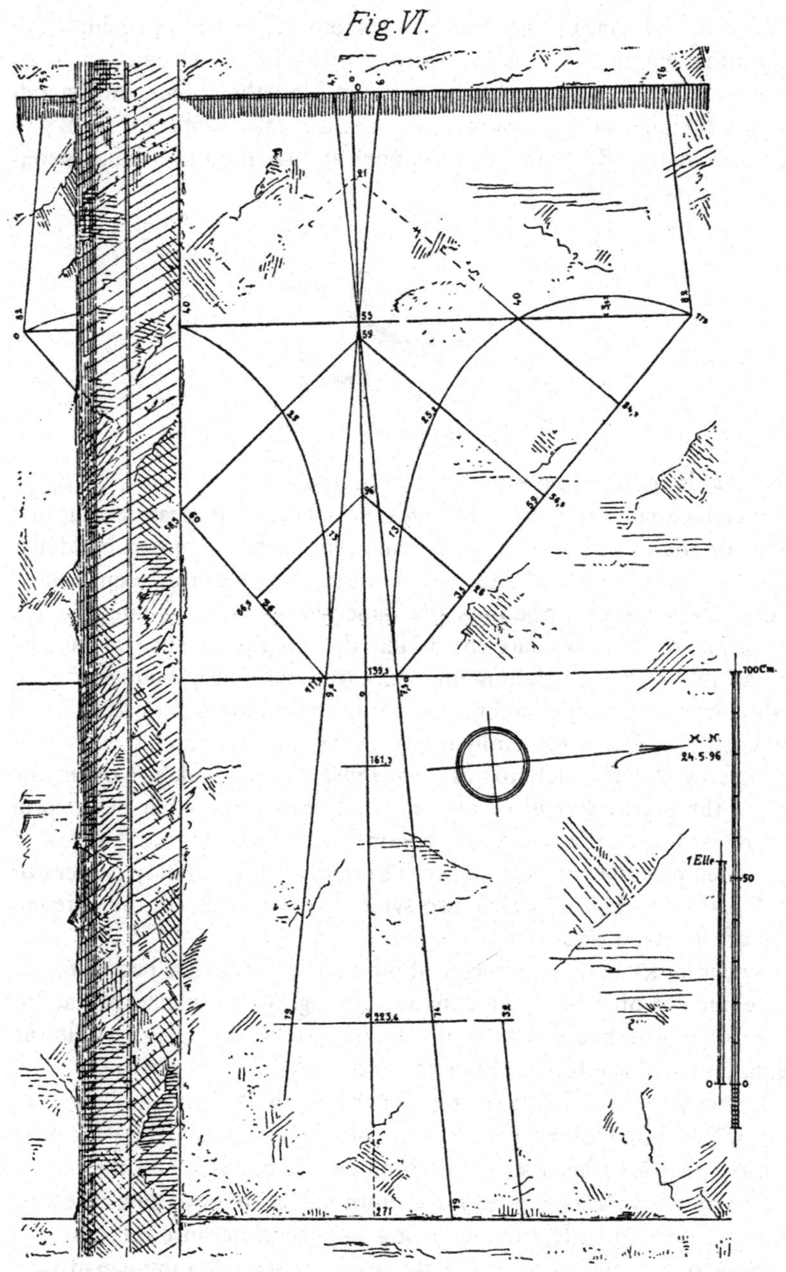

Figure 55: Another drawing provided by Ludwig Borchardt. (*Ibid.*, pl. V, fig. VI)

calculations, he came up with twenty years for the Meidum pyramid, which is a normal amount of time, compatible with the twenty-nine-year reign of Pharaoh Snefru, as given by the historian Manetho.[82] One understands why the building of these monuments did not take centuries, thanks to the use of ramps. Borchardt's calculations are based on the simultaneous use of two ramps.

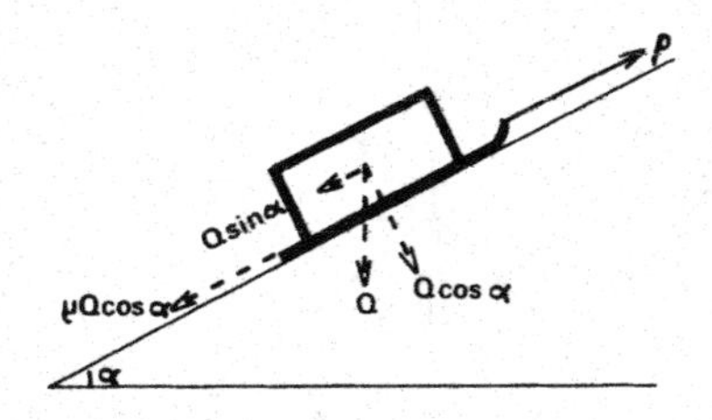

Borchardt, in the above-cited article, tried to find out, in part, the Egyptian architectural canon, in other words, the standard of measurement that would be the aliquot part of the dimensions of the Egyptian buildings. He found that the cubit (523 meters) does not meet this requirement, particularly when one examines the dimensions of the columns of the temples, even during the late epoch, like the temple at Philae; it must be stressed that even these late monuments were rigorously built according to the classical Egyptian architectural rules of previous periods. It is by studying the plans, purposefully drawn by the Egyptian architects on the monuments that they left for us—like those at Abu Fodah,[83] or on the roof of the hypostyle hall of the temple of Edfu, etc.—that he realized that the standard of measurement commensurate with all the dimensions is the cubit plus the geometrical series of fractions of a unitary numerator ($1/2 + 1/4 + 1/8 + 1/16$), which also symbolize, let us recall, the different parts of the eye of Horus.[84]

Thus, in order to set the height of a pillar, the architects had to take a whole number of cubits (9, for instance, in fig. 52) to which they added $1/4 + 1/8 + 1/16$. The diameter of the base could be $1 + 1/2$, while the thinning toward the top could measure $1 + 1/4$.

We have also reproduced the plan of the tomb of Ramses IV (figs. 56, 57), published by Howard Carter and Alan H. Gardiner.[85] The dark parts are those that have been spared by time on the papyrus, and the monument's symmetry has facilitated reconstitution, which is rigorous. The plan was not drawn to scale, but this is less important because the exact dimensions of the different parts of the tomb are given on the papyrus.

In the above-cited article, Flinders Petrie published the grid plan (a side view, so to speak) of a wooden altar, suspended in the frame of a *naos* and designed to be carried during processions. The document is a papyrus of the XVIIIth Dynasty.

In figures 58, 59, and 60, we have published a few types of Egyptian pillars, according to K. Richard Lepsius.

The Aesthetic Canon of Egyptian Art

The Egyptian aesthetic canon of the square section is at bottom, equivalent to the golden section; this explains why the latter can be rigorously applied to all works of Egyptian art. If this is so, it is because the square section is a convention that allows exact reproduction of the anatomical proportions of the human body, as we will see by analyzing the study of Ernest Mackay.[86]

The monuments analyzed are from the XVIIIth Dynasty or later, XXVth or XXVIth Dynasties.

Squares are evenly drawn on the area on which the drawing or the work of art is going to be applied, beforehand. The top of a person's head is always situated three squares above the shoulders; the upper head to the bottom of the forehead occupies one square unit;[87] from there to the base of the nose, one unit, that is, one square; from the base of the nose to that of the neck, one unit. The body, from the base of the neck down to the knee, ten units; from the knee to the heel, six units. In total, the human body occupies, from head to toe, nineteen units, or squares.

When a male figure wears the loin cloth (*calasiri*), its lower limit is at 12½ units from the top of the skull.[88] The depth of the opening of the neck of the garment worn by men is half a square, measured from the shoulder line. A vertical line passing in front of the ear, when it is not hidden by a wig, unequally divides the body into two parts and ends at a square behind the toe of the rear foot when the person is standing in a normal position. Most of the body is in the front of this line which divides the head into two equal parts. Another important vertical line is in the front of this first one; it goes through the eye's iris all the way down to the toe of the back foot.

When there are two individuals, a man and a woman, only the first can be executed according to the above rule, but six squares have to separate the two verticals that pass through the eye of each one. The vertical line that is situated two squares behind the one that divides the head into two is also of major importance, for it determines the position of the calf of the rear leg and the balance of the body in general.

The total length of the foot, from toe to heel, is generally three units; thus it is equal to the height of the head plus the neck. The toe of the rear leg touches the vertical line of the eye, while the heel, three units behind it, touches the vertical line that establishes the position of the calf. In general, a square and a half separates the heel of the front foot from the toe of the rear foot. When the arms are folded in front, the elbow is four units in front of the vertical line that divides the head and seven units below the top of the skull.[89]

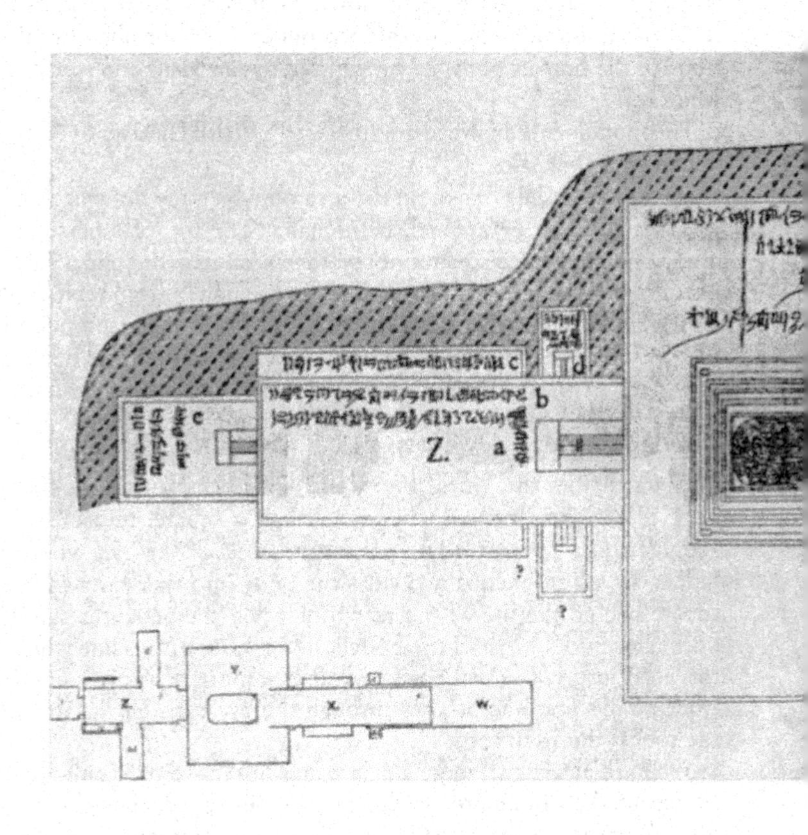

Figure 56: Diagrams of the tomb of Ramses IV, as they were conceived and drawn on papyrus by the Egyptian engineers of the XIXth Dynasty. (From the *Turin Papyrus*, restored by K. R. Lepsius. *See* the article by Howard Carter and Alan H. Gardiner, "Plans du

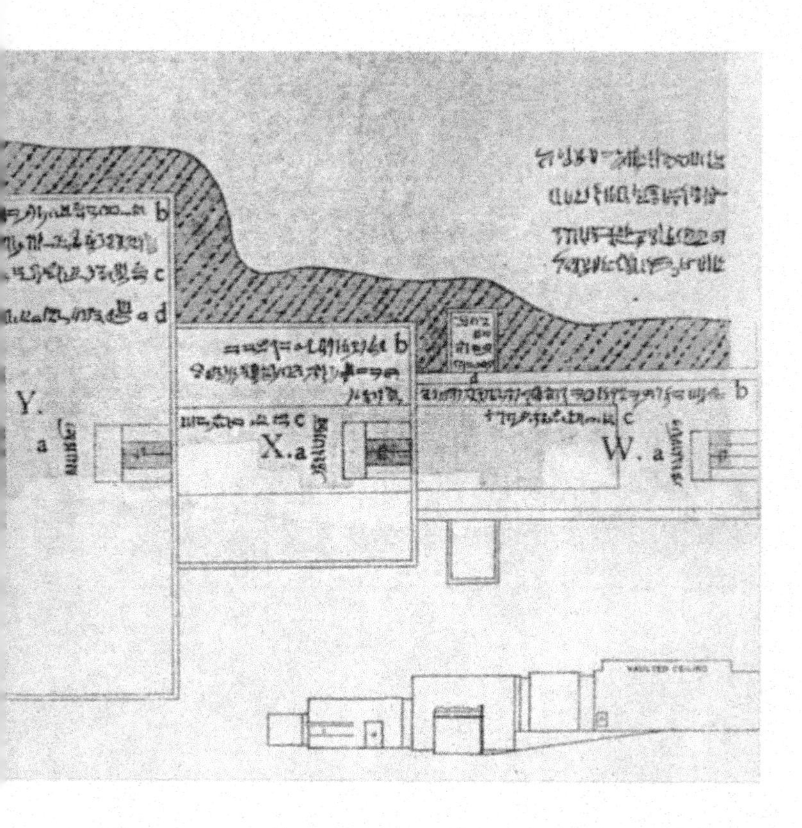

tombeau de Ramsès IV" in *Journal of Egyptian Archeology*, 4 (1917), pp. 130–58, pl. XXIX.) Notes at bottom left and right of the drawing: *Left*: Part of the diagram by Carter illustrating the papyrus *Right*: Part of the section by Carter illustrating the papyrus.

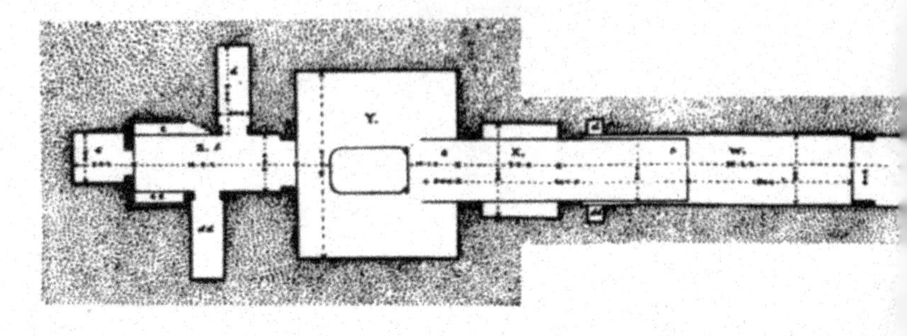

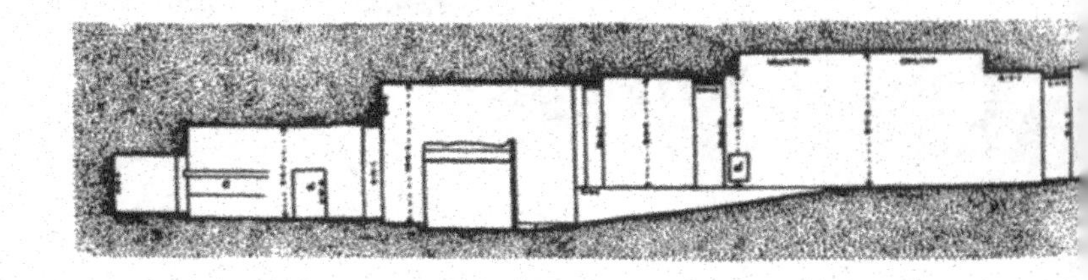

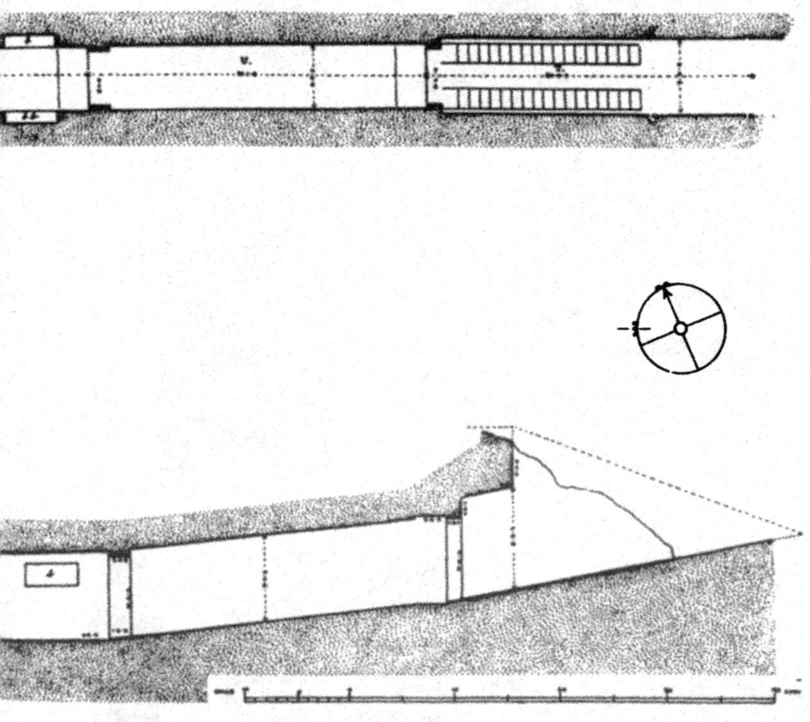

Figure 57: Blueprint and cross section of the tomb of Ramses IV at Bibân el-Molûk, Thebes. (*Ibid.*, pl. XXX)

Figure 58: Pillars of the great temple at Karnak. (K. R. Lepsius, Denkmäler aus Aegypten und Aethiopien, vol. I–II, part I, p. 81)

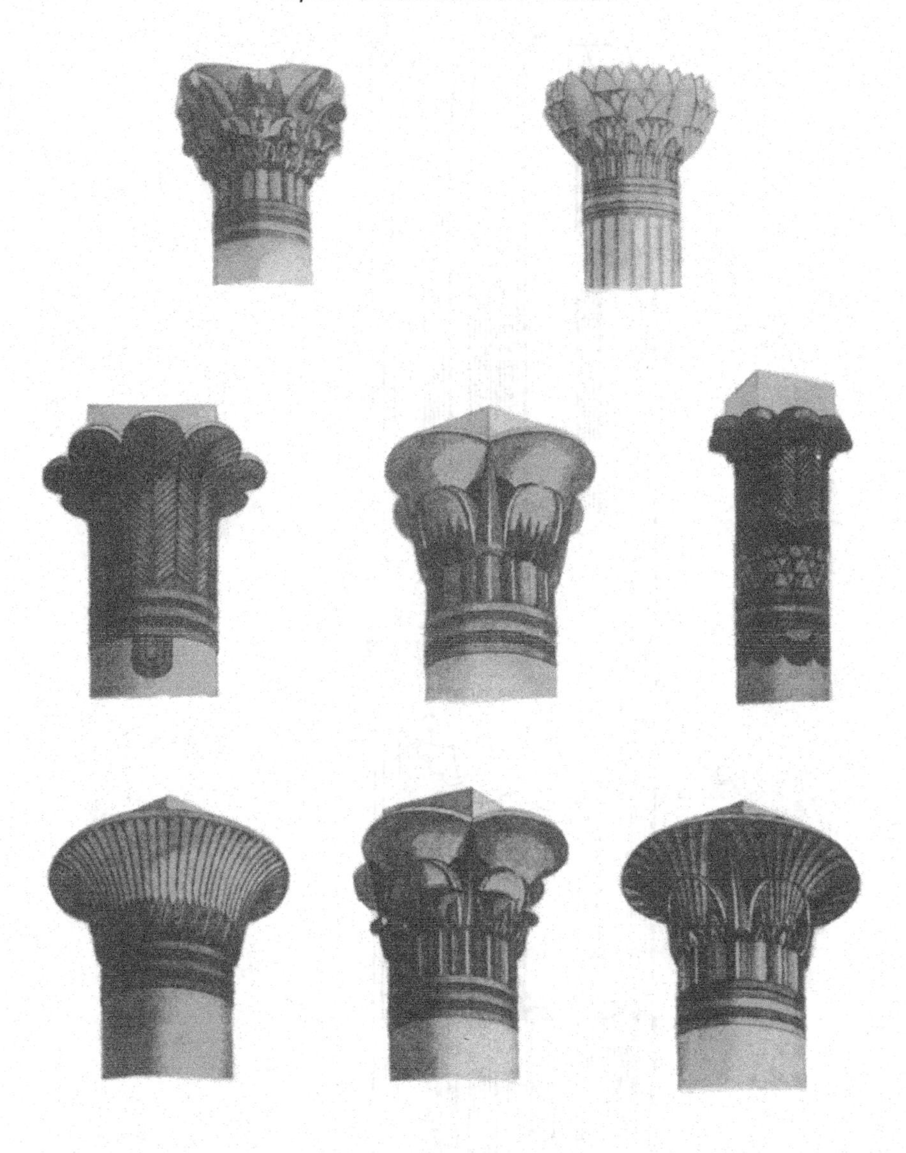

Figure 59: Capitals of the columns of the temple at Philae. (Ibid., p. 108)

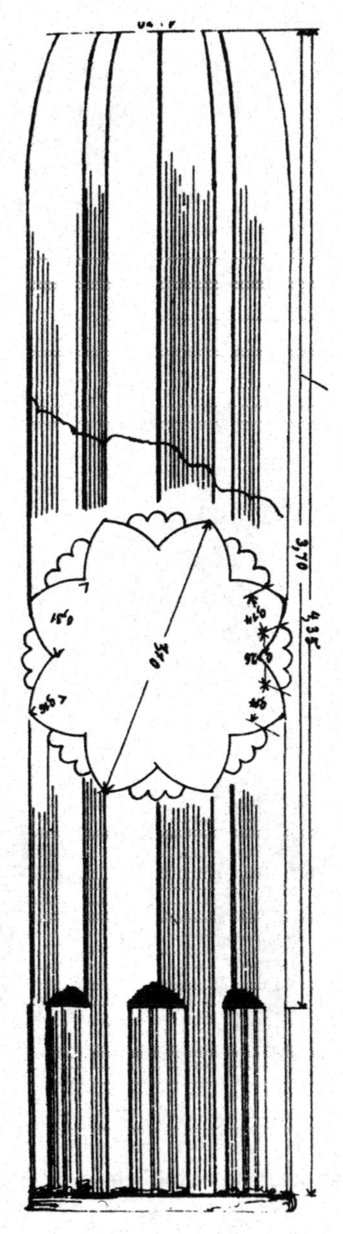

Figure 60: Cross section of a column, showing its geometric structure in a rosette form. (*Ibid.*, text, vol. I, p. 211)

Figures 61–65: The "squared section" in the sketches of the Egyptian painters of the XVIIIth Dynasty. The squared section is equivalent to the golden section, for, in both cases, there is the invention of a technique that permits the faithful reproduction of the anatomical proportions of the being. Thus, any Egyptian masterpiece achieved through the squared section is inscribable in minute detail in the rectangles corresponding to the golden section, meaning that the ratio of the length to the width is equal to 1.618 (Cheikh Anta Diop, *L'Antiquité africaine par l'image*, Dakar: IFAN, p. 8). The tiles in figures 61–65 are from the XVIIIth Dynasty; these are the sketches and the studies of the Egyptian painters of that time and not the work of modern specialists (Ernest Mackay, "Proportion Squares on Tomb Walls in the Theban Necropolis," in the *Journal of Egyptian Archeology*, 4, 1917, plates XV, XVII, XVIII).

Figure 61: Tomb 92, plate XVII.

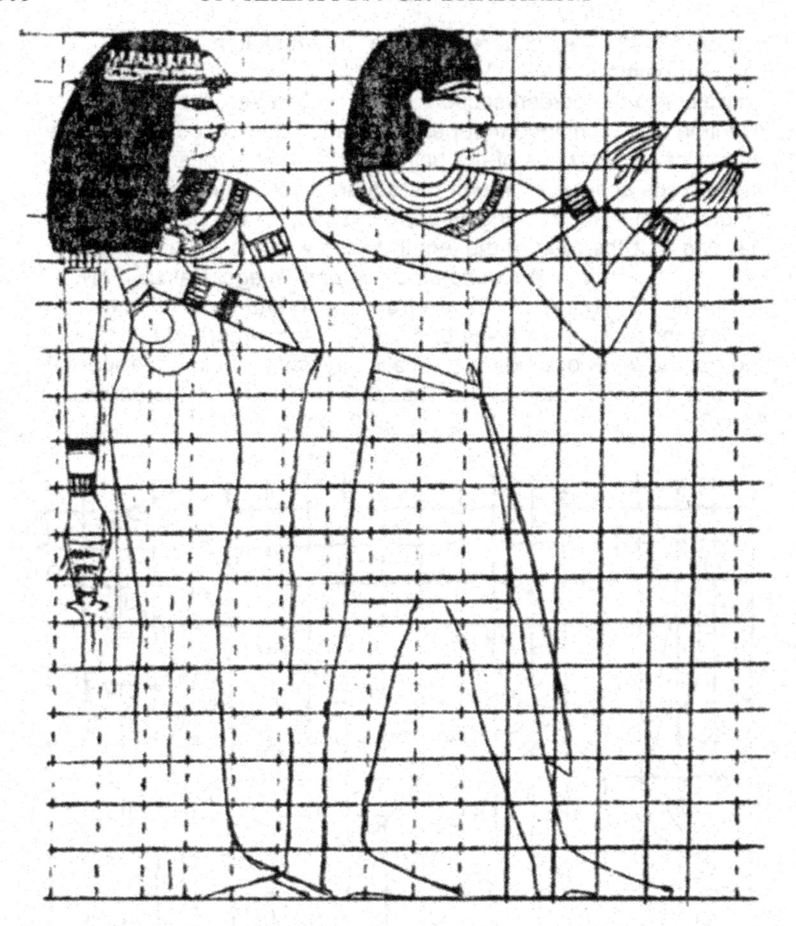

Figure 62: Tomb 52, plate XV.

Figure 63: Tomb 36, plate XVIII.

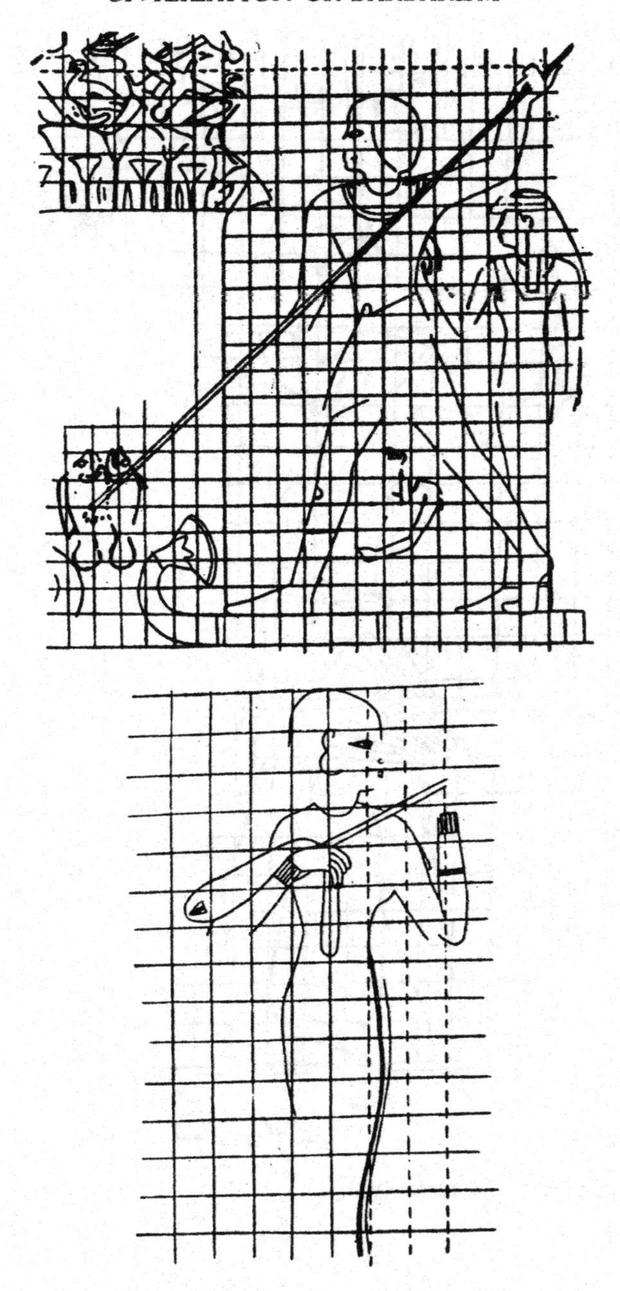

Figure 64: Tomb 92, plate XVII and tomb 93, plate XV.

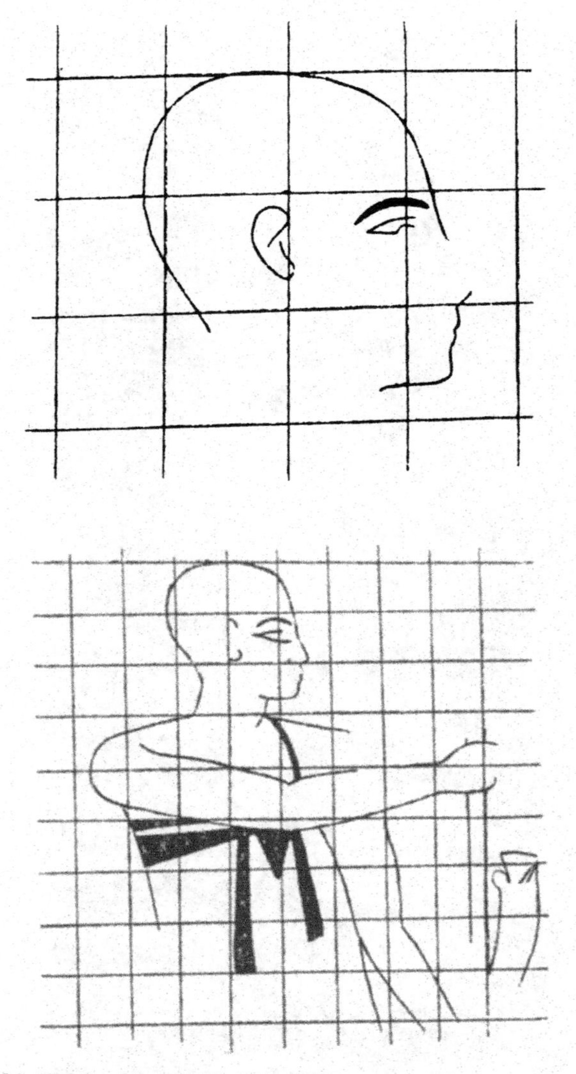

Figure 65: Tombs 95 and 55, plate XV.

Figure 66: Wooden statuette, end of the XVIIIth Dynasty. Notice the harmony of the pleats in the dress, a thousand years before Phidias had sculpted the friezes of the Parthenon (parade of the Panathenaea). A special study should be devoted to this detail of the pleats in the clothes and their transparency, permitting the body to become visible, in Egyptian art. (*Dictionnaire de la Civilisation égyptienne*, p. 191)

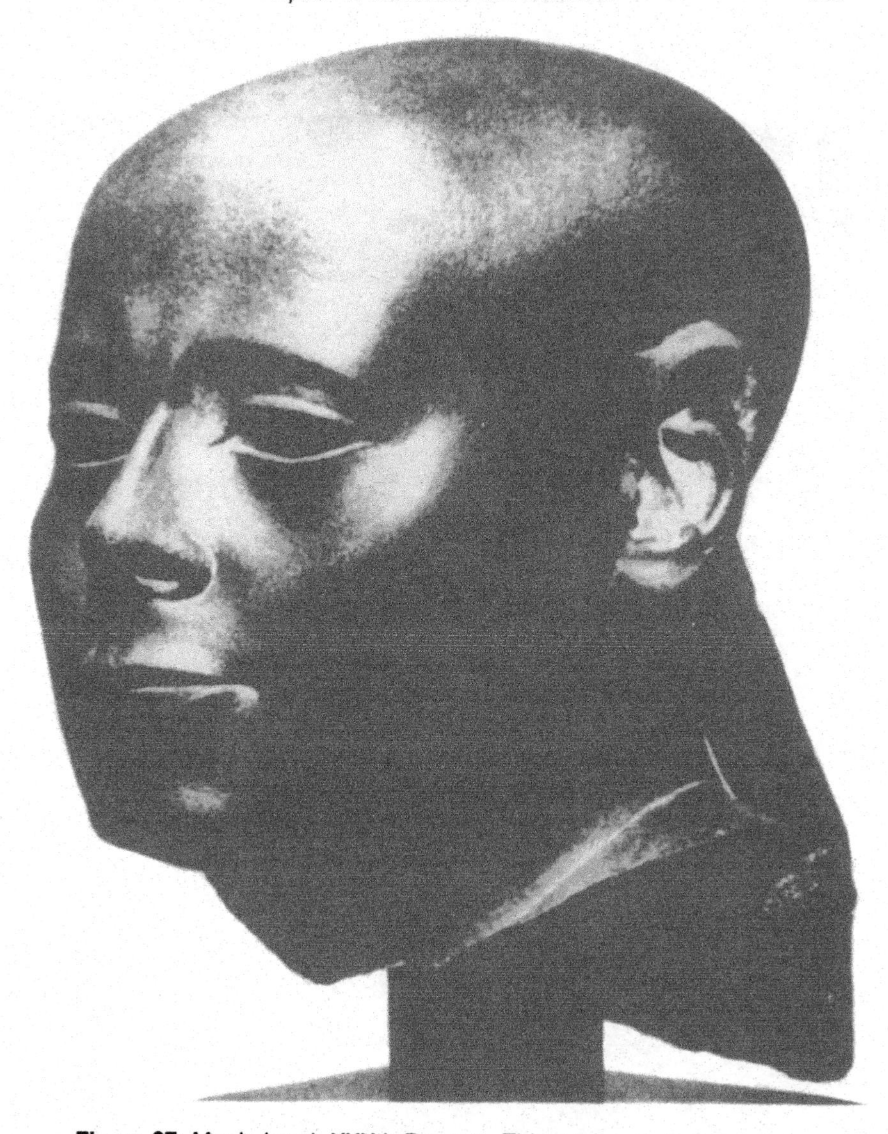

Figure 67: Man's head, XXXth Dynasty. This sculpture in the round rigorously conforms to the proportions of the golden section. It already is as naturalistic as future Greek art. One could compare this canon with that of Ife in Yorubaland. This would confirm the equivalence of the squared section to that of the golden section. (Brooklyn Museum, illustration taken from Jacques Pirenne, *Histoire de la civilisation de l'Égypte ancienne*, vol. III, fig. 57)

Figure 68: Bulls fighting, The New Kingdom. Egyptian profane art is an art of motion. The hieratic attitude characterizes mainly the monumental sacred art. (*Dictionnaire de la Civilisation égyptienne*, p. 101)

The total height of seated figures is fifteen units instead of nineteen. In Aba's tomb (XXVIth Dynasty), the total height of the body extends to 22⅓ units, the head now comprising 3⅓ units.[90] This is probably due to a change in the canon, which could have been a result of the renaissance of the arts during the XXVth Dynasty.

The other sketches[91] are similar studies executed by Egyptian artists of the XXVIIIth Dynasty.

17

DOES AN AFRICAN PHILOSOPHY EXIST?

THE EGYPTIAN CONTRIBUTION TO WORLD PHILOSOPHICAL THOUGHT

In the classical sense of the term, a philosophical thought must bear out at least two fundamental criteria:

1. It must be conscious of itself, of its own existence as a thought.
2. It must have accomplished, to a sufficient degree, the separation of myth from concept.

Through the examples given below, we will see how difficult it is sometimes to apply the latter criterion, even to classical Greek philosophy. Before evaluating the extent to which the African conceptual universe respected these two principles, let us delimit first, with precision, the cultural area to which our analysis applies. It includes Pharaonic Egypt and the rest of Black Africa.

Vis-à-vis Black Africa, Egypt has played the same role that the Greco-Latin civilization has played vis-à-vis the West. A European specialist, in any domain of the humanities, would be ill advised to conduct any scientific work if he cut himself off from the Greco-Latin past. Similarly, the African cultural facts will only find their profound meaning and their coherence in reference to Egypt.[1] We can build a body of disciplines in the humanities only by legitimizing and by systematizing the return to Egypt: in the course of this account, we will see that only the Egyptian facts allow us to find, here and there, the common denominator of the remnants of thought, a connection between the African cosmogonies in the process of fossilization.

Because Egyptian philosophical thought sheds a new light on that of Black Africa, and even on that of Greece, "the cradle" of classical philosophy, it is important to summarize it first, in order to bring better into focus, subsequently, its often unsuspected articulations, in other words, its loans. This manner of presenting the facts, by respecting the chronology of their genesis and their true historical connections, is the most scientific way of retracing the evolution of philosophical thought and of characterizing its African variant.

Egyptian Cosmogony

Egyptian "cosmogony" as summarized here is the one attested to by the texts of the pyramids (2600 B.C.), so that we may stick to sure facts, meaning, to the epoch when even the Greeks did not exist in history yet, and when the Chinese and the Hindu philosophies were meaningless.

One can distinguish three great systems of thought in Egypt that tried to explain the origin of the universe and the appearance of all that is: the *Hermopolitan* system, the *Heliopolitan* system, the *Memphite* system, and to this can be added the *Theban* system.

The summary below condenses the essentials of these four doctrines, but it is rigorously faithful to the Egyptian texts; it is not a tendentious interpretation.

According to these systems, the universe was not created *ex nihilo*, on a given day; but there has always existed an uncreated matter, without a beginning or an end (the *apeiron*, without limit and without determination, of Anaximander, Hesiod, etc.); this chaotic matter was, in origin, the equivalent of non-being, because of the sole fact that it was unorganized: thus, non-being is not, here, the equivalent of nothingness, from which would rise, no one knows how, the matter that would be the substance of the universe. This chaotic matter contained at the archetypal state (Plato) all the essences of the body of the future beings that, one day, would be called into existence: sky, stars, earth, air, fire animals, plants, human beings, etc. This primordial matter, the *nous* or the "primordial waters," was elevated to the level of divinity (called *Nun* in Egyptian cosmogony). Thus, from the start, each principle of explanation of the universe is doubled by a divinity, and as philosophical thought developed in Egypt, and more particularly in Greece (materialistic school), the latter replaced the former.

Primitive matter also contained the law of transformation, the principle of the evolution of matter through time, equally considered as a divinity: *Khepera*. It is the law of becoming that, acting on matter through time, will actualize the archetypes, the essences, the beings who are therefore already created in potentiality, before being created in actuality. (Thus Plato's "the Same and the Other," the theory of reminiscense, etc.; and Aristotle's matter and privation, potentiality and actuality, etc.).

Thus, carried by its own evolutionary movement, eternal matter, uncreated, by dint of going through the stages of organization, ends up by becoming self-aware. The first consciousness thus emerges from the primordial *Nun*;[2] it is God, Ra, the demiurge (Plato) who is going to complete creation.

Up to this point, the Egyptian "cosmogony" is materialistic in essence; for it is professing a materialistic faith when postulating the existence of an uncreated eternal matter, excluding nothingness and containing its own principle of evolution as an intrinsic property. This materialistic component of Egyptian thought will prevail among the Greek and Latin Atomists: Democritus, Epicurus, and Lucretius.

But with the appearance of the demiurge, Ra, Egyptian cosmogony takes a new direction with the introduction of an idealist component: Ra achieves creation through the word (Islam and Judeo-Christian religions), the *logos* (Heraclitus), the spirit (the objective idealism of Hegel).

As soon as Ra conceives beings, they emerge into existence. There is therefore an obvious, objective relation between the spirit and things. The real is necessarily rational, intelligible, because it is spirit; therefore the spirit can perceive external nature. Ra is the first God, the first demiurge of history who created through the word. All other gods in history came after him, and there exists a demonstrable historical relation between Ra's word, the *Ka*—or the universal reason that is present everywhere in the universe, and in every thing—and the *logos* of Greek philosophy or the Word of the revealed religions.

"The objective idea" of Hegel is nothing but the word (of Ra) of God, without God, a mythicized version of the Judeo-Christian religion, as Engels remarked.

Then, Ra creates the four divine pairs, according to Heliopolitan cosmogony:

1. *Shu* and *Tefnut* = air (space) and humidity (water).
2. *Geb* and *Nut* = earth and heaven (light, fire).[3]

In these first two pairs are found the four elements that make up the universe of the Pre-Socratic Greek philosophers (Thales, Anaximander, Heraclitus, Parmenides, Anaxagoras), namely, air, water, earth, fire; even Plato will still adopt them.

3. *Osiris* and *Isis*: the fertile human couple that will beget humanity (Adam, Eve).
4. *Seth* and *Nephthys*: the sterile couple that will introduce evil into human history; there is no notion of original sin here; evil is introduced by men, not by women; there is no pessimism, nor misogyny, typical of the Aryan-Semitic nomad societies.[4]

In conclusion, an idealistic (or spiritualistic) component is introduced into Egyptian cosmogony with the appearance of the demiurge Ra, and it is the basis for the concepts of the Greek idealist school (Plato, Aristotle).

Finally, a third component of Egyptian cosmogony is, historically speaking, at the origin of the revealed religions (the Judeo-Christian in particular).

In fact, Ra is, in the history of religious thought, the first God, autogenous (who was not created, who has neither father nor mother).

On the other hand, Seth, jealous because he is sterile, kills his brother Osiris (who symbolizes vegetation, from the discovery of agriculture to the Neolithic period). The latter rises from the dead to save humanity (from famine!). Osiris is the god of redemption.

In any case, Osiris is the god who, three thousand years before Christ, dies and rises from the dead to save men. He is humanity's god of redemption; he ascends to heaven to sit at the right hand of his father, the great god, Ra. He is the son of God. In *The Book of the Dead*, it is said fifteen hundred years before Christ: "This is the flesh itself of Osiris." Dionysus, Osiris's replica in the northern Mediterranean, will say five hundred years before Christ: "Drink, this is my blood; eat, this is my flesh." And one can see how the degradation of these types of beliefs can lead to the notion of the sorcerer who eats people in Black Africa.[5]

Egyptian cosmogony also states: "I was one; I became three"; this notion of trinity permeates all of Egyptian religious thought and is found again in the multiple divine triads such as Osiris-Isis-Horus, or Ra, in the morning, at noon, at night.

The term "Christ" is not an Indo-European root. It came from the Pharaonic Egyptian expression *kher sesheta*: "he who watches over the mysteries," and was applied to the divinities, Osiris, Anubis, etc. It was applied to Jesus only in the fourth century, by religious contamination.[6]

A ray from heaven descends upon the heifer (symbol of Hathor), who then "begets" the god Apis: without any possible doubt this is the prefiguration of the immaculate conception of the Blessed Virgin.[7]

Conception of the Being. According to Egyptian thought, the being is composed of three principles (Plato, Aristotle), to which a fourth one can be added: the shadow.

1. the *Zed* or *Khet*, which decomposes after death
2. the *Ba*, which is the body's corporeal soul (the "double" of the body throughout Black Africa)
3. the being's shadow
4. the *Ka* = immortal principle that rejoins the divinity in heaven after death. Thus was founded, on the ontological level, the being's immortality (three thousand years before the birth of the revealed religions). Each person possesses a portion of the divinity that fills the cosmos and renders it intelligible to the spirit. Perhaps it is on these grounds that the Egyptian cosmogony makes God say "that he made man in his own image."

Lastly, let us say that the Hermopolitan ogdoad is specifically composed of four divine pairs representing the opposing principles of nature that are supposed to be at the origin of things:

Kuk and *Kuket*	= the primordial darkness and its opposite: darkness and light.
Nun and *Nunet*	= the primordial waters and their opposite: matter and nothingness.
Heh and *Hehet*	= spatial infinity and its opposite: the infinite and the finite, the unlimited and the limited.
Amon and *Amonet*	= the hidden and the visible, the noumenon and the phenomenon.
Niaou and *Niaouet*	= emptiness and its opposite: the void and the replete, matter (later).

One can see how the universe can be constructed from these notions, which will also become the basis of Western philosophy and particularly of dialectical thought.

One can measure, from this account which only scratches the surface of this subject, all that Greek philosophy owes to the Egyptian thought of the Nile Valley's Blacks: Heraclitus' theory of opposites, Aristotle's dialectics . . . the diverse cosmogonies of the Pre-Socratic philosophers, etc.

Today's Black Africa

Dogon Cosmogony. Dogon cosmogony, described by the late Marcel Griaule in *Dieu d'eau*, recalls Hermopolitan cosmogony on many points: the same ogdoad, the same primitive divinity that supposedly was a reptile sometimes dancing in darkness.[8]

The Egyptian ideas equally shed light on the androgynous concept of the being in Dogon society and furnish the ontological bases for circumcision. For the Egyptians, God, particularly the god Amon (in Dogon: Amma), autogenous, was necessarily androgynous. This divine androgyny is found to a lesser degree in human beings, and it explains, in Pharaonic Egypt as in all of Black Africa, the practices of circumcision and excision in order to radically separate the sexes at puberty.

In their article entitled "A Sudanese System of Sirius,"[9] Marcel Griaule and Germaine Dieterlen give us an idea of the cosmic visions of the Dogon, the Bambara, the Bozo, and the Minianke, who all inhabit the region of the Niger River's loop: the Dogon in the cliffs of Bandiagara, the Bambara and the Bozo in the Ségou region and the Minianka in that of Koutiala (p. 273).

A principal idea that exists everywhere in Black Africa is that of initiation at different levels or degrees, and one which contributed greatly to the degradation and the fossilization of knowledge that was earlier considered to be quasi-scientific. There is a priestess of Amma (p. 273), god of water, rain, and the atmosphere, who has the same attributes as the Egyptian god Amon. Amon, great god of Thebes, was the only one of the Egyptian gods to shelter in his sanctuary a woman entirely dedicated to his service and who was called the divine adorer, the god's wife, the priestess of Amon, and who necessarily had to be of "Ethiopian" royal blood, that is to say, a princess of Kush, a Black.

Every sixty years the Dogon celebrate a ceremony called *Sigui*, corresponding to the renewal of the world and during which Amma and his son, the *nommo* or the world's demiurge, appear (p. 275). We will see below how interesting it will be to compare this sixty-year period to the Greeks' "great year," of the same duration and supposedly discovered by Oenopides.

The Dogon knew the syzygies: thus the world was created in seven twin years, which comes to fourteen years. They call Sirius, whose heliacal rising they knew, *Sigui tolo* = "The Star of Sigui," the feast of the world's rebirth marking the time when a new "sigui" priest had to be chosen for another sixty years.

What is even more extraordinary is that for the Dogon, the star Sirius is not the basis of the system; a minuscule star, called *Põ tolo* or *Digitaria*,[10] is the true center of the Dogon system. In modern astronomy, it is called the invisible companion of Sirius, which is also a double star. *Põ tolo*, its companion, is a white dwarf star, invisible to the naked eye, and its unsuspected presence explains the perturbations of the orbit of Sirius, the most brilliant star in the sky, and which is also the basis of the Egyptian sidereal calendar.[11] The density of matter in a white dwarf star is such that a volume that will fit into a thimble weighs around forty tons. This is a star that has burned up all its energy and collapsed, and then the colossal pressure that accompanies such a collapse pushes the electrons of the atomic processions to agglutinate at the nuclei of the atoms, and the usual spaces that separate the atomic nuclei from the electrons' strata disappear, filled with electronic matter: matter, which in our solar system ordinarily presents itself as a void, becomes particularly dense in a white dwarf star, and takes a new form called "degenerate."

Far be it from us to imply that the Dogon or the ancient Egyptians had already acquired the same scientific comprehension of these phenomena as modern scientists. But it is certain that the Dogon have acquired a precise knowledge of the existence of this white dwarf star, invisible to the naked eye, and of its enormous density; similarly, they know its trajectory and that of Sirius: "*Digitaria is the smallest of all things. It is the heaviest star*," say the Dogon.[12]

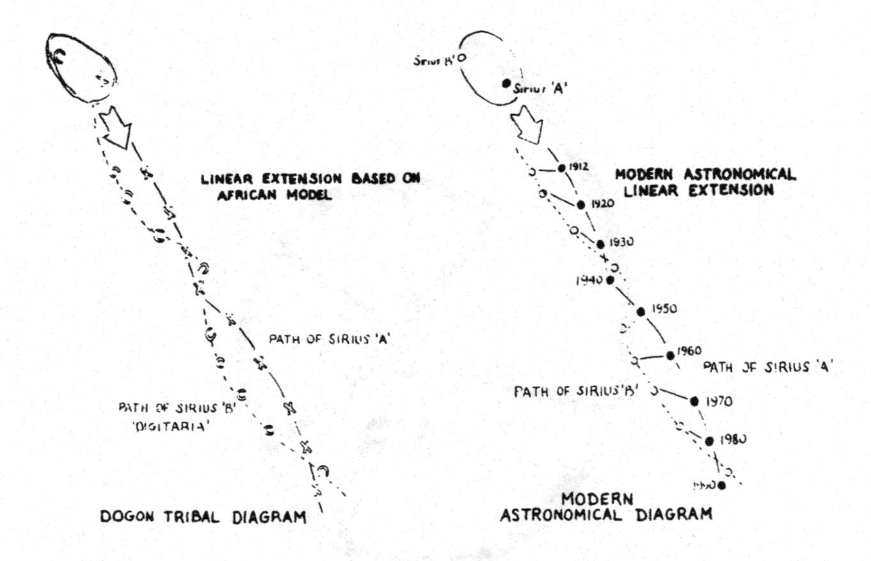

Figure 69: Linear development of the orbit of Sirius according to Dogon tradition and modern astronomy. (Hunter Adams III, in *Journal of African Civilizations*, vol. I, no. 32, November 1979)

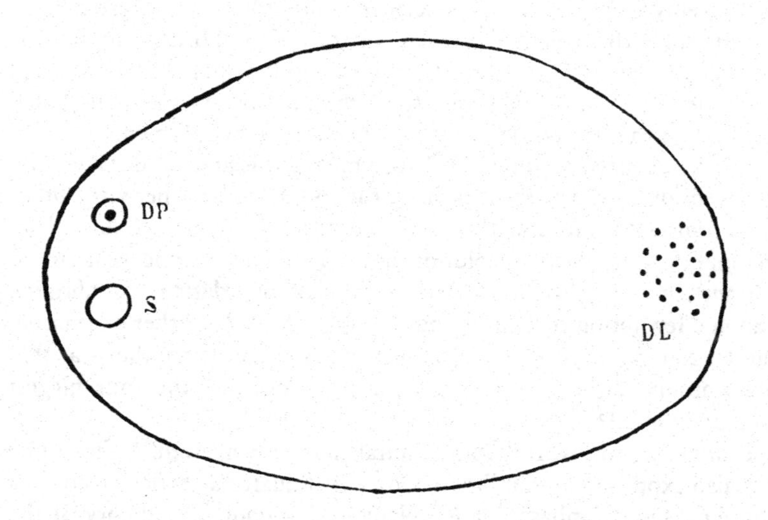

Figure 70: Trajectory of the star Digitaria around Sirius. (Marcel Griaule and Germaine Dieterlen, "Un système soudanais de Sirius," (*Journal de la Société des Africanistes*, vol. XX, fasc. II, Musée de l'Homme, Paris, 1950, fig. 3)

Figure 71: Origin of the spiral of creation. (Indigenous drawing from Marcel Griaule and Germaine Dieterlen; *op. cit.*, fig. 6.)

Only twenty years ago, modern science could not have contested these facts; but since then, with the recent progress in radio astronomy, it is known that there exist in interstellar space bodies that are heavier and even smaller than the white dwarf stars: the neutron stars and the black holes, though the reality of the latter remains to be confirmed.

The vivid language used by the Dogon must not lead us to devalue their comprehension of the phenomenon, for it could not be otherwise. Other than its translatory movement on its orbit around Sirius, *Põ tolo* or *Digitaria* makes a complete revolution around its axis in one year. Most importantly, modern astronomy is not capable of invalidating or confirming this annual revolution of *Põ tolo*, but it has confirmed another affirmation of the Dogon, namely the period of fifty years taken by another star that revolves around Sirius. They know Saturn's rings and the four biggest moons of Jupiter.[13]

The origin of the world from a spiral mass is perceived.[14] This same idea is also expressed by the Woyo people of Equatorial Africa, according to former Zairian Ambassador M. Nguvulu-Lubundi. The theory of the four elements is known.[15]

According to Griaule and Dieterlen: "Digitaria's orbit is situated at the center of the world; Digitaria is the axis of the whole world, and without its movement no heavenly body could maintain itself. This is to say that

Digitaria is the regulator of the celestial positions; notably, it regulates that of Sirius, the most uncoordinated star; it separates it from the other bodies by surrounding it with its trajectory."[16]

According to this text, one sees that for the Dogon the Earth is not the center of the world; similarly, the notion of attraction, meaning the action at a distance of one heavenly body on another, is clearly expressed. Griaule and Dieterlen add: "But Digitaria is not the only companion of Sirius: the star Emma ya, 'female-sorghum,' more voluminous than it, four times lighter, follows a much wider trajectory in the same direction and in the same time (fifty years). Their respective positions are such that the angle of their rays would be straight."[17]

Therefore, for the Dogon, stars are not simply luminous bodies suspended in space. They have trajectories and weight, dimensions that are to be determined, like the direction of their course, their rays, and their revolution's period, as well as the effect of their radiance on human behavior.[18]

The Dogon give the elliptical trajectory of Digitaria. When it is near Sirius, it appears more brilliant, and when it is far off, it gives the impression that several stars are shining.[19]

The Dogon speak of a male and a female soul, and of pairs of rays.[20] These are indeed principles of opposites—the syzygies of the *Hermopolitan* cosmogony—which are the basis of the creation of the universe.

In the following article, entitled "Bambara Writing of Numbers," by Solange de Ganay, it appears that the Bambara know the so-called "Pythagorean" symbolism of numbers and that they had even adopted an original system of writing or notation that we partially reproduce.[21]

> A first group of eight signs, called the secret count, reproduces the first seven numbers which, according to a Bambara myth, were engraved in space when, through his word, the creator formed the universe. It is said that they contain the whole universe, for they are an arithmetical summary of the creator and his work. The number *one* represents the primordial thought that formed the world; *two* symbolizes the splitting in two of the first principle. The number *three* corresponds to the element of fire and the masculine principle; it is the origin of life, movement, and time.[22] The number *four* symbolizes the female principle, born of the male principle, nature, and the element of water. Number *five* is the synthesis of the creator and his work (see Hermopolitan cosmogony, the five greats); *six* represents male as well as female twinship; *seven*, which is the sum of three and four, represents the couple, the person (both male and female), intelligence, fecundity, and the earth. As for the first of these eight signs called *fu gundo* or *foy gundo* (the secret of nothing), in some way it represents creation in potentiality, its starting point, in

other words, the primordial thought that secretly existed in "nothing." The fork λ represents the duality of the first principle generating itself; the cross represents the multiplicity of everything, the consequence of this division, while the bar placed at the end of the sign, called the "wind's nose" (*fyé nu*), means that the four elements of which beings are formed proceed from the divine substance itself, and initially from the air.

This is an arithmetical expression of the world's system and of the divinity that created it; thus the soothsayer, possessing full knowledge of the seven tablets and of the numerical representation of the four elements, is known as the "master of divinatory art."[23] Among the Dogon, the four elements (*kize nay*, literally, "four things") are also expressed numerically.[24] They are also the terms emphasized in the above text.

Here is a text that would be repudiated neither by the Pythagoreans, nor by the other Pre-Socratic philosophers, nor by Plato. The omnipotence of the number in the Dogon and the Bambara systems, as well as in the Pythagorean one, is beyond question. In Pythagorism, the first ten numbers were endowed with secret properties comparable to those attributed to them by the Bambara. The effort toward abstraction that leads to representing the four constituent elements of the universe in Dogon and Heliopolitan cosmogony by numbers curiously reminds us of Plato's speculations in the *Timaeus* (see p. 337). We will note that for the Dogon and the Bambara, if we refer to the above-cited text, the universe is a "number that moves" in the literal, rigorous, Platonic sense of the term.[25] One could believe that it concerns a primitive thought remodeled by Western brains or a surviving element of ancient philosophical doctrines introduced by the Arabs at Timbuktu in the Middle Ages. As a matter of fact, the count of the number of the Dogon *sigui* (period of sixty years) dates back to the first half of the thirteenth century A.D., based on the number of the ritual objects related to this ceremony and spared from destruction.[26]

The multiple intimate connections between the Dogon and the Egyptian cosmogonies require us to separate these suppositions. The different Dogon tribes have each specialized in the study of a particular domain of the sky: the Ono study Venus; the Dommo, Orion's shield; the Aru, the moon; and the Dyon, the sun. Thus the Dogon have the lunar, solar, and sidereal calendars just like the Egyptians. Their mythology, as described in Griaule's and Dieterlen's article, reveals in the sociopolitical domain, the passage from putting the "king-priest" to death, the *sigui*, every seven years, to the symbolic death, or to the renewal, every sixty years. "According to Dogon mythology, before the discovery of Digitaria, the supreme chief was sacrificed at the end of the seventh year of his reign (seventh harvest).

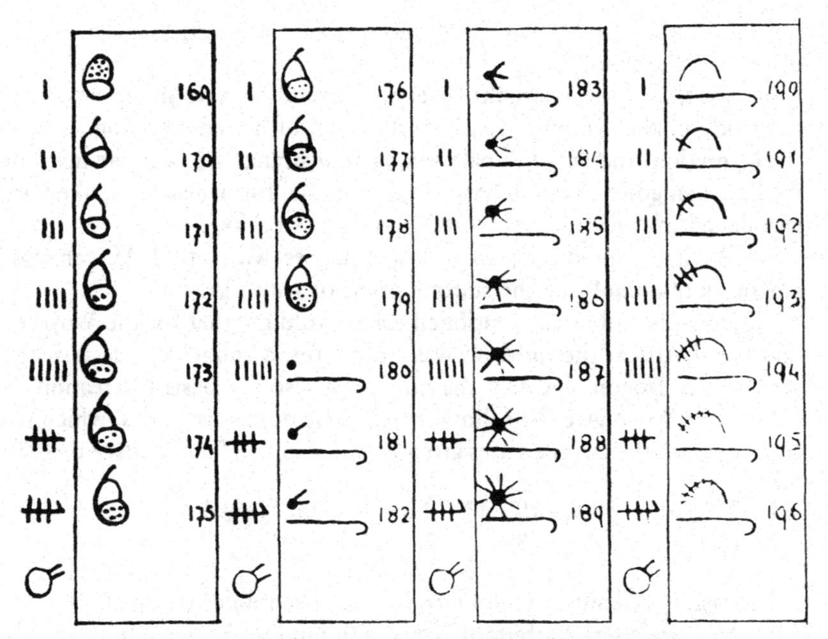

Figure 72: Bambara symbols for number notation. (Solange de Ganay, "Graphie bambara de nombres," in *Journal de la Société des Africanistes*, vol. XX, fasc. II, Musée de l'Homme, Paris, 1950, pp. 297–301)

Figure 73: "The secret of nothing" and the numbers 1 to 7 among the Bambara. *From left to right*: "The secret of nothing"; 1, 2, 3 (fire, male); 4 (water, female); 5, 6 (twinning); 7 (earth). Normally, these signs are written vertically. (Solange de Ganay, *op. cit.*)

But the eighth chief, having discovered the star, resolved to avoid the lot of his predecessors."[27]

In Egypt, it is the Pharaoh Zoser who seems to have inaugurated the ceremony of the symbolic death of the king, of his regeneration.

The myth of the Dogon's pale fox *yurugu* strangely recalls the myth of the Egyptian god Seth, who has the same animal form, and who, like him, introduced the creation of disorder, evil, and sterility.[28]

Finally, let us point out some resemblances with other African cosmogonies that could be the starting point of fruitful research.

M. Nguvulu-Lubundi, mentioned earlier, told me that for the Woyo of Equatorial Africa, the universe was born from a spiral matter, as is the case for the Dogon, and that the number is also the basis of creation.

Thus the Woyo give the following symbolic numerical series, which we compare with the cosmic series given by Plato in the *Timaeus* (see p. 349):

1 - 2 - 3 - 4 - 7 9 - 10 - 11 27 99 - 100 (Woyo)
1 - 2 - 3 - 4 9 - 8 27 (*Timaeus*)

The whole scientific community has not been able to explain, to this day, why Plato's series arbitrarily ends with number 27. Certainly nobody expected that the initiation rites of the Woyo would shed a new light on this question. Indeed, as with the Kongo also, number 27 plays a particularly important role; in their cosmogony, it corresponds somehow to the supertrinity of the Egyptian ennead: $3 \times 9 = 27$.

Thus the Woyo say that in order to change the cosmic order, in this case matrilineal filiation, in order to substitute it with patrilineal descendancy, one must harbor enough mystical power to be able to take possession of nine divinities three times, thus twenty-seven divinities. That is why one finds the symbolism of the twenty-seven copper rings among the Woyo as well as among the Kongo. The symbolism of the number is also the basis of the Yoruba cosmogony. The Egyptian ennead has also survived in Nyambism, in Zaire, in the form of nine principles of cosmic energy.

The Woyo have a hieroglyphic writing system the study of which has been recently undertaken by a Belgian enthnologist, according to Nguvulu-Lubundi. In Zambia, an Austrian researcher, Dr. Gerhard Kubik of the Vienna University's Institute of Ethnology, has recently discovered ideograms called *Tusona*, of a philosophic meaning that are known only by the old men who speak the Luchazi language in the Kabompo district; he is in the process of studying them. Therefore it is not by chance that a statuette of Osiris was found *in situ* in an archeological layer in Shaba, a province of Zaire.[29]

Going back to the sixty-year period of the Dogon *sigui*, Hunter Adams III writes: "Every sixty years, when the orbital periods of Jupiter and Saturn

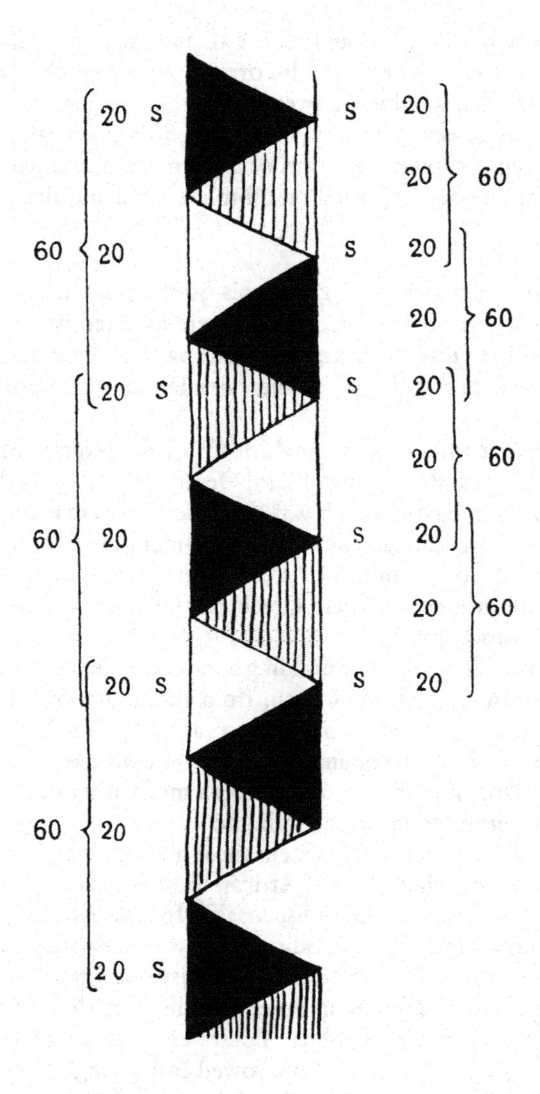

Figure 74: The count of the Sigui of the Dogon people. (Marcel Griaule and Germaine Dieterlen; *op. cit.*, fig. 2)

are synchronized, a ceremony called 'sigui' takes place."[30] What must be added is that this is the same sidereal period baptized "great year" that Oenopides, who went to Egypt to be initiated,[31] claimed to have discovered.

According to Paul Ver Eeke:

> Oenopides of Chios lived around 450 B.C. and, according to Eudemus, cited by Theo of Smyrna, discovered the ecliptic's obliquity whose measure had a value of twenty degrees. He had established in Greece the great year (μέγας ενιαύτος) of fifty-nine years, which, according to him, marked the return of all astronomical phenomena, discoveries that he had engraved on a bronze table and displayed in Olympia."[32]

By referring to the indicated pages in this book, one finds out that the process remains the same: the Greeks who were initiated in Egypt appropriate everything they learned once they went back to their country. The discovery of the ecliptic and even of the calendar were also attributed to Thales.[33]

From the above it follows that the Africans of the interior of the continent, like the Greeks (Pythagoras, Plato, Oenopides, etc.), were initiated to different degrees in Egypt, which was then the intellectual center of the world; only this view can explain the above-mentioned numerous encounters, which not only could not stem from chance, but which reestablish clarity and rationality where Greek plagiarism had created a zone of darkness and obscurity.[34]

A vigorous, valuable manner of building a modern science on the terrain of African tradition recognized as such, from the legacy of the past, for a young African astrophysician would be to tackle the verification of the annual rotation of Sirius' companion around its own axis, a movement predicted by the Dogon cosmogony and which modern astronomy has not yet been able to either confirm or invalidate.

Be that as it may, we see to what extent these ancient doctrines of Africa are invaluable for the archaeology of African thought, and, for this reason alone, their study will always be indispensable for the African thinker, if he wants to build an intellectual tradition based on historical terrain.

We have just shown that these doctrines constitute irreplaceable complements of the classical sources, in order to rediscover the winding paths followed by the ancient philosophical doctrines from Egypt. They shed an unexpected light on the Greeks' unavowed borrowings from Egyptian thought in the most diverse domains, and they therefore reveal that they necessarily or probably had the same status as Greek thought had at the time of Greek and African common initiation in Egypt.

But the African initiatory tradition degrades the quasi-scientific thoughts that it received during very ancient periods, instead of enriching them with time.

We could review, in the light of Egyptian thought, all the African cosmogonies and thus rediscover their often lost profound meaning.

Does this mean that today these cosmogonies have the status of a self-conscious philosophical thought? Certainly during precolonial epochs, when they were intensely lived, these cosmogonies were infinitely close to a self-conscious thought, but they have since become degraded, fossilized, and it would be excessive to take them for philosophical systems at this point in time. Similarly, it would be an error to conduct a bogus debate on them.

"Bantu philosophy" of Father Tempels. The "Bantu philosophy" studied by Father Placide Tempels is, according to the Abbé Alexis Kagame, characteristic of the Baluba of Kasai. It reveals vitalistic concepts that have become semiconscious at the basis of all the being's activity. The whole ontological universe is filled with a hierarchy of vital forces that have the property of being additive. The vital forces of an individual can increase with the wearing of a beast's tooth or decrease because of the negative effect of a magical practice. We see here also that this system of thought, of which its upholders are hardly aware, cannot be considered to be a philosophy in the classical sense.

Once more, Egypt will allow us to better penetrate the facts: in Egypt, the first concrete manifestation of vitalistic concepts goes back to Pharaoh Zoser (IIIrd Dynasty, 2800 B.C.). In the funeral domain of this Pharaoh at Saqqara, one can still see today the wall with rounded-off angles along which he had to run (among other practices) in order to demonstrate to the priests that he had recuperated his vital force during the ceremony of regeneration: the "feast of *sed*." Following this test, the Pharaoh was again able to reign; if not, he probably had to resign for insufficiency of his vital force. Another striking example is that of Pharaoh Unas of the Vth Dynasty who, after death, had to mystically reinforce his vital force so that he would be able to rejoin his "Ka" in order to become immortal: on his journey he swallows all beings possible in order to reinforce his vital force in the strict Baluba sense.[35] These vitalistic concepts that go back to the Ancient Empire are at the basis of all of the African monarchies and explain their structure. Everywhere in Black Africa, in the societies that have reached the monarchical organizational stage, there exists the act of actually or ritually putting the king (cf. Zoser) to death, after a reign of a certain number of years, generally eight.

The Pharaoh is the demiurge on earth, who recreates the universe by his ritual acts. If he does not have the vital force of a god, misfortune befalls the earth. It is the same all over Black Africa in the case of the traditional king, to the extent that in the whole Sudanese region, a king wounded in war was forced to leave the throne until he had recuperated; similarly, both in Egypt and in the rest of Black Africa, the interregnum periods are periods of chaos and anarchy because there is no intermediary between heaven and earth, between the divinities and humanity.

Other Osirian practices show that the Baluba come from the northeast and that they had been in contact with Egyptian thought. In fact, according to the Abbé Kagame, "pearls are put in the dead person's mouth in order to pay the ferryman of hell who will take the dead one across to the other shore," as in Thebes. It is certain that the Greek (river) Styx was borrowed from Egyptian mythology, for only the Egyptians had two towns, one for the living and another for the dead, separated by a river, the Nile: Karnak and Luxor on one side, Thebes on the other, western side.

Sometimes Egypt sheds some unexpected light on African cultural facts. One need only recall the magical efforts made by Sundiata, founder of the Mali Empire, who was born crippled, in order to regain his vital force, if not in the physical realm, at least in the ontological one: such practices are directly related to Pharaonic vitalism.

The numerous relics of metempsychosis of souls in Black Africa (Yoruba, Sara, etc.) could give an idea of the massive scale of the contact with Pharaonic Egypt. Everything seems to indicate that there did exist, here and there in the heart of Africa, secondary centers of the diffusion of the Egyptian religion. We know that it is in Egypt, and not in India, that the theory of reincarnation was first attested to: it concerned a quest for immortality. One could insist on many common points between the Yoruba and Egyptian religions: the trinitarian symbol in the form of a triangle, symbolism of the number almost in the Pythagorean sense, etc. It is these possible scraps of ancient beliefs, metempsychosis, vitalism, etc., that antagonize our young philosophers. But revolt is pointless when faced with these kinds of hard facts: only knowledge deriving from scientific investigation allows us to understand them, to restore their full meaning, and to place them in their true position in the spiritual evolution of Africa.

Only thus will the demon be exorcised; the *Muntu* will be surpassed instead of being vainly denied or ignored. Only then will the ghost no longer come to haunt the dream of the philosopher armed with the knowledge of his cultural past.

African philosophy cannot develop except on the original terrain of the history of African thought. Otherwise, there is the risk that it will never be.

Categories of the Being in "Bantu Philosophy" According to Abbé Kagame. Following a penetrating linguistic analysis, Abbé Kagame retains four great nominal classes corresponding to four categories of beings:

Mu-ntu = the intelligent being (human being)
Ki-ntu = the non-intelligent being (thing)
Ha-ntu = the localizing being (place—time)
Ku-ntu = the modal being (manner of being)[36]

Here too, philosophy is meant in the broad sense, because the least that can be said is that people who speak these languages are not aware of this implicit classification, even if it were to exist. But is it so?

My mother tongue, Wolof, spoken in Senegal, is a language with gradations, and as such, a semi-Bantu language. For several years now I have been interested in the fascinating peculiarity of the group of languages "with gradations." In *Parenté génétique de l'égyptien pharaonique et des langues négro-africaines*, I believe that I have furnished the quasi-rigorous scientific explanation of the origin of the languages with gradations, starting with a comparative analysis based on the earlier attestations of ancient Egyptians: it is precisely the classical language written since the era of the pyramids, from 2600 to 1470 B.C., from the IVth to the XVIIIth Dynasties.[37]

It seemed to me that the nominal classes have both a semantic and above all a phonetic origin, as shown in the examples below:

In Wolof we have the following pleonasms:

m̱us-m̱i = the cat
w̱und-w̱i = the cat
ḏanâb-ḏi = the cat
ṣîru-ṣi = the cat (wild)

Thus, with the first three examples, we have three beings or identical essences classified in three different categories, which can only be explained phonetically, by the initial consonant of the word, considered as the class morpheme.

Similarly, when we introduce a foreign word (French, for example), it obeys the phonetic laws.

Examples:
ḇoyet-ḇi = la boîte < French (box)
ṣûkar-ṣi = le sucre < French (sugar)

The absence of a metalanguage shows that this thought is not conscious of itself.

It happens that a researcher makes a more important discovery than the one he expected, and I believe that this is the case with the eminent scholar Kagame: he has done a first-rate job in the linguistic domain.

Medieval Timbuktu. In the Middle Ages, ancient philosophy was introduced in Timbuktu under the same conditions as in Europe of the same epoch, and in both cases by the Arabs. Aristotle was readily quoted at Sankore. The introduction of the trivium is attested: Sâdi, a well-read Black of Timbuktu, author of the celebrated work entitled the *Tarikh es Sudani*, cites among the subjects that he had mastered, logic, dialectic, grammar, rhetoric, not to mention law and other disciplines.

Several other literate people were in the same category; and the two *Tarikh** contain long lists of subjects studied and of the African scholars

*The other is *Tarikh el-Fettach* by Kati.

who taught them at the University of Timbuktu, during the era when Scholasticism flourished at the Sorbonne, in Paris, and when Aristotle reigned supreme.

The *quadrivium* was also introduced, and we have several proofs that are too many to expound here. Let us say that astronomical knowledge was necessary for the orientation of the religious buildings (mosques), and this led to scholarly measurements, calculations, and determinations. Gao's students decided one day to conduct a census of the town's population, which cannot be conceived of without calculations. Astrological practices also imply laborious calculations. But it is by analyzing the content of the works on the syllabus cited in the two *Tarikh* that one can do an exhaustive study of the question.

Let us say in conclusion that the cabala, still practiced by marabouts literate only in Arabic, gives one of the different ways in which the quadrivium was introduced: a Hindu number, up to 10, is made to correspond to every letter of the Arabic alphabet, then from 10 plus 10 up to 100, then from 100 plus 100 up to 1,000; and last, from 1,000 plus 1,000; altogether, the sum of the letters of the alphabet correspond to the number 5,995.

In order to make a talisman for somebody, the numerical weight of his name, so to speak, is calculated. Thus Cheikh Diop = 1,000 + 10 + 600 + 3 + 6 + 2 = 1,621. This sum must undergo diverse manipulations, additions, subtractions, divisions, according to the purpose of the talisman.

Thus the literate Africans of Timbuktu knew conceptual thought in the classical sense of the term: the teaching of grammar, which was common, required the conceptualizing and the creation of a metalanguage, in African languages, from where most often didactic images and examples were taken.

In the African cities of the eastern coast, on the Indian Ocean, the situation should be the same, and systematic research should lead to analogous results.

But can one speak of African philosophy when obviously this is an acclimation on African soil of Western thought, through the intermediary of the Arabs?

We have said, at the beginning of this account, that this thought was born first in Black Africa, then underwent a specific development in Greece and came back to Africa in the Middle Ages. What then was Greece's originality when she received, almost copied Egyptian thought? We will see the truly original stamp that Greece added to Egyptian philosophical thought. For this, let us come back to the two criteria posed earlier, to which, in our opinion, every philosophical thought must adhere: the first criterion was thoroughly verified in Egypt and, to a lesser degree, in the other African cosmogonies.

Egyptian Grammarians and Mathematicians

The Egyptian grammarians who, under the XIXth Dynasty, 1300 B.C., were having their students recopy exercises and literary texts of the Ancient Empire (2600 B.C.) on *ostraca*, knew conceptual thought, in the most rigorous sense, two thousand years before Aristotle, the "creator" of the logic of grammar, meaning of formal logic.

Similarly, it is impossible to establish a mathematical formula, even through empirical pathways, without having created from the outset a rigorous mathematical logic; well, the Egyptians are the only inventors of geometry, and Jamblichus tells us that "all the theorems of lines (geometry) come from Egypt." Contrary to persistent opinion, the Egyptians always ended their proofs with the expression: *momitt pw* = "this one also the same" = CQFD.

Consequently, even if the demonstration was not rigorous (but it was), the desire to prove was already present in the Egyptian mathematician; and that is enough in order for a logical apparatus to be consciously lived.

It is therefore by posing the problems in reverse that one can measure the importance of what the Greeks, Pythagoras and Aristotle in particular, Plato, Euclides, and others, borrowed from the Egyptian sciences all the while keeping completely quiet about it. The honest Herodotus also called Pythagoras a vulgar plagiarist of the Egyptians.

1. Can one teach grammar without having created a metalanguage, without conceptualizing, without discovering particularly at the level of syntax, the whole grammatical logic of the language taught? The Egyptians did all that, more than two thousand years before Aristotle.
2. Can one establish a mathematical formula, even through empirical means, without having invented beforehand a mathematical logic? Yet, the Egyptians were the sole inventors of elementary geometry.
3. Can one create an arithmetic, even an elementary one, without consciously relying on a mathematical logic?
4. Can one engage in solving routine mathematical operations (calculating the area, the volume, evaluating numerical quantities, etc.) without having radically separated the myth of the number from the concept of the number? Thus, if the two are brought together again, as in the lofty metaphysical speculations of the Egyptian priests, it can only be on symbolic grounds, and not as the result of mental confusion.

Therefore, as far as the second criterion is concerned, the separation of the myth from the concept, it was fully accomplished in Egypt at the level of the sciences, and often all that Greece did was to take credit for the Egyptian philosophy of the Nile Valley Blacks.

Such a separation of the myth from the concept equally took place in Black Africa in the realm of everyday life, without its being spoken of as rigorous science. Therefore, it is in the metaphysical domain that Greece distinguishes itself radically from the others.

If we consider the Greek school of idealism (Plato, Aristotle, the Stoics), there appears to be no essential difference with Egypt, because here, too, we are dealing with a barely modified Egyptian thought: everywhere in the Platonic cosmogony and in Aristotelian metaphysics, myth peacefully coexists with concept. Plato could even be called, and rightfully so, Plato the Mythologist. But things change radically with the Greek materialistic school; the principles, the laws of natural evolution become intrinsic properties of matter, which no longer necessitate coupling, even symbolically, with any divinity; they are self-sufficient. Likewise, any primary cause of a divine nature is rejected: the world was never created by any divinity; matter has always existed.

Even though this thought was the logical development of the materialistic component of Egyptian cosmogony, it did sufficiently deviate from its Egyptian model to become identifiably Greek. Atheistic materialism is a purely Greek creation; Egypt and the rest of Black Africa seem not to have known it. As for the sociopolitical conditions of its birth, this is another story.[38]

Throughout the European Middle Ages, religious spiritualism, the Catholic Church in this case, tried to accommodate itself to Greek philosophical idealism, particularly to Aristotelianism. But at the end of the Middle Ages, Scholasticism lost its vigor and the Renaissance inaugurated the era of Democritus, Epicurus, and Lucretius: Galileo, Descartes, Kant, Newton, Leibniz, Lavoisier. The modern Atomists have often been strongly inspired by this school, which, in its passing on of Egyptian African thought, is largely responsible for modern science, even if one pretends not to know this.

Details of the Egyptian Cosmogonies

In chapter XVII of the *Book of the Dead*, it is written, concerning the universal god Ra:

> Speak, Universal Master; he says after having become: It is I the becoming of Khepera, when I became the becoming of those who became after my becoming, for numerous are the desires coming out of my mouth, when the Earth had not yet been formed, when the sons of the Earth were not yet made, the snakes, out of whose dwelling I came, out of the Nun where I was among the dispirited, no place was found for me where I could stand up. I found in my heart that which should be useful to me: and in the void that (would serve me) as a foundation, when I was alone, when I had not begotten Shu (air, empty space), when I had not yet spat out Tefnut (water), when no other divinity that would have been made with me had yet

become. (Therefore) I conceived myself in my own heart and the becoming of my numerous becomings of my becomings in the becomings of the children, and in the becomings of their children. . . . Says my father Nun: "They have weakened my eye (my consciousness, my attention) behind them since the secular periods that have distanced themselves from me" [meaning the periods that have passed, during the stage of the creation of the universe in potentiality]. After having been only one God, it is three Gods that I became for myself and for Shu, certainly, and Tefnut came out of *Nun* where they were: they brought my eye after them. . . . Shu and Tefnut gave birth to Geb and Nut, Geb and Nut begat Osiris, Khar-khenti-merti [the prince of the two eyes, see p. 361], Set, Isis, and Nephthys; from the womb, one after another, they gave birth to [children] who then multiplied on the earth.[39]

Through the above excerpt from the *Book of the Dead*, whose conception probably goes back to the first dynasties, 3000 B.C.,[40] we can see what the revealed religions, Judaism and Christianity, owe to the Egyptian religion: the theory of creation by the word, by simple vision, by the representation of future beings in the divine conscience of Ra; creation in potentiality, first during an eternity (ever and ever), intelligible essences before their actualization into sentient beings, the object of a second creation. Finally, the divine trinity, expressed in this text for the first time in the history of all religions.

Emile Amélineau is right when, using this Heliopolitan cosmogony, he deciphers the following obscure passage from Plato's *Timaeus*, which all of a sudden becomes understandable: "The being, the place, and the generation are three distinct principles and are anterior to the formation of the world."[41]

In fact, the aforementioned passage from the *Book of the Dead* shows that "being," meaning the intelligible essences; "place," meaning space (Shu); "generation," meaning the act by which the god Ra engenders the first beings Shu and Tefnut, belong to the state of creation in potentiality, and consequently are anterior to the creation, in the second place, of the sensible world; thus the seeming paradoxes of Plato can be made clear and understandable only by going back to their Egyptian source of inspiration, which he conceals.

The word of Ra is the *logos* of Heraclitus and Plato; it is also the *nous* of Anaxagoras and the *koun* of the revealed religions.[42]

Osiris and Isis are Adam and Eve of the future revealed religions.

In the cosmogony of Thebes, the god Amon will say: "I am the God who became by himself, and who was not created."

Finally, the Heliopolitan cosmogony appears with traits of a "philosophy" of becoming, in the strict sense of *werden* (to become) in German.[43]

Ra will also say: "I am the great God, who became by himself—I, I am yesterday and I know tomorrow."

In reality, these phrases are questions that are asked of the dead, enigmas that they have to solve before they can enter "Paradise," the dwelling of the gods in the other world.

Osiris, the personification of the Good, is the son of Ra, as Christ is the son of God.

Similarly, the Gnostic philosophers of the second century were inspired by the old Egyptian religion, all the more so because they were Egyptians themselves and because Christianity first developed mainly in Egypt.

The Egyptian *Nun* and *tum* clearly correspond to Οὐκών of Basilides or to βὺθος, or treasures of seed, in other words, the archetypes and essences of Valentinus, the Gnostic heresiarch who was originally from Egypt and settled in Rome.

The Gnostics' ogdoad, apart from its chief, is nothing other than the Egyptian ennead: Valentinus' ennead is composed of four syzygies, of Æons plus the βὺθος. As in Egyptian cosmogony, the human being does not appear until the third syzygy in Valentinus's gnosis: intellect and truth, "the word and life," precede "man and the church."[44]

And Amélineau writes:

> One was right to admire the speculating genius of the Greek philosophers in general, and of Plato in particular; but this admiration that the Greeks deserve without any doubt, the Egyptian priests deserve even more, and, if we give them credit for the paternity of what they invented, we would only be committing an act of justice.[45]
>
> Egypt had inaugurated, from the first Egyptian dynasties onward and probably before that, a system of cosmogony that the first Greek philosophers, Ionian or Eleatic, reproduced in its essential lines, and from which Plato himself was not loath to borrow the basis for his vast speculations, which Gnostics, Christians, Platonists, Aristotelians, and Pythagoreans all did only decorate with more or less pretentious names and concepts, whose prototypes are found in Egyptian works, word for word in the case of both the ennead and the ogdoad, and almost that for the hebdomad.[46]
>
> Between (Aristotle's) doctrine, Plato's doctrine, and that of the Heliopolitan priests, I could see no difference other than a difference of expression.[47]

The Gnostics were filling the space between heaven and earth with all types of more or less fantastic worlds that they imagined. Later, they would be taken over by the Muslim gnosis—different from the true Koranic Word—whose survival in Black Africa shows that in that respect also, the chain has never been completely broken.

Paradise and Hell in Egyptian Religion

Without any doubt, the history and the accomplishments of each group of people are intimately tied to the manner in which they solve the problem of death, to the philosophy that they adopt in terms of human destiny.

The religion of Osiris is the first, in the history of humanity, to invent the notions of paradise and hell. Two thousand years before Moses, and three thousand years before Christ, Osiris, the personification of the Good, was already presiding over the judgment of the dead in the world beyond the grave, wearing on his head the *Atew* or *Atef*.[48] If the dead person during his terrestrial life had satisfied the different moral criteria that are too many to enumerate here,[49] he gained the *Aaru* or *Aar*, a garden protected by an iron wall with several gates, and a river running through it. This garden is tilled by the spirits, the blessed ones, who wander through it; the roads that lead to it are mysterious; the dead one has to cross a bridge suspended in space and made of a hideous snake who hangs above the gates of hell.[50] The vindicated dead man becomes an Osiris, immortal, and from then on lives among the gods eternally; it is thought that the *Aaru* field, the Egyptian paradise, was used as a model for the Elysian Fields of Homer, a contemporary of Piankhi or of Shabaka who is supposed to have visited Egypt, according to Greek tradition itself.

Paradise is also called "the land of the word's truth," or the *Amenti*, meaning the kingdom of Osiris; this subterranean world is also the one where Ra, the principle of the Good, engages every night in a fierce battle against the snake Apap or Apophis, the principle of Evil, the demon, so to speak, who is almost as powerful as he is and who, according to Amélineau, is supposedly a creation of *Nun*, independently of Ra.

But Ra, the Good, always triumphs and reappears daily on the Eastern horizon: thus Good is superior to Evil, although the latter is very powerful; this dialectical movement, symbolized by the unceasing struggle between two principles, one positive, the other negative, did contribute to the birth of Manichaeism, and, in short, of dialectics.

Hell is reserved for punishment of the impious, represented by souls, by shadowy figures plunged into fiery abysses in which one also sees severed heads. Female executioners watch over these abysses, goddesses with lionesses' heads, who "feed themselves on the screams of the impious, on the howling of the souls and the shadowy figures, who stretch out their hands to them from their abysses. These tortures are conducted under the orders of Horus, who, by punishing Evil, avenges his father Osiris, the Good Being." On the other hand, "it will not be until the second century B.C. that Judaism, under the influence of Iran and Egypt (namely of the Jewish colony of Alexandria), will definitively adopt the concept of life in the hereafter."[51]

Side by side these philosophical cosmogonies and the religion of the salvation of Osiris's soul, there reigned, naturally, popular superstition, as

Figure 75: Hell in the Egyptian religion represented in the tomb of Seti I, father of Ramses II (XIXth Dynasty, 1300 B.C.). A monstrous snake uses the coils of its body to form a hideous bridge hanging in space, above hell, whose jailers stir the flames. Death, on the right hand side, facing the snake's mouth, is held in space only by its past actions on Earth in order to cross this bridge and reach paradise. If Good wins out, he is saved. If not, he will be thrown into the flames of hell, which will devour him. This certainly is Islam's *siratal moustakhima*, 1,700 years before the birth of the prophet Muhammad, and one can grasp the undeniable historical connection that exists between the Egyptian ancestral religion and the revealed religions. One might have reproduced also the tribunal of Osiris (*Aras* in Islam), the day of the Last Judgment. (Photo by the author)

it does today in Black Africa: amulets already existed and constituted preventive weapons against the danger of ill-fated days, like the 19th of *Phamenoth*,[52] against the powers of enemies, like Apap, etc. There were many kinds that people wore, in the form of a scarab, a heart, Osiris's pillar, the ansate cross of Isis, etc:

"Recite the above over a figure of Apap drawn on a papyrus that has never been used and in the middle of which is written the name of the

Figure 76: The god Thoth inscribing the name of King Seti I on the sacred tree *ished* in the temple at Karnak (*Dictionnaire de la civilisation égyptienne*, p. 220). We find a similar scene in the *Denkmäler aus Aegypten und Aethiopien* by K. R. Lepsius (vols. V–VI, part III, p. 37) where the god Atum and the goddess Hathor guide Thutmose III toward the sacred tree, while the god Amon, sitting on the right, is inscribing their names on the leaves. We know that this sacred tree that grows in paradise plays a major role in the Senegalese Muslim mythology.

reptile, then burn it. . . .";[53] one would believe oneself in Senegal in the 1980s.

The Egyptian Sacerdotal System

Undoubtedly, the Egyptian priests are characteristically Black, and it is again Lucian, author of *Philopsuedes*, who describes them to us as such, in the story of the sorcerer-apprentice. "It is Pancrates whom you are talking about, said Arignotos, it is my master, a holy man, shaven, attired in linen, thoughtful, speaking Greek (but badly), tall, with a flat nose, prominent lips, spindly legs. . . ."[54]

The king is the demiurge Ra, on Earth, who mirrors and perpetuates creation; he is the intermediary between God (his father) and humanity, and as such, he guarantees cosmic order. Therefore, he must personally officiate in the temples; he, alone, should be face to face with God in his sanctuary inside the temple: but worshiping God is done daily in all the temples of Egypt, true states within the state, especially in the case of Amon's domain in Thebes; and as he cannot be everywhere at the same time, he delegates his religious functions to the priests of the different temples.

God's servants can approach him only when they are free of any physical blemish; therefore, twice each day and twice each night, they must perform their ablutions (this includes washing the mouth with natron) by the sacred lake, which, in every temple, symbolized the primordial water of the *Nun* from which creation emerged; the whole body is shaved every other day in order to avoid contamination by lice.

Royal baptism is done with lustral water. Christian baptism (John the Baptist and the water of the Jordan River), the Catholic priest's tonsure, and the Muslims' ablutions find their distant origin here. Eudoxus of Cnidus was shaven before being initiated by the Egyptian priests.[54]

Circumcision was the rule.[55] This practice is one of the most typically African, because the bodies in the predynastic tombs studied by Elliot Smith show that it was already practiced then; it is linked to an androgynous concept of the being (the uncreated god Amon), and therefore implies excision, equally present among the mummies, as confirmed by Strabo.[56] Therefore circumcision, even though abandoned here and there, is no less a trait specific to African ethnology: its presence in the Semitic world reveals a very ancient influence of the Black world on the Semitic one, as witnessed by Herodotus's statements.[57]

Fasting and prohibition from eating certain foods are no less revealing of the Egyptian legacy to the later religions, Judaism, Christianity, Islam: pork, fish, wine, etc., are forbidden to the priests; a tenacious legend among the Muslim astrologists of Senegal says that those who eat fish will not dream about the divinity, when it should rather be the opposite given the high percentage of phosphorous in fish.

According to Herodotus (II-64), "almost all men, except the Egyptians and the Greeks, make love in sacred places and then go from a woman's arms into the sanctuary without having washed themselves"; this is strictly forbidden in the Muslim religion.

The Egyptian priests, like those of the Catholic Church, wore prescribed vestments, which, in the Egyptian case, excluded wool as coming from tainted animals.

The administration of the temples, that of the domain of Amon at Thebes in particular, with its army of clerks, prefigured the skillful organization of the Catholic Church.

The Egyptian priest is married, generally monogamous, perhaps through abstinence, but women are not explicitly admitted to the caste: "The Theban institution of an earthly spouse of God, the divine worshiper, who occupies an eminent place in the clergy of Amon, remains an isolated case with no parallel in the other religious assemblies."[58]

The Passion and the Mysteries of Osiris were performed in front of the temple (see the paragraph on theater, p. 337).

The temple was a replica of heaven here on Earth, and its architecture was a vast symbol of the universe. Clement of Alexandria gives the list of subjects or works that the horologist-priest had to master:

1. A work on the arrangement of the fixed stars
2. Movement of the moon and the five planets
3. Conjunction and the light of the sun and the moon
4. Rising of the heavenly bodies[59]

Among the sacred writings in the library of the Temple of Edfu, one can quote as a confirmation of Clement of Alexandria's statements the following books: *Knowledge of the Periodic Returns of the Two Heavenly Bodies (Sun and Moon); Control of the Periodic Returns of the (Other) Heavenly Bodies; Book of Knowledge of All the Secrets of the Laboratory*; and also, *Magical Protection of the King in His Palace; Formulas to Repel the Evil Eye.*[60]

Science was in the hands of and developed by a body in service to the state, with which it was born; the clergy, source of science in Egypt, and the state that it serves can therefore not enter into conflict for the sake of science or anti-intellectualism and sectarianism as in continental Greece, in Athens, where Anaxagoras, Socrates, Plato, and Aristotle were all sentenced to death or almost were, because they taught scientific ideas received from Egypt and well ahead of local institutions. While the Egyptian religion engendered science, Athenian religious tradition protected itself from science of Egyptian origin, and this very special situation explains the differences in the compared evolution of the Egyptian and the Greek societies.

The Egyptian civilization was initiatory and elitist: modern freemasonry, its outgrowth, is the abusive denaturation of its model.

In the temple, the cult included three services: morning, noon, and evening, together with processions, prayers, chants, and music to the glory of the god—who at times came to dwell in his place, the statue in the sanctuary, the holy of holies—who received, as offerings, meals placed on the altar, which he consumed spiritually. These meals were then shared among the members of the clergy.

The god's outing in his sacred barge, carried by a group of priests followed by a procession, reminds one in many ways of the practices of the Catholic Church: the pope carried on a baldaquin.

Everything, including the use of the font and the spraying of incense for the purpose of chasing away the evil spirits, is identical.

The oracles pronounced by the god during his outings are expressed by the tilting of the boat in a positive (affirmation) or negative direction toward the back (negation, refusal): these movements are imposed on the carriers by a sudden and mysterious increase in weight that becomes unbearable; such a superstition has survived in Senegal where the dead person who is being transported to the cemetery on a stretcher is said to be endowed with the same power, not to pronounce any oracle, but to express a last wish, generally a refusal of something; the stock phrase in Wolof is *sîsou* = (the dead) refuses to move!

It would be interesting to renew the courageous experiment of Alain René, not for the purpose of criticism or denigration, but to better illustrate the Egyptian roots of the revealed religions, particularly of Christianity: it would involve the making of a film in which the Christian and the Egyptian liturgies would be shown in a parallel fashion.

In 1972, the Israeli archaeologists discovered in Jerusalem texts of the Roman epoch describing the person of Christ in a very precise manner. These manuscripts have, as it were, an explosive character, because their content differs from several of the versions of Jesus' life as told in the New Testament.

In order to avoid colliding with the Catholic Church's susceptibilities, the Israelis kept these discoveries secret and invited the Vatican to send a specialist to examine them: this was done. Since then, by shared agreement, secrecy has been maintained about these exceptional discoveries.

Moreover, Christ, in his youth, took a trip to Egypt where he was initiated into the mysteries.

> The Orphic myths (Thrace) told how Dionysus, cut to pieces by the Titans, the incarnations of Evil, was brought back to life by his father Zeus.... Those who propagated these myths were promising bliss in the life to come to all who would follow the physical and moral asceticism that was recommended to all men, whose death would separate the soul from the impure carnal element.[61]

Dionysus was nothing less than a lustful god, a wine drinker, who preached debauchery.

Egyptian and Greek Theater

In *l'Unité culturelle de l'Afrique Noire*, we showed the Egyptian origin of Greek theater from the Mysteries of Osiris, or of Dionysus, his replica on Greek soil.

Up to the first Tanite dynasty, the royal family itself acted in Osiris's drama, assimilated with the deceased Pharaoh. Then later, only the priests would act, before the royal family, in the passion of Osiris, the mystery of his death, and resurrection.

The British school of Egyptology has translated one of these plays written in hieroglyphics; a team of disguised British actors performed it, following the text faithfully. The film that was made of this unique document was shown by the dramatist and poet G. M. Tsegaye, during the 1973 Pan-African Congress in Addis-Ababa.

"The Athenian tyranny organized and made official the celebration of these (Dionysian) feasts, from whence came theatrical performances."[62] "The Dionysian feasts lead, through theater, to the literary life."[63]

It was through urban Dionysian celebrations, in the sixth century B.C., that the theatrical performances were instituted, which were later expanded to other subjects.[64] This Dionysian origin of Greek theater is confirmed by Jean Delorme:

> The origin [of the theater] as a literary genre is always argued about. One has wanted to take [tragedy] out of the cycle of Dionysus in order to link it to the funeral cult of the heros of the aristocratic society. But the fact is that it constitutes an integral part of the god's religion when it started in Athens in 534.
>
> Therefore, the action had to be very much reduced in relation to the choir's chants [only one actor needed to hold the dialogue with the chorist, then a second character in the following generation]. However, this progress perhaps does not precede Aeschylus, who won his first prize during the Dionysian competitions in 484.[65]

RELATIONSHIPS BETWEEN EGYPTIAN AND PLATONIC COSMOGONIES THROUGH THE *TIMAEUS*

For Plato, the world is made according to a perfect, immutable model, as opposed to the perpetual becoming of matter (being born and dying) which is the true materialization of imperfection: the demiurge (we would say the Ra of the Heliopolitan cosmogony), the worker who creates the sensible beings always has his eyes fixed on his model, which is an absolute, beautiful, perfect idea, the archetype, the eternal essence of being, which he copies:

> . . . Now, one can, in my opinion, in the first place make the following divisions. Who is the eternal being who is never born and

> who is the one who is always born and never exists? One is understood by the intellect and by reasoning, for he is constantly the same. As for the second one, he is the object of opinion combined with irrational sensation, because he is born and dies, but never really exists. (*Timaeus*, 28a) [The causality, the maker, the two models.]

One easily recognizes here the archetypes of all future beings as described in the Egyptian *Nun*, already created in potentiality and awaiting their actualization thanks to the action of Khepera, god of becoming or law of the perpetual transformation of matter: the Heliopolitan cosmogony is essentially a philosophy of becoming, more than two thousand years before Heraclitus and all the Pre-Socratic philosophers:

> . . . Now, if this world is good and if the maker is good, it is clear that he fixes his attention on the eternal model. Otherwise, what should not even be a permissable supposition, he would have looked at the model that was born; now, it is absolutely obvious to everybody that the maker contemplated the eternal model. For this World is the most beautiful of everything that was ever begotten and the maker is the most perfect of causes. (*Timaeus*, 29a)

The intelligibility of the world, of the universe, is founded in law, as in the Egyptian Heliopolitan cosmogony where the essences, the rational beings, lay in the uncreated primordial matter, a divinity itself, without beginning or end.

For Plato, the science of absolute truth is possible and accessible to humanity, but only by the intellect, which alone can think and grasp the archetypes, the essences of beings, to the exclusion of the misleading intervention of our senses.

The Platonic cosmogony is imbued with optimism as opposed to the Indo-European pessimism in general. This is obviously a heritage of the African school. During Strabo's time, the lodgings of the former "pupils," Plato and Eudoxus, were being shown at Heliopolis, in Egypt, where they spent thirteen years studying different sciences, philosophy, etc. Every Greek initiate or pupil had to write a final paper on Egyptian cosmogony and mysteries, irrespective of the curriculum that he had followed. This was the case with Eudoxus, who was one of the most brilliant Greek mathematicians and who translated, for the first time, Egyptian papers on astronomy into Greek and introduced in Greece the Egyptian theory of the epicycles.[66]

"The perfect causality of the world," for Plato, merges with its creator, the maker, the demiurge who identifies himself, point by point, with the god Ra of Heliopolis, a town founded by the Anu of Osiris's race in protohistoric times. Divine Providence, the cause of the World, is good and can only conceive of that which is good and beautiful, like Ra, Amon, Ptah, all the great divinities of Egypt who created the world at different stages. This creator, according to Plato, "had wanted all things to be born in his likeness, whenever possible. . . ."

"He expelled, as much as it was in his power, all imperfection, and also he took the whole visible mass, deprived of any rest, changing without order and measure, and he brought it from disorder to order, for he had deemed order to be worth infinitely more than disorder. And, never was it permitted, never is it permitted to the best to make anything but that which is the most beautiful" (*Timaeus*: 30a, b, c). These divine preoccupations that consist of loving the Good and hating Evil have passed on to the popular level as a moral ideal, in Egypt and all over Black Africa.[67]

Thus, the Platonic universe, as much later that of Leibniz, is optimistic, therein identical to that of Egypt and the rest of Africa.

The above-cited passage of Plato could be taken for an excerpt (without reference) from the Heliopolitan cosmogony: as a matter of fact, in this cosmogony the *Nun*, the chaotic primordial matter, was first the site of an indescribable disorder and it is the action of the god Khepera, through time, that will actualize the essence of Ra, who brought order by completing creation, in beauty and goodness. This is the reason why order (*Hu*), justice or truth (*Maat*) are of divine essence for the ancient Egyptians as they are for Plato.

Ra, like Plato's god, who is nameless, is the absolute idea of the Good, and the organizing principle of the world.

But, as Albert Rivaud points out in his exposition of the *Timaeus* (p. 35), there is a certain imprecision that prevails in Plato: one does not know where the ideas are, where they were in the beginning; are they distinct from sensible things? What are the relationships between the world of ideas, the living in itself, God, and the world-soul? This is not clear. Now, in the Egyptian philosophical cosmogony, all the analogous notions to which Plato alludes are clearly defined: the *Nun*, or primordial chaotic matter, is the living in itself, which potentially contains the whole universe in gestation, in the form of eternal essences or pure ideas, indestructible models, the archetypes of future beings, but also the necessary force for its own evolution toward the world's actualization; therefore one knows where the eternal forms were of which the *Timaeus* speaks, at the origin of things. Similarly, the universal *Ka*, present everywhere in the universe, will be, after the birth of Ra and the creation of the sensible world, the immortal soul of this universe, the objective spirit that animates it and makes it intelligible to the individual spirit of the scholar, the logos of Plato's world, as we will see below. The immortality of the individual's soul and that of the world, as affirmed in the *Timaeus*, is ontologically founded on the Egyptian cosmogony, because the individual Ka, meaning the perimeters of the intellect, are indestructible elements of the universal Ka. They are alien to the body. Joined to the *Ba*, the individual's sensible soul, and to the physical support which is the body, they form the living human being. After death, the Ka reunited with the Ba goes to heaven and the individual enjoys immortality, if his earthly existence was exemplary. Otherwise, the soul becomes reincarnated, as punishment, in the form of an animal, pig, dog, horse, mollusk, or as a plant, but salvation lies at the end of this long and painful expiation of the soul, in its essence immortal.

In any case, the individual Ka joins the universal Ka—the intellect or the world-soul—and never gets lost in the Great Whole: thus, the Egyptian philosophical cosmogony invented the immortality of the soul during the Ancient Empire, 2600 B.C. and even earlier, as witnessed by the pyramid texts, more than one thousand years before the first revealed religion. According to popular Egyptian belief, every individual soul was linked to a star in heaven, which fell from the sky when the individual died.

Plato, without citing them, uses in the *Timaeus* and in his other dialogues, all these Egyptian ideas to different degrees: archetypes (or the reality of ideas or essences), the world-soul, immortality of the world-soul and of the individual soul, composition of the world and of the individual soul, theory of the four elements—earth, fire, air, water—mathematical essence of the world conceived as a pure number, metempsychosis, the soul of the stars, sphere of the fixed stars, celestial equator, ecliptic, theory of the movement of the planets, notion of mathematical time, theory of the Self and the Other, or of the archetypes, as opposed to the perpetual becoming of matter as symbolized by Khepera.

It is because he does not name his obvious Egyptian sources that his philosophical system seems to be suspended in air, even and especially to his modern exegetes.

Even though Proclus of Lycia affirms that Plato was inspired by Locres's work entitled *Of the Soul of the World and Nature*, in order to write the *Timaeus*.[68]

Plato's demiurge is nothing other than the Egyptian god Ra, even though Plato does not say it: as Ra, he does not create *ex nihilo*, but limits himself, in principle, to actualizing preexisting essences, of all eternity, in the divine *Nun*, and even preceding his first appearance.

This essential principle of the Egyptian cosmogony, which Plato faithfully copied without admitting it, should always be kept in mind: the Egyptian cosmogonic philosophy is integrally evolutionist and transformist, though not, of course, in Spencer's sense. The eternal primordial matter, without beginning or end, is engaged in an evolution, a perpetual becoming, thanks to its intrinsic property which is the law of transformation, elevated to the level of a divinity. Matter, together with the evolutionary movement that always pushes it to change its form, to evolve, are both eternal principles. There did not exist in Egyptian cosmogony a period designated as zero, at which point the being, matter, arose out of nothing, out of non-being; being, in Heidegger's and Jean-Paul Sartre's sense, is eternal; its fullness excludes *a priori* even the hypothetical possibility of non-being, of nothingness, as supreme absurdity. Nothingness, non-being, in the Egyptian philosophical cosmogony, is equivalent to concrete matter in disorder, in the chaotic state of the *Nun*, of the primordial abyss. But this *Nun* contained in it, in the form of a desire toward order and beauty (so many notions allegedly Platonic), a force capable of assuring its evolution, in the same sense used by the Marxists (Lenin) when they say that movement is an intrinsic property of matter. We will also see that Aristotle's "final cause," responsible for the physical universe's movement, corresponds to matter's intrinsic property symbolized by the divinity Khepera[69] in the Egyptian cosmogony who only actualizes "forms," meaning the "essences" of the being in both the Aristotelian and Platonic sense.

It is true that Plato does not always copy to the letter the Egyptian texts that were written two thousand years before him, and which, at times, he interpreted with incomparable brilliance, as Amélineau puts it. In fact, the primordial *Nun*, under the action of the god of becoming, begets Ra, who is the first "eye," the first conscience that observes the world, and who becomes aware of his own existence. The *Nun* is Ra's father, and that is what Ra calls him in the Heliopolitan cosmogony. Therefore, it is *Nun*'s son, Ra, who after he is begotten, achieves creation as the demiurge, while his father, *Nun*, returns to his initial rest and does not intervene any further in creation. Here, everything is clear once one adopts the starting principles of the Egyptian cosmogony: Ra, the God-son, the demiurge, completes the creation of his father, *Nun*, who goes back to rest.

In the *Timaeus*, Plato tells us that the demiurge, after having fashioned souls out of preexisting ingredients, sowed them on the Earth, the moon, the stars, these instruments of time:

> And after having sown, he left to the young gods the task of making the perishable bodies. . . .
>
> And the God who had regulated all this remained in his accustomed state. While he was resting, his children, having assimilated his instructions, carried them out.[70]

Plato's theogony, in the *Timaeus* or in the other dialogues, does not explain the birth of the subordinate gods, the sons to whom the demiurge, the father-god, gives tasks to perform, and who, like his Egyptian counterpart the god *Nun*, was going back to rest, "his accustomed state," and to let his children finish creation.

Plato, in the above-cited paragraph, speaks of the sewing of souls; now, we know that this is how Ra created the "god-sons" or second divinities, eight in number, who had to finish creation through normal generation and to engender Osiris and Isis (or Adam and Eve), the human race: Shu (air), a divinity, came first out of Ra's seed, in a solitary and archaic way; but, as Amélineau remarks, how could it be otherwise? Then, it was the female divinity Tefnut (water), who was spat out by Ra: thus was born, through the demiurge Ra, the first syzygy, in other words, the first divine couple, made up of the dialectical union of two principles, or two constituent elements of the universe, the one male or active, the other female or passive.

This first couple begets the following, Geb (the Earth), a male principle in the eyes of the inventors of Egyptian cosmogony, and Nut, or heaven (the fire of heaven, the stars, and the ether), female principle; here is how appeared, in a vigorously clear and logical process, the four elements: air, water, earth, and fire, which will become the basis for the theory of the four elements in Greek philosophy, from the Pre-Socratic philosophers (Thales, Pythagoras, Empedocles, etc.) to Plato himself, who, precisely in the *Timaeus*, explains the formation of the universe from these four elements (*Timaeus*, 55e–61c).

In order to give the appearance of depth to his theory, Plato does not hesitate to abuse the Egyptian symbolic method introduced in Greece by Pythagoras, according to Plutarch (*Isis and Osiris*): the earth "element" corresponds to the geometric being that is the cube; because of its huge size, he writes, the tetrahedron or the pyramid corresponds to fire; because of its lightness, the octahedron represents air, and the icosahedron, water. According to Plato, metals are varieties of water (*Timaeus*, 59b), minerals come out of earth and water, etc. (*Timaeus*, 60c).

Thus, we have seen that Ra, "created" in potentiality for all eternity and dwelling as essence, archetype, within the primordial *Nun*, was actualized, meaning "created," in actuality, by the god of the raw becoming of matter, *Khepera* or *šopi* (in Coptic). And *sopi* in Wolof means "to transform," "to become," just as it does in the first two languages. Ra was first a solitary god, and he had to create in actuality, meaning that he had to actualize the essences of the first secondary divinities, Shu (air) and Tefnut (water); this is when he exclaimed, "I was one; I became three." Here we have the expression of the first divine trinity in the history of the religions. These notions, borrowed without any such admission, become in the other future religions inextricable mysteries that defy understanding.

Plato's god, like his prototype Ra, creates nothing but order and beauty, or the Good, by introducing harmony—mathematics—into evolution; neither he nor Ra creates *ex nihilo*: Beauty and Good merge together in both cosmogonic systems, which share the same optimism.

Similarly, in the *Timaeus*, next to the great god (Ra), there is a line of subordinate divinities: the Earth, the five planets, the stars, all of which have divine souls. This world-soul, that of the universe of stars and planets, of the Earth and the Sun, is made up of three substances, according to Plato:

> Thus the soul is made up of the nature of the Same [the "essence" of the Egyptian *Nun* or *Ka*, the universal *logos*] and the nature of the Other [matter in the process of becoming through Khepera's action] and the third substance (*Timaeus*, 37a). And composed of the mixture of these three realities, mathematically divided and unified [we will see in what artificial manner and based on the already acquired knowledge of Egyptian mathematics], it moves in a circle by revolving on itself. (Timaeus, 37a)

It is clear that here Plato takes up the Egyptian theory of being, composed of three elements: the *Ka* (the intellect), the *Ba*, (the vital force), the *Sed* (mortal body) by barely adapting it; and by changing the original names.

The Heliopolitan origin of Plato's doctrine is even more obvious in the ideas on astronomy that are put forth in the *Timaeus*, because they are integral copies of the Egyptian theories, as corroborated by the statements of Strabo, a chauvinistic Greek, who cannot be said to be generous toward the ancient Egyptians.

Through a mediocre and degraded, mystical account, Plato, in order to introduce mathematical time in the universe, reverts to the Egyptian ideas on sidereal and civil calendars, on a purely qualitative level:

> Now, when the Father who engendered it understood that this World moved and was alive, image born of the eternal gods, he rejoiced, and in his joy he thought of ways to make it resemble his model even more. . . . That is why its author thought of making a certain mobile imitation of eternity, and while organizing the heavens, he made, out of the one and immutable eternity, this eternal image that progresses according to the law of Numbers, this thing that we call time. In fact, days and nights, months and seasons never existed before the birth of heaven, but their birth was accomplished at the same time that heaven was constructed. Because all this comprises divisions of time: the past and the future are engendered species of time, and when we apply them out of the context of eternal substance, it is because we are ignorant of their nature. (*Timaeus*, 37d–e)

Plato then opposes the qualities of eternal substance—which, in brief, "is" as long as eternal "being," to which it is improper to apply the notion of physical time determined from the sensible world—to those of matter in the process of becoming: "And besides that, all the formulas of this kind: what became has become; what becomes is in the process of becoming; or else: the future is future, or again: non-being is non-being, all these expressions are never correct." (*Timaeus*, 38b) Here Plato uses a pure and simple language, the same sentences of Heliopolitan cosmogony in reference to the becoming of the god Khepera (see p. 328).

Plato then speaks of the conjunction and the oppositions of the planets, of the eight orbits of the then five known planets, the moon and the sun, their oblique course following the movement of the Other and that of the Same, of the origin of day and night, of the phases of the planets, and of the "great year": "Nonetheless, it is possible to conceive that the perfect number of time has achieved the perfect year when the eight revolutions, having equalized their speed, return to the initial point and give as common measurement to those speeds the circle of the Same, which possess a uniform movement" (*Timaeus*, 38b–39d, e).

There is no doubt that all these ideas were already known in Egypt two thousand years before the birth of Plato; and furthermore, by reading carefully, one realizes that Plato furtively puts forward the scientific concepts of Egyptian astronomy on a uniquely qualitative level by deforming them, precisely because he does not understand them well.[71] Plato vaguely wants to deal with astronomy without compromising himself: in the above citation, concerning the "great year," it is clear that he means to discuss the heliacal rising of Sothis (Sirius),[72] i.e., the 1,460-year period at the end of which the first day of the calendar year—that of the planets—coincides again with the first day of the sidereal year, that of the sphere of the fixed stars, which he calls "the circle of the Same."

With the invention of this calendar, the Egyptians had in the same way, from protohistory onward, made it common knowledge that the universe, the celestial mechanism, the world par excellence, is governed by the harmony of the pure number, which is the mathematical time spoken of by Plato, who develops this same idea of the omnipotence of the number (see the quote above).

This does not prevent the Western ideologists from crediting Pythagoras or Plato with this innovation, pretending to be ignorant of the Egyptian legacy.

The oblique ecliptic movement of the sun in relation to the celestial equator, and the eclipses of the celestial bodies (see Strabo's quote above), the planets' phases, the very anteriority of night in relation to day, in the creational process, are all Egyptian ideas copied by Plato, without any reference to his sources, as was the Greek custom.

Even at the beginning of the Hellenistic era, an eclipse of the sun sowed panic among the ranks of Alexander the Great's army as they fought against soldiers, Alexander did not call on Aristotle, his private tutor, or on any other Greek scientist, but on the knowledge of an Egyptian priest, who restored calm by giving the soldiers a scientific, natural explanation of the event.[73]

Plato and Eudoxus spent thirteen years in the Egyptian town of Heliopolis, where the so-called Heliopolitan cosmogony was born that heavily inspired Plato in the *Timaeus*, to the extent that he went so far as to reproduce sentences from the Egyptian texts without citing where the material came from, as when he writes: "That which became has become; that which becomes is in the process of becoming . . ." (*Timaeus*, 38b)

According to his biographers (Olympiodorus, *Life of Plato* and anonymous author, *The Life*), Plato went to Egypt precisely in order to be initiated in theology and geometry. Here are the terms in which Strabo, one of the greatest Greek scholars of his time (58 B.C. to A.D. 25), confirms Plato's and Eudoxus's voyage to Heliopolis, in Egypt:

> We saw over there [in Heliopolis] the hallowed halls that were used in the past for the lodging of the priests; but that is not all; we were also shown Plato's and Eudoxus's dwelling, for Eudoxus had accompanied Plato here; after arriving at Heliopolis, they stayed there for thirteen years among the priests: this fact is affirmed by several authors. These priests, so profoundly knowledgeable about celestial phenomena, were at the same time mysterious people, who did not talk much, and it is only after a long time and with skillful maneuvering that Eudoxus and Plato were able to be initiated into some of their theoretical speculations. But these Barbarians kept the best part to themselves. And if today the world owes them the knowledge of what fraction of a day (of a whole day) has to be added to 365 whole days in order to have a complete year, the Greeks did not know the true duration of the year and many other facts of the same nature until translators of the Egyptian priests' papers into the Greek language popularized these notions among modern astronomers, who have continued, up to the present time, to draw heavily from this same source as they have from the Chaldeans' writings and observations.[74]

According to Diogenes Laërtius, Eudoxus translated for the first time Egyptian scientific works into Greek "and he introduced for the first time in Greece accurate notions of the course of the five planets, badly construed until then, and whose true nature would have been taught to him in Egypt, undoubtedly the theory of the epicycles."[75]

From the above two texts, it appears that both Plato and Eudoxus experienced the same difficulties as Pythagoras in order to be initiated and taught by the Egyptian priests, and that in the end this initiation was only partial, especially as far as Plato is concerned (in spite of his long thirteen-year stay), who would turn out to be less of a mathematician than Eudoxus. And we have already said that it is for this reason that Plato keeps himself from engaging in serious, that is, consequential and detailed, mathematical digressions or developments. All the mathematical elements of his work are borrowed ones (in the *Theaetetus*, for instance) or are notions that he had learned in Egypt and which were already being taught in Greece, like the theory of the series (geometric, arithmetic, harmonic) of which he makes extensive use in his construction of the world-soul.

It is remarkable that neither Plato nor Eudoxus ever cite their Egyptian teachers, despite the formal testimony by Strabo. We have already said that one could believe Strabo without any doubt when he reveals to us the existence of the Egyptian priests who engage in theoretical speculations, those of a unique, genuine astronomy, from which both he himself and all the Greek scholars of his time were still drawing on; one can believe him when he says that before the translation into Greek of Egyptian scientific works, the Greeks knew almost nothing about astronomy and the theoretical and applied sciences in general, not even the exact duration of the year. One will notice that it is out of the question that a Greek scholar as chauvinistic as Strabo would present the Egyptians as being simple empiricists next to the Greeks as the true theoreticians. Such an idea could never cross the minds of the Greek scholars, who had all been pupils of the Egyptians at the birth of Greek science. Thales, who inaugurated the cycle by being the first to introduce Egyptian science into Greece, particularly geometry and astronomy, never dared to make such a claim, for it would have been ridiculous in his own eyes. Also, after he finished teaching Pythagoras all that he knew, he advised him to follow his own example, to go and complete his training with the Egyptian priests, the true keepers of scientific knowledge at that time. That is why Pythagoras spent twenty-two years in Egypt, obtaining information about all the sciences that he could; when he returned to Greece, he founded the sect that bears his name, characterized above all by the quasi-integral maintenance of the Egyptian methods: the symbolic method (cf. Plutarch, *Isis and Osiris*), the idea of the omnipotence of the Number that governs the universe (see pp. 270–72), the metempsychosis or transmigration of souls, which is also found in Plato, the so-called "Pythagorean" theorem, and the irrational numbers (see pp. 346, 258–60). All these facts made Herodotus say that Pythagoras was nothing but a vulgar plagiarist of his Egyptian masters.[76]

According to Jamblichus, his own biographer, "Pythagoras acquired in Egypt the science for which he is generally considered to be a scholar."

We have seen earlier that the Egyptians invented the sidereal and the civil calendars and that they divided the year into 365 days, having 3 seasons of 4 months each, and this, from protohistory onward, in 4236 B.C., that is, 3,600 years before the birth of Thales and 2,800 years before the emergence of the Greek people in history; yet, Diogenes Laërtius writes: ". . . it is said that he [Thales] discovered the seasons of the year and divided it into 365 days" (*op. cit.*, p. 53). Here we see the methods of the Greek plagiarists at work.

And Diogenes Laërtius continues: "He [Thales] did not take any lessons from any master, except in Egypt where he frequently kept company with the country's priests. Hieronymus says that he measured the pyramids by calculating the ratio between their shadow and that of our body."

This is the origin of the legend that attributes to Thales (who did not leave even one written line to posterity, except a few hypothetical letters, in one of which he said to Pherecydes that he does not write, that he is not in the habit of writing) the theorem that bears his name and that is illustrated by the figure of problem 53 of the *Rhind Papyrus*, thirteen hundred years before the birth of Thales (fig. 44).

One must imagine the inferior intellectual and moral figure that a Greek could make of himself in Egypt during Thales's epoch, around 650 B.C., in order to see the picture of a Thales supposedly taking scientific measurements at the foot of the Great Pyramid: it is truly the epitome of the ludicrous!

The Egyptian priests themselves had the habit of reminding the Greek scholars that it was in Egypt that they had learned the sciences that made them famous in their own country. It is all these facts that Western ideologists either innocently or cynically falsify today, when they dogmatically decree that Pharaonic science was merely empirical and that it was Greece that introduced theory. If Thales, Pythagoras, Democritus, Plato, Eudoxus, Strabo, Diodorus, Euclides, Eratosthenes, Archimedes, Clement of Alexandria, Heron of Alexandria, Diophantus, Hippocrates, Galen, if any of these Greek scholars, all contemporaries of the ancient Egyptians, had dared to make such an affirmation, it would have had enormous weight, and yet they did not lack pride. Such an attitude was, however, inconceivable for all the reasons mentioned above. Only the modern Westerners, with the passing of time, dare display such contempt for the facts, going so far as to deny the existence of an Egyptian astronomy, for ideological reasons.

Imagine that if in two thousand years the descendants of the African students in Paris and in London maintain "obstinately" that their ancestors had taught modern scientific theory to today's Western world, the situation would be identical!

Let us go back to the *Timaeus*. The world contains four species: gods, fish, birds, earthly animals (*Timaeus*, 40e). It is an analogous classification that we find in the Heliopolitan cosmogony, with the appearance of the beings with which Ra populated the universe.

Plato then gives the generation of Greece's common gods with contained irony: "Oceanus and Tethys were children of Gaia and Uranus . . ." (*Timaeus*, 40e).

One finds, in popular form in Greece, the Egyptian syzygy *Geb* and *Nut* = earth and heaven, in the Greek couple *Gaia* (the earth) and Uranus (heaven). And so on.

Plato then describes the world-soul. About this, Albert Rivaud notes: "By the fact that it does not imply a completely elaborated theology, the *Timaeus*'s doctrine can be interpreted, depending upon the disposition of the interpreter, as a kind of theory of procession, of a still confused and ill-defined doctrine of creation. It certainly seems that in Plato's mind a conflict of several different inspirations was taking place, among which he did not know how or want to decide."[77]

According to Plato, the world-soul is spherical "because the circular configuration is the most beautiful of all for it holds the most beings in the least space."[78] Plato wants to demonstrate that the entire heaven is organized according to mathematical laws and relationships, so many scientific notions that the Egyptians had put in place from protohistory onward with the invention of both civil and sidereal calendars.

All in all, the soul is composed of two principles, the one proceeding out of the indivisible, immutable essence of forms, the archetypes (the Egyptian *Nun*, the other from divisible matter involved in the becoming of the sensible world (according to the law of the Egyptian divinity of becoming, Khepera). The fusion of these two essences following a determined pattern yields a third principle, and the fusion of these three principles yields a fourth one. Such are the four principles that Plato calls the constituent ingredients of the world-soul, and even of human beings. Rivaud points out that Plato, who had espoused the transcendental point of view, now makes a concession to the doctrine of immanence, which alters the economy of its construction because the Immutable Form, the eternal idea, "itself descends into matter in order to organize it, through a direct action."[79]

God made the world with earth and fire, these two elements being joined by a third one in geometrical progression: we find ourselves here in a truly Egyptian universe.[80]

> Hence the fact that when God started forming the body of the World, he first began with fire and earth [Geb and Nut]. But it is not possible for two terms to form a beautiful composition by themselves without a third one, because between the two there must be some link that holds them together. Now, of all the links, the most beautiful is the one that gives the most complete unity both to itself and to the two that it united. And that is the progression that naturally accomplishes it in the most beautiful way. (*Timaeus*, 31b–c)

The unicity of the relationships or the mediators that Plato assumes between the means and the extremes is false, in the case of "linear numbers or planes," as Rivaud points out, but this is only one detail that shows that Plato was never a mathematician in the sense of discovering theorems; he was simply a learned person, who could follow mathematical reasoning that was not complicated and use it, if needed, in his mystical, superficial speculations, as in the passage below:

> But, in fact, it was convenient that this body [the body of the world] was solid, and, in order to harmonize two solids, one mediator is never enough: there must always be two.[81] Thus, God has placed air and water between fire and earth, and he has disposed of these two elements in regard to the others, as much as possible in the same relationship, in such a manner that what fire is to air, air was to water, and what air is to water, water was to earth. (*Timaeus*, 32b)

This is truly a mathematical version of Egypt's Heliopolitan cosmogony. Plato's god (Ra) also made the "visible and tangible" heaven with the aid of the four elements of the Heliopolitan cosmogony, according to a divine proportion.

The order of the elements indicated by Plato is identical to that of the Heliopolitan cosmogony: indeed, one knows that in the latter, *Geb* (the earth) and *Nut* (five, sky) were united and that *Shu* (air) had to separate them by suspending the sky in such a way that air and water find themselves interposed between heaven and earth; thus the order of the elements is identical: earth, water, air, and heaven, which also corresponds to the apparent order or to the order of the densities.

On the other hand, in the Egyptian cosmogony, the quandary of the solitary demiurge, Ra, ceased after he created the first syzygy, Shu and Tefnut; thus appeared the first triad forming a divine unity. It is indeed this idea of the divine trinity that Plato seems to want to recover at all costs in his constructions; and only this can explain a senseless affirmation such as this, cited earlier: "But it is not possible that two terms form by themselves a beautiful composition without a third one." The question is: why not?

But let us follow, along with Plato, the making of the world-soul by the demiurge (Ra). One recalls the three constituent principles of which the third is a mixture of the first two: the demiurge divides the obtained "composition" into "seven parts[82] which are between them like terms of two geometrical progressions, the one with the ratio 2 (1, 2, 4, 8) and the other with the ratio 3 (1, 3, 9, 27)" (*Timaeus*, p. 43). The demiurge recombines these two progressions in order to form a third one (1, 2, 3, 4, 9, 8, 27) in which, a significant detail, until now unexplained, the demiurge had inverted, according to Plato, the order of the terms 8 and 9, without explaining why.

This particular fact is singularly revealing as to the Egyptian origin of Plato's inspiration; in fact, such an inversion, called "respectful inversion," is imperative in Egyptian writing every time that the name of a god is implied: the sign that represents him must come before all other signs, even if, phonetically, it should normally be at the end of the word. Here, in the third progression, 9 is indeed the number of the Heliopolitan ennead, that is, of the eight primordial divinities created by Ra, the demiurge plus Ra himself:

Shu, *Tefnut* = air, water
Geb, *Nut* = earth, fire
Osiris, *Isis* = Osiris, Isis (Adam and Eve)
Seth, *Nephthys* = Seth, Nephthys

These eight gods form the Heliopolitan ogdoad, without Ra. When they are reunited with Ra, they form the ennead (or the 9) which thus ranks before the ogdoad, hence the probable mystical reasons for the inversion of the numbers 9 and 8 in the progression, respectively symbolizing the Heliopolitan ennead and ogdoad.

The demiurge fills the intervals in this last progression according to an arbitrary process that is laborious and elementary at the same time, which it is not useful to elaborate here: let us only note that Plato seems to be inspired by the so-called Pythagorean theories, because the progression's mathematical intervals are now considered to be musical intervals that he fills in with mediators, meaning arithmetic and harmonic means, in such a way that one passes, without sensing it harmonically, from one extreme to the other: the mathematical relationship or ratio that unites musical tones is called λόγος = logos; it deals with a harmonizing operation; there is a symphony when the intervals are all in tune.

In fact, only the name of the intervals is musical, but Plato fills them with purely mathematical and arbitrary processes that do not correspond at all to the true relations between the musical sounds of a scale.

Plato's series is longer than the musical scale, and "only the interval called δὶα πασῶξ (diapason) corresponds to two groups of four strings or to two tetra-strings, consequently, it assumes an instrument of eight strings" (Albert Rivaud, *Timaeus*, p. 50). Let us recall that the Egyptian harp of eight or nine strings reproduces the figures of the ogdoad or the ennead and that Pythagoras, who stayed for twenty-two years in Egypt, became very familiar with Egyptian musical theories.

Fragment 6 of Philolaus already contained musical considerations similar to those set forth by Plato on harmonies. Therefore, even if Philolaus does not precede Socrates, one notices that these types of ideas were already commonplace.

For Plato, while music uses only the 2/1 interval = the ratio δία πασῶν, going from the ϑπατη string, the deepest of the lyre's strings, to the νήτη, the harmony of the world-soul comprises all of the possible scales according to the above series. Thus the pure number constitutes the most important immortal part of our soul, if not the only one, and Rivaud shows that "Xenocrates remains faithful to the spirit of the *Timaeus*'s doctrines, by defining the soul by a number that moves" (*Timaeus*, p. 51).

The task of establishing that the number can govern all of the manifestations of the cosmos and its movements in general was already accomplished by the Egyptians in protohistory with the invention of the calendar, as we have already stated: consequently, all these Greek theories on the omnipotence of the number were obviously imported from Egypt, as revealed moreover by the introductory sentence of the *Rhind Papyrus* (see p. 274). African musicologists should study mathematically the relationship between the length or weight of the Egyptian instruments' strings, particularly of the harp, in order to see whether they will find relationships similar to those found in the *Timaeus* for the intervals: this would be a supplementary confirmation of the Egyptian origin of Plato's ideas (*Timaeus*, 36a, b, c, d).

Plato describes the manner in which the demiurge made the celestial equator, animated by the movement of the Same (eternal essence), and the ecliptic, animated by the movement of the Other, the matter that is involved in the perpetual becoming of births and deaths:

> Now, this whole composition, God cut it in two lengthwise, and, having crossed the two halves one on the top of the other at their centers, like a *chi* (*X*), he bent them in order to join them in circles, putting together the tips of each at the point opposite their intersection. . . . (*Timaeus*, 36c)
>
> The movement of the outer circle was designated by him to be the movement of the substance of the Same; that of the inner circle for the movement of the substance of the Other. He oriented the movement of the Same from left to right following the side of a parallelogram, and that of the Other from right to left in a diagonal. (*Timaeus*, 36b, c)

This is indeed the oblique trajectory of the ecliptic in relation to the celestial equator. Strabo has already told us (see pp. 273–274) that the Greeks did not know a single word of these ideas until the Egyptian works of astronomy were translated into Greek. These works are for the most part lost today, but their existence cannot be doubted in light of the precise testimony made by Strabo, who was a full-fledged scholar, and, moreover, a user of this Egyptian science of astronomy: therefore he knew what he was talking about, because he was speaking for himself; Strabo cited the ecliptic and the celestial equator precisely.

Likewise, Diodorus of Sicily tells us that Oenopides learned many secrets from the Egyptian priests and astronomers, and particularly the fact that the Sun has an oblique rotation (ecliptic, oblique in relation to the celestial equator) directed toward the opposite side of the other stars[83] (see p. 322).

In the same manner, Democritus spent five years in Egypt in order to study astronomy[84] and geometry.[85] From the above it is thus clear that the Egyptian origin of Plato's ideas on astronomy found in the *Timaeus* cannot be doubted, particularly those dealing with the theory of the movement of the "celestial spheres."

For Plato, the One, meaning the Same, and the Many, meaning the Other, cannot exist separately in the absolute, but they have to *necessarily* coexist in the being, according to laws, in order for them to form the universe (*Timaeus*, p. 65).

Plato considers the elementary solids—the cube (corresponding to the element earth), the tetrahedron or the pyramid (fire), the octahedron, and the icosahedron—as types of geometric atoms that make up the universe, but are susceptible to wearing out instead of being indestructible, because of the fact that necessity is present in them. These geometric figures of the elements participate in the nature of Ideas, but it is through their intermediary that the Idea becomes flesh or thing.

Plato constructs all these elements using the essence of the Same, represented by the right-angled isosceles triangle, always identical to itself, and the essence of the Other, represented by the right-angled scalene triangle, of which there is an infinite variety, corresponding to matter in becoming. With the help of these geometrical materials, he constructs—in his own way, as must be emphasized—the cube and the pyramid, meaning earth and fire, meaning *Geb* and *Nut*.

The demiurge unites these two elements through a geometric mediator, forming an implicit trinity, as we have already seen on page 349; finally, using the same process he constructs, with triangles, the octahedron, the figure of air, and the figure of water, the icosahedron, in other words, the Egyptian syzygy (*Shu* and *Tefnut*: *Timaeus*, 53c, d, e; 54; 55a, b, c).

Finally, the myth of Atlantis, which occupies the second part of the book, the *Critias*, is restored to science thanks to radiocarbon dating, which revealed that the island of Santorini in the Cyclades had been the site of a volanic explosion in 1420 B.C., probably under the reign of Amenophis III.

Thus, the "legend" of Atlantis definitely becomes part of history, and here again, the statements of the Egyptian priests of Sais, recorded by Solon with some probable errors and transmitted by Plato in the *Critias*, have proven to be of astonishing accuracy (see p. 84–85), contrary to Rivaud's opinion.

RELATIONSHIPS BETWEEN ARISTOTLE'S PHYSICS AND THE EGYPTIAN COSMOGONIES

Let us recall first that the Hermopolitan cosmogony, probably more recent than the Heliopolitan cosmogony, as Amélineau thinks, constructs the universe using eight or ten principles, represented in the form of four and sometimes five syzygies, which are at the origin of the future Greek dialectical method:

> *Nun* and *Nunet* = the eternally uncreated primordial matter and its opposite, thus, in the most rigorous logic, being in general and non-being; in other words, matter and nothingness. Nothingness does not signify the absence of matter, but rather matter in its chaotic state.
>
> *Hehu* and *Hehut* = temporal eternity and its opposite; others say: the spatial infinite and the finite.
>
> *Kuk* and *Kuket* = the primordial darkness and its opposite, thus darkness and light.
>
> *Gareh* and *Garehet* = night and its opposite, thus, night and day.
>
> *Niaou* and *Niaouet* = movement and its passive opposite, therefore movement and inertia, according to Amélineau;[86] others translate: "spatial emptiness" and its opposite.[87]
>
> *Amon* and *Amaunet* = the hidden and its opposite, thus rigorously: the noumenal world, inaccessible to the senses, and the phenomenal world: the noumenon and the phenomenon in the Kantian sense.

The demiurge of the Hermopolitan cosmogony is the god Thoth, who created the whole universe with the Word, the logos (Plato), and this from the period of the pyramids onward: he is the famous Hermes Trismegistus of the Greco-Roman epoch.[88]

There is no doubt that the theory of the dialectical movement due to the action of opposite couples (thesis, antithesis, synthesis) originates from the Hermopolitan cosmogony, which explains all the phenomena of the universe by the action of the laws of opposites.

Aristotle begins Book I of his *Physics* with a critique of the earlier (ancient) Greek philosophers, a critique that once more confirms the fact that all of them had borrowed the elements of their doctrines either from the Heliopolitan cosmogony (theory of the four elements: earth, fire, water, air) or from the Hermopolitan cosmogony, with the adoption of the abstract, or the sensible, physical principles: "the infinite, the finite" "the unlimited, the limited," etc.

> It is the same question posed by those who endeavor to find the number of beings, for it is on the subject of the components that they begin their research, by asking themselves if there is one unique component or several (air, water), and, assuming that they are many, are they then limited or unlimited; this amounts to researching whether the principle and the element are one or several.[89]

The whole of ancient Greek thought, from the poet Hesiod at the beginning of the seventh century B.C., through the Pre-Socratics, all the way to Aristotle himself, bears the marks of the Egyptian cosmogonies: "chaos, the gaping abyss" of Hesiod's theogony; "Thales suspected that water was the principle of things."[90]

The author of the work entitled "Περι ϑυσεως" (*Of Nature*) supposes that the first principle is water, fluid, humidity, all these substances being animated (hylozoism); the idea of passivity has not yet penetrated matter or substance; an exception is the Hermopolitan *Nun* which, at first, was inert, before it began to move; the inexhaustible, the unlimited, the *apeiron*, the matter without limit of Anaximander (of Miletus), is at the basis of things. For Anaximenes, the third Ionian philosopher after Thales and Anaximander, the first element is air.

The second generation of Greek philosophers after the Ionians is represented by Pythagoras, Heraclitus, and Parmenides. It is also the epoch of the Orphic movement, and orgiastic cult of Dionysus, coming from Thrace in the sixth century B.C. and invading Greece and its colonies in southern Italy (theory of reincarnation and of survival, already known in Egypt).

Philosophy becomes more abstract, with a detailed study of the soul, but its Egyptian origin remains obvious. For Pythagoras, the whole number is at the basis of the making of the universe, because with One all the other numbers can be constructed through addition.

For Heraclitus, nicknamed "the obscure," because everything that is supposed to have been said by him is obscure, the first element is fire. The world is in a perpetual state of becoming, only the law of transformation (Khepera) remains; while Parmenides opposes the One to the Many as the constituent principle of the universe; by exploiting the idea of the One, the immutable, the primordial principle, his pupil Zeno of Elea discovers the antinomies of the infinite: Achilles and the Tortoise; the being is "one" and is identified with thought (the Egyptian archetypes of the *Nun*).

Heraclitus affirms the struggle of opposites, but each of them is resolved in unity and harmony (Egyptian syzygies). A universal reason, the logos, governs the cosmos (Egyptian Ka). Heraclitus believes in reincarnation (Egypt). Empedocles (490–430 B.C.) is a follower of Orphism (Egypt) and of the theory of the four elements (fire, air, earth, water). The cosmic force that mixes and separates things—for nothing transforms itself—according to him is the result of the opposition between love and hatred (Egyptian syzygy). Fragments still remain of his doctrinaire poems: his writings on nature deal with physics ("φυσεως" = physis = "that which has become," literally). The very origin of this root could be Negro-African or Egyptian.[91]

Anaxagoras, a contemporary and a friend of Pericles, believes in an original chaos moved by an intelligent and ordering force of the universe, following a design; it is the νους = "nous" (the Egyptian *Nun*, Khepera and Ka).

Democritus (460–360 B.C.) believes in being and non-being, meaning, in matter and nothingness (*Niaou*, *Niaouet*, the syzygy of the Hermopolitan cosmogony). But for him there is neither chance nor finality in nature. The force that impels and orders chaos (*Nun*) is purely blind and mechanical; the soul is composed of atoms of "fire" (Egypt) that run throughout the body.

Following the mathematician Archytas of Tarentum, whose works were used by Plato in the *Timaeus*, the Pythagoreans had developed a mathematical atomism by reducing all geometrical bodies and beings to a punctual representation in space; everything is formed by the "limited" (point) and the "unlimited" (continuum). The regular geometrical bodies—tetrahedron (pyramid), cube, octahedron, and icosahedron—called "Plato's bodies," and above all the bodies of *Theaetetus*, are coordinated with the four elements: earth, fire, water, air (theory of the four elements, Egypt), as we have already seen. It is very curious that these bodies were attributed to Plato or to *Theaetetus*, when one knows that the Egyptians discovered these properties and calculated their volumes (for the cube and the pyramid at least, and probably also for the others) two thousand years before the birth of Greek mathematics! Better yet, the Greek word "pyramid" is certainly of Egyptian origin, like so many other Greek scientific terms, and comes from *pa mer* or *per m ws* in the Egyptian language.

Returning to Democritus, he adopts the atomic theory of matter and admits to the continuity of empty space, undoubtedly taking into account Zeno of Elea's antinomies of the infinite, and the difficulties raised thereby. But the Pythagoreans do admit to a material space, thus confusing matter and space as Descartes will later do in the seventeenth century.[92]

All throughout this review of the doctrines of the Pre-Socratic or even post-Socratic Greek philosophers, the influence of Egyptian thought is revealed in various forms, and remains obvious.

Aristotle criticizes almost all of these doctrines in Book I of his *Physics*, before presenting his own concept of a philosophy of nature, or of physics.

He refutes the theses of the Eleatics, of Parmenides, and especially that of Melissus on the infinite character of the "non-generated" being (*Physics* 3). He then critiques those he considers true physicists: Anaxagoras, Anaximander, Empedocles, etc. (*Physics* 4). After this he attacks the opinions of the ancients, who consider (borrowing from the Hermopolitan cosmogony) the opposites as the explanatory principles of the universe.

> In any case, all of them use the opposites as basic principles, those according to whom the whole is one and without movement (Parmenides, in fact, uses as principle hot and cold, which he calls, besides, fire and earth), and the partisans of the rare and the dense, and Democritus with his full and his empty, of which the One, according to him, represents being, and the Other non-being; and also with the differences that he calls situation, figure, order; those are the opposite types: the situation, for up and down, front and back; the figure, for the angular and the non-angular, the straight and the circular.
>
> One sees therefore that all of them, each in his own way, use the opposites as their principles; and with reason; for principles should not be formed either one from the other, nor from other things; and it is from principles that everything must be formed; now, this is exactly the group of the first opposites; first, they are formed from nothing else; opposites, they are not formed one from the other. (*Physics*, I-5)

One therefore sees how abusive it is to credit Heraclitus alone with the theory of opposites: this was a commonplace to all those Greek scholars who had studied under the Egyptian priests and who were using almost word for word the "laws of opposites" of the Hermopolitan cosmogony, or were contenting themselves with making variations on the same theme, as Aristotle shows:

> All [the ancients], in fact, use the opposites as elements and, as they say, as principles, although they adopt them without rational motive, as if truth itself were forcing them to do so. They distinguish themselves one from the other by using the first or the last ones, the most easily known according to reason, or according to feeling; some hot and cold, some humid and dry, others the odd and the even; while others pose friendship and hatred as causes of generation. (*Physics*, I-5)

Thus, if Heraclitus emerges from the group, it is due to a large extent to the fact that Marx consecrated him as the inventor of the dialectic, whereas he was essentially an obscure thinker.

Lastly Aristotle, even though he criticizes the ancients, when all is said and done accepts the opposites as principles, to which he adds matter, considered as subject, which, he writes, brings the explanatory principles of the universe to three instead of only two; for him, matter is accidental non-being, while privation, meaning the absence of form, is non-being in itself, a distinction that Plato does not make. Thus we have the following two opposites: form and privation (absence of form), joined together by matter, a subject that desires form like the female, the male.

It is almost a transposition on the physical plane of Plato's pair of terms, joined together by a geometric or arithmetic mediator. One will remember that Aristotle was Plato's pupil:

> This is why one must say that, in one sense, the principles (laws) are two, in another sense, three; and, in one sense that they are opposites, as if one is speaking of the literate and the illiterate, or of hot and cold, or of the harmonious and the inharmonious; in another sense, not, for there cannot be any reciprocal passion between opposites. But this difficulty is in turn overcome by the introduction of another principle, the subject . . . thus, in a certain way, the principles are not more numerous than the opposites, and they are, one can say, two as to their number; but they are not absolutely two either, but three. (*Physics*, I-7)

Aristotle thinks that one of the opposites will suffice by its presence or its absence, in order to cause movement.

In order to get an idea of the subject, one need only think of "how bronze is related to the statue or wood (matter) to the bed" or the "relation of that which lacks form to that which has form, prior to the reception, to the acquiring of form; such is the relation of matter to being" (*Physics*, I-7).

Aristotle shows or maintains, in Book 7 of his *Metaphysics*, that it is the form that is substance and not the subject. Matter is eternal:

> The spheres of reality are classified according to degrees, from matter, the first term, whose being is only a being in potentiality, to the pure form, the divinity that is the Prime Mover, the principle and at the same time the goal of the evolution of the world, the efficient cause and the final cause.[93]

Throughout the above quote, we find the concepts of the Egyptian cosmogony, rejuvenated, embellished perhaps, but always recognizable: the theory of opposites of the Hermopolitan school, the creation in potentiality and in actuality, the pure form, meaning the eternal essence, the archetype, as last reality and final cause of the world's evolution, all this sends us back to Egypt. As a matter of fact, is it not to actualize the essences, the archetypes, the pure forms of the *Nun* that evolution got started with the law of the transformation of matter? [Khepera → šopi (Coptic) → sopi (Wolof)];[94] therefore, in Egyptian philosophy, it is indeed the divine essence, the pure form that is the final cause of the movement of matter and of its evolution, its goal: the movement of matter has no other finality than to make these essences, these pure forms, go from potentiality to act; and Aristotle adopts the "Kheperian" concept of movement, that is, accompanied by change, by transformation, instead of ending up with an infinity of identical displacements. There is present, indeed, this desire of matter to take form in the *nous*, of which Aristotle speaks, also this passage from potentiality to act, because all beings, even the divinities, including Ra, were first created in potentiality and waited for "centuries and centuries," meaning an eternity, before they were created in actuality: therefore, Aristotle very often contents himself with reversing a little the direction of evolution, and not even, since the pure form, final cause of the universal movement was already there, in the beginning, in the Egyptian system as well as in that of Aristotle.

Matter and form (essence of the Egyptian *Nun*) are uncreated and eternal; the Prime Mover is immobile (such as the *Nun* in origin) and is pure form; natural beings, objects of physics, are made of matter engaged in form, therefore of beings in action. Word for word, the Egyptian ideas are used.

Aristotle was not at all a mathematician; he only knew "the direct proportions and sometimes was in error when he wanted to write the inverse proportions" (Henri Carteron, *Aristotle*, *Physics*, Introduction, p. 16); he also never succeeded in his physics in giving a quantitative, mathematical description of movement. He contented himself with defining, in a more explicit but still qualitative manner, the notions that assume the evolution of matter conceived of as movement, such as: the infinite, the location, meaning space (which Plato had already tried to define in a more nebulous way in the *Timaeus*), the void, time, the continuum, so many notions already explicitly present but to different degrees in the Heliopolitan and the Hermopolitan cosmogonies.

On a psychological level, the soul, according to Aristotle, as with all the ancient Egyptians, is composed of three principles: the intellect (the Egyptian *Ka*), the sensitive soul (the Egyptian *Ba*), the vegetative soul (the Egyptian *Sed*). The Egyptians add the body's image to these elements, or the shadow, and these four principles have to be reunited in the afterlife in order to reconstitute the complete eternal being in the dwelling of the gods.

INEXHAUSTIVE LIST OF EGYPTIAN PHILOSOPHICAL CONCEPTS THAT HAVE SURVIVED IN WOLOF

Egyptian	Wolof
Ta = earth	*Ta* = inundated earth, the very image of Egypt, of the Nile Valley
Ta tenen = The earth that rises, the first mound that appeared within the *Nun*, from the primordial water, in order to serve as the place where the god Ra appeared in the sensible world.	*Ten* = a formed mound (in clay), as God made to create Adam; emergence, earth mound *Ta-ten* = to collect rain water *Tenden* = edema

Egyptian	Wolof
Kematef = mysterious initial snake that encircles the earth and eats its own tail (?)	*Kemtef, Kematef* = the limit of something; could apply to the mythical snake encircling the world and feeding each day off its own tail.
Etbo = the "floater" = the emergent mound where the sun appeared at the beginning of time = the town of Edfu.[95]	*Temb* = to float (a parasitic "m" before "b").
Ermé = Ra's tears through which he created humanity, hence the name of the Egyptians.	*Erem* → yeram = mercy; the feeling of compassion often accompanied by tears.
Ermé = men par excellence	
Aar, aaru = Paradise, Elysian Fields	*Aar* = divine protection *Aaru* = protected by the divinity
Khem-min(t) = the god Min's sanctuary. = *kemmis* in Greek	*Ham "Min"* = to know Min; can also be applied to the prophet of Min, meaning, his first priest.
Anu = Osiris's ethnic group; word designated by a pillar	*Enou* → yenou = to carry on the head *K-enou* = pillar
Di Ra = Ra made.	*Dira* → *dara* = something; the being, and also the non-being, depending on the case.
Di ef = he does.	*Di-ef (na)* = one will do *def* = action
Irt = to do (make) = Ra's eye = Ra's conscience, which is his tool used to create the world, in potentiality and in act.	*Def dara* = to do something. *Ir* → *yer* = to look. One now grasps the etymological auxilary verb signifying "to make" (to do), the only one that I thought had not been attested to in Wolof.[96]
Tefnut = the divinity that Ra created by spitting him out.	*Tef-nit* = to spit out a human being; to have a human being come out of one's spittle, by spitting him out, hence *Teflit* = saliva.[97]
Shou = *šou* = space, the first divinity created by Ra.	*Daw* = space (š → d[98]).
Nuter-kher = god's country or *ntr-kher*: *ntr* = protecting god, *twr* = libation	*Ker* = house *Twr* = protecting god, totem. *Ker-twr* = the house of the protecting god *Twr* = libation
Geb = the earth, the divinity	*Gab* = to dig the ground *Goub* = stalk *Gob* = harvest, harvesting stalks of wheat or millet
Nwt = the sky, the shining divinity, the fire of heaven	*Nît* = the evening light
Khepera = šopi (Coptic) = to transform, to become	*Sopi* = to transform, to become
Nun = the muddy and black primordial water	*Nûl* = black *Ndoh um ñûl* = the water of "Black," of the black (river), of the Nile (?)[99]
Nen or *nwn*: the inert primordial water	*Nen* = nothingness, non-being *Nenn* = inert

Egyptian	Wolof
Wsr = Osiris = the being, the god whose limbs were cut off and dispersed by his brother Seth so that he would not rise again.	*Wasar* = to disperse *Wasar* = family name in the Serer language; for instance, *Wasar Ngom*, an ancient Lamane or Serer landowner who, it is said, was generous, hence his name that would symbolize the habit that he had of giving away his goods with prodigality! Here is an example of popular etymology that is probably false.
Dn d = to fall without impetus.	*Dëll* = to fall without impetus (n → l) *Dëll—dëll* = multiple falls *Dân* = to cause to fall *Dânou* = fallen
Tum = the god who no longer is; Ra in the underworld when he cannot even see or recognize his way, and is guided by the infernal divinities, who are divine personages coming back to life for a moment in order to give him light as he passes through and then returns to eternal obscurity immediately afterwards.	*Toum* = the blind person's stick that he uses to guide himself. *Tul* = that which no longer is, verbal suffix indicating the end of an action.
Tem = to stop doing something; non-being complete stop	*Tem* = to stop doing something; absolute immobility; complete stop
Ka or *Kau* = the universal reason	*Ka* = Peul etymon
Kau = the upper part, above	*Kaou* = high, heaven
Ba = vital force, soul	*Ba* = Peul and Tukulor etymon *Ba* = ostrich; semantic confusion with the hieroglyphic sign.
Sa = the god who nourishes the intelligence of truth; god of knowledge	*Sa* = to teach, to instruct
Kwk = primordial darkness	*Kwk* = darkness
N heh = (waiting?) time of the beings before they were created in potentiality and in act; eternity; spatial-temporal infinity. (The prothetic *n* of the word exists since the epoch of the pyramids.)[100]	*Neg* = to wait *Eleg* = tomorrow[101]
New = emptiness	*Nèw* = rarity, rare, faction
New = agitate(?)	*Leww* = flat, calm
Atef, atew = Osiris's headdress when judging at the tribunal of the dead.	*Ate* = to judge, judgment
Set = Isis = woman	*Set* = spouse (wife)
Sat = girl	*Sat* = descendence (uterine, at the origin?)[102]
Wer = great (Thoth)	*Wer* = trustworthy personality
Tiou = five	*Diou-rôm* = five
Oudjat = sacred eye of Horus whose different parts constitute a geometric series of the ratio 1/2, going from 1/2 to 1/4	*Dia* = to see clearly, to fix one's gaze

Egyptian	Wolof
Harkhentimerti, Khenti-merti = the prince of two eyes	*Harkanam* = the human face
Tn-r = to remember[103]	*Dênêr* = to see by imagining, to imagine
Seh, sih = noble	*Seh* = dignitary
Seke(t) (?) = female noble	*Seket* = goat (semantic noble confusion?)
[hieroglyphs] = *kouchet* = *koush* (Amelineau, p. 98)	*Kous* = midget
Dtti = the desert, the savage country	*Datti* = the savage brush, the uninhabited open country
Hab = *sed* = the king's revitalization feast	*Hab-tal* = the action of vitalizing or conditioning a human being or an animal, in order for him or it to become capable of attacking, with a chance at success, a subject of a naturally superior species.
	Hamb = canary (for ritual libations) (flat m between h and b; occurs frequently in Wolof)

[hieroglyphs] = ikw—T3 = [ikouta] Pyr: *als Name des Osiris* (*Pyr:* as Osiris's name) (Wörterbuch, *op. cit.*, vol. 1, p. 139).

To be likened to the following Yoruba term:

Ojo-Jakouta = "the day of the person who melts stones," meaning the god Shango who throws lightning on the earth (Leo Frobenius: *Mythologie de l'Atlantide*, Paris: Payot, 1949, pp. 127, 177).

In fact, the Egyptian term could etymologically mean: "that which lifts," "that which seizes the earth," and Shango-Jakouta is the god "who throws stones on the earth."

Shango's lightning is also symbolized by the double hatchet of his head-dress; a symbol to be likened to the *labris* labyrinth (Crete). Labyrinth = "dwelling of the *labris*," meaning the double hatchet, which is the most sacred symbol of the Minoan religion and is engraved several times on the walls and the pillars of the palace of Minos (Cnossus). A tablet in *Linear B* has revealed the existence of the cultural title "Our Lady of the Labyrinth" (Costis Davaras, Le Palais de Cnossos, Ed. Hannibal, Athens).

This last fact, together with the presence of Poseidon's trident among the MBoum of Cameroon, tends to give credence to the idea of ancient maritime contacts between West Africa and the eastern Mediterranean, in Frobenius's sense.

PERSPECTIVES OF RESEARCH FOR A NEW PHILOSOPHY THAT RECONCILES MAN WITH HIMSELF

Could Africa, with the warmth of her social fabric, save Western man from his pessimism and individualistic solitude? Is it true, as Ernest Renan said, that only pessimism is fecund?

But does it have to be demonstrated that this African sense of solidarity is a psychological and social trait capable of surviving revolution, a cultural invariant? Does it not belong to an ideological superstructure condemned by history and progress, and having to be entirely engulfed by the revolutionary wave that will drastically change the social order? Is it not incompatible with the revolutionary conscience of the new African in gestation in all of the surrounding action, oriented toward the elucidation of all social relations? Is it comparable to that permanent trait of human nature (insatiability) on which Faust had intimately based his bet with the devil, Mephistopheles? A bet that he eventually won, because at no moment did he ever feel enough satisfaction for him to say: "Stop now, supreme moment, you are so beautiful."

An in-depth analysis would show that the African is dominated by his social relations, because they reinforce his equilibrium, his personality, and his being.

It is therefore correct that the individualist or communal superstructures are transitory and that they evolve in relation to the material conditions that brought them into existence? Put another way, all the specific traits of the African societies analyzed in *l'Unité culturelle de l'Afrique Noire* have no permanence; they are very profound traits, but they are not fixed forever. Nature, the material conditions that forged them, can reshape them by changing themselves; thus, I do not plead for a petrified African psychological nature; the sense of solidarity so dear to the African could very well give way to an individualistic, egocentric behavior of the Western type, if conditions were modified.

It is no less true that today we are witnessing a hypertrophy of the individualistic structures in Europe and the opposite in Africa to the extent that, if Western neuroses come from the former, those of Africa could be linked to the excess of communal life, which erases even the boundary of private life.

However, it is important to distinguish two components of the Western malaise:

> The one, of individualistic and social origin, is mentioned above, and here lies the African contribution, and vice versa.
>
> And the other, of a metaphysical nature, is a result of scientific progress and of the development of philosophical thought.

The discovery of spatial-temporal infinity during the Renaissance (Galileo, Copernicus) and the decline of Western religious faith, mainly since Nietzsche, have brought about the metaphysical malaise that characterizes all of modern Western thought, by "suddenly" putting man face to face with himself, with his destiny.

We will not analyze the different unsatisfactory responses that have been given to this last issue up to now.

On the other hand, it is extremely interesting to approach this problem from the angle of the transformation of human reason and of man as a biological being, in order to see if there is any glimmer of hope.

We are going through a period of crisis in reason following the dizzying development of the sciences; what will come out of it?

Usually the distinction is made between constituent reason and organized reason. In other words, there is on the one hand "the human spirit's aptitude" to organize provisional data of experience according to rules that are equally provisional, a logical transitory grammar, in order to acquire a more or less adequate comprehension of the real, and on the other hand these very data of experience and the above-cited rules, including also the extrapolations, all form organized reason.

Thus there is reason and its content of the moment, or more correctly, the aptitude, the ability to reason, on the one hand, and on the other hand, the more or less consistent, provisional materials brought to light by the sciences which are affected by this ability to reason: there is reason's permanent structure and its always outmoded content, directly caused by scientific progress and which condition the operating rules of the logic of the moment. Only, reasoning reason is permanent; its content becomes modified with time.

Scholarly antiquity only knew the logic of the excluded third, formal logic, for that is all that was permitted by the scientific level of the time.

Aristotle turned over in his grave the day that scientific progress allowed the invention of trivalent logic, better yet, polyvalent and modal logic.

Modern physics first imposed, as a matter of experience, the wave/corpuscle duality, two apparently irreducible forms, one from the other, even though both are of the same reality: light, or in a more general way, the electromagnetic ray.

Such a crucial experience called into existence a new logico-mathematical formalism that will raise, for the first time in the history of the sciences, "doubt," "uncertainty" at the level of logical value.

The philosophy of "everything happens as if" had already seen its day. At the beginning of the century, physics raised the "as if" to the dignity of an operational scientific and philosophical concept, of a logical concept.

Scholarly antiquity could not raise doubt, uncertainty to the level of a logical value, in order thus to create a trivalent logic; for the progress of physics, meaning the scientific knowledge of the real, did not allow it.

One had to wait for the advent of quantum physics in order for mental habits to arduously but assuredly change.

Engels says that it is always nature that corrects the spirit and never the other way around. The process of knowledge, the perfecting of the instrument used for the acquisition of knowledge, which is logic, is therefore infinite.

Reason, the brain, appears like a programmed computer that is using exploiting data according to obsolete rules.

One can suppose that with scientific progress, unsuspected aspects of the real appear every day in the field of experience, mainly at the quantum and the subquantum level of matter, and also at the level of cosmic observations of radio astronomy, and in the realm of molecular biology:

> The light's mass is of a banality that no longer amazes anybody.
>
> One can theoretically set time back into a black hole.
>
> What would be the philosophical implications of the neutral current?
>
> What do Plato's eternal essences of the archetypes become in the face of the hybridization of animal and vegetable cells?

It is a new essence, a new living biological being, who thus is created by humanity, in the laboratory, and this success shows that the barrier between species, between kinds or kingdoms, does not exist in nature at the cellular level: the cells of the animal kingdom do not secrete antibodies that reject the vegetable kingdom's cells; there is fusion of both kingdoms that gives rise to a new zoo-vegetable cellular being capable of reproducing and multiplying itself. Here is what is needed to profoundly modify our thinking habits, a real opening toward an infinite development of our mental structures, our logic, our reason.[104]

The opposites in logic such as:

being/nothingness or
being/non-being
finite/infinite
matter/emptiness
natural/supernatural
etc.

are pure concepts of the spirit that seem to have an *a priori* obviousness only by improper assimilation with pairs of real opposite terms such as: light/darkness or day/night, which are data of experience.

For the philosophers of antiquity, the pairs:

natural/supernatural
matter/emptiness
being/nothingness
light/darkness, etc.

stood out with an equal obviousness. They seemed to derive from the logical structure of the human mind, and from the nature of things.

However, the progress of the sciences forces us today to consider the first two as being simple appearances that do not conform to the intimate nature of things: in fact, even the "ulta-vacuum" obtained in the laboratory still contains some matter and definitely is nothing but a relative notion, and is philosophically or scientifically improper.

Matter is present at different levels everywhere in the universe: an absolute vacuum does not exist. But the philosophy of antiquity, which could not know this, had elevated the void to an absolute, to the level of a scientific and philosophical category. Thus, scientific progress shows us every day that what seemed to be a specific trait of the human mind was nothing but a mental habit that one has difficulty eliminating.

Likewise, the fundamental contradiction that is the basis of the creationist theories comes to light more and more with time.

The absurdity of the notion of nothingness will progressively impose itself in view of the plenitude of matter. Perhaps humanity will one day solve the fundamental problem of philosophy, that of being (why being rather than nothing?), a question posed by Heidegger throughout his life and also by Sartre after him.

In the same way, the present naive and contradictory notion of the infinite will be susceptible to successive revisions, as an element of organized, not constituent, reason. It is directly or indirectly implicated in the quasi-totality of mathematical paradoxes.

The incapacity of language to embrace exactly the contours of the real is often the cause of errors in philosophical, scientific, or even mathematical reasoning.

The accumulation of all these new data of science cannot leave the habits of reasoning and thinking untouched. Logic will necessarily evolve and will indefinitely pass from one stage to another.

Gödel's theorems on the indecisiveness of arithmetic, the indecisiveness or the paradoxes of the infinite only reflect, perhaps, the unfinished character of mathematical logic.[105] We know the famous controversy between formalists and intuitionists on the subject of the foundations of mathematics: For the formalists, particularly David Hilbert, any mathematical problem ultimately can be resolved, even if it cannot be resolved right now due to the fact that the progress of mathematics does not yet allow it. The intuitionists (empiricists or realists) think that everything beyond that which is countable must be suppressed in mathematical formalism. The continuum is no longer, in essence, a present infinite; it is only a medium of free becoming. One must also do away with the theorem of equivalence; the Bolzano-Weierstrass theorem; Zermelo's theorem on the existence of a right order for every set.[106]

The number of the first twin numbers is either finite or infinite: a still irresolvable question. Every even number is either the sum of two first numbers (Goldbach) or it is not: irresolvable for the moment.

There is at least a triplet of integers x, y, z for which $x^n + y^n = z^n$ ($n = 3, 4, 5, \ldots$), or there is none (Pierre de Fermat's theorem): this question has remained undecided since the seventeenth century.[107]

In the context of the general evolution of thought, Black Africa stated the thesis, *idealism* (in the general sense), Greece, the antithesis, *materialism*, and the elements of a synthesis and beyond are only beginning to show up on the scientific horizon: What are the conditions of change in the brain's grammatical rules or in the always provisional logic? What can destiny, humanity's salvation, expect from such a modification relative to the malaise that originated from the enigma of being, and of being in the world, from the conception of the spatial-temporal infinite, from the idea of death?

Lacking a solution in relation to the evolution of the logical structure of thought, would man be able to reconcile himself with himself through the biological path? Would molecular biology be the way to salvation? Man is a metaphysical animal, and it would be catastrophic if a genetic or chemical manipulation were to take away his innate anxiety; this would be equivalent to inflicting on him an infirmity that would make him cease being himself, a being with a destiny, no matter how tragic.

Perhaps the full use of the associations of the brain's billion neurons remains the hopeful path of an evolution that would make the human being a god on Earth, without his having to artificially create a super-*Homo sapiens sapiens* who would endanger the survival of his creator.

The adaptation to a more and more complex environment is perhaps the last evolutionary path that is left for humanity and which leads to progressively putting to work man's tremendous cerebral potential by the triggering of new genetic orders, new associations of neurons that have remained latent until now and whose effects will be beneficial to the whole species.

Credit to Parapsychology

Parapsychological phenomena have entered the laboratory, where reputed scholars (physicists, biologists, physicians, etc.) are studying them.

The second International Congress of Psychotronics took place in Monaco from June 30 to July 4, 1979, and brought together two hundred specialists from twenty-two countries. The president of the International Association of Psychotronics is Professor Zdenek Redjak, researcher in the Department of General Medicine at Charles University in Prague.[108] He affirms that "man, as living matter in general, is capable of action from a distance."

M. M. Martiny, medical anthropologist and president of the International Metaphysical Institute, notes that: "Phenomena such as telepathy, premonition, and clairvoyance do exist at the savage state." At the present time, gifted subjects of transmission are said to be on board Soviet and

American submarines in order to undergo tests designed to verify the possibility of communicating with other receptive subjects situated in laboratories on land where the arriving signals are recorded with all the desired chronological precision! Harold Puthoff, a physicist specializing in lasers, and Russel Targ have been conducting research on vision from a distance since 1973 at the Stanford Research Institute, and they have published a book entitled *Within the Limits of the Spirit*, cited by Pierre Thuillier in *La Recherche*:[109] "The authors demonstrate in an indisputable manner that subjects locked in a room are capable of describing with precision the sites where other subjects are." Olivier Costa de Beauregard thinks that relativist quantum mechanics could aid comprehension of the phenomena of parapsychology.

> If one isolates in two different rooms two people who are very close friends, and if one of them is shown a document, a photograph for instance, that triggers in this person an emotion measured by the plastimograph (invented by Professor Figar to measure the volume of blood running through the arteries), identical changes are observed, at times, in the other person. This is a case of biological or unconscious telepathy.

A Soviet electrician discovered "the Kirlian effect," which bears his name: "By placing a photographic film with an object between two metallic plates connected to a very high frequency electrical current, one obtains a photograph of that object surrounded by a halo. In the case of a hand, the halo seems to vary with the emotional state of the subject."

To underscore the strictly scientific character of their studies, the Eastern scholars preferred to call the new concept "psychotronic" (semantically close to electronic) rather than using the term parapsychology, of Anglo-Saxon origin, or that of metapsychism, of French origin.

The press reported in the last few years that a woman from Lyon dreamed about the winning numbers for the tiercé: 14, 15, 18, which her husband played twenty times the following Sunday and won the jackpot: 2,070,000 francs were paid to him by the chief of the PMU center in Lyon, Mr. Arnaud.

Our point of view on these extremely delicate questions is that the parapsychological phenomena implying simultaneity are not embarrassing to science, for, in the final analysis, they could all be brought back to known physical facts such as the transmission of cerebral electromagnetic waves; this would explain all of the cases of telepathy. It is a different matter in the case of premonition. Only one true case of premonition, meaning the revelation of the future, would be too much for today's science; all its bases would be ruined, as would those of philosophy. The premonitory dream ought not to exist and everything ought to be, in the final analysis, an illusion; otherwise it would certainly mean the revelation of a natural, objective order, independent of us. This then would mean the death of the whole notion of metaphysical freedom, hence, the death of any concrete liberty, of liberty in all its aspects, that liberty so dear which made Goethe's Faust say:

> It is the supreme lesson of wisdom: the only one who deserves life and liberty is the one who has to conquer them each day.
>
> I want to see such a swarming, to live in a free land with a free people. To the passing moment I could then say: stop now, you are so beautiful!
>
> In the presentiment of such a noble happiness, I am now enjoying the supreme moment.[110]

Max Jammer[111] recalls that classical physics is founded on three principles that quantum physics has proven wrong: determinism, objectivity, and completeness. The principle of determinism postulates that all the phenomena of nature obey vigorous laws, in such a way that by knowing the initial conditions of a system, namely its position and its momentum, one can rigorously determine its future evolution.

In quantum mechanics, Werner Heisenberg's uncertainty principle forbids the simultaneous knowledge of two conjugated quantities such as the position and the momentum of a [subatomic] particle. From this then derives an essential impossibility, meaning an impossibility of principle, that of knowing with precision the initial conditions that would permit the tracking of the evolution of a system.

Classical physics affirms that it can describe physical reality independently of its observation. Niels Bohr's theory of correspondence (wave/corpuscle) denies the objectivity of the observations of physics at the quantum level.

Finally, the completeness principle is satisfied when a theory is capable of representing all the aspects of the real.

Albert Einstein, who wanted absolutely to prove quantum physics wrong, because he did not want to renounce the above-stated three principles, tried to demonstrate its incompleteness in a famous article published in 1935 with his collaborators, Boris Podolsky and Nathan Rosen, hence the name often given to this publication: "EPR Paradox," reproducing the three initials.[112] According to Einstein, two correlated particles governed by the function of Max Born's wave interact then move away from each other; by successively determining the position and the impulse of one, without disturbing the other, one nevertheless obtains respectively analogous information about the other. David Bohm took up the same experiment of thought by replacing the two particles with a system represented by a molecule whose two atoms are moving away from each other; the total rotation being nil, one measures on the perpendicular xy axes the components of the atomic rotations of only one of the atoms. Bohr responded by demonstrating that the conjugated quantities chosen by Einstein and his collaborators for their article were not simultaneously observable and that the definition of reality in the EPR thesis was improper.

In 1932, John von Neumann[113] wanted to salvage determinism in quantum mechanics by introducing "hidden variables," meaning unobservable factors. But he ended up with the conclusion that a theory with hidden variables is incompatible with the predictions of quantum mechanics.

However, in 1952, David Bohm proved the opposite by introducing a coherent theory of quantum mechanics with hidden variables. But meanwhile, J. S. Bell's works had removed the difficulties that von Neumann's theses had identified. From then on it was legitimate to apply the theories with hidden variables to quantum mechanics. Bohm tried to reinterpret the EPR argument using the theory of hidden variables, by supposing that the instantaneous transmission of uncontrollable perturbations from one particle to another was possible, whereas the maximal speed of propagation of a signal is that of light, according to the theory of general relativity.

The notion of instantaneity has drawn attention to those of validity and locality, which are, as principles, already contained in Einstein's EPR argument. The "validity" of any theory supposes the confirmation through experiment, and the "locality" postulates that two systems separated in space and that are no longer interacting with each other do not influence one another. Einstein's EPR thesis showed that a theory could not respect at the same time the four principles of reality, completeness, validity, and locality.

A theorem advanced by Bell (Bell's inequality) "implies that the principle of locality is incompatible with that of validity. If quantum mechanics is correct, nature does not verify the principle of locality: two correlated particles, even if they are separated from each other by light-years, are each influenced by the impact of the other. However if nature satisfies the principle of locality and if Bell's inequality is respected, there must be, somewhere, something that is wrong with quantum mechanics. Only experience can decide between these two alternatives."[114]

In the United States and in France, these considerations very rapidly led to the setting up of experiments designed to show the existence of supraluminous phenomena, meaning instantaneous interactions from afar. If one wants to believe their authors, the results obtained thus far confirm the validity of quantum mechanics. If it were really so, modern physics would require us to admit the idea that nature is subject to nonlocal causality (action from a distance), to quantum interconnection and to the inseparability or even "the undivided unity of the universe in its entirety," as Bohm prefers to call it.[115]

In order to avoid the idea of nonlocality, "Olivier Costa de Beauregard uses the reversal of time to account for the EPR correlations between two particles. . . . It [his theory] supposes that information is spread from particle I along a time vector directed toward the past. The message, after having reached the particle that would disintegrate (positron), would go back toward the future in order to reach particle II."[116]

Alain Aspect, of l'Institut d'Optique d'Orsay (see fig. 77), supposes a supraluminous interaction without any transfer of either energy or signal, in order to agree with the notion of general relativity. He set up an experimental device that changes in a shorter period of time than that of the propagation of light, between the two instruments of measurement, so that the correlations would only be due to a supraluminous interaction.

In fact, of all the experimental devices put forth, this is the only one capable of isolating the supraluminous instantaneous phenomena. Alain Aspect's experiment is in progress, and if it confirms the predictions of quantum mechanics, the nonlocality of microphysics will be confirmed.

If it were so, by changing the referential, cause would become effect! Thus, it is the causality of physics in the classical sense that is at stake in these experiments.

From the above one sees that the development of microphysics has contributed powerfully to the advent of the crisis of reason: *a priori* it is no longer rationally absurd to conceive of the interchangeability of cause and effect, born of the dependence of two correlated systems, even at fantastic distances of thousands of light-years. Quantum mechanics is on the verge of negating the local physical causality of classical physics in order to admit the possibility of instantaneous interactions on the scale of the dimensions of the universe.

The same discipline now allows the most advanced research of our time to contemplate going back into the past with a signal, and then changing the direction toward the future. Thus Olivier Costa de Beauregard estimates that the properties of physics revealed by quantum mechanics and by relativity make possible and thinkable the parapsychological phenomena of vision or of action from a distance.[117]

The principles of determinism and locality of classical physics, which Einstein held so dear, are hardly applicable to quantum mechanics, which remains indeterministic, nonobjective, nonlocal, but valid and complete.[118]

Thus, modern physics has created the right situation to teach us that classical logic is nothing but the sum of mental habits, of provisional rules that can change when sovereign experience requires it. Reason lapses, but it does not get caught in a vicious circle; it progresses; it is accomplishing under our eyes the most formidable qualitative leap that it has ever made since the origin of the exact sciences.

The reasoning reason, supported by the experience of microphysics and astrophysics, is going to give birth to a super-logic that will no longer be hampered by the archaeological materials of thought, inherited from the previous phases of the evolution of the scientific mind.

A new philosophical concept has to be forged, that of the "logical availability" of the mind. Tomorrow, sovereign experience will be able to transform into rational fact what seems to us logically absurd or impossible today. The absolute absurd no longer exists with regard to reason. In fact, it is remarkable that the sense of logic is on hold today, and that it awaits the verdict from the laboratory experiments in progress, before it either maintains or rejects the fundamental logical category, that is, the causality of classical physics: this is a remarkable corroboration of Engels's thought, according to which *it is nature that corrects the mind and not the reverse.* And we can add that such a process of the perfecting of reason is infinite. It is the "real" that helps the mind to refine its rationality. Hence, the rationality of the "real" is based on facts and ceases to be inconceivable, and this no matter what the given to the notion of "reality" by quantum mechanics.

There is therefore a moment when reason, having exhausted all the resources of the sum of past scientific experiments and knowledge, remains on hold—mathematical theories then open diverse and equally possible paths—without being able to do anything but stay in the background, while awaiting the only decisive results of experience. It is this new attitude of the scientific spirit, arrived at only with the help of the progress made in quantum mechanics, that merits special designation of a nature that will put its novelty in the limelight: we thought the concept of "logical availability" would fit well.

The unsuspected aspects of the real that are exposed in the field of experiments in microphysics, in astrophysics, and in molecular biology expand the horizons of reasoning; the systematizing theories of the real thus have much richer data, potentially allowing theory to sometimes go as far as predicting some other unknown aspects of the real, before reaching the limits allowed by the facts that were its basis, in other words, before being replaced by a new integrating theory on still broader bases.

The tangibility of such complex parapsychic facts, linked to the ardent desire for survival present in each individual, led renowned physicists such as Jean E. Charon[119] to attempt to make physics take a new leap by endowing it with a bit of psyche, of soul, or of conscience implicit in the electron. Professor Francis Fer holds a similar point of view in an article that appeared in *Science et Vie.*[120] But he does not go so far as to attribute a psyche to the electron; he only confers on it an implicit memory and represents it as an orbital fluid, which allows him, he says, to rediscover the results of quantum mechanics starting from different principles. We must take him at his word, because the calculations could not be explained here in a simple article for the layman. He reminds the reader that the existence of a memory in raw matter in physics has been known since the beginning of the century. Let us illustrate Professor Fer's idea by citing

Figure 77: Here are two types of experiments intended to show the principles of "non-locality" and of "non-separability" in quantum mechanics. Correlations between polarizations of two photons emitted in series by a source (S) are studied in general. In either case, one has to prove that the number of correlations, measured in a circuit of coincidences where the polarizers are rotatable, violates the inequality of Bell, which supposes separability.

In the classic case, by carrying out three series of measurements A, B, C, of the same duration, each corresponding to a direction different from the polarizers, one has $A < B + C$, and in the case of quantum processes, $A > B + C$; this latter measurement, in particular, is reproducible, and the difference in the values exceeds the rate of statistical fluctuations.[1]

The second experiment, by Alain Aspect, would give more convincing results due to the fact that it eliminates, by the introduction of two symmetrical commutators (Ca and Cb) between the polarizers and the source, all interaction between these two. The calculation shows that if the commutators are located each at a distance of six meters from the source and if the commutation time is on the order of twenty nanoseconds, it will be lower than the time of propagation of light from the commutators to the source.

On the other hand, the circuit of coincidence is double, based on the commutators, in such a way that if the polarizers of the two circuits are directed in the same fashion, the photomultipliers (PM) must register the same number of coincidences. Therefore, if with such a device, based on three different directions of the polarizers, one registers, during the same span, three series of measures of coincidences A′, B′, C′, so that the inequality of Bell is violated ($A' > B' + C'$), this would then tend to prove that there exist interactions much faster than light (supra-luminous phenomena) between the source and the polarizers.

It is the principle of separability and even that of causality that would then be questioned seriously.

But in order to avoid violating the fundamental principle of relativity (characteristic limit of the speed of light), Alain Aspect supposes that the supra-luminous communication carries neither signal nor energy: But then how can it be understood as a causal interaction that could modify results of the measurements of events?

Parallel to this, the school of Louis de Broglie attempts to give a causal interpretation of quantum mechanics, by supposing the reality of the pilot wave; but the account of this theory is not within the scope of this book.

1. See Bernard d'Espagnat, *A la recherche du réel* (Paris: Gauthier-Villars, 1980). The two inequalities above are copied from those of Bell.

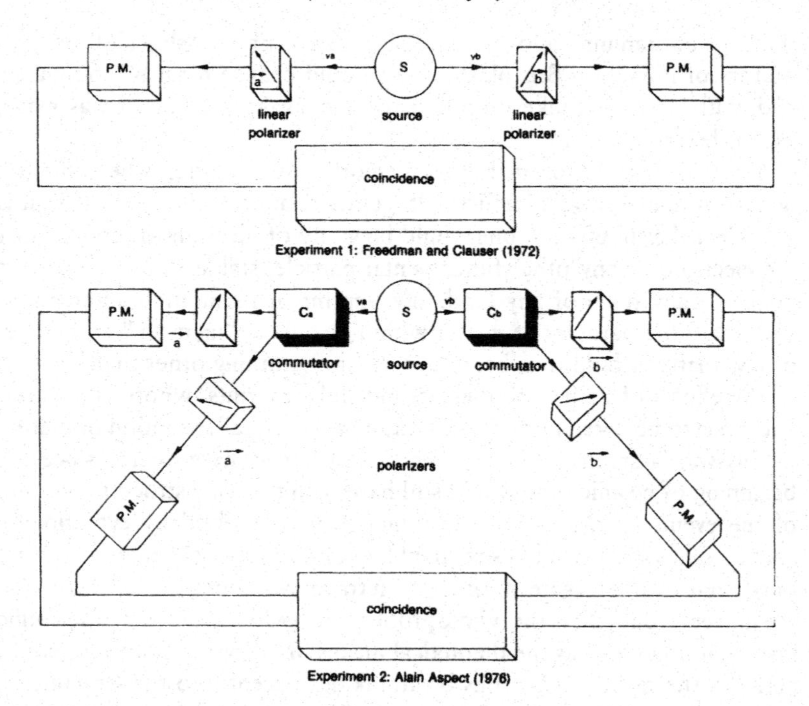

Figure 77: Locality, nonlocality, separability. (Max Jammer, "Le paradoxe d'Einstein-Podolsky-Rosen," in *La Recherche*, no. 111, May 1980, p. 515.)

the "nickel-titanium" alloy. According to Dr. Kenneth Ashbee of the Laboratory of Physics in Bristol, this alloy could change form by cooling off and, with reheating, take on primitive form again in which it was made, as if it had recall of it.

It is very delicate to attribute a memory to raw matter; one easily understands that this is an implicit, altogether relative notion. However, it is very clear that in physics, one would be guilty of idealism to suppose that the electron, or any other fundamental particle, stable or unstable, does not leave any trace of any kind, any imprint of its multiple interactions with the other particles of matter within its milieu; "memory" at the level of raw matter would thus be, in our opinion, nothing other than the sum of the effects of its interactions, its indelible imprints, whose cumulative effect has to be taken into consideration in the overall evolution of matter. In this way, a stable elementary particle that may have existed since the beginning of cosmic time would still have within its fine structure the sum of the events of the universe in which it was involved by evolutionary chance. Thus there would exist an infinity of cosmic clocks that one would only need to interrogate in order to retrace evolution, or the history of the universe. But that is the whole problem: today's instruments of scientific investigation as well as the theoretical means of analysis do not yet permit, perhaps, the realization of this breathtaking descent into the structure of matter and the accounting of the events that have unfolded by a modeling or a quantitative representation: today only the qualitative necessity of the facts is grasped.

So many entities of physics are mastered at the level of mathematical formalization, without their having revealed the secret of their intimate natures. This is the case in all fields: gravitational, electromagnetic, nuclear. How does the gravitational field act "instantaneously" from distances of several billions of light-years? In what intimate, that is, exact, way does the star Vega retain instantaneously within its field of attraction the entire solar system at a distance of several light-years? What is the particle of the gravitational field that is responsible for this attraction? What is the mode of action of gravitation, if it does exist? How does a neutral mass, electrically speaking, attract another neutral mass?

Einstein's powerful answer to all of these questions, through his theory of general relativity and of the geometrization of space, no matter how grandiose, does not account for the intimate mechanism of the interactions of field/matter, and the mystery of the intimate nature of the gravitational field still remains unfathomed. However, its direction, its volume, its diverse effects, etc., can be calculated. It can even be created or eliminated locally; it can be broken away from; its value can be multiplied by *n*; it can be controlled by placing satelitious artificial "moons" around planets, or "planetons" around the Sun, but its intimate nature still remains an enigma to science.

What is the nature of this magnetic force that goes through my hand without causing any damage, and that holds, on the other side, in space, I mean suspended in the air, one ton of metallic matter?

The physicist is not the naturalist who describes in detail the intimate and functional arrangement of the organs of a biological being in order to account for life; that is why he limits himself to representing the electromagnetic field with a tri-rectangular trihedron moving in space.

All of the above shows that classical philosophy, as promoted by men of letters, is dead. A new philosophy will rise from these ashes only if the modern scientist, whether a physicist, a mathematician, a biologist, or anything else, ascribes to a "new philosophy": in the history of thought, the scientist up to now, has almost always had the status of a brute, of a technician, unable to extract the philosophical importance from his discoveries and his inventions, while this noble task always fell to the classical philosopher.

Philosophy's present misery corresponds to the time interval that separates the death of the classical philosopher and the birth of the new philosopher; the latter undoubtedly will integrate in his thought all of the above-signaled premises, which barely point to the scientific horizon, in order to help man reconcile man with himself.

The Ethical Foundations of the Behavior of Modern Man

Ethics stem from philosophy as the practical behavior comes out of the idea that one has about things.

Only scientific knowledge differentiates modern man's ethics from those of primitive man.

It is possible to demonstrate the originally "rational" foundation of all moral behavior, for any given mental level. That which is feeling and moral was first conceived as saving knowledge in the natural order.

A new ethics that largely takes into account objective knowledge (in Jacques Monod's sense) and, in short, the interests of the human species is in the process of being built; it is only difficult to internationalize it because of conflicts of national interests.

Ecology, defending the environment, tends to become the foundation of a new ethnic of the species, based on knowledge: the time is not far off when the pollution of nature will become a sacrilege, a criminal act, even and mainly for the atheist, because of the one fact that the future of humanity is at stake; what knowledge or the "science of the epoch" decrees as harmful to the whole group thus becomes progressively a moral prohibition.

Progress of the Ethical Conscience of Humanity

Humanity's moral conscience progresses, slowly but surely, after all the crimes committed in the past, and that is an opening toward others and a powerful element of hope foreseeing tomorrow the blooming of an era of genuine humanity, a new perception of humanity without ethnic coordinates.

The end of genocide coincides with the emergence of an international opinion. This fact has brought about a modification of the behavior of the capitalist universe toward the weak; and the phenomenon is irreversible; the result is a forced progress of the world's ethical conscience. The Americans did not spontaneously become better than in 1932, the period of the Ku Klux Klan and of quasi-official lynching. It was the appearance of an adversary of their own caliber that imposed on them the revision of their behavior, and so much the better if social and moral progress comes out on top. The young white American, Slain, who drove his car into a meeting of the wizards of the Ku Klux Klan, performed an important civilizing act. In essence, it is a peacemaking, nonviolent act.

It is the worldwide dissemination of information that forces the ethical conscience of humanity to stick to "acceptable" limits, in the absence of radical change.

18

GREEK VOCABULARY OF BLACK-AFRICAN ORIGIN

INVENTORY OF NEGRO-AFRICAN ROOTS IN CLASSICAL GREEK (Method to Follow)

It is necessary first to recall some important facts that will help to illustrate our spiritual endeavor.

"The Greek language has adopted some words that are neither Indo-European nor Semitic; they come from a language that is perhaps more ancient than the Cretan language; in any case, the Cretans and the Mycenaeans had used them."[1]

We know with certainty that Pythagoras, who spent twenty-two years in Egypt in order to be initiated by the Egyptian priests, Plato and Eudoxus (thirteen years), Democritus (five years), and many others received their training in the Pharaonic language, which was that of the priests, their teachers, all the more so because in those periods the insignificance of Greece, in all domains, rendered the necessity for the Egyptian priests to learn Greek absurd.

Thus Diogenes Laërtius tells us that: "Pythagoras learned the Egyptian language, as Antiphon tells us in his book on men of exceptional merit."[2]

With Strabo, we know that the translation of Egyptian works into Greek had become commonplace and that Eudoxus, in particular, did several translations of this kind (see p. 345). This fact is again confirmed by this statement by Diogenes Laërtius: "Eratosthenes in his writings to Bato tells us that he [Eudoxus] composed 'The Dialogues of Dogs'; others say that they were written by the Egyptians in their own language and that he translated and published them in Greece."[3]

These facts were so obvious to the Greeks themselves that Diodorus of Sicily, from antiquity, tried to establish a list of Greek words of Egyptian origin.[4]

These translations not only existed, but, based on an essential difference between the Greek and Pharaonic languages, the Egyptians were already warning against the deformations and the obfuscations that these translations would ultimately engender.

> Thus Hermes, my master, in the frequent talks that he held with me . . . had the habit of telling me that those who would read my books would find their content very simple and clear, whereas, on the contrary, the content is obscure and hides the true meaning of the words, and that it will become even more obscure later when the Greeks will get it in their heads to translate it from our language into theirs, which will lead to a complete distortion of the text and to its total obscurity. On the other hand, expressed in the original language, this discourse conserves in all clarity the meaning of the words: and in fact, even the peculiarity of the sound and the proper intonation of the Egyptian terms retain in themselves the energy of the things that are being said.[5]

Here, then, is a method that one could follow in searching for the Negro-African words that, in the course of these contacts between languages and particularly in these translations, could have passed into the Greek language:

1. After analysis, the Greek term must not be of Indo-European or Semitic origin: in some cases, it can be both African and Semitic.
2. It must be attested to in the Egyptian language.
3. The ideal is that it is attested to in Egyptian, in Greek, and in one or more modern Negro-African languages, to the exclusion of the Indo-European and the Semitic languages; otherwise check the empty boxes with question marks, so that the research will continue.
4. Thus the concepts that would be passed on from the Negro-African languages, particularly from Egyptian to classical Greek, would deal mainly with the different domains of civilization and of science: mathematics, physics, chemistry, engineering, astronomy, medicine, philosophy, etc. . . .[6]

Greek Terms of African Origin (Via the Ancient Egyptian Language)

The following list has, at this point, only a suggestive value. The Greek words cited here are not of Indo-European origin (see P. Chantraine, *Dictionary of Greek*).

EGYPTIAN	GREEK	WOLOF
noh	Νικη = *dorsen:* the one who achieves victory	*noh* = the one who inflicts a defeat
nwn	Νελος = the Nile[7]	*ñul* = black
ba = soul, vital force	Βια = vital force Βα	*Ba* = proper name
tak = to light up	Θαλυκρος = hot, burning	*tãl* = light up *tak* =light up
per = house	Περας = limit[8]	*per* = the fence that surrounds the house, that limits it
p(a)mer = pyramid	Πυραμις = pyramid	*ba-meel* = tomb, tombstone (see p. 276 on the formation of this word)
gen = phallus	Γηγος = patrilinear line, clan[7], stock	*geño* = patrilinear line, stock, or clan
	Βαρβαρος = barbarian. The Romans were barbarians (Strabo). *onom*: anciently attested to in Sanskrit (?) and in Semitic	*bar* → *barbar* = the one who talks fast.
	αναξ = *wanak* (in Mycenaean ϝαναξ language): Sir, lord, master, protector	*wanak* = court of the royal palace, private court, hence: toilets
	Βακχος = name of Dionysus, the branch held by those initiated in the cult of Dionysus, hence the changing of the name to Bacchus.	*bankhas* = branch

NOTES

INTRODUCTION

1. Jacques Ruffie, *De la biologie à la culture* (Paris: Flammarion, 1976), pp. 392–93.

2. *See* figure 7.

3. A street in the business section of Dakar, where Lebanese and Syrian immigrants are a majority.

4. *See* chapters 16 and 17, and figure 75.

5. *See* pp. 405ff.

6. *See* chapters 5–13.

CHAPTER 1

1. A campaign of sampling geological cores in both the Strait of Gibraltar and the two trenches around Sicily would permit C14 dating of the fossilized marine sediments and the determination of the ages of these depressions. The same process would allow precise dating of the formation of the Nile Delta.

Isotopic analysis ($^{18}O/^{16}O$) would seem to prove that the Gibraltar depression is relatively ancient (Duplessy). But that does not exclude the existence of a chain of islands. On the other hand, since the Congress of the UISPP (1976) in Nice, it is known that the earliest navigations date back to the Upper Paleolithic period, 20,000 to 30,000 years ago. The example of the peopling of Australia now stands as proof.

2. Cheikh Anta Diop, "L'apparition de l'*Homo sapiens*," in *Bulletin de l'IFAN*, vol. XXXII, series B, no. 3 (Dakar, 1970), p. 627. *See also* H. Alimen, *Préhistoire de l'Afrique*. (Paris: Ed. Boubée & Cie., 1955).

We share the opinion of Leo Frobenius who thinks that, at the very least, a part of this art is from the Upper Paleolithic period, and the research conducted by Africans should confirm this important opinion. Here is how Frobenius puts it:

> No province of rock painting is as extensive and as fertile in specimens as South Africa. The number of images that are found between the Zambezi River and the Cape, on the one hand, and between the mountains bordering Southwest Africa and those of the East, on the other, far exceed all the other works of prehistoric times and earliest historic times in the whole world. Attempts have been made to explain this fact by saying that the rock paintings of South Africa have an ethographic meaning, that they were all done in a recent time by the Bushmen, and that consequently they were not exposed to the wear and tear of the centuries.
>
> This theory, based on a form of naive enthusiasm of conquest, cannot withstand in-depth study.
>
> The South African engravings, executed with great care, are true artistic marvels. The shapes of the antelopes, the hippopotami, and the rhinoceroses are so finely engraved, the folds of the skin, covered with fur or not, so skillfully rendered that the reliefs almost give one the impression of works in color. The color of the stone (basalt, diabase, diorite) is uniform in both the places that have been worked on and those that have not. This proves their very old age.
>
> By their technique, these rock images are related to the Nubian desert style and to the oldest as well as the most recent styles of the Saharan Atlas Mountains. Their art makes them unique. Both at Klerksdorp and at the Orange River, stone tools of a typically Capsian character have at times been unearthed. No relationship can be discovered between the style of these engraved works and that of the paintings. The two styles are foreign to one another. Sometimes engravings were found underneath the paintings. Leo Frobenius, *Histoire de la civilisation africaine*, translated from the German by H. Back and D. Ermont (Paris: Gallimard, 1952, third edition), pp. 50–52.

3. Museum of Monaco, *see* fig. 13.
4. Cheikh Anta Diop, *op. cit.*, pp. 623–41.
5. Kim Marshall, "The Desegregation of a Boston Classroom," in *Learning*, August–September 1975, p. 38.
6. Asiatic invaders from the East.
7. Karl Richard Lepsius, *Denkmäler aus Aegypten und Aethiopien.*
8. "*Kennst du das Land, wo die Zitronen blühn,*
   Im dunkeln Laub die Gold-Orangen glühn,
   Ein sanfter Wind vom blauen Himmel weht,
   Die Myrte still und hoch der Lorbeer steht,

Kennst due es wohl?
Dahin! Dahin
Möcht ich mit dir, o mein Geliebter, ziehn."
(Goethe, *Gedichte*. Stuttgart: Reclam, 1978, p. 88.)

9. Marija Gimbutas, *Gods and Goddesses of Old Europe 7000–3500 B.C.: Myths, Legends and Cult Images* (Berkeley: University of California Press, 1982). *See also* the article by the same author in *La Recherche*, no. 87, March 1978, pp. 228–35.

10. Marcellin Boule and Henri V. Vallois, *Les Hommes fossiles* (Paris: Masson, 1952), fourth edition, p. 378.

11. Gimbutas, in *La Recherche*, *op. cit.*, p. 234.

12. Gimbutas supposes that this chariot could well be a borrowing made by the hypothetical Kurgans from the Mesopotamians, which implies a nonnegligible Oriental cultural influence on Europe even at that period.

13. What does this vague term mean?

14. *La Recherche*, *op. cit.*, p. 234.

15. *Ibid.* p. 229.

16. Charles Mugler, *Dictionnaire archéologique des techniques* (Paris: Ed. de l'Accueil, 1964), vol. II, p. 682.

17. Raymond Furon, *Manuel de Préhistoire générale* (Paris: Payot, 1958), fourth edition, p. 374.

18. Furon, *op. cit.*, p. 375 (quoting Charles Autran, *Mithra, Zoroastre et la préhistoire aryenne due christianisme*, Paris: Payot, 1935).

See also Cheikh Anta Diop, *Nations nègres et Culture* (Paris: Présence Africaine, 1954) paperback, 1979, pp. 119–20, and *L'Antiquité africaine par l'image*, no. 145–46 of the series "Notes africaines" (Dakar: IFAN, 1976), p. 38, fig. 54; p. 42, fig. 63; and p. 43, map concerning the black virgins.

19. K. Schreiner, *Crania Norvegica*, II, Institutet for sammenlignende Kulturforskning, series B XXXVI, 1946.

20. Boule and Vallois, *op. cit.*, p. 238.

21. *Ibid* pp. 385–86.

22. Gimbutas, *La Recherche*, *op. cit.*, p. 235.

23. *See* note 18 above.

24. This would throw a strange new light on some passages of the *Iliad*; the apparent gap is about thirty years.

25. Except the language of the Luwi or Lui people which is attested to by a few words and the few samples of the Hittite writing in cuneiform: 1700 B.C.

CHAPTER 2

1. Hallam L. Movius, Jr. (Peabody Museum, Harvard University, Cambridge, Massachusetts), "Radiocarbon Dating of the Upper Paleolithic Sequence at the Abri Pataud (Les Eyzies, Dordogne, France)" in *L'Origine*

de l'homme moderne, Paris Symposium, 1969 (Paris: UNESCO, 1972), pp. 253ff.

2. René Verneaux, *Les Origines de l'humanité* (Paris: F. Riedder & Cie., 1926).

3. The "Piltdown fossil" was discovered in 1912 by the British geologist Charles Dawson and principally studied by Smith Woodward, Elliot Smith, A. Keith, and other scholars.

4. Marcellin Boule and Henri V. Vallois, *Les Hommes fossiles* (Paris: Masson et Cie., 1952), fourth edition, p. 193.

5. Contrary to Vallois's conclusion, although quoting the same authors as we: Oakley and Hoskins (Vallois, *op. cit.*, pp. 182, 183, 191).

6. Kenneth P. Oakley, "Analytic Methods of Dating Bones," Report of the British Association for the Advancement of Science, meeting at Oxford, 1954.

7. J. S. Weiner, *The Piltdown Forgery* (Oxford, England: Oxford University Press, 1955).

8. Boule and Vallois, *op. cit.*, p. 196.

9. *Ibid.*, pp. 198–99.

10. *La Recherche*, no. 91, 1978, p. 695.

11. "Datations absolues et analyses isotopiques en préhistoire. Méthodes et limites," printed in *IX*ᵉ Congrès UISPP, Symposium I, Nice: 1976, published by the CNRS, edited by J. Labeyrie and C. Lalou. *See* pp. 46ff.

12. *IX*ᵉ Congrès UISPP, guide book for tour A5 Pyrenees-Nice, 1976, pp. 72ff. Since then, this fossil has been given an older age, estimated at 500,000 years old, which does not change anything. Dating by gamma rays, according to the new method of Yuji Yokoyame and Huu-Van Nguyen, provides nothing new, and merely allows us to assume that the age is greater than 200,000 years (*Le Monde*, April 25, 1981, p. 16).

Likewise, there are too many uncertainties about the fossil recently discovered at Petralona, in Greece. Even if it were a true *erectus*, dated 700,000 years old, this would make no change in the African data which are much older. There has been no radiometric dating. The skull picked up by peasants was not found *in situ*. The age of the teeth, alone, might warrant assigning it a putative age of 700,000 years. Yet these teeth, picked up separately from the fossil, might be those of a bear, according to some specialists. Measurement of fluorine becomes a must.

13. Boule and Vallois, *op. cit.*, pp. 169–78.

14. "There would then be in Europe only a single lineage, that of the Neanderthals, which ended at the close of the Mousterian period. The *pre-Sapiens* lineage, which led to modern man, would have to be found in other regions. It is the one that particularly gave rise to the Cro-Magnons who appear in Europe around 37,000 years ago and who are now known to be of Oriental origin." Bernard Vandermeersch in *La Recherche*, no. 91, 1978, p. 696.

15. Boule and Vallois, *op. cit.*, pp. 477–84. The three reconstructions of the cranial volume of Boskop respectively give 1830 cm^3 (Haughton), 1950 cm^3 (Broom), and 1717 cm^3 (Pycraft).

16. Boule and Vallois, *op. cit.*, p. 395.

17. "The amino acid racemization ages listed in table 3 for Skhul and Tabuzs are consistent with radiocarbon dates and other age estimates for these sites. Oakley lists A.2 dates on charcoal of 39,700 + 800 years (Gr N-2534) for Tabun Layer B and 40,900 + 1,000 (Gr N-2729) for Tabun Layer C. Faunal bone from lower Layer C gives an amino acid age of 44,000 years." Jeffrey L. Bada, in *IX*ᵉ Congrès UISPP, Symposium I, preprinting, p. 51.

18. *L'Origine de l'homme moderne*, Paris Symposium, 1969, UNESCO, 1972. Communications of L. S. B. Leakey, "Homo Sapiens in the Middle Pleistocene and the Evidence of Homo sapiens' Evolution," pp. 25ff.; M. H. Day, "The Omo Human Skeleton Remains," p. 31.

19. Diop, "L'apparition de l'*Homo sapiens*," in *Bulletin de l'IFAN*, vol. XXXII, series B, no. 3, Dakar, 1970, p. 625.

20. *L'Origine de l'homme moderne*, *op. cit.*, p. 217.

21. Andor Thoma, "L'origine de l'homme moderne et de ses races," in *La Recherche*, no. 55, August 1975, p. 334.

22. *See below.*

23. Thoma, *op. cit.*, p. 335.

24. *Ibid.* Prognathism and width of the nostrils are controlled by the same gene.

25. C. Petit and E. Zuckerkandl, *Évolution génétique des populations. Évolution moléculaire* (Paris: Hermann, 1976), p. 178.

26. Jacques Ruffie, *De la biologie à la culture* (Paris: Flammarion), *op. cit.* p. 398.

27. Thoma, *op. cit.*

28. *IX*ᵉ Congrès UISPP, Symposium XXII: La Préhistoire Océanienne. Communication by A. J. Mortlock, "Thermoluminescence. Dating of Objects and Materials from the South Pacific Region," p. 187.

29. Vallois, *L'Anthropologie*, 1929, pp. 39, 77.

30. Carleton S. Coon, *The Origin of Races* (New York: Knopf, 1962).

31. Thoma, in *Anthropologia Hungarica*, no. 5, 1962, pp. 1–111.

32. Thoma, *La Recherche*, *op. cit.*, p. 332.

33. Yves Coppens, F. Clark Howell, Glynn L. Isaac and Richard E. F. Leakey, "Earliest Man and Environment in the Lake Rudolf Basin," in *Prehistoric Archeology and Ecology Series*, Karl W. Butzer and Leslie G. Freeman, eds. (Chicago: University of Chicago Press, 1976), pp. 19–20.

34. *See Nature*, July 20, 1969.

35. Vallois, *op. cit.*, p. 464; *see also* "Early Human Remains in East Africa," in *Man*, April 1933.

36. Diop, *op. cit.*, pp. 627–28.

37. Movius, *op. cit.*, pp. 253ff.

38. The following table is taken from the article by Movius, *op. cit.*, pp. 258–59. The abbreviation B.C. means "before Christ," whereas B.P. means "before present" (1950 taken as year zero).

—Layer 14 (Base Aurignacian): more than 7m deep, 34,000 B.P. or 32,050 + 675 B.C.

—Layer 13 (Base Aurignacian), no date.

—Layer 12 (Base Aurignacian), 32,250 B.P. + 500 or 30,300 B.C.

—Layer 11 (Base Aurignacian), 32,600 B.P. + 800 or 30,650 B.C.

—Layer 7 (Intermediate Aurignacian), 32,800 B.P. + 500 or 30,850 B.C.

—Layer 5 (Perigordian IV) 27,900 B.P. + 260 or 25,950 B.C.

—Layer 4 (Noaillian or Perigordian Vc), 27,060 B.P. + 370 or 25,110 B.C.

—Layer 3 (Perigordian) VI) 23,010 B.P. + 170 or 21,000 B.C.

—Layer 2 (Proto-Magdalenian), 21,940 B.P. + 250 or 19,990 B.C.

39. *GrN—2526* according to Vogel and Waterbolk, in Movius, *op. cit.*, p. 259.

40. Boule and Vallois: *op. cit.*, p. 297, p. 51.

41. François Bordes, in *L'Origine de l'homme moderne*, *op. cit.*, pp. 211ff.

42. Bordes, *op. cit.*, p. 214. Diop, *op. cit.*, p. 631.

43. Movius, *op. cit.*, p. 259, note I. Reindeer Cave (Arcy-sur-Cure), *GrN—1736*: 33,720 B.P. + 410 or 31,770 B.C.; *GrN—1742*: 33,860 B.P. + 250 or 31,910 B.C. These samples were collected at level VIII which belonged to Perigordian I.

44. D. de Sonneville-Bordes, "Environnement et culture de l'homme du Périgordien ancien dans le Sud-Ouest de la France. Données recoltées," in *L'Origine de l'homme moderne*, *op. cit.*, pp. 141ff.

45. In other words, Negroid (underlined by author).

46. Boule and Vallois, *op. cit.*, p. 311.

47. *IX*[e] Congrès UISPP, Symposium XVI: "L'Aurignacien en Europe." Edited by Janusz Kozlowski, Nice, 1976, pre-printing.

Finally, the recent discovery of the Saint-Césaire Neanderthal pointedly confirms our stance in regard to the nonexistence of a *Homo sapiens sapiens* indigenous to Europe and anterior to the Grimaldi Negroid. This Neanderthal who lived only 35,000 years ago is found associated with the most typical forms of Castelperronian industry, of which he is the true inventor. A crossbreeding with *Homo sapiens* becomes probable: Brno, Predmost. (François Lévèque and Bernard Vandermeersch, in *La Recherche*, no. 119, February 1981, pp. 242–44.)

48. "Étude et remontage due massif facial du 'Négroïde de Grimaldi,'" by F. Mantelin, University of Paris VII, 1972, 71pp.

"Reconstruction de la denture de l'adolescent du Grimaldi," doctoral dissertation in dental surgery, Max Banti, University of Paris VII, 1969.

Articles in journals, P. Legoux, "Étude odontologique de la race de Grimaldi," in *Bulletin du Musée d'anthropologie préhistorique de Monaco*, no. 10, 1963, pp. 63–121. L. Barral and R. P. Charles, "Nouvelles données anthropométriques et précision sur les affinités systématiques des négroïdes de Grimaldi," *Ibid.*, no. 10, 1963, pp. 123–39. G. Olivier and F. Mantelin, "Nouvelle reconstitution du crâne de l'adolescent de Grimaldi," *Ibid.*, no. 19, 1973–1974, pp. 67–82.

49. Boule and Vallois, *op. cit.*, p. 301.

50. *Ibid.*, p. 301.

51. *Ibid.*, pp. 299–300.

52. *L'Origine de l'homme moderne, op. cit.*, pp. 287ff. *See also* Diop, *op. cit.*, pp. 636ff.

53. *La Recherche*, no. 55, August 1975.

54. *See La Recherche*, no. 108, February 1980.

55. *Archeologia*, no. 123, October 1978, p. 14. *See also* Kia Lan-Po, *La Caverne de l'Homme de Pékin*, People's Republic of China, first edition, 1978, p. 2.

56. Boule and Vallois, *op. cit.*, p. 405.

57. *Ibid.*, p. 406.

58. Diop, *Parenté génétique de l'égyptien pharaonique et des langues négro-africaines* (Dakar: IFAN, 1977), pp. xxix–xxxvii.

59. *La Recherche*, no. 89, May 1978, p. 447.

60. *Raison Présente*, no. 53, pp. 135–36. Data prepared by Georges Chappaz, Jean-Paul Coste, and France Chappaz.

61. Thoma, in *La Recherche*, *op. cit.*, p. 333.

Nothing is more contrary to the truth than the assertion that "Coon's theory has been quasi-officially accepted by the anthropologists assembled by UNESCO in 1969 in Paris" (*Race et Intelligence*, p. 45); and that "the polycentric theory is now supported by the majority of the votes among specialists, as demonstrated by the Symposium of Paris on the origins of *Homo sapiens*" (p. 88). In fact, the opinion of the majority of the participants at this symposium cannot be confused with that of the majority of all the specialists who were absent and are of the opposite opinion. Everything depends on the organizers and on the manner of the invitation. Many specialists did not wish to participate in this symposium for a variety of reasons.

62. Jean-Pierre Hébert, *Race et Intelligence* (Paris: Éditions Copernic Factuelles, 1977), p. 90.

63. Thoma, in *L'Origine de l'homme moderne*, *op. cit.*, p. 84.

64. *Race et Intelligence*, *op. cit.*, p. 91.

65. *Ibid.*

66. *Ibid.*

67. WASP: White Anglo-Saxon Protestant.

68. In the last century, Black children were sold by the pound in America.

69. Diop, *Parenté génétique de l'égyptien pharaonique et des langues négro-africaines*, *op. cit.*, "Processus de sémitisation" chapter.

70. Nobuo Takano, M.D. *See* p. 55.

71. *Le Monde*, February 4–5, 1979, p. 2.

72. *Ibid.*

73. Diop, "Pigmentation des anciens Égyptiens. Test par la mélanine," in *Bulletin de l'IFAN*, vol. XXXV, series B. no. 3, July 1973, pp. 515–31.

74. Petit and Zuckerkandl, *op. cit.*, pp. 190–91. *See* fig. 7.

75. Certainly a regrettable prejudice, which Montesquieu in his time was already citing, but which leaves no doubt about the fact that the people who behaved in this way were not white-skinned.

76. *See* Diop, *L'Antiquité africaine par l'image*, *op. cit.*, p. 28, figs. 40 and 41.

77. Gaston Maspero, *Histoire ancienne des peuples d'Orient* (Paris: Hachette, 1917), twelfth edition, p. 259.

78. Raymond Mauny, *Tableau géographique de l'Ouest africaine au moyen âge* (Dakar: IFAN, 1961), p. 59. A. Lucien Guyot, *Origine des plantes cultivées, "Que sais-je?"* Series (Paris: Presses Universitaires de France, 1942), p. 69.

CHAPTER 3

1. Dragoslav Ninkovich and Bruce C. Heezen (Lamont Geological Observatory), *Columbia University contribution*, no. 819.

2. Jacques Pirenne, *Histoire de la civilisation de l'Égypte ancienne* (Boudry, Switzerland: Ed. de la Baconnière, 1961), p. 203.

3. *Ibid.*, p. 205.

4. *Ibid.*, p. 206.

5. *Ibid.*, p. 209.

6. *Ibid.*, p. 213 (quoting Breasted).

7. *Ibid.*

8. James H. Breasted, *Ancient Regime*, Vol. II, p. 493 (quoted by Pirenne).

9. *Ibid.*, p. 446.

10. *Ibid.*, p. 449.

11. *Ibid.*, pp. 484–85.

12. *Ibid.*, p. 509.

13. *Ibid.*, pp. 510–11.

14. *Ibid.*, p. 447.

15. *Ibid.*, p. 482.

16. Gaston Maspero, *Histoire ancienne de peuples d'Orient*, *op. cit.*, pp. 236–37.

17. *Ibid.*, p. 237.

18. A slightly elevated pillar without either a base or a head: a kind of small architectural monument commemorating an event, a victory, for example.

19. Maspero, *Histoire ancienne des peuples d'Orient*, *op. cit.*, p. 237.

20. *Ibid.*, pp. 237–38.

21. *Ibid.*, p. 242.

22. *Ibid.*, pp. 239–40.

23. *Ibid.*, pp. 257 and 259.

24. *Ibid.*, p. 268.

25. *Ibid.*, p. 269.

26. Herodotus, *Histoires*, Book II, pp. 102–103.

27. An exclusively Egypto-Ethiopian practice that dates back to prehistory. Elliot Smith has verified that the predynastic Egyptians of the protohistorical era were circumcised. (*See* Herodotus, *Ibid.*, pp. 104–105.)

28. The goddess Isis is the figurehead of the prow of a ship that is the coat of arms of the city of Paris. This latter influence may well date back to the era of the navigations of the Phoenicians of Sidon. *See* B. Stavisky, "Cultural Ties Between Ancient Central Asia and Pre-Islamic Egypt," in *Ancient Orient* (Moscow: Editions Naura, 1975).

29. Herodotus, *op. cit.*, p. 106.

30. The Wolof word *Naar* (Syrian), of an unknown, but not Arab, etymology; does it come from *Nahr el-Kelb*?

31. Gustave Lefebvre, *Grammaire de l'égyptien classique*, Cairo, 1940, p. 34.

32. "Secret writing or cryptography, known perhaps since the Old Kingdom, had been practiced in the Middle Kingdom as well as under the Eighteenth and Nineteenth Dynasties. It is in this writing that we must look for the principle of innovations contained in the writings of the Greek and Roman epoch. Taking into consideration the particular character of this writing, which is above all a game, its processes come down to the core of those of non-coded writing.

Here indeed are some of its principal characteristics: it uses extraordinarily developed alphabetical signs, the list of which increases inordinately according to whim of the scribes; the new uniliteral phonograms grew out of the well-known process of acrophony." (Gustave Lefebvre, *Grammaire de l'égyptien classique*, Cairo, 1940, p. 38.)

33. *See* p. 113, the poetic hymn of Amon.

34. Around 2340 B.C., Sargon I of Akkad attempted the unification of the Mesopotamian city-states in order to realize the first national Semitic state by regrouping several towns. It was a short-lived attempt at national unification, not an attempt to create an empire in the true sense of this term.

CHAPTER 4

1. a) The Oriental Institute, *News and Notes*, no. 37, November 1977.
b) *International Herald Tribune*, March 9, 1979, "Nubian Monarchy May Be World's Oldest," by Boyce Rensberger.

2. Otto Muck, *Cheops et la Grande Pyramide*, translated from the German by Georges Rémy (Paris: Payot, 1978), p. 36 (quoting Scharff).

3. *Ibid.*, p. 37.

4. *See* Cheikh Anta Diop *Parenté génétique de l'égyptien pharaonique et des langues négro-africaines*, *op. cit.*, p. 287.

5. *Voyages d'Ibn Battuta*, vol. IV, translated by C. Défremery and B. R. Sanguinetti, 1922, p. 388.

6. *Ibid.*, p. 417.

7.

EGYPTIAN	WOLOF
šema = south; *our medj*	*dëm* = to go toward
šema = *wr md sma* = (counsel)	to orient oneself toward
from the ten greats of the South	(the South)

8. Émile Amélineau, *Prolégomènes à l'étude de la religion égyptienneé* (Paris: Ernest Leroux, 1908), pp. 133–34.

9. *Ibid.*

10. *Ibid.*, p. 90.

CHAPTER 5

1. For more extensive treatment of these ideas, *see* Cheikh Anta Diop, *L'Unité culturelle de l'Afrique noire* (Paris: Présence Africaine, 1959).

2. Exception: The Massai people of East Africa, who have no ancestral cult and leave their dead to predators, but who are, in fact, seminomadic.

3. *See* Émile Benveniste, *Le Vocabulaire des institutions indo-européenes: Économie, Parenté, Société* (Paris: Éditions de Minuit, 1969), pp. 155–56.

4. Polyandry is encountered among certain marginal societies in the process of regression and of physical degeneration.

5. Hadid of the Koran and the Bible.

CHAPTER 6

1. Edward E. Evans-Pritchard, A. R. Radcliffe-Brown and Forde, *Systemès familiaux et matrimoniaux en Afrique. Parenté et communauté locale chez les Nouers*, p. 483.

2. Category of the name that he is known by.

3. Alphonse Tiéron, *Le Nom africain ou Langage des traditions* (Paris: Maisonneuve et Larose, 1977), pp. 74–75.

4. Robert H. Lowie, Traité de sociologie primitive, translated from the English (Paris: Payot, 1936), pp. 75–76.

5. *Ibid.*, p. 76.

6. *See* Pierre Clément, "Le Forgeron en Afrique Noire," in *Revue de Geographie humaine et d'Ethnologie*, no. 2, April–June 1948.

7. Cheikh Anta Diop, "Introduction à l'étude des migrations en Afrique Centrale et Occidentale. Identification de berceau nilotique du peuple sénégalais," in *Bulletin de l'IFAN*, Vol. XXXV, series B, no. 4, Dakar, 1973.

8. *Ibid.*, pp. 769–92.

9. Émile Benveniste, *Le Vocabulaire des institutions indo-européennes: Économie, Parenté, Société* (Paris: Éditions de Minuit, 1969), p. 217.

10. *Ibid.*, p. 218.

11. *Ibid.*, p. 223.

12. *Ibid.*, p. 279.

CHAPTER 7

1. Friedrich Engels. *L'Anti-Dühring*, translated by Émile Bottigelli, second edition, (Paris: Éditions Sociales, 1963), p. 215.

2. Louis Halphen, *Les Barbares, peuples et civilisations*, vol. V, second edition (Paris: Felix Alcan, 1930), p. 56.

3. *Ibid.*

4. Joseph Arthur Gobineau, *Essai sur l'inégalité des races humaines*, first edition, 1853–1855.

5. A. Cuvillier, *Introduction à la sociologie* (Paris: Armand Colin, 1967), pp. 152–53ff. The weaker the cephalic index, the more prominent the dolichocephaly.

6. *Ibid.*, pp. 153–54.

7. *Ibid.*, p. 154.

CHAPTER 8

1. Some authors have felt that they could speak of the birth of African states within zones of contact with other people, owing to the control of commerce at the level of these boundaries, while forgetting that the efficiency that permits the control of commerce as well as the notion of boundaries imply the prior existence of a state.

2. And more generally, to the whole Christian West engaged in the Crusades against Islam or the "Saracens"; from this angle it would be interesting to have an African rereading of the epic literature of the Middle Ages, and of the *Song of Roland* in particular. That is where this dialectical opposition that marks the awakening consciousness of the West vis-à-vis the Arab world is especially clear.

CHAPTER 9

1. J. Chesneaux, in *La Pensée*, no. 114, Paris, p. 36, note 6.

CHAPTER 10

1. Jacques Pirenne: *Histoire de la civilisation de l'Égypte ancienne, op. cit.*, vol. I, pp. 328–29.

2. "Thieves become owners and the former rich are robbed. Those wearing fine linen are beaten. Ladies who have never set foot out of doors now go out. The children of nobles are beaten against the walls. People try to get out of the city. Gates, walls, columns are set afire. The children of the great are thrown into the streets. The great are hungry and in distress. Servants are now served. Noble ladies are running away . . . [their children] bow down for fear of being killed. The country is full of factionists. The man who goes to till the fields carries a shield. A man kills his own brother born of the same mother. Roads are spied upon. People hide in the bushes until [the farmer] returns in the evening in order to steal his load: beaten with sticks, he is shamefully killed. Cattle herds roam haphazardly, there is nobody to gather them. The wealthy class is completely dispossessed. Those who owned clothes now wear rags. The great are employed in stores. The ladies who were in their husbands' beds now lie on animal skins, suffering like servants. . . . Noble ladies are hungry. They offer their children on beds [for prostitution]. . . . Each man takes away the animals that he has branded with his name. Harvested crops rot on all sides; there are shortages of clothes, spices, oil. Filth is everywhere. [State] stores are destroyed and their guards slammed to the ground, people eat grass and drink water. They are so hungry that they steal food from the mouths of pigs. The dead are thrown into the river; the Nile is now a sepulcher. Public archives are divulged.

"Let's go! say the ushers, let's go and loot. The archives of the sublime chamber of justice are taken away, the secret places are divulged, public offices are violated, declarations [acts of the cadastre of vital statistics] are taken away, so serfs becomes masters. Civil servants are killed, their documents stolen. . . . The king's silo belongs to anyone who yells: Here I am, give me that. The king's entire household has no more revenues. The laws of the chamber of justice are thrown into the vestibule. They are trampled on in the public squares; the poor tear them to pieces in the streets. Things happen that never took place in the past: the king is kidnapped by the poor. What the pyramid had hidden is now empty. *A few men with neither hearth nor home have plundered the country of the royalty.*

"The poor make an attempt against the state of the divine ennead. . . . The son of the mistress now is the son of the servant."

Following this reversal of social situation, the former class of the poor kept, for a certain time at least, the positions thus conquered, for economic life and commerce resumed their normal course; wealth reappeared but had changed hands: ". . . there is luxury in the country, but it is the former poor who have the wealth. He who had nothing now has wealth. He who had nothing now has treasures and the great flatter him. . . . He who had no maid now has servants." (*op. cit.*, p. 392.)

3. Until then, only the Fari rose from the dead and could rejoin his *ka*, or *kau* (the eternal part of him) in heaven.

4. On different levels, this reminds one of the antique and Germanic "modes" of ownership described by Engels and recalled by Godelier (*see* p. 246).

5. R. Grousset, *Histoire de la Chine* (Paris: Fayard, 1942), chapter 20, pp. 203–207.

6. N. D. Fustel de Coulanges, *La Cité antique* (Paris: Hachette, 1930), p. 243.

7. Zeno, Socrates . . .

CHAPTER 11

1. The battle of Ra against Apap.

2. Referring to pp. 226–67, one realizes, for instance, the gross errors that could be made by applying glotto-chronology to the evolution of Latin.

3. M. I. Fineley, *Les anciens Grecs* (Paris: Maspéro), 1977, p. 19.

4. Victor Bérard, *Résurrection d'Homère. Au temps des héros.*

5. Fineley, *op. cit.*, p. 30.

6. Jean Delorme, *La Grèce primitive et archaïque* (Paris: Armand Colin, 1969), collection U2, pp. 64–66.

7. *Ibid.*, pp. 66–67.

8. *Ibid.*, p. 68.

9. *Ibid.*, p. 72.

10. Fineley, *op. cit.*, p. 50.

11. Delorme, *op. cit.*, p. 75.

12. Fineley, *op.cit.*, p. 68.

13. *Ibid.*, p. 73.

14. *Ibid.*, p. 79.

15. *Ibid.*, p. 84.

16. Rudyard Kipling.

17. Cheikh Anta Diop, *L'Afrique Noire précoloniale* (Paris: Présence Africaine, 1960), pp. 113–14.

CHAPTER 12

1. *Antériorité des civilisations nègres: Mythe ou vérité historique?* (Paris: Présence Africaine, 1967). The others have been cited.

2. *See Jeune Afrique*, no. 475, February 10, 1970, p. 26.

3. N. Ngono-Ngabission reports in this article that M. Malam Adi Bwaye, a fifty-year-old Nigerian of the Jukun tribe from central Nigeria, former secondary school teacher of sience, did not close his eyes for two years, since 1967 to be exact. He was *aku uka*, meaning king of the Jukun,

and had been chosen as of 1961 from among several candidates. He was then enthroned with all the pomp required by his rank. But the Jukun tradition requires that the *aku uka* reign for seven years only and the king must be sacrificed at the end of his term. During the last month of his reign, he is strangled in his sleep by the priest of the cult. Now, the seventh year had expired as of December 1967. Refusing to comply with the rite till the end, Malam slept only with a loaded revolver under his pillow.

Nigerian public opinion was divided upon learning this. A poll conducted by the *Lagos Sunday Times* revealed that, out of 500 responses including that of the party involved, 55 percent was against carrying out the sentence, but 45 percent was for it. Toward the end of his life, which terminated through natural causes on January 18, 1970, he was guarded twenty-four hours a day by the Nigerian federal police.

4. Leo Frobenius, *Histoire de la civilisation africaine*, *op. cit.*

5. Otto Much, *Cheops et la Grande Pyramide*, *op. cit.*, p. 85. *See* the end of the chapter, note II, pp 236–37.

6. *See* Cheikh Anta Diop, *Nation nègres et Culture* (Paris: Présence Africaine, 1954) (revised paperback, 1979), p. 210.

7. Charles G. Seligman, *Egypt and Negro Africa: A Study in Divine Kingship* (London: George Routledge & Sons, 1934).

8. J. P. Vernant, *Les Origines de la pensée grecque.*

9. *See* Théophile Obenga, *La Cuvette Congolaise: Les hommes et les structures* (Paris: Présence Africaine, 1976). *See below* the analysis of the political organization of the Cayor of the Damels.

10. King of a region of precolonial Senegal: the Cayor.

11. Diop, *L'Afrique Noire précoloniale*, *op. cit.*, p. 39.

12. Diop, *L'Antiquité africaine par l'image*, *op. cit.*, p. 36, fig. 91.

13. *See* page 217, the reproduction of the map of the "correspondences between the dominant economy of a region or of a given group and the attitude of that group toward the blacksmith," taken from Pierre Clément: "Le forgeron en Afrique Noire," in *Revue de Géographie humaine et d'Ethnologie*, no. 2, April–June 1948, p. 51.

14. Diop, *L'Afrique Noire précoloniale*, *op. cit.*, pp. 84–87.

EGYPTIAN	WOLOF
Per-aa = Pharaoh	*Fari* = supreme king *Fara* = officer in charge *Fara* lĕku = keeper of the harem
P(a)our = the chief > *P-our* = the king	*Bur* = the king *P* (Egypt) → *b* (Wolof)
Π-oȣpo = *P.ouro* = (Coptic) king	

EGYPTIAN	WOLOF
N D(e)m = the throne	*NDam* = glory *NDamel* = glorification whence *NDamel* = kingship in the Cayor and *Damel* = the king of the Cayor
Remen = cubit, unit for measuring the fields	*Laman* = landowner *r* (Egyptian) → *l* (Wolof)

15. Clément, "Le forgeron en Afrique Noire," *op. cit.*, p. 51.

16. *Ibid.*, pp. 43–44. Note the survival of the king-blacksmith among the Malinke people of the Sahel.

17. The name of Ghana has caused much ink to flow: we only know that it was probably not an indigenous name; similarly, the name *Ganâr* by which we, Senegalese, designate Mauritania is alien to the language of this country, the Arabic or the Berber; therefore, the name of the former empire of Ghana and that of today's Mauritania could well have an etymological origin that is identical and foreign. In fact, during the Roman epoch, not only were the inhabitants of the Canary Islands called *Canari*, but those of the country south of Morocco as well, by assimilation with the first.

The Roman historian Pliny the Younger (Book V, chapter I), referring to the expedition by the praetor Suetonius Paulinus against the Getulies (a western group of Lybians living in the south of Morocco) in A.D. 41–42, says that: "The Romans pushed south into the territory of a people called the Canarii, who mainly ate dogs and the meat of wild animals. . . . These Canarii lived near Perorsos south of the Getules, near the Salsum River, Oued-el-Melh (rio Salado), more precisely across from the Canary Islands." The Gannaria Cape, which Ptolemy (*Geography*) mentions on the African coast, at 20°11′ latitude north, at the exact level of the Canaries, must have derived its name from these people, the Kannurich of the Arab authors.

Taking into account what has been said above, it is not implausible to propose the following diagram, based on Ptolemy's statement:

Gannaria → { *Ganâr* ; = Mauritania
Gana = ancient Ghana }

18. *See L'Afrique Noire précoloniale*, *op. cit.*, p. 85.

19. *Ibid.*, p. 51.

20. Herodotus, *Euterpe*, "Description de la société égyptienne"; *see also L'Afrique Noire précoloniale*, *op. cit.*, pp. 7–14.

21. *See L'Antiquité africaine par l'image*, *op. cit.*, pp. 45–53.

22. Diop, *Parenté génétique de l'égyptien pharaonique et des langues négro-africaines*, *op. cit.*, chapter entitled "Processus de sémitisation."

23. *See above*, chapter 3.

24. Diop, *Parenté génétique de l'égyptien pharaonique et des langues négro-africaines, op. cit., p. 88.*

25. *Diawerigne* and *Diaoudine* are two variants of the same word.

26. The voyage of the Portuguese Cadamosto to Wolof country, in 1455, is a reference, because the author already found the kingdom of the Damels of the Cayor in place.

27. Seligman, *Egypt and Negro Africa: A Study in Divine Kingship, op. cit.*, p. 52.

28. Flinders Petrie, *The Making of Ancient Egypt* (London: The Sheldon Press, 1939), pp. 69–70. *See also* Diop, *Anteriorité des civilisations nègres* (Paris: Présence Africaine, 1967), p. 73.

29. Seligman, *Egypt and Negro Africa: A Study in Divine Kingship, op. cit.*, p. 3. The Mashona (Zimbabwe, ex-Rhodesia), Balobedu (North Transvaal), Bakitara, Banyankole, Wawanga, Zulu, Jukun, Bambara, Mbum, etc.

30. *Ibid.*, p. 60.

31. *Ibid.*, p. 10.

32. Edward E. Evans-Pritchard, *Les Nuer* (Paris: Gallimard, 1937), translated from the English.

33. Otto Muck, *Cheops et la Grande Pyramide, op. cit.*, pp. 85–86.

CHAPTER 13

1. *Sur le "mode de production asiatique"* (Paris: Éditions Sociales, second edition, 1974). Published under the direction of the Centre d'Etudes et de Recherches Marxistes (C.E.R.M.).

2. *Ibid.*, p. 299.

3. *Ibid.*, pp. 305–306.

4. *Ibid.*, p. 294, note I.

5. *Ibid.*, p. 47.

6. *Ibid.*, p. 66.

7. *Ibid.*, p. 67.

8. *Ibid.*, p. 283. Marx quoted by Charles Parrain.

9. *Ibid.*, p. 81.

10. The danger is real but avoidable.

11. *Ibid.*, p. 81

12. *Ibid.*, pp. 91–92.

13. *Ibid.*, p. 89.

14. *Ibid.*, p. 96.

15. *Ibid.*, p. 124.

16. *Ibid.*, p. 257.

17. *Ibid.*, pp. 263–64.

18. *Ibid.*, p. 267.

19. *Ibid.*, pp. 271–72.

20. *Ibid.*, p. 273.
21. *Ibid.*, p. 273.
22. *Ibid.*, p. 285.
23. *Ibid.*, p. 289.
24. *Ibid.*, p. 473.
25. *Ibid.*, pp. 290–92.
26. *Ibid.*, p. 293.
27. *Ibid.*, p. 180.
28. *Ibid.*, p. 297.
29. Was not the exiguity of England and of the Netherlands a factor for success of the revolution, recalling, to some extent, the case of the Greek city-state and of the Latin state (from the sixth to the third century B.C.)?
30. The exception confirms the rule: Spartacus, Bagdad (ninth century), Toussaint Louverture.
31. *Ibid.*, p. 301.
32. *Ibid.*, p. 302.
33. *Ibid.*, p. 302.
34. *Ibid.*, p. 301.
35. Long after the Egyptian cosmogonies, and particularly after the Hermopolitan cosmogony.
36. *Ibid.*, p. 303.
37. *Ibid.*, p. 369.
38. Kautilya, *Arthashastra* II, 16.
39. *Sur le "mode de production asiatique," op. cit.*, p. 195.
40. *Ibid.*, p. 169.
41. *Ibid.*, p. 170.
42. Cheikh Anta Diop, *Nations nègres et Culture*, *op. cit.*, chapter VII.
43. Karl Marx, *Capital*, Book III, Vol. VIII, p. 172.
44. This is what we compare to the general mobilization in modern states.
45. *Sur le "mode de production asiatique," op. cit.*, p. 175.
46. *Ibid.*, p. 178.
47. J. P. Vernant, *Les origines de la pensée grecque*, *op. cit.*, p. 14.
48. Charles Parrain in *Sur le "mode de production asiatique," op. cit.*, p. 179. One will note that = *dmi* = town, city, habitation in ancient Egyptian.
49. *Ibid.*, p. 187.
50. *Ibid.*, p. 189.
51. *Ibid.*, p. 190.
52. Giacomo Devoto, *La Crisi del latino nel V°* secolo a. Ch., Studii, Clasice, VI, 1964.

53. One can thus measure the errors to which glotto-chronology is exposed as a method of dating in linguistic archaeology.

54. Karl Marx, Friedrich Engels, *German Ideology*, p. 24, as well as note 2 of the first part of *L. Feuerbach et la fin de la philosophie classique allemande*.

55. André Aymard et Jeannine Auboyer, *Rome et son Empire* (Paris: Presses Universitaires de France, 1959), pp. 140–50.

In the Roman Empire, it was in order to escape fiscal insecurity that the small peasantry put itself under the protection of the great landowners, thus losing, little by little, its land and its liberty, in order to become serfs later in the Middle Ages. In fact, when with the barbarian invasions, physical insecurity prevailed in the countryside, the right conditions for the birth of the feudal system were in place.

CHAPTER 14

1. Georges Hardy, *Une conquête morale: l'enseignement en A.O.F. (Paris: Armand Colin).*

2. *Satire*, XV, verses 126–28.

3. Joseph Arthur Gobineau, *Essai sur l'inégalité des races humaines, op. cit.*, Book II, chapter VII.

CHAPTER 15

1. Jean-Paul Sartre, *Situations III*, "Orphée noir" (Paris: Gallimard, 1949), p. 245.

2. *Ibid.*, p. 246.

3. *Ibid.*, p. 243.

4. *Ibid.*, p. 248.

5. *Ibid.*, p. 247.

6. *Ibid.*, p. 248.

7. *Ibid.*, p. 244.

8. André Malraux, *Le Musée imaginaire* (Paris: Gallimard, 1965).

CHAPTER 16

1. Paul Ver Eecke, *Les Oeuvres complètes d'Archimède* (Paris: Albert Blanchard, 1960). Introduction, pp. xliv–xlv.

2. Ver Eecke, *op. cit.*, p. xlix.

3. V. V. Struve, *Mathematischer Papyrus des Staatlichen Museums der Schönen Künste in Moskau.* (Quellen und Studien zur Geschichte der Mathematik; Abteilung A: Quellen, Band I) Berlin, 1930.

4. "*Die Aufgabe Nr 10 hat uns aber zusammen mit der Formel für die Kugeloberfläche auch die Formel für den Kriesumfang gebracht.*" (Struve, *op cit.*, pp. 177–78.)

5. Ver Eecke, *op. cit.*, p. xxxi.

6. *See* pp. 345–46.

7. Struve, *op. cit.*, p. 190.

8. *See* pp. 323–24.

9. Ver Eecke, *op. cit.*, vol. I, p. XXIX.

10. *See* L. Croon, *Lastentransport beim Bau der Pyramiden (Transport de charges lors de la construction des pyramides)* (Hannover: Diss, 1925).

11. "So mussen wir jetzt zugeben, dass die Ägypter in der Mechanik mehr Kenntnisse hatten, als wir es ihnen zutrauen wollten." (Struve, *op. cit.*)

12. "Die ägyptischen Werkzeichnungen erweisen sich ebenso genau wie der modernen Ingenieure." (Struve, *op. cit.*)

13. *See* "Die Bewertung eines auf ein Papyrus des Turiner Museums erhaltenen Planes des Felsengrabes von König Ramses IV" by Howard Carter and Alan H. Gardiner in *Journal of Egyptian Archeology*, IV, pp. 130ff.

See also Flinders Petrie's research: "Les plans des Égyptiens" in *Ancient Egypt*, 1926, pp. 24–26. The exactness of the architectural plans of the ancient Egyptians had already been stressed by Ludwig Borchardt in A.Z. 34, p. 72.

14. Ver Eecke, *op. cit.*, p. XXXVIII.

15. Didorus of Sicily, vol. II, book V, chapter XXXVII, p. 39 (quoted by Paul Ver Eecke).

16. Ver Eecke, *op. cit.*, pp. XIV–XV. Strabo, *Géographie*, translated by Amédée Tardieu, vol. III, book XVII, p. 433 (cited by Ver Eecke).

17. P. H. Michel, *La Science antique et médiévale* (Paris: Presses Universitaires de France, 1957), p. 233.

18. "Wenn die Deutung Borchardts einer Zeichnung an einer der Wände des Luqsortempels zu Recht besteht, so hatten sich auch die Ägypter das Problem gestellt, den Inhalt einer Ellipse zu berechnen." (See *A.Z.* 34, pp. 75–76; Struve, *op. cit.*, p. 180, note 1.)

19. "Der M.P. der uns unter vielem anderen interssanten auch das Zeugnis liefert, dass eine berühmte Entdeckung des Archimedes den Ägyptern zugeschrieben werden muss, bestätigt auf die glänzendste Weise die Angaben der grieschen Schriftsteller von der mathematischen Kenntnis der ägyptischen Gelehrten. Wir haben also keinen Grund mehr die Behauptung der grieschen Schriftsteller, dass die Ägypter die Lehrmeister von Hellas in der Geometrie waren, abzulehnen." (Struve, *op. cit.*, pp. 183–84.)

20. "Da wird aber eine der grössten Entdeckungen des Demokrit uns etwa 1,400 Jahre zurückdatiert. Diese neuen Tatsachen, durch welche der Pap. Adwin Smith und der M.P. unser Wissen bereichern, zwingen uns zu einer radikalen Revision des bis jetzt bestehenden Werturteils über die ägyptische Wissenschaft. Probleme, wie die Untersuchung der Funktionen des Gehirns oder der Oberfläche einer Kugel gehören nicht mehr in den Kreis der Fragen hinein, die sich die praktische Wissenschaft einer prim-

itiven Kultur stellt. Da sind schon rein theoretische Probleme die davon zeugen, dass auch das ägyptische Volk, ebenso wie das griechische, um eine rein wissenschaftliche Weltanschauung gerungen hat." (Struve, *op. cit.*, pp. 185–86.)

21. "Diese Tatsache der Genauigkeit der ägyptischen Geometrie die sich durch keine neuen Funde wegdisputieren lassen wird, war auch zweifellos der Grund, dass nach griechischer Tradition, die Geometrie nicht aus Babylonien, sondern aus Ägypten nach Hellas kam." (Struve, *op. cit.*, p. 183).

22. "Wir haben deshalb das volle Recht anzunehmen, dass in den ägyptischen Schreiberschulen sich im Laufe der Jahrtausende weitere umfangreiche mathematische Kenntnisse aufgespeichert haben, die aber zusammen mit den grossen Tempel und Königsbibliotheken zum grössten Teil für immer verloren sind." (Struve, *op. cit.*, p. 181).

23. "Das Word Wird mit der Hieroglyphe *nbt*, dem *t* des weiblichen Geschlechts und einem vertikalen Strich geschrieben. Dieser vertikale Strich zeigt an, dass die Hieroglyphe, der sie folgt, tatsächlich das Ding, das sie darstellt, bezeichnet. Da die Hieroglyphe *nb* einen halbkugelförmigen Korb darstellt, so wird das Wort *nb.t* hier in der Aufgabe 10 auch einen Krob entsprechen." (Struve, *op. cit.*, p. 158).

24. T. Eric Peet, "A Problem in Egyptian Geometry," in *Journal of Egyptian Archeology*, t. 17, 1931, pp. 100–106.

25. Struve, *op. cit.*, p. 166.

26. *Ibid.*, p. 159.

a) See *Rh 58 i,* where one finds *mr pr-m-ws n-f imi m* 93 1/3 = a pyramid that has a height of 93 1/3.

b) *st 3W...m hj mh* 60 = a slope with a height of 60.

27. Peet, *op. cit.*, p. 100.

28. *Ibid.*, pp. 100–101.

29. *Ibid.*, p. 102.

30. *Wörterbuch der ägyptischen Sprache*, Erster Band (Berlin: Akademie Verlag, 1971), p. 98.

31. Richard J. Gillings, *Mathematics in the Time of the Pharaohs* (London: M.I.T. Press, 1972), p. 201.

32. According to Diodorus, the first Chaldean astronomers were only a colony of Egyptian priests settled around the Upper Euphrates.

33. Book I, 69, 81.

34. Aristotle, *Metaphysics*, A 1, 981 b, 23.

35. Herodotus, Book II, 109.

36. Clement of Alexandria, *Stromata*, Ed. Poller, I, 357.

37. T. Eric Peet, *The Rhind Mathematical Papyrus*, The University Press of Liverpool, 1923.

38. *Berlin Papyrus*.

39. Gillings, *op. cit.*, p. 208.

40. "Die Aufgabe *Rh.* 48 hat uns schon lange gezeigt, dass das Problem der Quadratur des Kreises den ägyptischen Mathematikern bekannt war." (Struve, *op. cit.*, p. 178).

41. Peet, *The Rhind Mathematical Papyrus*, pp. 93–94.

42. Gillings, *op. cit.*, p. 139.

43. Peet, *The Rhind Mathematical Papyrus*, pp. 80–82.

44. Borchardt, A.Z., 35, pp. 150–52. See also critiques by Peet, *op. cit.*, p. 83.

45. Peet, *The Rhind Mathematical Papyrus*, pp. 121–22.

46. Peet, *Ibid.*, p. 78.

47. Ferdinand Hoefer, *Histoire des Mathématiques* (Paris: Hachette, 1895), fourth edition, pp. 99, 129–30.

48. Plutarch: *Isis and Osiris*, § CLVI.

49. Gillings, *op. cit.*, p. 175.

50. Gillings, *op. cit.*, p. 181.

51. *Pesou* (literally: kitchen). Examples:

$$pesou = \frac{\text{number of breads}}{\text{amount of grain used}}$$

52. Literally, *Aha* means: bunch, piece, quantity, number, abstract number.

53. "The factorizations are always, at one point or another, simpler than any other possible factorization." (R. J. Gillings, *op. cit.*, p. 48.) While a detractor like T. E. Peet would say that the recto (of the papyrus on which is found the table of the factorization of the fractions) is a monument to the lack of altitude of scientific spirit. (*Ibid.*, p. 48.)

54. Gillings, *op. cit.*, p. 52.

55. Thus: $2/41 = 1/24 + 1/246 + 1/328$ (*Rhind Papyrus*, p. 37).

Note: 𓂋 = *ro* = fraction = the morsel that is swallowed = the portion. In Wolof, we have *roh* = to swallow with gluttony (?).

56. Jean Vercoutter in *La Science antique et médiévale* (Paris: Presses Universitaires de France, 1957).

57. *Rhind Papyrus*, problem 4: seven loaves of bread to be divided among ten persons.

58. Cheikh Anta Diop: *Parenté génétique de l'égyptien pharaonique et des langues négro-africaines, op. cit.*, p. 258.

59. *Ibid.*, p. 168, for additional explanation.

60. Flinders Petrie, *Papyrii* (cited by R. J. Gillings, *op. cit.*, p. 162).

61. Alan H. Gardiner, *Egyptian Grammar* (London: Clarendon Press, 1927), p. 145.

62. Vercoutter in *La Science antique et médiévale, op. cit.*, p. 38. See also Charles Mugler, *Dictionnaire archéologique des Techniques* (Paris: Éditions l'Accueil, 1963), pp. 97–98.

63. The Gregorian calendar was introduced in October 1582 in Rome by Pope Gregory XIII. France adopted it in December 1582, Great Britain

in 1752, Russia in 1918, and Greece in 1923. Based on the tropical year of 365.2425 days, it has a slight lag of 3 days in 10,000 years, as opposed to the most exact duration of 365.2422 days.

64. Otto Neugebauer, *The Exact Sciences in Antiquity* (New York: Harper, 1962), p. 81 (cited by R. J. Gillings, *op. cit.*, p. 235).

65. If four years are equal to a lag of one day, one must have then 4 × 365 = 1,460 years in order for the civil year to coincide again with the astronomical year, meaning for the first day of both calendars to fall on the same day and to coincide with the heliacal rising of Sothis, or Sirius, or "Sepedet."

66. A.D. 139: Heliacal rising, according to Censorius.

1471–74 B.C.: Religious feast (advent?), under Thutmose III.

1555–58: 1st or 9th year of the reign of Amenophis I, second king of the XVIIIth Dynasty.

1885–88: 1st or 7th year of the reign of Senusret, XIIth Dynasty.

67. 1 day = 4 years.

68. *Papyrus dêmotique Carlsberg 1* and 9. *Carlsberg 9* was written during the Roman epoch, after 144 A.D..

69. Muck, *op. cit.*, p. 40.

70. Great pyramid of Khufu (Cheops): 2′28″
Pyramid of Chephren: 2′28″
Pyramid of Mycerinus: 9′12″
Rhomboidal Pyramid 24′25″
Pyramid of Meidum: 14′3″.

71. Example: *Mentou m hat*, written with the sign of God, holding a veil, symbol of navigation, the two signs being respectively homophones of "Mentu" and "hat" (Gustave Lefebvre, *La Médecine égyptienne*, p. 39).

72. *Papyrus Ebers 2*.

73. *Djat, lemu* in Wolof.

74. *Djat u djt* = the magical formula that heals the scorpion's bite (in Wolof, Senegal); *lugg daan* = to bring down the venom of the snake through magical means.

In Egypt, a cooked mouse heals the troubles of teething; in Black Africa, in order to have beautiful teeth, a child has to throw his baby teeth, which fall to the mice hidden in the hedgerow.

75. We are told that it was Herophilus of Alexandria who first counted the heartbeat in the pulse, in the third century B.C. All the scholars who have made the reputation of Greek science in antiquity have become aware of their "discoveries" during their contacts with Egyptian scholars, in Egypt itself and never in Greece. To this rule there are practically no exceptions. We will come back to this question.

76. Among the cases studied are cited: the dislocation of the jaw, of a vertebra, of the shoulder, the perforation of the skull, of the sternum,

a broken nose, jaw, clavicles, humerus, ribs, a fracture of the skull without rupture of the meninges, with a crushing of a cervical vertebra, etc.

77. Lefebvre, *La Médecine égyptienne*, *op. cit.*; Vercoutter in *La Science antique et médiévale*, *op. cit.*, p. 50.

78. Robert Maddin, James D. Muhly, and Tamara S. Heeler, "Les débuts de l'âge du fer," in *Pour la Science* (the French edition of *Scientific American*), no. 2, December 1977, p. 17.

79. Diop, "La métallurgie du fer sous l'Ancien Empire égyptien," in *Bulletin de l'IFAN*, series B, vol. XXXV, no. 3, July 1973, pp. 532–47. "L'âge du fer en Afrique," in *Notes africaines*, no. 152, October 1976, IFAN, University of Dakar.

80. Borchardt, in *A.Z.* (*Z.A.S.*), XXXIV, 1896, pp. 69–76.

81. For an inclined plane at angle $\alpha = 20°$, using the formula $p = Q \text{ sine } \alpha + \mu Q \text{ cosine } \alpha$, one finds, for a block weighing 1,150 kg, a final weight of: $p = 1150 \text{ sine } 20° + 0.25 \times 1{,}150 \text{ cosine } 20° = 390 + 270 = 660$ kg for traction (μ = coefficient of friction). By supposing that each maneuver can pull up along the inclined plane a weight of 15 kg, one has: $660/15 = 44$ workers.

82. L. Croon, in *Beiträge zur Ägyptischen Bauforschung und Altertumskunde*, Heft 1, 1928, pp. 26–39.

83. On fig. 53, see the reproduction of table III, fig. 5, of the article by Borchardt.

84. *See* figs. 52 to 55.

85. Howard Carter and Alan H. Gardiner, "Plans du tombeau de Ramsès IV," *Journal of Egyptian Archeology*, no. 4, 1917, plates XXIX–XXX.

86. Ernest Mackay, "Proportion Squares on Tomb Walls in the Theban Necropolis," in *Journal of Egyptian Archeology*, no. 4, 1917; see figs. 61 to 65.

87. *See* fig. 61, a drawing of tomb 92 (pl. XVII).

88. *See* fig. 62, tomb 52 (pl. XV).

89. *See* fig. 63, tomb 36 (pl. XVIII).

90. *See* fig. 64, tombs 92 (pl. XVII) and 93 (pl. XV), and fig. 65, tombs 95 (pl. XV) and 55 (pl. XV).

CHAPTER 17

1. Cheikh Anta Diop, *Nations nègres et Culture* (Paris: Présence Africaine, 1954, revised paperback, 1979).

2. *Nun*: The muddy black waters of the Nile during the time of cosmic creation. *See Nations nègres et Culture*, *op. cit.*, paperback edition, 1979, p. 169.

3. Diop, *Parenté génétique de l'égyptien et des langues négro-africaines*, *op. cit.*, p. 228.

4. Émile Amélineau, *Prolégomènes à l'étude de la religion égyptienne*, *op. cit.*

5. *See* "La sentence des cannibales," pp. 183–84 in this text.

6. *Wörterbuch der Aegyptischen Sprache*, IV, (Berlin: Akademie Verlag, 1971), p. 298.

7. *See* Jacques Pirenne, *op. cit.*

8. Diop, *Nations nègres et Culture, op. cit.*, p. 213.

9. *Journal de la Société des Africanistes*, vol. XX, fasc. II (Paris: Musée de l'Homme, 1950). *See also* the excellent analysis of this article by Hunter Adams III in the *Journal of African Civilizations*, vol. I, no. 32, November 1979, edited by Ivan Van Sertima, Douglass College, Rutgers University, New Brunswick, New Jersey.

The Dogon people include four tribes who in the past assumed different roles: The Aru (fortune tellers), the Dyon (farmers), the Ono and the Dommo (merchants). (Marcel Griaule and Germaine Dieterlen, *op. cit.*, p. 275).

10. Griaule and Dieterlen, *op. cit.*, p. 280. The *po* = the *Digitaria exilis*, an African cereal that has the popular name of foñio.

11. *See* the section "Calendar" in this text, pp. 279–82.

12. *Põ tolo kize woy wo gayle be dedemogo wo sige be.* (Griaule and Dieterlen, *op. cit.*, p. 287, note 2). *See* figs. 69 and 70.

13. *See* Adams, *op. cit.*, p. 3.

14. *See* fig. 71.

15. Griaule and Dieterlen, *op. cit.*, p. 284.

16. *Ibid.*, p. 287.

17. *Ibid.*, p. 287.

18. For the impact of the stellar matter on the instability of man's temper, *see* Griaule and Dieterlen, *op. cit.*, p. 284.

19. *Ibid.*, p. 281. *See* fig. 70.

20. *Ibid.*, p. 288.

21. *See* figs. 72 and 73.

22. According to Proclus of Lycea, for the Pythagoreans, three is the first of the order of numbers (Paul Ver Eecke: *Proclus de Lycie* (Paris: Albert Blanchard, 1984), introduction, p. XVII.

23. Solange de Ganay, "Graphie bambara des nombres" in *Journal de la Société des Africanistes*, vol. XX, fasc. II (Paris: Musée de l'Homme, 1950), pp. 297–301.

24. *Ibid.*, p. 301, note 3.

25. Griaule and Dieterlen, *op. cit.*, p. 279.

26. *Ibid.*, pp. 282–84. *See* fig. 74.

27. *Ibid.*, pp. 282–84.

28. *Ibid.*, pp. 291–92.

29. R. Grauwet: "Une statuette égyptienne au Katanga," in *Revue Coloniale Belge*, no. 214, 1954, p. 622.

30. Adams, *op. cit.*, p. 3.

31. *See* p. 352 as well as Diodorus, *Book I*, 98.

32. Ver Eecke, *op. cit.*, p. 57, note 6.

33. *See* quotations of Diogenes Laërtius, p. 347.

34. It would be interesting to further the study of certain terms such as:

Faro (Bambara) = *nommo* (Dogon)
Faro < *Fari* = pharaoh (?)
Aru = name of a Dogon tribe, tribe of the fortune tellers
Aru = paradise (in Egyptian, *see* p. 416)
Minianka = men of Min = name of a Dogon tribe (Could it be the men of the Egyptian god Min?)

Finally, Hunter Adams III (*op. cit.*, p. 10) cites:
Numu = forge (Dogon)
Inumu = iron (Dravidian)

and one can add to these two names from the works of Cheikh Tidjane Ndiaye:
Nem = ancient Egyptian knife
Nam = to sharpen a knife (Wolof)

The etymological study of such terms as *nommo* and *kora* (harp) must be furthered.

35. *See* "La Sentence des cannibales," pp. 183–84 of this text.

36. Alexis Kagame, *La Philosophie Bantu comparée* (Paris: Présence Africaine, 1976), p. 122.

37. Diop, *Parenté génétique de l'égyptien pharaonique et des langues négro-africaines*, *op. cit.*, pp. XXVI–XXVIII; 1–24.

38. *See* chapters 8 and 11 in this text.

39. Amélineau, Prolégomènes à l'étude de la religion égyptienne, *op. cit.*, pp. 152–56.

40. *Ibid.*

41. Plato, *Timaeus*, XXIX.

42. *Kun* (Arabic) = let such (thing) be; let there be light, and there was light.

43. *Kheper* → *šopi* (Coptic) → *sopi* (Wolof) = to become. *Werden* = to become (German); an auxiliary verb that plays a fundamental role in expressing German thought.

44. Amélineau, *op. cit.*, pp. 209–10.

45. *Ibid.*, p. 219.

46. *Ibid.*, p. 221.

47. *Ibid.*, p. 213.

48. *Ate* = to judge, judgment (Wolof); *atew* = judged (Wolof).

49. Diop, *L'Antiquité africaine par l'image*, *op. cit.*, p. 37, figs. 51 and 52.

50. This bridge is, in all aspects, comparable to the *siratal moustakhima* of Islam (*ibid.*, p. 34, fig. 59). *See* fig. 75.

51. Pirenne, *op. cit.*, vol. 3, p. 352.

52. The Egyptian texts say: "on this day the Nun gave birth by producing happy breaths"; an idea picked up almost word for word from two places, in the Bible (Genesis 1.2 and Genesis 7.20 ff.: "the breath of God moved over the abyss").

See also the Egyptian calendar of the ill-fated days.

53. Amélineau, *op. cit.*, p. 147.

54. Serge Sauneron, *op. cit.*, p. 35. Diogenes Laërtius, *op. cit.*, Book VIII, 8(87) 3.

55. Herodotus, Book II, 37.

56. Diop, *Nations nègres et Culture*, *op. cit.*, pp. 206–207.

57. Herodotus, *Euterpe.*

58. Sauneron, *op. cit.*, p. 67.

59. *Ibid.*, p. 150. Let us add that the periodic return of the stars probably concerns the theory of the epicycles and the eccentrics that allowed the accounting for apparent abnormalities of the movements of the stars: particularly the stations and the retrogradations of the small planets. In fact, the two systems (epicycles/eccentrics) are equivalent. In an epicycle, the Earth occupies the center of a big circle all of whose points on the circumference are covered by the center of another circle of a radius r and whose circumference is described by the planet.

60. *Ibid.*, p. 136.

61. André Aymard and Jeannine Auboyer, *L'Orient et la Grèce antique* (Paris: Presses Universitaires de France, 1961), p. 274.

62. *Ibid.*, p. 274.

63. *Ibid.*, p. 350.

64. *Ibid.*, p. 350.

65. Delorme, *La Grèce primitive et archaïque*, *op. cit.*, p. 94.

66. According to Strabo.

67. In Egyptian, one finds the typical sentence: *Ink mr f nfrt msd f dwt* = I love that which is good (beautiful) and detest that which is bad.

In Wolof, there exists an identical sentence: *Bëgg bu baah ban lu bon* = (I) love that which is good (beautiful) and detest that which is bad.

68. Ver Eecke, *Proclus de Lycie*, *op. cit.*, introduction, p. xii.

69. The principle of the evolution of matter (*see* p. 310 in this text).

70. Plato, *Timaeus*, 42e.

71. *See below* the quotes from Strabo.

72. Theme already developed in the preceding chapter, pp. 279–82.

73. Ernst Curtius, *Histoire d'Alexandre*, IV, 10.

74. Strabo, *Géographie*, Book XVII, 1, 29.

75. Serge Sauneron, *Les Prêtres de l'ancienne Égypte* (Paris: Éditions du Seuil, 1957), pp. 114–15.

76. A letter supposedly from Thales to Pherecydes, cited by Diogenes Laërtius: "But we who do not write, we willingly travel through Greece and Italy." (*Vies, doctrines et sentences des philosophes illustres*, p. 59.)

77. Albert Rivaud, *Platon, Oeuvres*, vol. 10, "Timée," "Critias" (Paris: Les Belles Lettres, 1956), note, p. 39.

78. *Ibid.*, p. 40.

79. *Ibid.*, p. 41.

80. *See* p. 340, the exercise on geometrical progressions, in order to see that these mathematical notions were taught by Egypt to the Mediterranean world: the *Rhind Papyrus* goes back to 1800 B.C. and is a copy of a more ancient text, according to the scribe Ahmes himself.

81. This is incorrect.

82. Why seven parts? Most probably because the relationships coming out of these considerations will explain, among other things, the (supposed) distances between the planets (5 + 2: Sun, Moon).

83. Diodorus, *Book I*, 98.

84. Diodorus, *Book I*, 98.

85. Diogenes Laërtius, *op. cit.*, "Democritus," 3 (cited by Sauneron, *op. cit.*, p. 114).

86. Amélineau, *Prolégomènes à l'étude de la religion égyptienne*, *op. cit.*, pp. 227–28.

87. Serge Sauneron and Jean Yoyotte, *La Naissance du monde*, "Égypte ancienne" chapter (Paris: Le Seuil, 1959), p. 53.

88. Egyptian: *dhwt* = *thot* = *ibis*
Wolof: *dwhat* = bird of exceptional height
toh = *hod* = *ibis*

89. Henri Carteron, *Aristote—Physique* (Paris: Les Belles Lettres), I–2, 184 b.

90. Diogenes Laërtius, *op. cit.*, p. 52.

91. *Fes* = to become, appears, visible, as opposed to hidden (in Wolof).

92. Ernest d'Astier, *Histoire de la philosophie*, translated by Marcel Belvianes (Paris: Payot, 1952).

93. *Ibid.*, p. 388.

94. The Wolof term probably derives from the Egyptian causative of the same verb:
hopir = to change (Egyptian)
shopir = to have a change made (Egyptian)
šopi = to change (Wolof)

95. Sauneron and Yoyotte, *La Naissance du monde*, *op. cit.*, p. 35.

96. Diop, *Parenté génétique de l'égyptien pharaonique et des langues négro-africaines*, *op. cit.*

97. One knows that *n* → *l* in many cases, as one goes from the Egyptian to the Wolof language. (*See Parenté génétique de l'égyptien pharaonique et des langues négro-africaines*, *op. cit.*, pp. 3, 11, 73).

98. *Ibid.*, p. 29.

99. *Ibid.*, errata.

100. Amélineau, *op. cit.*, p. 224.

101. Diop, *Parenté génétique de l'égyptien pharaonique et des langues négro-africaines*, *op. cit.*

102. *Ibid.*, p. 287.

103. Raymond O. Faulkner, *A Concise Dictionary of Middle Egyptian*, p. 306. *See* Amélineau, *op. cit.*, p. 192 (Malinke, Sama-nke, etc.).

104. The physicists James Watson Cronin and Val Logdson Fitch (Nobel Prize 1980; *see Le Monde* of October 16, 1980) have demonstrated, in a very complex manner, the partial nonconservation of the product (C.P.). One must understand that this means the product of the operation of parity (exchanging up and down, right and left) and the conjugation of charges (replacing particles with their anti-particles).

The operation (C.P.) is mathematically equivalent to a reversal of the direction of time. In terms of physics, it means that because the law of invariance (C.P.) is not good, if there were a corresponding physical universe in which time ran toward the past, that universe would not be rigorously symmetrical to ours, far from it.

For our development, it is important to emphasize the fact that the notion of a reversibility of time, of its going back toward the past, far from being absurd, has become an integral part of the conceptual apparatus of the modern physicist.

On the other hand, the partial asymmetrical structure of matter would mean that the evolution of the universe does not follow a periodic function: an "initial" explosion (*big bang*), ten billion years ago, followed by an expansion and new condensation of matter, and so on.

Thus, even if the "initial" *big bang* belongs to an absolute past and cannot repeat itself, it is only a relative beginning, and reason and imagination continue to be intrigued by the anterior evolutionary process of matter that started it. The universe, instead of being stationary as general relativity would have it, has momentum, is in expansion and constantly in disequilibrium. However, the study of the nuclei of the galaxy, which has just begun, allows one to hypothesize the existence of black holes that would be sources, centers of extreme condensation of matter throughout cosmic space. Could each one of these diverse black holes (if they really exist) snatch up all the galactic matter that surrounds it, in order to fuse more and more closely by mutual attraction, so as to finally reconstitute a huge ball comparable to that of the supposed initial *big bang*, and have the absurd evolution start over again? It seems unlikely. The little that is known, or more precisely, that is assumed, about the thermodynamics of black holes would seem to forbid that kind of infinite growth in their size; the latter supposedly has a maximum limit. In reality, we are in the world of hypotheses, and everything can still be questioned in this domain.

It is only important to stress the fact that the characteristics of the universe are no longer deduced from esthetic or moral principles that are laid down *a priori* (Plato), but rather from scientific experience. The universe is not *a priori* symmetrical by pure speculative and allegedly rational exigency of the mind; it is rather asymmetrical, as revealed by experience.

105. The theorem of Gödel says that if a theory is founded on a finite number of axioms rich enough to allow the constructing of arithmetic, it is possible to find in this theory an indefinable proposition, meaning one that, as related to this theory, is neither true nor false.

Thus the theorem of Gödel ruined Hilbert's hope to demonstrate the internal coherence of arithmetic while bypassing the infinite. Therefore Gödel showed that it was necessary to depend on the notion of the infinite, in other words, to go beyond the framework of the original axioms, in order to prove the coherence of arithmetic. It is therefore a theorem of nonfulfillment indeed, of the same kind, of the same finality as the one that Einstein tried to establish concerning quantum mechanics. In order to conduct his word well, Gödel found himself obliged to create recursive functions, which are the basis of modern logic and of the theory of computer science.

From Gödel's theorem of nonfulfillment follows the fact that complete "axiomatization" of mathematics is impossible, particularly that of arithmetic and of fractions. More precisely, every axiom in the system can be associated with an indecidable equation, but decidable in another, different system of axioms. Therefore, every axiom is incomplete, whence the theory of nonfulfillment.

Since the works of Gödel, completed by P. J. Cohen, we know that two axioms, the "axiom of choice" and the "hypothesis of the continuum," are quite independent of the other axioms of the theory of sets. For that, Gödel created constructible sets, which are an extension of the recursive functions and which are at the basis of the logic of sets.

The axiom of choice postulates that a straight line contains an immeasurable part, and the hypothesis of the continuum postulates that there does not exist any infinite strictly located between that of the natural numbers and that of the points of a straight line.

106. J. Breuer, *Initiation à la théorie des ensembles* (Paris: Dunod, 1961), pp. 105–106.

107. *Ibid.*, p. 102.

108. *Le Monde*, July 6–7, 1979, p. 8, article by Dominique Dhombres.

109. *La Recherche*, no. 111, May 1980, p. 582.

110. Goethe, *Faust*, translated by Gérard de Nerval (Paris: Flammarion), p. 29.

111. *La Recherche*, no. 111, May 1980, pp. 510–19.

112. *Physical Review*, May 15, 1935.

113. John von Neumann, *Les Fondements mathématiques de la mécanique quantique*, Alcan, 1946 (original edition, 1932).

114. Max Jammer, *op. cit.*, p. 516.

115. *Ibid.*, p. 516.

116. *Ibid.*, p. 516.

117. Pierre Thuillier, "La physique et l'irrationnel" in *La Recherche*, no. 111, May 1980, p. 583.

118. Jammer, *op. cit.*, p. 519.

119. Jean E. Charon, *L'Esprit, cet inconnu* (Paris: Albin Michel, 1977).

120. *Science et Vie*, no. 728, May 1978, pp. 42–46.

CHAPTER 18

1. André Aymard and Jeannine Auboyer, *L'Orient et la Grèce antique*, *op. cit.*, p. 231.

2. Diogenes Laërtius, *Vies doctrines et sentences des philosophes illustres*, *op. cit.*, Book VIII, I (1–4).

3. *Ibid.*, 8, 89.

4. Diodorus, *Book I*, 96–8

5. Serge Sauneron, *Les Prêtres de l'ancienne Égypte*, *op. cit.*, p. 124. "Écrit hermétique" (Treatise XVI, 1–2).

6. The contribution of the Latins to the exact sciences is almost nonexistent contrary to that of the Greeks, because the former had less contact with Egypt.

7. According to an ingenious theory, the sum of the numerical values of the letters that make up the Greek word "Neilos" supposedly is equal to 365, the number of days in the year, marking the return of the flooding of the Nile. If this were the case, the word would have been recent in the Greek language and therefore absent in the archaic language.

8. However, these two words are considered to be of Indo-European origin.

BIBLIOGRAPHY

Adams III, Hunter. Article in *Journal of African Civilizations*, vol. I, no. 2 (November 1979). Edited by Ivan Van Sertima, Douglass College, Rutgers University, New Brunswick, New Jersey.

Alimen, H. *Préhistoire de l'Afrique*. Paris: N. Boubée and Co., 1955.

Amélineau, Émile. *Prolégomènes à l'étude de la religion égyptienne*. Paris: Ernest Leroux, 1908 (2d ed. 1916).

Antoniadis-Bibicou, Hélène. "Byzance et le M.P.A." In *Sur le mode de production asiatique*. 2d ed. Paris: C.E.R.M.–Éditions Sociales, 1974.

———*Archeologia*, no. 123 (October 1978).

Archimedes. *The Method, On the Sphere and the Cylinder, On the Measurement of a Circle, On the Equilibrium of Planes and Their Center of Gravity*. From the complete works of Archimedes translated by Paul Ver Eecke.

Aristotle. *Physics*.

d'Astier, Ernest. *Histoire de la philosophie*. Translated by Marcel Belvianes. Paris: Payot, 1952.

Auboyer, Jeannine. *See* Aymard, André and Auboyer, Jeannine.

Autran, Charles. Cited by Raymond Furon in *Manuel de Préhistoire générale*.

Aymard, André and Auboyer, Jeannine. *L'Orient et la Grèce antique*. Paris: Presses Universitaires de France, 1961 (1st ed. 1953).

———*Rome et son Empire*. Paris: Presses Universitaires de France, 1959.

Ba, Oumar. *La Pénétration francaise au Cayor*. vol. 1. Nouakchott, 1976.

Bada, Jeffrey L. *IX*[e] Congrès UISPP, Symposium I.

Banti, Max. "Reconstruction de la denture de 'l'adolescent du Grimaldi.' " Paris: Université de Paris VII, 1969.

Banu, Ion. "La formation sociale 'asiatique' dans la perspective de la philosophie orientale antique." In *Sur le mode de production asiatique*. 2d ed. Paris: C.E.R.M.–Éditions Sociales, 1974.

Barral, L. and Charles, R. P. "Nouvelles données anthropometriques et précisions sur les affinités systématiques des négroïdes de Grimaldi." In *Bulletin du Musée d'Anthropologie préhistorique de Monaco*, no. 10 (1963).

Batutta, Ibn. *Voyages d'Ibn Battuta. vol. IV.* Translated by C. Défremery and B. R. Sanguinetti, 1922.

Baumann, Hermann. and Westermann, D. *Les Peuples et les Civilisations de l'Afrique*. Paris: Payot, 1948.

Benveniste, Émile. *Le Vocabulaire des institutions indo-européennes, Économie, Parenté, Societé*. Paris: Éditions de Minuit, 1969.

Bérard, Victor. *Resurrection d'Homère. Au temps des héros.*

Blackman, A. M. and Fairman, H. W. "The Myth of Horus (II): The Triumph of Horus over His Enemies; a Sacred Drama." *Journal of Egyptian Archeology*, vol. 28 (1942): 32–38; vol. 29 (1943): 2–36; vol. 30 (1944): 5–22.

Borchardt, Ludwig. *Zeitschrift für Ägyptischer Sprache, XXXIV*. Band, 1896, (Ägyptischer Zeitung, nos. 34, 35).

Bordes, François. *See* UNESCO.

Boule, Marcellin and Vallois, Henri-Victor. *Les Hommes fossiles*. 4th ed. Paris: Masson, 1952.

Breasted, James H. *Ancient Records of Egypt*. Chicago, 1906.

Breuer, J. *Initiation à la théorie des ensembles*. Paris: Dunod, 1961.

Carrel, Alexis. *L'Homme, cet inconnu*. 1st ed. Paris: Plon, 1936.

Carruthers, Jacob H. *Orientation and Problems in the Redemption of Ancient Egypt*.

Carter, Howard and Gardiner, Alan H. "Plans du tombeau de Ramsès IV." *Journal of Egyptian Archeology*, no. 4 (1917).

Carteron, Henri, ed. (Aristote) *Physique*. Paris: Les Belles Lettres.

Césaire, Aimé. *Cahier d'un retour au pays natal*. Paris: Présence Africaine, 1956.

Charles, R. P. *See* Barral, L. and Charles, R. P.

Charon, Jean E. *L'Esprit, cet inconnu*. Paris: Albin Michel, 1977.

Chesneaux, J. Article in *La Pensée* (Paris), no. 114.

Clarke, John Henrik. Introduction to *The Cultural Unity of Black Africa* by Cheikh Anta Diop. Chicago: Third World Press, 1978.

Clément, Pierre. "Le forgeron en Afrique Noire," *Revue de Géographie humaine et d'Ethnologie*, no. 2 (April–June 1948).

Clement of Alexandria. *Stromata*. Éditions Poller.

Confucius. *Lun-Yu*. Translated by M. G. Paul. Paris: Garnier.

Contenau, Georges. *La Civilisation des Hittites et des Mitanniens*. Paris: Payot, 1934.

Coon, Carleton S. *The Origin of Races*. New York: Knopf, 1962.

———Article in *La Recherche*, no. 89 (May 1978).

Coppens, Yves; Howell, F. Clark; Isaac, Glynn L.; Leakey, Richard E. F. *Earliest Man and Environments in the Lake Rudolf Basin* (Prehistoric Archeology and Ecology Series). Edited by Karl W. Butzer and Leslie G. Freeman. Chicago: University of Chicago Press, 1976.

Cronin, James Watson and Fitch, Val Logdson. Physicists cited in *Le Monde* (October 16, 1980).

Croon, L. *Lastentransport beim Bau der Pyramiden.* Hannover: Diss, 1925.

———*Beiträge zur Ägyptischen Bauforschung und Altertumskunde.* Heft 1, 1928.

Cuvillier, A. *Introduction à la sociologie.* Paris: Armand Colin, 1967.

Dambuyant, Marinette. "Un État à 'haut commandement économiqué'—l'Inde de Kautilya." In *Sur le mode de production asiatique.* 2d ed. Paris: C.E.R.M.-Éditions Sociales, 1974.

Davaras, Costis. *Le Palais de Cnossos.* Athens: Ed. Hannibal.

———Article in *Musée d'Hérakleion.* Athens: Ekdotike Athenon.

Davies, Norman de Garis. *Tomb of Rekh-Mi-Rè at Thebes.* vol 2. New York: The Metropolitan Museum of Art, 1943.

Day, M. H. "The Omo Human Skeletal Remains." In *L'Origine de l'homme moderne*, Paris Symposium, 1969. Edited by UNESCO, Paris, 1972.

Delorme, Jean. *La Grèce primitive et archaïque.* Paris: Armand Colin, 1969.

Devisse, Jean. *L'Image du Noir dans l'art occidental.* vol 2. Fribourg: Office du Livre.

———"Le passé de l'Afrique dort dans son sol." In *Recherche, Pédagogie et Culture*, no. 39 (January–February, 1979).

Devoto, Giacomo. *La Crisi del latino nel V°.* secolo a. Ch. Studii Clasice, VI, 1964.

Dhombres, Dominique. Article in *Le Monde* (July 6–7, 1975).

———*Dictionnaire archéologique des techniques* (see Mugler, Charles).

Dieng, Amady Aly. *Hegel, Marx, Engels et les problèmes de l'Afrique Noire.* Dakar: 1979.

Diodorus of Sicily. *Bibliothèque historique* in 40 books. Books 1–5, *Égypte*, etc.

Diogenes Laërtius. *Democritus*, Book 3.

———*Vies, doctrines et sentences de philosophes illustres* in 10 books. Book VIII.

Diop, Cheikh Anta. *L'Afrique Noire précoloniale.* Paris: Présence Africaine, 1960. (*Precolonial Black Africa*, Lawrence Hill, 1987.)

———*Anteriorité des civilisations nègres. Mythe ou vérité historique?* Paris: Présence Africaine, 1967.

———*L'Antiquité africaine par l'image.* Dakar: IFAN, 1976.

———*Nations nègres et Culture.* Paris: Présence Africaine, 1954. Pocketbook edition, 1979.

———*Parenté génétique de l'égyptien pharaonique et de langues négro-africaines*. Dakar: IFAN, 1977.

———*L'Unité culturelle de l'Afrique Noire*. Paris: Présence Africaine, 1959.

———"L'âge du fer en Afrique." *Notes Africaine*, no. 152 (October 1976).

———"L'apparition de l'Homo Sapiens." *Bulletin de l'IFAN* (Dakar), vol. XXXII, series B, no. 3 (1920).

———"Introduction à l'étude des migrations en Afrique Centrale et Occidentale. Identification du berceau nilotique du peuple sénégalais." *Bulletin de l'IFAN* (Dakar), vol. XXXV, series B, no. 4 (1973).

———"La métallurgie du fer sous l'Ancien Empire égyptien." *Bulletin de l'IFAN* (Dakar), vol. XXXV, series B, no. 3 (1973).

———"Pigmentation des anciens Égyptiens. Test par la mélanine." *Bulletin de l'IFAN* (Dakar), vol. XXXV, series B, no. 3 (1973).

Diophantes. *Arithmetic*.

Einstein, Albert; Podolsky, Boris; Rosen, Nathan. "EPR Paradox." *Physical Review* (May 15, 1935).

Eisenlohr, trans. *Rhind Papyrus*.

Eliade, Mircea. *Traité d'histoire des religions*. 1949.

Engels, Friedrich. *L'Anti-Dühring*. 2d ed. Paris: Éditions Sociales, 1963. *See also* Marx, Karl and Engels, Friedrich.

d'Espagnat, Bernard. *A la recherche du réel*. Paris: Gauthier-Villars, 1980.

Evans-Pritchard, Edward E. *Les Nuer*. Paris: Gallimard, 1937. Translated from the English.

Evans-Pritchard, Edward E.; Radcliffe-Brown, A. R.; Forde. "Parenté et communauté locale chez les Nouer." *Systèmes familaux et matrimoniaux en Afrique*.

Fairman, H. W. *See* Blackman, A. M. and Fairman, H. W.

Faulkner, Raymond O. *A Concise Dictionary of Middle Egyptian*. Oxford, 1962.

Fer, Francis. Article in *Science et Vie*, no. 728 (May 1978): 42–46.

Fineley, M. I. *Les anciens Grecs*. Paris: F. Maspéro, 1977.

Fitch, Val Logdson. *See* Cronin, James and Fitch, V. L.

Forde. *See* Evans-Pritchard, Edward E.; Radcliffe-Brown, A. R.; Forde.

Frobenius, Leo. *Ekade Ektab. Die afrikanischen Felsbilder*. Graz, Austria: Akademische Druch U. Verlagsanstalt, 1963.

———*Histoire de la civilisation africaine*. 3d ed. Translated by H. Back and D. Ermont. Paris: Gallimard, 1952.

———*Mythologie de l'Atlantide*. Paris: Payot, 1949.

Furon, Raymond. *Manuel de Préhistoire générale*. 4th ed. Paris: Payot, 1959.

Fustel de Coulanges, N. D. *La Cité antique*. Paris: Hachette, 1930.

de Ganay, Solange. "Graphies Bambara des nombres." *Journal de la Société des Africanistes*, vol. XX, fasc. II. Paris: Musée de l'Homme, 1950.

Gardiner, Alan H. *Egyptian Grammar*. London: Clarendon Press, 1927.

———*See* Carter, Howard and Gardiner, A. H.

Gillings, Richard J. *Mathematics in the Time of the Pharaohs*. London: M.I.T. Press, 1972.

Gimbutas, Marija. *Gods and Godesses of Old Europe 7000–3500 B.C.: Myths, Legends and Cult Images*. Berkeley: University of California Press, 1982.

———Article in *La Recherche*, no. 87 (March 1978).

Gobineau, Count Joseph Arthur de. *Essai sur l'inégalité des races humaines*. 1st ed. 1853. Translated by Adrian Collins as *The Inequality of Human Races*. New York: G. P. Putnam's Sons, 1915.

Godelier, Maurice. "La notion de 'mode de production asiatique' et les schémas marxistes d'évolution de sociétés." In *Sur le mode de production asiatique*. Paris: C.E.R.M.-Éditions Sociales, 1977.

von Goethe, Johann Wolfgang. *Faust*. Translated by Gérard de Nerval. Paris: Flammarion.

———*Gedichte*. Stuttgart: Reclam, 1967.

Grauwet, R. "Une statuette égyptienne au Katanya." *Revue Coloniale Belge*, no. 214 (1954).

Griaule, Marcel. *Dieu d'eau. Entretiens avec Ogotemmêli*. Paris: Éditions du Chêne, 1948.

Griaule, Marcel and Dieterlen, Germaine. "Un système soudanais de Sirius." *Journal de la Société des Africanistes*, vol. XX, fasc. II. Musée de l'Homme, Paris, 1950.

Grousset, R. *Histoire de la Chine et de l'Extrême-Orient*. Paris: Fayard, 1942.

Guan-Zi. *Gouan-Tzy*. Translated by V. M. Stein.

Guyot, A. Lucien. *Origine des plantes cultivées*. Paris: Presses Universitaires de France, 1942. *Que sais-je?* series.

Halphen, Louis. *Les Barbares: peuples et civilisations*. 2d ed. Paris: Felix Alcan, 1930.

Hardy, Georges. *Une conquête morale: l'enseignement en A.O.F.* Paris: Armand Colin.

Hazoumé, Guy Landry. *Idéologies tribalistes et nation en Afrique: Le cas dahoméen*. Paris: Présence Africaine, 1972.

Hébert, Jean-Pierre. *Race et Intelligence*. Paris: Copernic-Factuelles, 1977.

Heezen, Bruce C. *See* Ninkovich, Dragoslav and Heezen, Bruce.

Herodotus. *Book II*.

Hesiod. *Les Travaux et les Jours. Théogonie*.

Hoefer, Ferdinand. *Histoire de Mathématiques*. 4th ed. Paris: Hachette, 1895.

Homer. *The Iliad*.

Howell, F. Clark. *See* Coppens, Yves; Howell, F. Clark; Isaac, Glynn L.; Leakey, Richard E. F.

Ipuwer. Egyptian author of "Admonitions of a Sage," cited by Jacques Pirenne.

Isaac, Glynn L. *See* Coppens, Yves; Howell, F. Clark; Isaac, Glynn L.; Leakey, Richard E. F.

Jacquard, A. *Éloge de la différence. La génétique et les hommes*. Paris: Seuil, 1978.

Jamblichus. *Vie de Pythagore.*

James, George. *Stolen Legacy*. San Francisco: Julian Richardson Associates, 1988.

Jammer, Max. "Le paradoxe d'Einstein-Podolsky-Rosen." *La Recherche*, no. 111, Paris (May 1980).

Juvenal. *Satir XV*.

Kagame, Abbé Alexis. *La Philosophie Bantu comparée*. Paris: Présence Africaine, 1976.

Kautylia. *Arthashastra*, vol II.

Kia Lan-po. "La caverne de l'Homme de Pékin." 1st ed. Printed in People's Republic of China, 1978.

Kozlowski, Janusz. "L'Aurignacien en Europe." in *IX*[e] Congrès UISPP. Nice, 1976.

Labeyrie J. and Lalou, C. "Datations absolues et analyses isotopiques en préhistoire. Méthodes et limites." In *IX*[e] Congrès UISPP, Symposium I. Nice, 1976.

Langaney, André. "Anthropologie: faits et spéculations." *La Recherche*. No. 92 (September 1978).

Lao-tze. *Tao-te-ching*.

Leakey, Dr. L. S. B. "Homo Sapiens in the Middle Pleistocene and the Evidence of Homo Sapiens' Evolution." In *L'Origine de l'homme moderne*. Paris Symposium. Paris: UNESCO, 1972.

Leakey, Richard E. F. *See* Coppens, Yves; Howell, F. Clark; Isaac, Glynn L.; Leakey, Richard E. F.

LeFebvre, Gustave. *Grammaire de l'égyptien classique*. Cairo: IFAOC, 1940.

———*La Médecine égyptienne*.

———*Romans et Contes égyptiens de l'époque pharaonique*. Paris: A Maisonneuve, 1976 (1st ed. 1949).

Legoux, P. "Étude odontologique de la race de Grimaldi." *Bulletin du Musée d'Anthropologie préhistorique de Monaco*, no. 10 (1963).

Lepsius, Karl Richard. *Denkmäler aus Ägypten und Äthiopien*. Geneva: Éditions de Belles-Lettres, 1972.

Lévèque, François and Vandermeersch, Bernard. Article in *La Recherche*, no. 119 (February 1981).

Locres. *De l'âme du monde et de la nature*. Cited by Paul Ver Eeke.

Lowie, Robert H. *Traité de sociologie primitive*. Translated from the English. Paris: Payot, 1936.

Lucretius. *On the Nature of Things.*

Mackay, Ernest. "Proportion Squares on Tomb Walls in the Theban Necropolis." *Journal of Egyptian Archeology*, no. 4 (1917).

Maddin, Robert; Muhly, James D.; Heeler, Tamara S. "Les débuts de l'âge du fer." *Pour la Science* (French edition of *Scientific American*), no. 2 (December 1977).

Malraux, André. *Le Musée imaginaire*. Paris: Gallimard, 1965.

Mantelin, F. "Étude et remontage du massif facial du 'Nègroïde de Grimaldi.' " Université de Paris, 1972.

———*See* Olivier, G. and Mantelin, F.

Marinatos, Spyridon. *Fouilles de Théra*, VI.

Marshall, Kim. "The Desegregation of a Boston Classroom." *Learning* (August–September 1975).

Marx, Karl. *Capital*. Books I and III.

———*Pre-Capitalist Formation.*

Marx, Karl and Engels, Friedrich. *The German Ideology.*

Maspero, Gaston. *Histoire ancienne des peuples d'Orient*. 12th ed. Paris: Hachette, 1917.

Mauny, Raymond. *Tableau géographique de l'Ouest africain au Moyen-Age*. Dakar: IFAN, no. 61, 1961. (Reprint: Swets, Holland.)

Melekechvili, G. A. "Esclavage, féodalisme et MPA dans l'Orient ancien." In *Sur le mode de production asiatique*. Paris: C.E.R.M.–Éditions Sociales, 1977.

Melissus. *On Being.*

Michel, P. H. Article in *La Science antique et médiévale*. Paris: Presses Universitaires de France, 1957.

Moore, Carlos. "Interview with Professor Cheikh Anta Diop." *Africascope*, Lagos (February 1977).

Morgan, Lewis H. *Ancient Society*. New York: *Labor News*, 1978.

Mortlock, A. J. "Thermoluminescence. Dating of Objects and Materials from the South Pacific Region." In *IX*e Congrès UISPP. Symposium XXII. Nice, 1976.

Movius, Hallam L., Jr. "Radiocarbon Dating of the Upper Paleolithic Sequence at the Abri Pataud (Les Eyzies, Dordogne)." In *L'Origine de l'homme moderne*. Paris: UNESCO, 1972.

Muck, Otto. *Cheops et la Grande Pyramide*. Translated from the German into French by Georges Rémy. Paris: Payot, 1978.

Mugler, Charles. *Dictionnaire archéologique des techniques*. vol. II. Paris: Éditions de l'Accueil, 1964.

Naville, Édouard. *Textes relatifs au mythe d'Horus recueillis dans le temple d'Edfu*. plates I–XI. Geneva, 1870.

Neugebauer, Otto. *The Exact Sciences in Antiquity*. New York: Harper, 1962.

———*Vorlesungen über Geschichte der antiken mathematischen Wissenschaften*. vol I. Berlin: Julius Springer, 1934.

von Neumann, John. *Les Fondements mathématiques de la mécanique quantique*. Alcan, 1946 (1st ed. 1932).

Ngono-Ngabission, N. Article in *Jeune Afrique*, no. 475 (February 10, 1970).

Ninkovich, Dragoslav and Heezen, Bruce C. *Columbia University Contribution*, no. 819.

Oakley, Kenneth P. "Analytic Methods of Dating Bones." In *Report of the British Association for the Advancement of Science*, meeting at Oxford.

Obenga, Théophile. *La Cuvette Congolaise: Les hommes et les structures*. Paris: Présence Africaine, 1976.

Olivier, G. and Mantelin, F. "Nouvelle reconstitution du crâne de 'l'adolescent de Grimaldi.' " *Bulletin du Musée d'Anthropologie préhistorique de Monaco*, no. 19 (1973–74).

Papyri of Upper Egypt:

———Two very fragmented papyri from the Middle Kingdom, dating from 1900 to 1800 B.C.: the *Papyrus of Kahun*, short and remarkably restrained; and the *Papyrus of Berlin*, containing sorcerers' formulas and incantations.

———The *Ebers Papyrus*, of the XVIIIth Dynasty. The *Smith Papyrus* deals with 48 cases of bone surgery with a quasi-scientific precision.

———Two longer and more recent papyri are evidently copies of earlier texts: the *Rhind Mathematical Papyrus*, which dates back to 1800 B.C.; and the *Papyrus of Moscow*, which dates back to the XIIth Dynasty, around 2000 B.C.

Other similar documents:

———The "Leather Roll." Manuscript on leather. British Museum.

———Two wooden tablets. Cairo Museum.

———Inscription from the IIIrd Dynasty, 2778 B.C., discovered at the Metjen mastaba, and has a surface calculation (e.g. of a house or field) executed according to the same method as the one on the *Rhind Papyrus*.

Parmenides. *On Nature*.

Parrain, Charles. "Protohistoire méditerranéenne et mode de production asiatique." In *Sur le mode de production asiatique*. Paris: C.E.R.M.–Éditions Sociales, 1977.

Peet, Eric T. *The Rhind Mathematical Papyrus*. Liverpool: The University Press of Liverpool, 1923.

———"A Problem in Egyptian Geometry." *Journal of Egyptian Archeology*, vol. 17 (1931).

Petit, C. and Zuckerkandl, E. *Évolution génétique des populations. Évolution moleculaire*. Paris: Hermann, 1976.

Petrie, William M. Flinders. *The Making of Ancient Egypt.* London: The Sheldon Press, 1939.

Pirenne, Jacques. *Histoire de la civilisation de l'Égypte ancienne.* vol. 1, *Des origines à la fin de l'Ancien Empire*; vol. 2, *De la fin de l'Ancien Empire à la fin du Nouvel Empire*; vol. 3, *De la XXIe dynastie aux Ptolémées.* Boudry, Switzerland: Éditions de la Baconnière, 1961.

Plato. *Critias.*

———*Phaedrus.*

———*Theaetetus.*

———*Timaeus.*

Pliny the Elder. *Natural History.*

Pliny the Younger. *Letters* (10 books).

Plutarch. *The Parallel Lives.*

———*Moralia.*

Podolsky, Boris. *See* Einstein, Albert; Podolsky, Boris; Rosen, Nathan.

Posener, Georges. *Dictionnare de la civilisation égyptienne.* Paris: F. Hazan, 1959.

Puthoff, Harold and Targ, Russel. *Aux confins de l'esprit.* Translated from English into French. Paris: Albin Michel, 1978.

Puttock, M. J. "A Possible Division of an Egyptian Measuring-rod." National Standards Laboratory, CSIRO. Sydney, Australia.

Radcliffe-Brown, A. R. *See* Evans-Pritchard, Edward E.; Radcliffe-Brown, A. R.; Forde.

Rensberger, Boyce. "Nubian Monarchy May Be the World's Oldest." *International Herald Tribune* (March 9, 1979).

Rivaud, Albert, ed. *Platon, Oeuvres.* vol. 10, *Timée, Critias.* Paris: Éditions Les Belles Lettres, 1956.

Rosen, Nathan. *See* Einstein, Albert; Podolsky, Boris; Rosen, Nathan.

Ruffie, Jacques. *De la biologie à la culture.* Paris: Flammarion, 1976.

Rufus, Curtis. *Histoire d'Alexandre.* vol. IV.

Sâdi, Abderrahman ben Abdallah es-(Sâdi). *Tarikh es-Soudan.* Paris: Maisonneuve, 1964. (1st ed. 1898–1900.)

Sakellarakis, J. A. *Musée d'Hérakleion.* Athens: Ekdotike Athenon.

Sartre, Jean-Paul. "Orphée noir." In *Situations.* vol. III. Paris: Gallimard, 1949.

Sauneron, Serge. *Les Prêtres de l'ancienne Égypte.* Paris: Éditions du Seuil, 1957.

Sauneron, Serge and Yoyotte, Jean. "Égypte ancienne." In *La Naissance du monde.* Paris: Éditions du Seuil, 1959.

Schreiner, K. *Crania Norvegica.* vol. II, series B, no. XXXVI, Institutet for sammenlignende Kulturforskning, 1946.

Seligman, Charles G. *Egypt and Negro Africa: A Study in Divine Kingship.* London: George Routledge and Sons, 1934.

Seneca, Lucius Annaeus. *Naturales Quaestiones.*

de Sonneville-Bordes, D. "Environnement et culture de l'Homme du Périgordien ancien dans le Sud-Ouest de la France. Donées récoltées." In *L'Origine de l'homme moderne*. Paris Symposium, 1969. Paris: Éditions UNESCO, 1972.

Spady, James G. Afterword to *The Cultural Unity of Black Africa* by Cheikh Anta Diop. Chicago: Third World Press, 1978.

———"The Cultural Unity of Cheikh Anta Diop, 1948–64." *Black Image*, vol. I, no. 3–4 (1972).

———"Negritude, Pan-Banegritude and the Diopian Philosophy of African History." *A Current Bibliography on African Affairs*, vol. 5, series II (January 1972).

Stavisky, B. "Liens culturels entre l'Asie Centrale ancienne et l'Égypte préislamique." In *Ancien Orient*. Moscow: Editions Naura, 1975.

Strabo. *Geography*.

Struve, V. V. *Mathematischer Papyrus des Staatlichen Museums der Schönen Kunste in Moskau*. Quellen und Studien zur Geschichte der Mathematik, Abteilung A, Quellen, Band I, Berlin, 1930.

Suret-Canale, Jean. "La société traditionnelle en Afrique tropicale et le concept de mode de production asiatique." *La Pensée*, no. 117, Paris (1964).

Targ, Russel. *See* Puthoff, Harold and Targ, Russel.

Tempels, R. P. Placide. *La Philosophie bantoue*. Translated by A. Rubbens. Paris: Présence Africaine, 1949.

Le Temple d'Edfou. VI, pp. 60–90; X, plates CXLVI–CXLVIII; XIII, plates CCCCXCIV–DXIV.

Thoma, Andor. "L'origine de l'homme moderne et de ses races." *La Recherche*, no. 55 (August 1975).

———Article in *Anthropologia Hungarica*. no. 5, 1962.

Thuillier, Pierre. "La physique et l'irrationnel." *La recherche*, no. 111 (May 1980).

Tiéron, Alphonse. *Le Nom africain ou Langage des traditions*. Paris: Maisonneuve et Larose, 1977.

Titus Livius. "Tarquinius the Elder." In *Books from the Founding of Rome*, book I.

UNESCO. *L'Origine de l'homme moderne*. Paris Symposium. Edited by François Bordes. Paris: UNESCO, 1972.

Vallois, Henri-Victor. *L'Anthropologie*. 1929.

———"Early Human Remains in East Africa." *Man* (April 1933).

———*See* Boule, Marcellin and Vallois, Henri-Victor.

Vandermeersch, Bernard. Article *La Recherche*, no. 91 (July–August 1978).

———*See* Lévèque, Francois and Vandermeersch, Bernard.

Van Sertima. *They Came Before Columbus: The African Presence in Ancient America*. New York: Random House, 1977.

Vercoutter, Jean. Article in *La Science antique et médiévale*. Paris: Presses Universitaires de France, 1957.

Ver Eecke, Paul. *Les Oeuvres complètes d'Archimède*. Paris: Albert Blanchard, 1960.

———*Proclus de Lycie*. Paris: Albert Blanchard, 1948.

Vernant, J. P. *Les Origines de la pensée grecque*.

Verneaux, René. *Les Origines de l'humanité*. Paris: F. Riedder & Co., 1926.

de Vries, Carl E. "The Oriental Institute Decorated Censer from Nubia." In *Studies in Honor of George R. Hughes*. Studies in Ancient Oriental Civilization series, no. 39. The Oriental Institute, Chicago, January 1977.

Vulindlela, Wobogo. "Diop's Two Cradle Theory." In *Black Books Bulletin*. Edited by Haki R. Madhubuti, Institute of Positive Education. vol. 4, no. 4 (Winter 1976). Chicago: Third World Press.

Weiner, J. S. *The Piltdown Forgery*. Oxford: Oxford University Press, 1955.

Westermann, D. *See* Baumann, Hermann and Westermann, D.

Williams, Bruce. *News, Notes*, no. 37. The Oriental Institute, Chicago (November 1977).

Wittfogel, Karl A. *Oriental Despotism: A Comparative Study of Total Power*. New Haven: Yale University Press, 1957.

Wörterbuch der Aegyptischen Sprache, Erster Band, Berlin: Akamedie Verlag, 1971.

Yoyotte, Jean. *See* Sauneron, Serge and Yoyotte, J.

Zuckerkandl, E. *See* Petit, C. and Zuckerkandl, E.

INDEX